Learning
to Become
Turkmen

Central Eurasia in Context

Douglas Northrop, Editor

Learning to Become Turkmen

Literacy, Language, and Power, 1914–2014

Victoria Clement

University of Pittsburgh Press

Published by the University of Pittsburgh Press, Pittsburgh, Pa., 15260
Copyright © 2018, University of Pittsburgh Press
Manufactured in the United States of America
Printed on acid-free paper
10 9 8 7 6 5 4 3 2 1

Cataloging-in-Publication data is available from the Library of Congress

ISBN 13: 978-0-8229-6463-6

Cover art: Statue of a Turkmen woman reading
Cover design by Melissa Dias-Mandoly

To my parents, who made everything possible

MAP 1. Map of Turkmenistan. From https://www.cia.gov/library/publications/re
sources/cia-maps-publications/map-downloads/turkmenistan-physiog.jpg/image.jpg

Contents

Acknowledgments

Researching and writing this book has been a magnificent adventure. I am pleased to have this opportunity to thank the individuals and institutions who lent support over the many years I have worked on this project.

As a doctoral student at the Ohio State University I had the good fortune to work with Nicholas Breyfogle, Eve Levin, and Harvey Graff, each of whom read large sections of this manuscript multiple times. I am forever indebted to them. While an undergraduate student at the University of Massachusetts I met Audrey Altstadt, who took me under her wing, taught me Turkish, and mentored me over the years. She remains my valued friend. Dona Straley taught me to read the Arabic script. My study of Jadid-inspired Turkmen would not have been possible without her guidance.

A number of colleagues have contributed to my thinking over the years. Laura Adams, Erik Dahl, Marianne Kamp, Adeeb Khalid, Paula Michaels, Daniel Moran, and Pamela Pennock read and commented on sections of the manuscript. Adrienne Edgar generously shared research notes and advice at various stages and read much of the manuscript. I have been lucky to have been friends with her over these many years. I also thank Peter Kracht, the editorial staff at the University of Pittsburgh Press, and Douglas Northrop for their encouragement and guidance with the manuscript. Nurmukhamed Eldosov was an invaluable research assistant.

The International Research and Exchanges Board (IREX), American Councils for International Education, the Social Science Research Council (SSRC), and the National Endowment for the Humanities funded this project at various stages. Awards from these institutions allowed me to conduct research in Aşgabat and Moscow. A postdoctoral fellowship at the University of Illinois, Urbana-Champaign, allowed me to begin the writing process. Time spent as a Title VIII Research Scholar at the Kennan Institute of the Woodrow Wilson Center for International Scholars allowed me to conduct research at the Library of Congress and to finish writing the manuscript.

My deepest appreciation goes to the friends and family members who believed in this project. My parents, William and Susan Clement, were unwavering in their love and support. Heartfelt gratitude goes to my sister, Tina Ross, my best friend, who believed in this project from the beginning. My thanks to Keith and Donovan Ross, who enthusiastically rooted for my research and always kept track of where I was traveling. Other friends offered encouragement and hospitality over the years. They include Gözel Amangulyýeva, Begench Atayev, Muriel Atkin, Yusup Azmun, Geraldine Bouchet, Christa Dahl, Ambassador Joseph Hulings, Anton Ikhsanov, Liliya Karimova, Ambassador Laura Kennedy, Elmira Kochumkulova, Professor Kenesbay Musaev, Bob Pennock, Ejegyz Saparowa, Uli Schamiloglu, Professor Myratgeldi Söýegow, Ayna Täçmammedowa, Professor Tagangeldi Täçmyradow, the Garryýew family in Aşgabat, and the İpekyuz family in Istanbul. I thank the librarians at The Ohio State University, the National Library of Turkmenistan, the Library of Congress, and the Woodrow Wilson Center Library, especially Janet Spikes and Michelle Kamalich.

Finally, my husband, Brian Pollins, has been a champion of this study for as long as he has known me. He read and commented on multiple drafts of each chapter, attended conference presentations, and even swam in the Caspian with me. I could not ask for a greater partner.

This book features material that appeared in the following articles: "Articulating National Identity in Turkmenistan: Inventing Tradition through Myth, Cult and Language," *Nations & Nationalism* 20, no. 3 (2014): 546–62; "Emblems of Independence: Script Choice in Post-Soviet Turkmenistan," *International Journal of the Sociology of Language* 192 (2008): 171–85. I thank the publishers of these two journals for permission to reproduce this material here.

Note on Transliteration

Over the past century Turkmen have used three distinct writing systems: Arabic, Latin, and Cyrillic. In the post-Soviet period (1993) Turkmenistan's government once again adopted a Latin-based script and this remains in use. Transliterating these alphabets has been a challenge. Despite the unique nature of Turkmenistan's current Latin alphabet (*Türkmen Milli Elipbiýi*), I have used it as the basis for my transliteration in part to convey some of the flavor of the language that is at the heart of this study. For sources written in Turkish, I have used the Turkish alphabet.

Russian is transliterated according to the Library of Congress system.

Learning to Become Turkmen

Introduction

Tradition is a process: it lives only while it changes.

The history of Central Asia's Turkmen as they evolved from a set of loosely connected tribes at the beginning of the twentieth century to a sovereign state at the start of the twenty-first century is a fascinating one. Tracing the long-term development of Turkmen identity and sociocultural practices—with a particular focus on literacy, language, and learning—places the Turkmen experiences with modernity into a global context and sheds light on a nation that regional analysts have often described as "opaque," "incomprehensible," or "perplexing" since its foundation as an independent country on 27 October 1991.[1] This study spans the years from early twentieth-century social reform to significant education reform in 2014 and, in the process, probes the intersections between cultural and social power in the historical context of shifting politics though the transformation, acquisition, or loss of cultural knowledge. These intersections are not recent phenomena in Turkmen history but have drawn new attention since the end of the Soviet Union and the establishment of Turkmenistan as a sovereign state.

Beginning in the early twentieth century, Turkmen identified mass literacy and learning as the means by which their people could become a modern nation.[2] The Turkmen nation's experiences with language and education reform support the argument that elements of everyday life—even those as seemingly innocuous as alphabets—are fraught with political value and serve as components of social power. In each era examined, political considerations and intellectual struggles redefine the meaning, the conceptualization of Turkmen identity, modernity, and literacy, what it meant to live as a Muslim, and indeed, what it meant to be a citizen of the world.

Knowledge of a language or alphabet became equal to possessing cultural capital, as defined by Pierre Bourdieu, who equated such intangibles as cultural capacity, political power, experience, talent, and skill with actual wealth.[3] Through a history of cultural policy and education reform, the Turkmen language became emblematic of twenty-first-century Turkmen national identity when, only a generation earlier, it was not even an identifying marker. At various times, different actors (reform-minded Muslims, Soviet authorities, independent Turkmen) held the predominant degree of cultural capital and thus could dominate the scene, and some actors, over time, possessed the cultural capital needed to shape Turkmen identity and ultimately a Turkmen nation. Examining the relationship between language and power enhances our understanding of national identity construction not only in Turkmenistan but also throughout Central Asia. Among Turkmen, as with other national groups, the educated elites and intellectuals—"the producers and transmitters of culture"—engaged modernity on behalf of the people.[4] They began in earnest in the 1910s, and over the following years shifts in education and cultural policies were often dramatic enough to trigger a reassessment of the Turkmen national identity, whereby identity, language, and learning became tightly linked.

Twenty-five years after the end of the USSR, there is a paucity of research about Turkmenistan, and little of what there is employs Turkmen language sources. Typically confined to the periphery of scholarship, the Turkmen are situated at the heart of this analysis, which brings in Turkmen language sources, taking into account the local culture within the context of global designs and drawing out the Turkmen voices. Western studies of power in Turkmenistan are typically limited to that of the state or individual leaders.[5] There are very few works that cover cultural power or the role of language or education as factors in social relations.[6] The focus here is on the power of language and education as social determinants, bringing in the voices of average citizens and taking the examination beyond the role of the state to include the agency of the people. The reader is encouraged to think in terms of a specifically Turkmen experience. Although Turkmen were not unique in history, they were exemplary in their use of language and education to underscore identity.

The work of Adrienne Edgar has been invaluable. Her work on Turkmenistan in the 1920s and 1930s demonstrates that culture was heavily politicized in the Soviet Union. She aptly illustrates the many ways in which identity was shaped in those years, involving not only Soviet officials but locals too.[7] Here a new perspective takes a long view, integrating these early years of the twentieth century in a broad context that includes Turkmen's experiences in late tsarist and the post-Soviet periods. My perspective is not only grounded in Soviet archival information and Turkmen language sources but also based on my personal observations and interviews with local residents while I was living in Turkmenistan and on my research in the Turkmen State National Archive and Turkmenistan's Manuscript Institute Archive.

Turkmen Identity

The history of the Turkmen nation and its struggle with modernity illustrates some of the nuances of Turkmen identity. Turkmen are part of the ethnolinguistic Turkic continuum that stretches from western China to western Turkey. They share a claim to western Turkic (Oguz) heritage, which is found in today's Azerbaijan, Iran, Iraq (Turcomans), Afghanistan, Turkey, and small areas in China.[8] Despite the development of a distinct twenty-first-century identity, Turkmen culture and traditions historically overlapped with that of all other Turks. The term "Turkic" refers to the cultural and linguistic heritage shared by all Turkic-language speaking groups.[9] While all Turkic people speak languages with fundamental similarities, a separate Turkmen sense of identity was born out of their particular historical experience.[10] A nomadic heritage, Oguz dialects, genealogical claims, and distinctive tribal traditions contributed greatly to the identity that sets Turkmen apart from other Turkic groups and has characterized a specifically Turkmen sense of identity.[11]

For millennia, the peoples living throughout the vast lands of Central Asia grouped themselves according to ancestry, religion, lifeways, or patronage. Until the early twentieth century, Turkmen identified themselves according to lineage and ancestry—or nomadic versus settled. Turkmen claim their identity in distinction from other Turks based on patrilineal descent from the semimythical, eponymous Oguz Han, whose legacy lives on in oral traditions.[12] As a result of this claim, genealogy was the organizational norm of Turkmen society long before the modern language became a matter of identity. Only in the 1910s did a small coterie of Turkmen begin to explore expression of their identity through language. Before this time, language was not politicized.

The earliest evidence of a Turkic writing system is the runic script that Turkic groups used before they adopted Islam in the tenth century.[13] Chiseled into stone stelea that record the history of the Gök Türk empire (from the sixth to the eighth century AD), these signs show that, long before Turks reached the borders of modern Turkey, the written language reflected a Turkic identity. Upon adopting Islam, Turks began using the Arabic script of the Qur'an to reflect their membership in the *umma*, which bound them to the community of believers.[14] It also facilitated access to great traditions of learning, poetry, literature, and treatises on governance, which were often written in Persian.

At the beginning of the twentieth century, Turkmen still did not yet conceive of themselves as a unified people. Turkmen society was not a stable coherent entity with a singular political leadership. Organized according to tribes and clans spread throughout Transcaspia, Bukhara, and Khiva, the notion of being Turkmen was based primarily on the Oguz genealogical claim.[15] As they encountered modern ideas, Turkmen began to examine their society and group identity. While "modernity" is an amorphous and highly contested term among scholars, educated Turkmen conceptualized it in a Turco-Muslim way that shaped their collective responses to global change.[16] The ongoing reconceptualization of the Turkmen "self" had much to do with what was taking place throughout the Muslim world. Muslims in the Russian empire identified education as the vehicle that would transport them to modernity. More specifically, they pinpointed literacy as the key to that vehicle.

But before Turkmen could promote mass literacy, they needed to standardize their language and unify the speech community.

The language of modern Turkmenistan is known as the literary language (*Turkmen edebi dili* or *häzirki zaman dili*).[17] What makes it a literary language is that it has been standardized and codified over the past century, primarily in the 1920s and 1930s, prior to which language was not represented by an official or agreed upon version but, rather, reflected the many dialectical variances. Turkmen dialects reflect variants that correspond to tribal identity; that is, there is variation in vocabulary and some differences in the grammar of spoken Turkmen dialects. Tribal identity has always been complex among Turkmen because the distribution of power among them has led to contention. This was mostly so during the nineteenth century when there was actual warfare among the tribes, but it continues to this day. There is a palpable imbalance in the distribution of power, with the Ahal Teke in a dominant position in part because of President Berdimuhamedov's own Teke identity and hiring practices that favor them. As a result of this imbalance discomfort over tribal dialects persists.

Tribal identity includes but is not limited to Teke, Ýomut, Gökleň, Salyr, Saryk, Ärsary, Çowdur, Nohur, and Änew; Teke and Ýomut are the greatest in number. Tribal identity corresponds closely to geographic location due to the history of migration and power over the centuries.[18] Turkmen dialects persist and are regional. In this way, it is possible to find local concepts and cultural traditions reflected in the language. All regions contributed terms related to local handicrafts and ways of life. For example, the Ýomut live in the northern and western regions near the Caspian Sea and contributed fishing terms.

The literary language is essentially a blending of Teke and Ýomut characteristics, but its content is closest to the spoken language of the Teke tribe, especially the Ahal subdialect spoken in Aşgabat, because in the first half of the twentieth century many of the individuals involved in writing and publishing were Teke.[19] The influence of the Teke's Ahal subdialect spoken in Aşgabat is especially prominent today because the majority of officials and intellectuals who use the language live in Ashgabat.[20] Yet Ýomut influence is seen in grammatical usage, especially in the use of the phoneme [r] at the end of the present tense: *bermek* (to give) is *berýär* in the official literary language from the Ýomut, but it is *berýä* without the [r] in the Teke dialect. The dative case and verbal infinitive in Teke and Ýomut is *bermege*, but is *bermene* in other dialects.[21]

The dialects are mutually intelligible, but there is noticeable variation in everyday life. The Teke words *oňat* and *gowy* mean "good" or "fine" and are the appropriate responses to the question "Nähili?" or "How are you?" But the Ýomut word *ýahşy* is also heard. For the concept "sister" one may hear *aýal dogan*, *gyz*, *bajy*, *ejeke*, or *uya*. There have been a number of variants for father as well: *kaka*, *ata*, *däde*, *aba*, *eke*, and *akga*.[22] There is a dramatic difference in the pronunciation of the graphemes "s" and "z," which most dialects pronounce with the interdental fricatives "th" [ð] and "th" [θ] where the tongue is placed between the teeth. This results in the sounds found in "this" (voiced dental fricative [ð]) and "thin" (unvoiced dental fricative [θ]). Yet there are some that do not employ the interdental fricative and pronounce the letters "s" and "z" as one would expect, with a dental fricative as in "sun" and "zero." Because of such differences native Turkmen speakers are able to identify each other's tribal affiliation. This contributes to the imbalance among tribes and perpetuates the Teke dominance. At the beginning of the twentieth century, the Turkmen speech community was not unified in all aspects of their everyday language. However, language planners did create a standardized written language, which is now found in schools, newspapers, and official documents.

By 2014 Turkmen were a literate people, many of whom had experienced socialism as well as an independent state. Although there are continuities that allow a people to self-identify under a rubric such as national identity (Turkmen, Uzbek, Irish, Mexican), there are also transformations, local and global, that alter a group over time. Identity is an ongoing process. Michel Foucault describes the nation as a "discursive formation." He notes how "statements different in form, and dispersed in time, form a group if they refer to one and the same object," but he concludes that this "does not enable one to individualize a group of statements, and to establish between them a relation that is both constant and describable."[23] That is, one must examine the interplay, the processes, and the transformations among historical clues to understand a discourse or a term over time. In this case the term was "Turkmen," and the discourse was becoming a Turkmen nation.

Modernity

As Turkmen have worked to fit aspects of their society into broad global patterns over the last century, the nature of "modernity" has come into question. Various ideas were rooted in Western societies, but Turkmen viewed them as global, even Muslim, because these notions arrived via other Muslim groups such as Azerbaijanis, Ottomans/Turks, Tatars, and Uzbeks, who all played important roles. Indeed, the concept of "multiple modernities" suggests that we see modernity as variegated and having authenticity in societies that are not Western.[24] One constant is that modernity "is inherently future-oriented," but it is not a coherent or integrated whole. "Multiple" is also an appropriate adjective here because the concept of modernity, as with others such as literacy, can be interpreted in multiple ways by diverse subjects.[25]

As political circumstances fluctuated, so did the parameters by which "modern" was defined as well as the concepts of learning, literacy, and power. These fluctuations were connected to recognition of change in the world and a reconsideration of tradition, with a sense of the individual and his or her rights in contrast to the group's rights, and with possibilities for societal growth. Over the period under study here we see both reinterpretation and transformation of symbols, institutions, and self-conceptualization. The Turkmen experience offers the opportunity to revisit the concept of modernity and the processes of becoming modern and to ask what they mean in specific historic contexts.

The end of the nineteenth and beginning of the twentieth century was a time in which Muslims around the world debated and experimented with various concepts, forms, and expectations of modernity.[26] Early twentieth-century Turkmen reformers believed that education and literacy were essential in the engagement of modernity. The Bolshevik/Soviet understanding of modern was incompatible with the Muslim modern.[27] Both agreed that the established order had to go, but they disagreed over how and who would oversee the project. Even in independent Turkmenistan (post-1991), with its full literacy rates, the state and a cadre of intellectuals believed that converting their Cyrillic alphabet to a modified Latin script was an appropriate way to mark the birth of the sovereign state. The post-Soviet Latin-based writing system conveyed Turkmen national consciousness in a manner worthy of the country's new international standing, elevating it from the former Soviet periphery where it previously had languished. Literacy, language, and learning offer lenses through which to see modernizing forces at work into the twenty-first century.

The concepts of modernity, power, identity, and literacy recur throughout the following chapters. The ultimate aspiration of many historical actors was to make Turkmen society modern. However, the means of getting there varied. Even Turkmen intellectuals in any particular era did not always agree on the best pathway to modernity, and they certainly were not always in step with St. Petersburg/Moscow. The notion of Turkmen modernity was not static, but in the historical records there is an underlying sense that certain Turkmen intellectuals believed they could progress if only they could codify their language just right, spread literacy, and educate the Turkmen people. If they could perfect their alphabet to reflect Turkmen speech and if they could combat illiteracy among their people, they would all become "modern." I therefore use the terms "modernity," "progress," and "internationalism" as they apply to each "phase of modernity" or sociopolitical era under discussion.[28]

Literacy Studies and Sociolinguistics

Every reader will be able to identify with the task of learning to read and write. What may surprise many, though, is how such mundane cultural aspects as an alphabet or a vocabulary can serve both as a sharp implement for nation building and as a powerful political tool.[29] Speech communities around the world have experimented with script change. That is, one or more groups within a society determined that changing the writing system would bring benefits—if not material, then at least symbolic gains. In the modern era, such change often has been linked to expressions of national identity. Turkmen have used forms of language and writing as a means to position their local society in response to or in opposition to various global designs.

Before adopting Islam in the tenth century, Turkmen, like other Turkic peoples, employed a runic script. The adoption of the Arabic writing system marked their people as Muslim and situated them within the *umma,* or community of Muslim believers. Even in these early years, writing marked the Turks' place in the world. Since then, the modern Turkmen language has been written with three distinct systems of writing as Turkmen shifted from Arabic to Latin (1928–1940), to Cyrillic (1940–1993), and back to Latin (1993–present), with modifications also taking place in 1923, 1925, 1928, 1995, and 2000.[30] Each alteration was tied to the continuing politicization of culture either by such broad political forces as Soviet nationalities policy or by such internal shifts as the desire to symbolize an anti-Russian cultural stance after independence in 1991.[31] Each reform dramatically affected the lives of the Turkmen people and acted as an important marker of the transformation of the Turkmen people. For example, in the 1910s, modification to their Arabic alphabet signified Turkmen membership in the larger Turco-Islamic world, but it also promoted a specifically Turkmen identity. This is a story that takes place on four intersecting and mutually influential levels of identity and political power: Turkmen, Turco-Islamic, Russian/Soviet, and global modern.

The details illustrate how a universal concern such as literacy is addressed at the local level. Language and education are particularly useful historical lenses because they were consistently important to Turkmen along their path toward modernity. Exploring the varying Turkmen responses to universal literacy and learning over several generations reveals both continuity and change over time, especially as their responses paralleled political eruptions and intellectual breaks. Through exploration we can see the intersections of language, politics, and cultural power.

Literacy is not a constant but is ever transforming. As the work of scholars in literacy studies demonstrates, using literacy as a means for transforming a people has not been limited to the modern era.[32] Nevertheless, literacy is closely linked to conceptualizations of progress and modernity across diverse cultures. As Harvey Graff explains, "the rise of literacy and its dissemination to the popular classes, therefore, was, and is, associated with the triumph of light over darkness, or liberalism, democracy and universal unbridled progress; literacy takes its place among the other successes, and causes, of modernity and rationality." But he also warns us of the "problems in treating literacy as an independent variable."[33] Graff encourages scholars to contextualize analyses of literacy and to problematize the definition therein. This study does that by examining the role of literacy in modern Turkmen history as it related to language, education policy, and power more generally, illustrating that the very concept of literacy is not a constant but is ever transforming within larger contexts.[34]

Decisions about language (language reform, official language policy) are frequently guided not by linguistic considerations but by social or political considerations.[35] "Language development" or "language planning," for example, entails deliberate efforts to shape language via public policy.[36] Ideological or political realities can demand new usages of language and culture—such as when the Soviet state began injecting the Turkmen language with Soviet-international vocabulary so that the language could keep pace with sociopolitical and economic change in the Turkmen Soviet Socialist Republic (TSSR). The language of instruction in schools is as much a political choice as a technical one.[37] New functional expectations—for example, an emergent technology or administration of a new state policy—may require language to adjust, and adjustments may include taking in new terminology or symbols, standardization in spelling or grammar, or adoption of a new writing system. In the end, members of the speech community (usually intellectuals or political elites) make efforts to adapt the language so as to meet social exigencies.[38] Pierre Bourdieu refers to this as bodies of specialists competing for a monopoly over legitimate cultural production. The history of such efforts is one way that language reflects the social experiences of a speech community.[39]

My work is inspired by Professor Joshua Fishman's call for language-related studies of power.[40] As Fishman's enterprising *International Journal of Sociology of Language* reveals, languages around the world have undergone transformations and amendments similar to those in Turkmenistan, and the pathways taken by the Turkmen in language reform and national identity formation are well traveled by other communities around the globe. Sociolinguistics is the study of the relationship between society and language, which illustrates that point through the many histories of official language creation, grammar codification, adoption of alphabets, language planning, the emergence of print cultures, and the innumerable histories of peoples' wielding language to manifest a group identity. Turkmen, like so many nations, have constructed a modern national identity, tinkered with the emblems reflective of that identity, and sought to experience the human condition through the prism of modernity.

Language and Power

My analysis is deeply influenced by the work of Pierre Bourdieu, including the idea that language endows a speaker with social capital. Within a speech community, facility in a language provides an individual with an important tool so as to function in that society. Bourdieu writes also of "linguistic capital," asserting that "speakers lacking the legitimate competence are *de facto* excluded from the social domains in which this competence is required, or are condemned to silence."[41] An individual who lacks capacity in a community's language or is illiterate is fundamentally disadvantaged and will likely remain politically marginalized and struggle to participate in everyday life. In Turkmenistan, it was not merely a question of knowing one particular language, either Russian or Turkmen, but also about being proficient in the writing system and alphabet employed for Turkmen, which were Latin-based in the 1920s, but then Cyrillic in the 1950s. It also meant being adept in the political language of the time, "speaking Bolshevik" in the 1930s or knowing the language of the president's nationalistic book *Ruhnama*—in a new Latin-based script—after the year 2000. As Bourdieu explains:

> Symbolic power [is] power of constituting the given through utterances, of making people see and believe, of confirming or transforming the vision of the world and, thereby, action on the world and thus the world itself . . . [whoever] makes "social solidarity" dependent on the sharing of a symbolic system [such as language or alphabet] has the merit of designating the *social function* . . . it is an authentic political function which cannot be reduced to the structuralists' function of communication. Symbols are the instruments *par excellence* of "social integration": as instruments of knowledge and communication . . . they make it possible for there to be a *consensus* on the meaning of the social world, a consensus which contributes fundamentally to the reproduction of the social order.[42] [original emphasis]

In other words, forms are socially determined; they are notions conceived when society agrees upon a definition for a term or concept. Power relations are embedded in everyday life and cultural practices.[43] Cultural policy was more than a question of how people would read or what alphabet letters they would use. Culture posed questions as to who rose or fell; in some cases, as in the 1930s purges, it was about life and death. A few years after the fall of the Soviet Union, for example, Turkmenistan changed its script from Cyrillic to a Latin-based one. The state moved away from all Soviet symbols, including the Russian language. This put Russian speakers at a great disadvantage. President Nyýazow's language policies disrupted the country's workforce by enacting regulations that advantaged Turkmen speakers and augmented their social power. These policies undermined the socioeconomic place of Russian-only speakers by dispossessing them of their ability to work when state jobs required employees to speak Turkmen.

Bourdieu asks, "What creates the power of words and slogans, a power capable of managing or subverting the social order?" His answer is "symbolic power," by which he means the ability to create meaning or the power to convince, and "confirming or transforming the vision of the world, and thereby, action on the world and thus the world itself."[44] Bourdieu suggests that within society there is a constant struggle for meaning, knowing, and possessing the power to define society's norms through the definitions of "culturally valued knowledge."[45] In the pre-Soviet era, education or possession of knowledge was gained through Islamic ways of learning. The ability to say prayers, even without a formal education, earned one the title *molla*. In the Soviet era, knowledge was defined by ideology and one's relationship to the state. Both the understanding of knowledge and the access to it was in constant flux throughout the Soviet era. In the post-Soviet era, the definition of useful knowledge underwent a complete transformation.

Power appeared in a variety of guises. One method to gain power is to reduce others' access to it. Early twentieth-century reformists challenged the authority of traditional Muslim clergy by expanding the social meanings of literacy and transforming access to knowledge. In the twentieth century President Nyýazow likewise claimed the legitimacy of his rule through the semiotics of sovereignty (flag, anthem, and alphabet), while some members of society resisted by avoiding the new Turkmen script.[46] In the early post-Soviet years, language and education were among the greatest social concerns of Turkmenistan's citizenry. Some were empowered while others were disempowered due to a lack of access to language skills or education.

Continuity and Change

In order to understand the dis/continuities, it is necessary to delve into the intricacies of education and alphabet reform—should the alphabet have one letter or two to represent long vowel sounds? Should Turkmen write in the Cyrillic script or reform to a Latin-based one? What does it mean that some Turkmen do not know the Turkmen language? Fine-grained details are tightly embedded in real and serious political issues that confronted the Turkmen nation, issues that frequently challenged and focused Turkmen social power during tumultuous historical periods. Over the decades, the politics changed and the historical agents were transformed or forced out of the picture, but the aim of Turkmen intellectuals, nationalists, and others remained constant: to transport Turkmen society into modernity via literacy, and this led to calls for an alphabet that accurately reflected a refined, standardized language and an education system that taught it.

Historians look for turning points upon which to pivot their narrative, and this can sometimes lead to more emphasis being put on change rather than continuity. While I have organized the chapters in this book around moments of cultural change, I underscore the continuities among eras, historical actors, processes, institutions, and symbols. This method allows the reader to absorb the general history, with its accent on linkages, while tracing the most important transformations in its cultural currency.

There are shifting interpretations and uses of cultural capital and the application and appreciation that linked literacy and learning to cultural and social power, including Auguste Comte's concept of cultural knowledge as "wealth" and Bourdieu's concepts of "cultural capital" and "symbolic power."[47] In Turkmenistan cultural power changed as access to it changed hands through the possession of knowledge, language, or ethnicity in each respective era. At times, it paid to privilege or emphasize being Turkmen; at other times it was more profitable to be "Russian" (a Russian speaker)—or at the very least conversant in the Russian language. There are three principal reasons to emphasize continuity: (1) to situate the Turkmen in historical context; (2) to stress that people's lives and local cultures traverse the boundaries of political regimes, and periodization of history is complex when individuals are taken into consideration; and (3) as a reminder that there are often historical precedents for behavior, leaving few ages unique. Bourdieu extended the idea of capital to such constructions as social capital, cultural capital, symbolic capital, and even linguistic capital. For Bourdieu, each individual is defined not solely by class, gender, or religious group but also by the kind of capital, the amount of social currency, that individual can bring to a social situation. Bourdieu's theories help to illustrate and situate the historical realm of the Turkmen language and learning. They illuminate the historical turning points and trajectories as political affairs affected the value of cultural capital, thereby altering the ability to profit from accumulated social "wealth."

Organization of the Chapters

In chapter 1 the focus is on education and print culture as primary sites where Turkmen focused on social reform and on how language became symbolic of their group identity in the early twentieth century. Throughout the Russian empire in the late nineteenth and early twentieth centuries, Muslim reformers who wished to modernize Islamic cultural and social institutions through new methods of teaching (*usul-i jadid*) and socialization became known as *jadids*. Jadid activities attracted the attention of a small number of progressive Turkmen (I call them "Jadid-inspired" Turkmen). In response to the nineteenth-century perception that universal education and functional literacy possessed transformative modernizing powers, early twentieth-century Turkmic intellectuals proposed modifications to their schools and pedagogy and employed a modified, expanded Arabic script in the belief that it would expedite learning. Turkmen simultaneously explored pedagogical reform.

Drawing particularly upon the newspaper *Ruznama-i Mawera-i Bahr-i Hazar*, chapter 1 traces Jadid-inspired Turkmen as they articulated many of the cultural conceptions that later informed the work of early Soviet institutions. Turkmen believed that literacy could transform their society. Influenced by the reforms that moved across Central Asia, reform-minded individuals founded new schools and promoted a new pedagogy, opposing traditional schools that emphasized rote learning instead of functional literacy.

The next three chapters illustrate that Moscow also stressed the fundamental importance of literacy, but in later years this was political, not functional literacy. As political or cultural powers shifted, various sectors of Turkmen society used education, literacy, and writing systems to inculcate a socialist outlook in the masses. One could not function in Soviet society without at least a rudimentary familiarity with Marxism-Leninism, whether it was in the classroom or at a parade. Bolsheviks shared basic ideals about the role of literacy with Turkmen reformers, albeit within a different ideological framework.[48] Moscow expanded and intensified its control over Turkmenistan (and Central Asia more generally) when the Arabic writing system was supplanted first by a Latin-based script and then by Cyrillic. It was not tanks that rolled into Aşgabat, but the Russian alphabet. Moscow employed and manipulated the symbolic power of alphabets, creating meaningful change in people's everyday lives. The Cyrillic script and the Russification of language that accompanied it forced a new nexus in Turkmen speech, which suppressed the Islamic aspects/components of the Turkmen language so as to support the centralization of Soviet power through linguistic Russification.

Chapter 2 explores cooperation and competition between indigenous and Moscow-directed elites over how social arenas such as schools and print culture were employed to promote political objectives among Turkmen in imperial Russia and then in the Soviet Union. The overlap existed only so far; each group had different expectations of who would possess cultural power in Soviet Turkmenistan. The change in the political atmosphere and the purges of the 1930s reflected the limited correspondence of reformist and Bolshevik ideals. The groups had all agreed that literacy was a strategic solution in creating a progressive society, but ultimate goals, processes, and especially decisions about who was in charge differed wholly.

Chapter 3 tells two stories. The first is the Jadid-inspired story of creating a modern Turkmen nation within the larger, modern Muslim and Turkic worlds, an idea that continued more or less through 1930. The second story is the Soviet-inspired vision of converting Turkmen into a Soviet and socialist people and placing them in the socialist variant of modernity, embedded within the Soviet Union. These are two different visions of the future of Turkmen identity. Each one is about forging a Turkmen identity, but each is a very different type of Turkmen-ness and Turkmen future.

Chapter 3 also examines the introduction of a Cyrillic alphabet, which was infused with the capacity to situate the Turkmen within the Soviet Union. In the 1920s the transnational Latin alphabet was chosen specifically to modernize and internationalize Turkic peoples. By 1940 Turkmenistan's use of a Cyrillic-based writing system was emblematic of the *sliianie* (merging) of the Soviet peoples; Cyrillicization illustrated Russification of culture more broadly. The new Soviet person (*sovetskii chelovek/täze sowet adamy*) spoke at least some Russian and wrote their native language in the Russian script.[49]

In chapter 4, we see that during the rest of the Soviet era, local dialects and Russian at times vied for dominance whereas at other times coexisted amicably in

Turkmenistan as well as throughout the USSR. This meant that the languages in which people learned to read and write gained or lost currency according to political standards. Identity, too, was closely linked to the politics of language. Local sentiment reflecting frustration with the status of the Russian language was based less on the republicwide use of Russian and more on its dominance in official arenas. Calls for parity between Russian and national languages were focused more on language status and prestige than on actual daily usage.[50] Russification swept across the Soviet Union. Turkmen continued to speak the Turkmen language in their private lives, but cultural capital was vested in the Russian language as the Soviet lingua franca and it held sway in official arenas and public spaces. Soviet language policy was permissive of many national languages, but Russification was real both as national languages were infused with Russian vocabulary and as there was a steady expansion of the teaching of Russian.

As chapter 5 illustrates, reforms in the 1980s allowed ordinary citizens to discuss publicly their positions on language status. Mikhail Gorbachev's rule made space for demands for cultural autonomy that led to a reevaluation of the role of the Russian language vis-à-vis local languages. Debates over which would be the language of instruction in schools, in each of the Soviet regions, represented a continuity of language considerations found in earlier eras. Appeals for change in the status of Turkmen during glasnost and after 1991 bore witness to the fact that the symbolic place of language and alphabet was just as important as actual language conventions. Turkmenistan's president, Saparmurat Nyýazow, was slow to reject the Soviet era, but once he did his policies reflected an intense nationalism.

In asking how the Soviet experience changed Turkmen language and learning and what continuities there were in the post-Soviet period, this study problematizes the history of independent Turkmenistan. Placing Nyýazow's policies of language and education in a broad historical context, this study does not reduce the Nyýazow period to the bizarre dictatorship of a megalomaniac as so many other studies do.[51] In this way we see that his concepts were not without precedent.

Chapter 6 vividly illustrates the late 1990s and early 2000s when President Nyýazow took control over the appearance of the alphabet, content of textbooks, parameters of public speech, and content of academic research in Turkmenistan. Inspired by the power of information technology in the world, he formulated an alphabet that he believed would suit computers—changing the focus of literacy to computer literacy. Nyýazow developed a cult of personality around himself that pervaded public expression in newspapers, television, statues, and signage. Just a few years later, an intensification in the nationalism and Nyýazow's role in public, verbal, and visual discourse turned Turkmenification into Nyýazowization. Even after his death in 2006, Turkmen citizens could employ or express their alphabetic, political, and cultural literacies only within the parameters of Nyýazow's nation-building policies.

Chapter 7 highlights cultural policies of Turkmenistan's second president, Gurbanguly Berdimuhamedow (2007–present). The focus is primarily on education because the question of literacy was rarely a topic of discussion in this regime. Revealing a period of reform, this chapter suggests that although things in the education sector changed for the better in 2014 the country was still awaiting a Krushchevian "thaw."

Becoming modern has been an extended process for the Turkmen nation. The conclusion in this history will revisit the book's major themes, underscoring that the Turkmen historical experience provides an example of the enduring connection between culture and power. Despite the historical development of the Turkmen nation, Turkmen have shared their quest to become modern with all nations; language and education reform have been crucial components in that experience.

Chapter 1

Jadid-Inspired Paths to Modernity, 1914–1917

Without education no one advances. One stays behind, blind.

In the final years of the Russian empire, an intellectual awakening among Muslims stretched across Crimea, the Volga region, and Azerbaijan reaching Turkestan, and finally Transcaspia, where reformists, in their aim to make society modern, encouraged new methods of teaching and advanced social norms such as universal literacy or the education of women.[1] Turkmen added their voices to the deliberation at the beginning of the twentieth century, most prominently in the pages of the Turkmen/Persian bilingual newspaper *Ruznama-i Mawera-i Bahr-i Hazar*, published from 1914 to 1917, in Aşgabat. Writing about the need to change overall social conditions, they argued that Turkmen needed actively to engage modernity and pursue such ideals as the shaping of society through learning, through privileging secular knowledge over religious authority, and through the empowerment of the ordinary person by way of education.[2]

This debate continued into the Soviet period, blending with Bolshevik projects that aimed to change society through a modern education combined with socialist values. But even before Bolshevism made its way to Turkmen lands, modernist thinkers favored sociocultural reform and, like Turks around the Russian empire, urged their fellow Muslims to "wake up [and] open schools . . . become literate and seek progress [tarakgy]!"[3] To this end, a handful of Turkmen began setting up schools and publishing their ideas. Following the example of reform-minded Muslims throughout Eurasia, these Turkmen sought out modernity and attempted to situate themselves within the greater world, a world that was both Russian and Muslim.

Scholarship has traditionally left Turkmen out of the histories of Central Asian reformism—or Jadidism, as it is called in the literature. For example, Adeeb Khalid posits that cultural reform "never emerged as a viable phenomenon in Turkmen society."[4] However, a form of cultural activism among Turkmen obligates historians to include Turkmen in comprehensive studies of early Central Asian reform. The Turkmen belong in the historical record; their voices, ideas, and social activities should be acknowledged to more fully develop our access to Central Asian history. If we incorporate the Turkmen experience into the history of Jadidism more broadly, we widen our lens on that discourse and enhance our ability to understand its important role in Muslim Turks' relationship with modernity and can then access the experiences of a people who straddled multiple worlds: territorially and culturally, the Turkic world; politically, colonial Russia; and spiritually and culturally, the greater Muslim world. Jadid-inspired Turkmen wanted to traverse all of them.

Turkmen had been actively participating in a Jadid reform discourse for only a few years when the Bolshevik Revolution took place. But Jadidism was short-lived among Turkmen, as just over a decade later, purges of Turkmen cultural workers caused a serious rupture in cultural affairs. The story of the Turkmen participation in the debates over tradition, modernity, Islam, and social transformation of the 1910s illustrates how Jadidism informed Turkmen thinking on all of these matters. Experiences within the greater Muslim world led Turkmen reformers to draw connections between literacy, learning, and Turkmen identity that would continue to be relevant throughout the twentieth and into the twenty-first century.

Traditional *Mekdeps*

Muslim children usually began studying around age five to seven. Boys could enter the *mekdep* (elementary school) and girls could begin studies with the wife of the *molla* (a learned person who teaches), but only if their families were well enough off that they could spare the children's labor. The first stages of learning varied between rituals such as ablutions and prayers and memorizing the alphabet.[5] Traditional Muslim schools relied on rote memorization of Islamic subjects in Persian or Arabic. This meant that students did not possess functional literacy (they were unable to read and write freely) and could only recite memorized passages.

Traditional elementary school teachers were clerics whom the community recognized as educated men: mollas, imams, and *ahuns*.[6] These instructors had no training in pedagogy, but they did possess cultural authority. In addition to their duties in the mekdep, they performed such sacred acts as life-cycle rituals at weddings, funerals, births, and holidays, and they would perform administrative services for the community such as record keeping, handling testaments, and settling inheritances. They did this into the Soviet era.[7] This aspect of the clerics' role did not come into question as much with Turkmen reformers, who were not against Islamic ritual, but who did contest the influential social power that clerics held as an unchallenged intellectual authority.

The organization of traditional schools was uniform. There were no desks or blackboards. Texts included the Qur'an and other religious books that introduced the basic theory and practice of Islam. When studying, students sat on the floor in a half circle with the instructor in the center facing the entrance. In this configuration, an instructor's *taýak* or stick could reach each student, disciplining and encouraging them. Most of the time, students studied their lessons and made progress individually without the teacher's oversight; older students often helped younger students. Graduates gained the ability to recite passages from memory, but most students never acquired functional literacy skills.[8] The ability to cite a suitable passage from the Qur'an or a hadith (sayings of the Prophet Muhammed) in appropriate circumstances was a respected quality in a gentleman and a highly venerated Islamic tradition. Most students did not leave the mekdep to become gentlemen, however, but ultimately took on herding or a trade. In the end, the lessons learned at the mekdep were soon forgotten, and Turkmen reformers began to think that the lessons did most students little good, unless they were lucky enough to have a relative at home who helped them advance their skills.

There were two basic ways of funding mekdeps in late-tsarist Turkestan. Schools could rely on a *waqf,* or religious endowment (but those were typically committed to *medreses*); or, most common for mekdeps, parents paid money or sometimes paid in kind.[9] The location and housing of mekdeps was another question. *Waqf*-supported schools included living quarters for the teacher and a space for instruction. They were sometimes located in a mosque, a yurt, or for some nomads under the open sky, in the desert. There were also itinerant mollas who traveled with pastoral and nomadic families, teaching the alphabet or basic religious concepts to the children for a while before moving on.[10] For the majority of Turkmen it is most likely that a mekdep education would have been in a village setting.

Russian-Native Schools for Turkmen

Aside from mekdeps, there were also a handful of Russian government schools called *russko-tuzemnye shkoly,* or Russian-native schools, founded for Turkmen in 1895, though there were few graduates in the early years. The Russian Ministry of Education opened russko-tuzemnye shkoly—or as they were sometimes called in official documents, *inorodecheskiia uchilishcha* (schools for aliens)—as an alternative set of schools for the "eastern nationalities" starting in 1870. These were four-year institutions offering both Russian and traditional Muslim education in Russian and the local language.[11] The curriculum was designed so that, upon graduation, students would be able to read and write in Russian. Knowledge of Russian would be central to individuals' assimilation into the empire as well as their contribution to the acceptance of Russian cultural hegemony. The reason for this was not simply to help them align with Russian values but also to train cadres of native administrators who would be able to handle Russian-language documents.[12]

After the revolution of 1905, which expanded religious toleration, any goals of assimilation to the majority culture of the empire no longer included conversion. Regulations of 1907 underscored this, outlining the intention to promote Russian ways of thinking via Russian language but without converting natives to Orthodoxy.[13] The orientalist Vasilii V. Radlov, editor of the Russian Ministry of Education's journal *Zhurnal Ministerstva Narodnogo Prosveshcheniia* (ZhMNP) wrote that the russko-tuzemnye schools would act as "a middle ground between our state education system and the Muslim population . . . [showing] the Muslims that the government in no way desires to concern itself with their religious notions, but is trying only to raise the level of their development, for their own good."[14] With this statement he describes the empire's civilizing mission. Nikolai Petrovich Ostroumov (1846–1930) wrote frequently in ZhMNP and also used the gazette he edited, *Turkistan wilayatining gazeti*, as a tool for "enlightening natives."[15] Various Russian administrators sought ways of integrating Muslims into the empire while engendering the least amount of resistance. Education was an important site for employing this tactic.

Adrienne Edgar explains how the Russo-native schools were designed to "educate the natives in the spirit of respect for the throne and state, Russian law and power" and "to prepare future Russian-speaking translators, clerks, military officers, and teachers."[16] Kurbanov and Kuz'min note that these schools aimed to graduate "faithful subjects."[17] This underscores the pragmatic side of the equation but does not contradict the Turkmen scholar Kurbanov, who focuses on natives as culture brokers. Kurbanov writes that "Russko-tuzemnye schools were designed to bring the Turkmen people closer to the Russian language and way of life. In that way, an influence slowly developed over time translating Russian culture to the Turkmen populace."[18] It was for this reason that the *ulema* (religious scholars) had a healthy "mistrust" of the schools, fearing that they were designed "to convert students to orthodoxy"; that was in addition to undermining their positions in society and "stealing their jobs."[19]

Russia needed local administrators who were proficient in Russian. Edgar elaborates, asserting that the influence of the tiny group of tuzemnye-educated Turkmen was significant in that they produced a Russian-speaking, culturally Russified group who "later became the key political figures in the Soviet Turkmen republic." Ivan Alexander Beliaev (d. 1920), the chief school inspector for Transcaspia as well as editor of the Transcaspian newspaper *Ruznama-i Mawera-i Bahr-i Hazar*, hoped that the russko-tuzemnye schools would spread "culture among Turkmen."[20]

Turkmen scholar Hezretguly Durdyýew notes, however, that the number of students enrolled in tuzemnye schools in Transcaspia was small.[21] This is supported by the Russian administration's count of a total of 228 students in 5 tuzemnye schools in 1908; only 100 of these students were ethnic Turkmen.[22] A year later, according to Count Pahlen, there were 10 tuzemnye schools in the Transcaspian region with 328 students.[23] By the 1914/1915 academic year, the number had indeed grown to 58 tuzemnye schools in the Turkmen territory, but this was compared to 209 mekdeps.[24] And Russian imperial and Soviet documents reveal that mekdeps continued to grow in number for at least a decade after 1917; the traditional schools far outnumbered the Russian-native schools. In 1910 in Transcaspia there were 557 mekdeps with 9,560 students (900 girls) and 56 medreses with 911 students.[25]

Jadidism

Muslims throughout the Russian empire had identified education as a social condition in need of immediate change in order for their people to become modern. Growing dissatisfaction with Islamic and Russian state education available to Muslims in the Russian empire prompted reformers to advocate new methods of teaching as part of a greater discourse addressing the needs of a modern society.[26] New-style mekdeps (elementary schools) were more than reformed schools, they were sites for the reconfiguration of knowledge and the transmission of modern ideas. This is most visible in the works of Tatars, Uzbeks, and Azerbaijanis, but Turkmen also targeted literacy as a means to align their community with the modern world. Historians adopted the term "Jadidism"—from *usul-i jadid*, "new method," or the term for the pedagogy that began in the 1880s with a new set of Tatar schools most closely associated with the Tatar scholar Ismail Bey Gasprinskii (1851–1914).[27] Among Tatars such reformers as Gasprinskii came to be known as Jadids and the new pedagogy paralleled the discourse (Jadidism) surrounding social change and a striving for modernism. However, Turkmen, like most Turkestanis, did not use the term "Jadid" or *jadidçilar*. They used the term *tarakgy* (progress) to refer to the process of modernization they hoped to engender. I refer to the Turkmen who promoted such ideas as Jadid-inspired Turkmen; they were not part of Central Asia's first wave of Jadids, but they certainly espoused an appreciation for progress.

Turkmen came to accept the Jadid notion that "identity was linked to language."[28] Indeed, in the 1910s there was an intellectual exchange about literacy and how Turkmen should learn to read and write. Moreover, because Jadids viewed literacy as crucial to a people's ability to become modern, Turkmen engaged questions of language and alphabet.

Jadid-Inspired Turkmen before 1917

When the Bolsheviks took power in October 1917, a small number of Turkmen were already engaged in questions concerning literacy, language, and learning, confronting issues such as education, women's rights, and identity. The Jadid-inspired Turkmen's ideas are notable even if their numbers were not great. The situation accords with Khalid's suggestion that "those who seek to revolutionize society are scarcely its most typical representatives, nor are they ever the majority."[29]

Although Turkmen lived far from the urban centers where Jadids typically operated, they were not, as Edgar writes, "culturally isolated" from reformist goals.[30] There was a long tradition of Turkmen studying in such centers of Islamic learning as Bukhara, Istanbul, and Ufa, which introduced Turkmen to ideas about Jadidism, modernity, and new ways of learning.[31] Those traditions continued into the twentieth century so that the Turkmen who contributed to new ways of thinking about progress and identity in the 1910s had the benefit of interacting in multicultural settings before returning to Turkmen lands to set up new schools or write newspaper articles. Turkmen not only participated in Jadidism but also, having been educated in other Turkic regions, returned home eager to transfer their knowledge to the next generation of Turkmen.

It was not only the colonial experience with Russia that caused Turkmen to examine their social conditions and ask questions of their place in the world. Influences from around the Muslim world shaped Turkmen thinking as these societies were interactive.[32] Munawwar Qari, Mahmud Khoja Behbudiy, Rizaeddin ibn Fakhreddin, Namık Kemal, Alı Suavi, Ahmed Agaoğlu, Sayyid, Jamal al-Din al-Afghani, and Qasim Amin represented modernist movements from Turkistan, Tatarstan, the Ottoman Empire, Azerbaijan, Iran, and Egypt respectively. Their works provide examples of writing about identity in the Muslim world in the late nineteenth to early twentieth centuries. The works of these representatives aptly illustrate that Turkmen were sometimes chronologically a step behind, but not out of step with the rest of the Muslim world.[33] Comments by Muhammetguly Atabaý oglu (1885–1916) in his article "Much of the work among Turkmen is derived from other people," acknowledged the important influence that other Turks had on Turkmen thinking.[34] Turkmen credited the Tatar Gasprinskii, but they recognized the many voices that had contributed to the arrival of Jadid discourse in Transcaspia. This was underscored by the fact that many Turkmen intellectuals had traveled beyond Turkmen lands to obtain an education. Still, it was the local level that required their attention; many returned home for just that reason.

Educated in Tashkent, Muhammetguly Atabaý oglu and Kümüşaly Böriýew (1896–1942) were two such men.[35] Atabaý oglu, a teacher and publicist, wrote such newspaper articles as "Schools and Türkmen Mekdeps" and "The New School Method," in which he encouraged teachers to use the new phonetic method of teaching promoted by the Tatar Gasprinskii.[36] Men like Böriýew and Aliýew helped directly in the establishment of new method mekdeps in their home villages.[37] Atabaý oglu also set up schools. His were in Nohur, Çeleken, and Şagadam (Türkmenbaşy); the latter two schools were for girls.[38] What these men had in common was a desire to see society reformed.

Abdullah Gelenow, along with the well-known Turkmen poet Berdi Kerbabaýew, studied at a Bukharan medrese before attending St. Petersburg University. Allahguly Garahanow (1892–1938) and Muhammet Geldiýew (1889–1931), authors of early Turkmen language texts, were students of a Bukharan medrese; Geldiýew went on to the Jadid medrese Galiya in Ufa. Abdulhäkym Gulmuhammedow (1885–1931) graduated from a Bukharan medrese, as well as universities in Istanbul and St. Petersburg. Each of these men contributed to new ways of thinking about Turkmen literacy, language, learning, and identity through their poetry, polemics, textbooks, or patronage of schools.

Slightly younger, Hojamurat Baýlyýew (1905–1946) attended a Jadid mekdep in 1914 in his own village in Mary region before entering a Russian state teachers' training school in Mary. He would go on to be a professor at the Institute of History, Language and Literature in Aşgabat, which would later be named for him. The playwright Ayitjan Haldurdyýew attended the Tashkent Pedagogical Institute. There the director, Aliýew mentored Haldurdyýew, advising him to take new approaches to Turkmen themes in literature.[39] Haldurdyýew returned to Transcaspia where his dramatic plays such as "Without a Brideprice" challenged what he saw as "conservative" Muslim ideas.[40]

Muhammetgylyç Biçare (Nizami) (1885–1922), a graduate of a Turkmen new method mekdep in Kaka, used the traditional format of poetry to link the question of education with traditional values and general social needs. Commenting on the antiquated methods of traditional mekdeps and the cultural authority held by clerics, he wrote:

> Hey friends, if you graduate from [an old style] Turkmen mekdep
> No matter how hard you work, in the end you'll be poor
> The imam holds great prestige in the mosque,
> No matter how hard you work, in the end you'll be poor.[41]

Poetry held a special and powerful place in Turkic culture. It was thus an appropriate format for transmitting reformist ideas.

Even some who did not have a Jadid-inspired education contributed to reformist ways of thinking. Molladurdy Annagylgyç (1860–1922), Biçare, and Allahberdi Hojanyýaz oglu (Mollamurt; 1885–1930) obtained their education in local mekdep-medreses. Others such as Süphanberdi Öwezberdi oglu (Körmolla; 1876–1934), and Durdy Kylyç (1886–1950) joined these poets in using their art to promote reformist thinking through Turkmen poetry.[42]

While not positioning themselves against Islam as a tradition, Jadid-inspired Turkmen did want to see changes in Islamic culture. They saw the ulema as an obstacle to progress but did not want to tear down the existing structures as much as they wanted to build up new ones. It was not an anti-Islamic movement but, rather, a reorienting of the social power away from the ulema or clerics and a basic change in attitude toward women. However, this reconfiguration of knowledge and cultural transmission did *not* indicate a move away from Islam. Rather, as Khalid's work demonstrates, these reforms attempted to save Muslim culture by improving from within.[43] Jadid proposals aimed to pull education into a middle space between religious-based instruction and the demands of the secular modern world without completely rejecting Islamic identity. Jadids did not intend to separate instruction into secular and religious with hard divides; rather, they meant to create a merger between epistemological spaces. The fresh intellectual environment taught European sciences as well as Islamic doctrine, redefining knowledge and the social restrictions on access to knowledge. The Russian language was a particularly useful point of accommodation for the Muslims of the empire and one that the reformers incorporated into their new method schools.

Literacy, Schools, and Ulema

In the 1897 census the Russian government estimated Turkmen literacy to be at less than 1 percent.[44] Locals and Russian administrators alike blamed this low number on the traditional Turkestani educational system: the tight social power held by the ulema as teachers, the authority over knowledge the ulema possessed, and the teaching techniques that the mollas used in traditional mekdeps. The general method of instruction—rote memorization of sacred texts rather than functional literacy—was considered the greatest problem. In the end a student was disciplined in Islamic theory and etiquette (*edep-terbiýe*) but had little formal erudition.[45] Russian government schools—or tuzemnye schools (for *tuzemtsy*)—were also an educational option for the Turkmen, although few attended them.[46] An increasing number of educated Turkmen felt that neither school system could serve their children. In a world where literacy was fast becoming a marker of a modern man, reformist Turks perceived traditional Turkestani education to be "deficient."[47] Turkmen reformers' desire to promote mass literacy and to empower Muslims through a reformulation of what defined knowledge required social shifts that realigned the place of the ulema.

As Turkmen came to see older forms of Islamic pedagogy as "deficient" the mollas were identified as the cause of the social deficiencies. Muhammetguly Atabaý oglu attacked mollas, viewing the power they held over knowledge to be one of the greatest problems of the Turkmen people:

> The mollas will awaken in us absolutely nothing useful.
> The mollas have kept your people backward.
> They don't even know right from wrong, yet they receive lots of money.
> Hey, people, don't lend your ears to these mollas.
> Wake up from your sleep![48]

In the 1910s, as the Turkmen questioned traditional methods of pedagogy, they also challenged traditional social status of the teachers—the ulema—and thereby the structure whereby culture and knowledge had been inculcated.

Jadid-educated Turkmen writers referred to their efforts to reform education as "their struggle against the 'numbing' social sickness that had spread among Turkmen." They offered poems and prose that they anticipated "would 'medicate' the tragic condition this sickness had wrought upon their people."[49] In an article titled "The New Method," Öwez Muhammetýar oglu wrote, "We Turkmen passed a lot of time senselessly as if in a deep sleep, in ignorance, like animals. Now, in this century if we observe we will open our eyes to a great world. And realizing this all the tribes will study and learn a skill."[50] Muhammetýar oglu, like Atabaý oglu, represented a new way of thinking about Turkmen society at a time when teachers and poets, linguists, and playwrights experimented with conceptualizations of progress (*tarakgy*), endeavoring to merge Turkmen life and values into the modern world.

Tatars and Uzbeks had earlier spearheaded social and educational reforms while adopting modern Western styles of theater, publishing, or education. They provided models for the Turkmen to follow, encouraging them to preserve their religious and ethnic identity while engaging facets of modern life. Turkmen likewise targeted the mekdep as an arena in which to initiate reforms. In the 1910s they wrote newspaper articles, poetry, and textbooks addressing the new method of teaching, customs concerning women, the role of culture, and the importance of teaching in the Turkmen language (as opposed to Russian or Arabic).[51]

In the nineteenth century and into the twentieth century throughout the Turkic world, a common point of contention was the amount of time it took children to learn to read the alphabet in the traditional Muslim school. A prolific contributor to reformist discourse, Muhammetguly Atabaý oglu highlighted important points in an article:

> Boys, in school are not even able to say their "ABCs" [*elip-bi*]. . . . Mugallym [teacher] Aliýew published a good book in the Turkmen language which adheres to the new school method and its rules, and . . . if children are taught with this book they will be able to read and write in two months' time.[52] After such an education the children will quickly understand writing and will be able to explain the Qur'an and or any other book you put in front of them. Compared to the Turkmen, other peoples have had these new method schools for a long time. That is why they have so many literate people and in their homeland trade/commerce and all profitable things are in their own hands, while we remain behind.
>
> Of course, not every child entering the mekdep and medrese is going to graduate to be a great molla. The majority will finish uninformed and useless. However, if they are taught according to the new system [*emma täze düzgün bilen okadylsa*] none of them will leave without knowing the Muslim writing system. Their learning the alphabet in one place [school] will be of benefit to them.[53]

This sort of article fueled debates among Jadid-inspired Turkmen over methods for teaching literacy in schools. The name for schools, "mekdep," remained, but the qualifier "new method" (*täze usul, yeni usul, täze düzgün*) signified that the author of a newspaper article or a poet was referencing the new teaching style. Some polemicists complained bitterly about old-style mekdeps, teachers who were clerics, and the age-old pedagogy, which, though once revered, they deemed in this age to be insufficient for what the modern world would demand of Turks.

The tradition of learning was one greatly respected in the Muslim world. Turkmen writings leave no doubt that within their value system education of youth ranked highly even though many families could not afford to send their children to school. Atabaý oglu wrote numerous articles about the need for school reform. He argued that in order to effect change in social conditions, the Turkmen community first needed to address instruction of reading and writing, general education, and the modernization of Turkmen culture: "The thing the Turkmen people need more than anything else, more than food and drink, even, is education. Without education one does not advance but stays behind blind . . . [and as the] Qur'an reads in the first sura 'Ya Muhammed! Recite, be!' These words command us to learn. But, which method is easiest to teach children to write and read letters? This is the question."[54] Holding special social authority, teachers (mollas and imams) were elevated to the status of a parent, but even the molla's authority came into question as methods of instruction in traditional mekdeps came under debate. For example, it was no longer enough to be trained in the traditional mekdep or even the medrese system to be a teacher, so Turkmen mekdeps began hiring teachers with the pedagogical training offered at new method schools. Some reformers also stopped referring to teachers with the Persian term *molla* (mawla) and began to use the Arabic term *mugallym* (mu'allim) as a symbolically modern term for teacher.[55]

Changes within education, which had been under the purview of the ulema for centuries, meant disempowering ulema both individually and as a corporate body. Jadids encouraged social change by shifting the authority over formal knowledge away from Islamic texts to broader, secular curricula, adding the Russian language, and punctuating the social shifts that emerged with cultural reform. Cultural capital was shifting.

Awakenings in Turkmen New Method Schools

The first new method mekdeps to open in Transcaspia taught Russian, arithmetic, and geography as well as the local language.[56] There were several points that made these new-style schools different from traditional mekdeps. First, the Jadid-style of teaching was based on a phonetic approach to literacy where students learned to read based on the pronunciation and enunciation of every letter, as opposed to the conventional, syllabic approach used in the traditional mekdeps. Second, the new method's goal was to teach students to read and write in their own language rather than in Arabic or Persian. Third, the new method mekdep "offered its students an expanded curriculum which, besides the time-honored instruction in correct Qur'anic recitation, catechismal study, and calligraphy, also included courses in

Turkic grammar, the fundamentals of arithmetic, the history of Islam, geography, world history and hygiene."[57]

The reason for the founding of these new method schools is succinctly covered in a 1915 news article by Muhammetguly Atabaý oglu in which he argued:

> In our traditional Turkmen schools nothing has changed since the time of Adam. After four to five years children still cannot read or write a letter. However, if children are taught according to the new [method] they learn to read and write inside of one year and in one school. If they learn to read and write according to the new [method] then they will be able to read every sort of book; [even] the Noble Qur'an will be easier to read. It is much easier to teach according to the new method [*täze düzgün boýunça*] because the teacher Aliýew and others have published books according to this method. These books were used to teach other nationalities in their schools, but in ours there was nothing and our children in the mekdeps from morning to evening rocked back and forth, and even the talented ones could not read the ABCs. In three to four years' time they did not know a single thing. . . . Because of this 90 percent of our people cannot read. In some villages there is not a single literate person and they have to go to another place entirely if they want to learn their letters. Our [Turkmen] are unschooled in trade and every profitable thing is in the hands of other nationalities, and in every way we were left behind, . . . Slowly, *Inşallah*, we are embarking upon that road and joining those nations . . . moving toward change.[58]

That same year, Muhammetýar oglu wrote about the success one would find in a new-style mekdep: "For a long spell I studied our mother tongue in a Turkmen mekdep that was teaching with the traditional method [*köne usul bilen sapak berýän Türkmen mekdepde*]. When I graduated I could not read or write a thing. However, I attended a new school in Tejen where I took classes from our respected teacher Alyşbek Aliýew and in just a short time I learned to read both Turkmen and Russian. Because of the new method [*ýeni usul*] I can now read and write anything."[59] The definition of literacy was shifting from recitation to functional literacy (reading and writing on any subject). Literacy was becoming operational rather than just ceremonial.

Reformist discourse often employed "sleep" or a state of ignorance as a trope. This metaphor referred to the social and cultural backwardness from which reformers believed enlightenment could "wake" people and put them on the path to modernity. The writer Orazmämmet Wepaý oglu was living in the northern Daşoguz region when he wrote poetry that invoked the image of a sleeping Turkmen in which he addressed Berdi Kerbabaýew, who was living in Aşgabat. The manner in which he addressed Kerbabaýew was part of the Socratic question/answer (*sorag/ jogap*) format that many polemics took and was in fact the name of this section of the newspaper.[60]

Hey, esteemed Kerbabaý, I have a question for you
How many years is it going to take to open the Turkmen eyes?
You take a look around and then get back to me.
Which language do we need to wake our people from their sleep?[61]

Turkmen began adopting such language after attending Jadid mekdeps and medreses in Ufa, Bukhara, and Istanbul, and after being influenced by other Muslims such as the Young Turks.[62]

Muhammetýar oglu also described a Turkmen awakening as if from a deep sleep. In his article titled "New Method," he referenced the new century and underscored the usefulness of learning to read and write in both Russian and Turkmen:

> For a long time, we Turkmen were useless and in a deep sleep. That is, we were ignorant.... Now, in this century if we take stock of the world our eyes will open and the tribes will be educated, they will learn skills and everything will be before us. Because of all of this, in the world there is pleasure and people are living comfortable lives. At this time in history with our great White Tsar's permission we Turkmen are living well.... In our cities and in our villages with his permission schools were opened for us, in them very good mollas have been assigned and are teaching our Turkmen boys the necessary academics. Besides giving classes in the Russian language the molla also offers proper classes in sharia and our mother tongue.[63]

Again we see the reconceptualization of literacy. Here the author clearly values functional literacy over the recitation of limited passages from memory.

Gasprinskii maintained that traditional Muslim schools had become "asylums for the infirm and unemployed." He wrote, "Industries have been paralyzed and are on the decline. We have become a negligible quantity in commerce, finance and the merchant marine."[64] This complaint recurs in the writings of Turkmen authors who focus on "prosperity" and the connection between society's levels of education and literacy and their access to trade and commerce; their writings underscore that literacy is the mechanism for achieving material wealth. Authors lamented their situation in the newspaper *Ruznama-i Mawera-i Bahr-i Hazar* with one author writing, "If we remain uneducated we will starve [*ylymsyzlyk derdinden özlerimizi horlaýaris*]."[65]

Another article began, "For how long were you taught that to study in the—scholarly—language of our Russian enemy or that to learn Russian or other languages is a sin? We Turkmen have opened our eyes and realized that we are behind all of our neighbors and brethren [*taýpalardan*].... People!" It went on to excoriate the Turkmen people for allowing themselves to be duped into believing there was nothing useful in Russian. The author praised schooling, the sciences, and the trades and cited a Turkmen proverb (*nakyl*) about not forgetting that it is the educated who are the friends of God (*Hudaý*). He reminded his fellow Turkmen that without "language," by which he means erudition, they will remain like animals. But with schooling and by learning trades they could overcome the wretchedness that their people once faced.[66]

Acknowledgment of change in the world led to an increasing recognition of the need for knowledge of secular subjects. Some reformers followed Gasprinskii in arguing for a wholly secular education, but the great majority retained a strong personal identification as Muslims and sought not to separate students from their Islamic heritage but, rather, to save that heritage from decline. Reformist Turkmen built upon social concepts from other cultures—and Tatars were influential, introducing such ideas as universal education, mass literacy, and Western methods of schooling. It was with these concepts that Turkmen sought to preserve their ethno religious heritage.[67] Gasprinskii's discourse in European Russia equated modernity with secularization, but among Turkmen the reformist discourse was not anti-Islamic. Turkmen sources expressed desires to reform the curriculum of mekdeps and medreses and aspirations for increased literacy and general knowledge among Turkmen, but they did not argue that the mekdeps should be secularized or that Islamic values should be abandoned. In fact, they argued that Islamic values should be expanded—for example, that the schools should take in more students, especially women.

Educating Women as part of the Turkmen *Millet*

An important topic discussed in Jadid-inspired Turkmen literature was that of women in society. Authors pushed for better social conditions, education, and the rights of women. Turkmen, like Tatars and Uzbeks, wrote about the need to reform society "to make life better for women in the interest of the greater millet."[68] It was still early to speak of a Turkmen nation. But the term *millet*, which would come to mean "nation" proper, was already being used to recognize the Turkmen apart from other groups or peoples.[69] This included distinguishing between themselves and other Turkic peoples.[70] For example, they wrote of "we Turkmen [*biz Türkmen*]" and "other peoples [*başga milletler*]" and of the "boys and girls of their own Turkmen millet [*öz Türkmen milletleriň gyz oglanlary*]."[71] Molladurdu Nizami wrote:

There is no greater work in the world than service to one's people [*il*]
With knowledge your youth will bring prosperity to the group [*millet*].[72]

Newspaper articles refer not only to the "Turkmen *millet*" and "our *millet* [*milletimiziň*]" but also to the *Türkmen dili* (language). In 12 percent of newspaper articles the qualifier *Teke* was used to indicate a tribal identity, 85 percent of articles used the word *Türkmen* to describe a school, language, person, or idea; 4 percent of news articles used both terms. Although *millet* did not yet signify the conceptualization of a nation among the Turkmen tribes, it does seem to indicate an awareness of distinction between other Turkic peoples, on one hand, and those who spoke a Turkmen dialect in addition to possessing a Turkmen genealogy, on the other.[73]

Jadid-inspired Turkmen focused on elevating the entire Turkmen community, and in their opinion women needed specific attention, since "traditional" customs left women undereducated and with underdeveloped skills. The reformist Turkmen writers wanted Turkmen women to modernize, to progress, to have access to better education, and to be free of customs such as bride-price (*galyň*). Atabaý oglu addressed these questions in his article "Newly Opened Turkmen Schools," writing: "I am told that among the Ýomuts of Çeleken sixty-plus women and girls study and learn to write in the new educational framework. . . . A new school system has been founded in Çeleken. Seven-year-old girls will begin studying at these new schools within the next five to six months. . . . Thank God! Turkmen have [also] established new method schools in Ahal, Mary, and Tejen."[74] Later articles focusing on the social condition of women included titles that translate as "Human trade among Turkmen from the perspective of the bride-price" and "A good new custom."[75] Such men as Muhammet Atabaý oglu argued that women should be educated for the sake of the community.[76] However, most of the discussion was about women, not by them.

Bride-price (*galyň*) was a tradition that came under attack in the early Soviet years.[77] But even before that, debates had been taking place among Muslims as to its worth. Some authors wrote specifically of the inequities of galyň and how it could reduce women to an exchange at the bazaar.[78] Like Atabaý oglu and Sabyr Söýün, Öwezgeldi Mämetgurban oglu from Tejen wrote that Turkmen should eliminate galyň. Mämetgurban oglu related a detailed story of a family who had been in court fighting over a bride-price. It concerned the question of whether the bride's father or the man she had run off with had a right to the bride-price. Mämetgurban oglu explained that there had been no Islamic scholarly (*kazy*) decision (*karar*) on this topic and the Turkmen people needed one. Better yet, he suggested that the custom be eliminated.[79]

One of the main differences between Turkmen and other Turkic groups seems to be the degree of emphasis placed on women and the amount of time devoted to women's issues in literature. Marianne Kamp and Adeeb Khalid demonstrate that the role of women was a major focus of Jadidism among Uzbeks, but there is nowhere near the weight placed on this issue in the Turkmen sources. From the small and scattered information about women and the miniscule amount written by women in the Turkmen publications, it is clear that they were not as involved in the reformist movement as extensively as other Turks. The number of Jadidist or reformist sources in the Turkmen language is not nearly as large as in Tatar, Uzbek, or Azerbaijani. However, what is extant is indicative of the broader ideas connecting the advancement of the *millet* or *il* (people) with the betterment of women's lives. Efforts to include women in the push for modernity reflected pains to address society as a whole. Print culture reflected these broad social aims.

Jadidism and Print Culture

New method classrooms provided locations for direct presentation of reformist ideas to Turkmen students, while print media carried Jadid-inspired discourse beyond the classroom. The term "new method" referred primarily to the pedagogy of literacy and soon came to denote the new style of mekdep that utilized it, and it was also heavily associated with a greater reform discourse especially that found in print culture.[80]

Newspapers and textbooks were crucial in heralding and explaining the aims of reformist projects. In Gasprinskii's 1881 publication *Russkoe musul'manstvo*, he assessed the condition of life for Muslims in the Russian empire and the traditional form of Islamic higher education in the medrese. Later, his bilingual Russian/Turkic gazette *Terjüman/Perevodchik* (1883–1915) became his most important publication as it was read by Turks around the empire. Beginning as a weekly subscription in 1904, it grew to a daily paper by 1912, disseminating Jadid ideas throughout the Turkic world.[81] The thrust of *Terjüman* was simply that "the more knowledgeable and cultured a people are, the more they will progress, strengthen themselves, and increase their wealth. The greater the number of schools, libraries, books and newspapers that a people have the more knowledgeable and cultured they will become."[82] Literacy was Gasprinskii's means for getting both children and adults to join him on his journey to modernity.

Central Asian reformers used the press to discuss their concerns publicly. The bilingual Turkmen/Persian newspaper *Ruznama-i Mawera-i Bahr-i Hazar* began in December 1914.[83] Published for just over two years (it closed in April 1917), it reveals a great deal about Turkmen society at that time. On 14 December 1914, in an article titled "To the Turkmen People," Muhammetguly Atabaý oglu announced that "today is a great, genuine holiday for us!" and that it was the duty of the Turkmen people to put out the brand-new newspaper *Ruznama-i Mawera-i Bahr-i Hazar*, "in our own language, to broaden the thinking of our uneducated Turkmen."

> This newspaper, published for our people in our language and [designed] to reform them, will open the thoughts of our uneducated, illiterate Turkmen. Thank God it is our duty. Thank God our people [*millet*] got in line with the other nations [*millet*]. Every nation was putting out a newspaper except for the Turkmen who did not know how to do anything well. Among all the nations in every way Turkmen could not recover [from their ignorance]. Perhaps . . . now, if we gradually open our eyes and join the [other] nations [*il*], reading the newspaper for all the news, if we are able to work and . . . if we repair the things in which we are deficient . . . and of course if people who [do] learn to read will read the articles in this newspaper and other works to those who cannot read, we, with God's blessing, will slowly set forth on the path of religion

[Islam]. Thank God these days [the numbers of] learned among the Turkmen . . . boys studying in schools, and people who can read is increasing daily. . . .

What gets printed in this Turkmen language newspaper will be accurate. [Whether about] war, the market, education, farming, customs and laws, or any other such topic. This newspaper will announce all local news as well as useful news from around the world. For that reason, I advise all my schooled Turkmen brothers, [that] it would be a great blessing [*sogap*] to all those who straight away subscribe to this newspaper in their name and then share it with those in their neighborhood who cannot read themselves.[84]

The paper covered several categories of news, which it announced in the first issue. First, always, came news from the government of the Transcaspian oblast announcing, for example, long lists of names of brave men who had received medals in World War I or when the state was in need of donations to host a religious commemoration (*Hudaý ýoly*). This section also included *uruş habarlary* (news about the war), a section that grew longer and longer with each issue, keeping Turkmen abreast of important details such as the Battle at the Dardanelles in the Ottoman empire. Reformists considered newspapers to be repositories of information about the world and themselves as signs of progress. Articles about the evolution of other societies and the need for Turkmen to catch up to them were common. A specific concern, perhaps the most important to reformist Turkmen, was literacy. This is reflected in articles such as the one that discussed how useful it was to have a newspaper in the Turkmen language so that the people could understand the world and "get out of the rut of illiteracy [*sowatsyzlyk*]" in which they had been stuck.[85]

A section titled "News" (*Habarlar*) reported with jubilation any time *Ruzna-ma-i Mawera-i Bahr-i Hazar* reached yet another hamlet of Turkmen society. During World War I there was a paper shortage, so increasing the number of papers printed and getting them out to the villages was a victory with each issue. The news from the *uezds* (district governments) had a personal touch to it, including various telegrams, often from soldiers wishing the people at home well or sending greetings to a specific person, or begging an old friend to write to them. The most pragmatic articles were about agriculture, animal husbandry, and general issues concerning cultivation, such as the irrigation of crops or the price of cotton around the world. Any of this would have been of interest to a great many readers—or listeners, in the case of those who had the newspapers read aloud to them—as most families were engaged in some form of farming or animal husbandry. News from villages was a category the editors promised to cover, but it was typically mixed in with the rest, especially regarding schools.[86]

This newspaper was an important source of information about schools, both those established by the tsarist government to teach Russian language and culture and the new method schools established by locals with private funds.[87] Some notices were as simple, as "In Aşgabat village, in a school where both Russian and Turkmen languages are taught, there are now Russian students studying Turkmen language."[88] But even the tiniest bits of news were more detailed sometimes because they were actually serving as advertisements: "At Aşgabat's school for older girls [*Uly gyz şkolynda*] the Turkmen Ata molla's wife in the carpet-weaving school is teaching the landlord's daughter and other girls the 'molla alphabet' [Arabic script] very quickly so that they will be able to go and teach Turkmen [*Turkmen milletleriň*] boys and girls. This woman is taking a salary like any other molla."[89] The example is worthy of note as it not only shows the typical sort of notice that appeared in the newspaper but also tells us a little about the ways schools were advertised. This carpet-weaving school taught literacy and promised to do so well enough that the students would be able to become teachers themselves. The instructor was a woman and was advertising to both boys and girls. Gender segregation did not apply in this school, which is interesting for the time but clearly was part of the change that schools were going through.

When authors argued that it was for the good of society to educate women, or that the very concept of literacy was one that should be embraced, they were taking part in the debate that had been rousing the Turkic world. When a Russian-language teacher arrived to work at a new method mekdep, the name of the instructor, the number of the school, and its location were all announced so students could begin attending. "In the village of Aşgabat a large mekdep which teaches in both Turkmen and Russian has been opened and a lot of boys are coming to this mekdep to study. In this [newly] opened mekdep those teaching the Turkmen language will be such mollas as Meret Işan Körata oglu, while Tejenli Ata Kelewmyrat oglu has been assigned to teach the Russian language. That is why every day more boys are enrolling in this school."[90] The articles are full of detail and frequently plead with the Turkmen readers to seize the opportunity of progress (*taragky*) and not to be left behind the other peoples (*milletler*) again.

Within just a few months of its initial publication, *Ruznama-i Mawera-i Bahr-i Hazar* was already full of letters from the public.[91] There was a section for Turkmen to write to the paper, titled "Bize näme ýazýarlar?" and especially for poetry to be printed. Letters, articles, and poems reveal much about everyday life as well as about the social change that reformers were hoping to stimulate. Letters came in from readers singing the praises of the gazette and emphasizing the fact that it was being published in the vernacular:

> I am from the village of Kaka. Because there is no newspaper in Turkmen I get the daily from Baku, but I do not understand this very well. One day while walking around the bazar I came across a man holding a newspaper in his hand and I asked if I could look at it. I asked immediately, "Where did you get this newspaper?!" He said, 'In the city of Aşgabat there is a new newspaper being published in this Turkic language."

> I heard the man's answer with great pleasure, then I bought my own newspaper and
> I read that very Turkmen newspaper every day. In that paper, I read the intellectual
> words of the poet Molla Durdy written in our own language [*dilimiz*]. Every person
> will be able to read this Turkmen newspaper.[92]

This man's letter showed great enthusiasm for reading the news as well as for the
Turkmen language. This attitude toward the vernacular, underscored by such references as "our language [*dilimiz*]," indicate that language was beginning to act as
a marker of identity.

The Modified Arabic Script

The Turks of Central Asia had been using the Arabic script roughly since the ad-
vent of Islam in their region, but by the mid-nineteenth century reform-minded
Turks began to debate its perceived inadequacy for the Turkic languages.[93] Because
their new pedagogy relied no longer on memorization but on a phonetic method
of teaching functional literacy, instructors became "sensitized" to the unphonetic
nature of the Arabic script and identified it as a "poor instrument for mass education."[94] Several intellectuals independently proposed Turkified forms of writing
in an Arabic-based script. They did not wish to abandon the sacred script of their
religious community, but they wanted their writing to reflect Turkic sounds and
the immediate demands of literacy. They added diacritics, creating letters, to make
the alphabet more specific for clearly identifying Turkic vowel sounds. They also
eliminated some consonants.

Accurate representation of the Turkmen vernacular became key to Turkmen
writing in the Arabic script. A point of concern was long vowel representation. In
spoken Turkmen there are prominent long vowels.[95] Why should Turkmen have
been bothered over such a small detail when there was so much work to do toward
basic literacy? This level of detail was precisely the point. Denotation of long vowels
in writing became a way to chronicle Turkmen identity alphabetically. It was one
local response to the universal consideration of literacy.

The phonetic method appealed to Turkmen primarily because Turkic languages have more vowel sounds than the traditional Arabic orthography can represent.
For example, the three Arabic vowels (و, ى, ٱ) do not suffice for: [a], [ä], [e], [i],
[y], [o], [ö], [u], [ü]. Furthermore, in addition to these nine vowel sounds shared
by all Turkic languages, the Turkmen language possesses five distinct long vowels.
The traditional orthography did not reflect these long vowels. But an expanded,
modified alphabet—with the addition of diacritics—could reflect all the sounds
of Turkmen.

The authors of this reform believed that a greater representation of the spoken
word in print would increase intelligibility and aid in literacy.[96] Moreover, it would

assert a Turkmen identity since it took the Arabic script used by all Muslims and refined it according to the vernacular. The alphabet represented Turkmen-ness in a concrete way. Written language became pivotal to Turkmen self-expression while the details of language content, alphabets, and even punctuation symbolized the speech community's positioning of itself within the world.

As Turkmen became concerned with increasing literacy they also thought about teaching it more efficiently. Reformers considered the phonetic method of teaching to be the quickest means to literacy. This core component of Jadidism was Gasprinskii's pedagogical approach, and Jadid-inspired Turkmen came to see it as the quickest means to expedite literacy and enlightenment more generally.[97] This method required every phoneme (sound) to be marked by a distinct grapheme (symbol). The idea stemmed from nineteenth-century Turkic efforts to stimulate mass literacy and the resultant belief that accurate representation of speech would ease teaching and expedite literacy.[98]

While constructing new versions of the alphabet, these Turks were also molding important symbols of group identity that would later support a national consciousness. These efforts carried over into the Soviet period and intensified when Turkification splintered into such aspirations for national language development as Turkmenification for Turkmen and Uzbekification for Uzbek.

Conclusion

By the nineteenth century, European romantic nationalism had solidified justifications for distinctive national identities based on cultural properties such as language. Nevertheless, at that time, language was still not the definitive marker of identity in Central Asia. It was not until the early twentieth century that language began to emerge as but one variable of identity, along with religion, genealogy, territory, legal category, and colonial status.[99] The Jadid-inspired Turkmen's generation was the first for which language was a marker of identity. Khalid writes that, while romantic notions of identity promulgated change in concepts of identity, "the real change [in the use of the term *millet*] came with schooling." That is, until the influence of Jadidism arrived in Central Asia, Turkmen mekdeps relied primarily on books in Persian and Arabic. However, one of the central tenets of Jadidism was that students should be taught in their mother tongue. Khalid writes, "If functional literacy was a desired goal, it had to be achieved only in the child's native language."[100] The vernacular, both in schools and in the press, was the medium for reaching the people and spreading modern ideas.

Cultural capital was shifting from information transmitted orally to erudition that would be reproduced in written or printed form.[101] The definition of knowledge was changing, and the understanding of literacy was undergoing revision. Whereas it had earlier been enough for a student to recite from memory excerpts from a limited number of books, reformers expected students to learn to read and write on any number of subjects.

One area where the Turkmen reformers differed from the Tatar Gasprinksii, the father of Jadidism, was on the topic of a unified or pan-Turkic language, which had been a central tenet of Gasprinskii's philosophy. Turkmen gratefully acknowledged Gasprinskii's many other unique ideas and contributions but disagreed with his proposal to unify the Turkic languages because Turkmen chose to underscore their group identity with their written language and the alphabet. They saw the written language as being a reflection of their group identity and insisted on denoting the peculiarities of their regional speech in writing. Modernizing Turkmen society identified itself as both Islamic and Turkic, as well as a Russian colony; but in reforming their alphabet and schools, they asserted a Turkmen identity. The Turkmen *millet* was not yet synonymous with a national identity but was the concept of being Turkmen that linked those Oguz Turks who did not see themselves as Ottoman or Azerbaijani. This concept came to share much in common with what did develop into a national identity, though it remained primarily based on genealogical and—increasingly in the twentieth century—linguistic factors.

As Jadidism made its way throughout Russia it eventually made its way to Transcaspia. It was brought home by learned men, such as those Turkmen who had traveled abroad, and many who had been educated in Tatar and Uzbek Jadid schools, returning to open new method schools for Turkmen. These patrons and the parents who sent their children to the new method schools wanted to see Turkmen educated in an innovative way, and they drew a direct connection between literacy, language, and modernity. Understanding Jadidism and any activism leading up to 1917 helps us to better perceive ways that Turkmen intellectuals dealt with the possibilities and pressures the Soviet policy of *korenizatsiia* (indigenization) presented to them in the 1920s. Moreover, an awareness of the construction of Turkmen identity and the nation enhances our understanding of today's Turkmenistan.

Chapter 2

Partners in Progress

Turkmen Intellectuals in Soviet Space, 1917–1930

Literacy will facilitate the brotherhood of the many Soviet peoples.

From the earliest days after the Bolsheviks took power from the Provisional Government in October 1917, they recognized the power of education and literacy as tools of "cultural transformation."[1] One of the Bolsheviks' core goals was to make the peoples of the former Russian empire literate.[2] At the end of the Civil War (1918–1921), in addition to the challenges of material reconstruction, the Bolsheviks faced the need to gain control over the disparate political insurgencies that had surfaced around the former empire; they needed to repair a failing economy and unite a vast land full of cultural and ethnic diversity. Considering the material demands the new government faced, it was an extraordinary time for Moscow to support programs related to language and education. Yet these were central to the concepts of socialist progress, and the Party would not forgo them. Indeed, the Party used literacy, language, and learning to transform the former imperial subjects into Soviet nations and nationalities.[3] At the same time, the Bolsheviks also used these cultural programs to aid military measures in solidifying their control.[4]

In the 1910s literacy had referred to functional skills of reading and writing, but into the 1920s and 1930s the Bolshevik leadership aimed for *political* literacy. They were concerned not simply with functional literacy but also with knowledge of Party ideology, which would push the "backward" Turkmen forward to become literate in socialism.[5] Lenin had said, "As long as there is such a thing in the country as illiteracy it [was] rather hard to talk about political education."[6] He needed people to be able to engage political philosophy as well as read and write. Literacy was fundamental to the plan to build a new socialist state. Thus, illiteracy became an "enemy of the state."

After 1917 educated Turkmen continued to work toward fostering an enlightened population—only now within a socialist framework. Bolsheviks, like the Jadid-inspired Turkmen, believed that enlightenment (*prosveshchenie/bilimlik*), education (*obrazovanie/magaryf*), and upbringing/learning (*vospitanie/terbiýe*) would produce a progressive modern society. Even as they transformed them, the Bolsheviks fortified Jadid-era beliefs. They also encouraged exploration of the connection between language and group identity in Central Asia.

A decade earlier, a handful of educated Turkmen approached the twentieth century with a desire to participate in the changing world. Yet they struggled with questions about their identity and the preservation of their heritage. Jadidism allowed for the exploration of both of these and offered attractive approaches for several Turkmen intellectuals. By the early 1920s, as Turkmen cultural elites approached Soviet central policy in a manner that addressed local concerns about culture and identity, they adapted to a socialist framework. Like many other intellectuals around the former empire they negotiated a space for their local concerns within central state policy by creating a partnership.[7] Moscow forged an alliance with local representatives like Jadid-inspired Turkmen who wanted to reform society.

As Turkmen reformism began to merge with Soviet socialism, Turkmen intellectuals worked in a new atmosphere, within wholly new institutions, and under unstable, unpredictable pressures. They worked toward constructing a progressive, literate society that dovetailed with Soviet aspirations to shape a modern, socialist people. For many Turkmen participants this partnership would not last beyond the 1930s when an ideological shift created a rupture in cultural work, and the "partners" found themselves persecuted as "counterrevolutionaries" and "bourgeois nationalists" in Party purges.

It is interesting to continue the exploration of the intersections of culture and power as Turkmen began working within the Soviet system. While Turkmen reformist efforts continued into the Soviet period, there were important sociopolitical differences between tsarist Central Asia and Soviet Central Asia. The Soviet state was an "activist, interventionist, mobilization state" that aimed ultimately to achieve a utopian, classless state.[8] Through the merger of nationalities (*sliianie*) the state also aimed to eliminate the ethnic differences among peoples. Since Russian was the "language of international communication," this merging of all Soviet cultures into one society was going to take the form of Russification.[9]

Modernization was expected to take place at an accelerated rate. Many undertakings such as the standardization of languages, establishment of education, creation of print media, and the carrying out of literacy campaigns were historical experiences shared by others around the world, but the role of the state and the speed with which the Soviet state undertook to remake society distinguished the Soviet experience.[10] Through these years, the political setting changed and the fortunes of Turkmen intellectuals were altered, offering another occasion to apply Bourdieu's concepts of linguistic capital and symbolic power.

Transcaspian Dialects

In October 1917 the Bolsheviks began to take control over most of what had been the Russian empire. The people endured enormous upheaval, including years of illness, famine, and civil war before the Bolsheviks were in full control. In mid-

1918, not long after the signing of the Treaty of Brest-Litovsk, which pulled Russia from World War I, civil war broke out in the former empire. An alliance between Turkmen locals under the leadership of Serdar Oraz and Russian White troops established the Socialist Revolutionary Transcaspian Provisional Government in Transcaspia. That political coalition appealed to the British for assistance, and together they fought the Bolsheviks for control of the area through July 1919.[11] Despite such pockets of resistance, the Bolsheviks began their formal administration of Central Asia in 1918 with the establishment of the Turkestan Autonomous Soviet Socialist Republic (1918–1924).[12] Within this entity a great many Turkmen lived in the Transcaspian oblast or region. On 7 August 1921, the Transcaspian oblast was renamed the Turkmen oblast. Then, in 1924, as part of the policy of delimitation (*razmezhevanie*) of Turkestan, Moscow created the Soviet Socialist Republic of Turkmenistan out of the regions where most Turkmen had lived: Transcaspia, Khiva, and Bukhara. Among the Turkmen who lived in what became Turkmenistan when the borders were drawn in 1924, 43 percent had previously lived in the Turkmen oblast of Turkestan (or Transcaspia), 27 percent had lived in Bukhara, and 30 percent had lived in Khiva.[13] As Edgar points out, these three populations "had been exposed to different historical experiences and influences over a period of several centuries."[14] Thus Turkmenistan was not homogeneous; it was tribally diverse, and each tribe spoke a distinct dialect.

Building Socialism (*Sotsialisticheskoe stroitel'stvo*)

Despite the tumult the first years of Soviet power constituted a period of great cultural enterprise. The Bolsheviks wanted to be in control both militarily and politically but, also, to wield symbolic power that would mobilize the masses to support socialist power throughout the Soviet Union. They wanted control over the means of production as well as the symbols of power: language, architecture, music, even alphabets. To this end Bolsheviks established relationships with local intellectuals both for practical purposes and in the hope that the appearance of management of the national regions by local cadres would allay any potential bitterness toward the new centralized government in Moscow, which wanted to distance itself from the image and memory of its imperial predecessor.[15]

Upon gaining power, Bolsheviks immediately issued numerous decrees to revolutionize everyday life and to reform society. They put forth reforms dealing with land, workers' rights, sports, and the body; family matters such as divorce, and the rights of women and children; they even altered the Russian alphabet.[16] However, to see these decrees through Bolsheviks and the state needed experienced and trained intellectuals, scientists, doctors, teachers, and the like. In order to strengthen the numbers of "specialists" and "experts" the Party would have to recruit every source of talent. The only way of meeting long-term needs was through the rapid creation and education of a new socialist intelligentsia.[17] Yet people not only in Turkestan but around the former empire were, in Lenin's opinion, "distressingly backward."[18]

Old Bolsheviks disliked the partnership, but until new, "loyal" cadres could be trained (especially in technical areas) the Party would continue to rely on the expertise of the old specialists and intellectuals.[19] Lenin shared his fellow revolutionaries' disdain for "bourgeois experts" and the old intellectuals against whom they would soon wage a "class war," but noted that as long as there was widespread illiteracy it would be impossible to build socialism.[20] In the short term, the Bolsheviks needed the old specialists; in the long term, however, they wanted to create cadres loyal to the Soviet state to replace them. Thus, Moscow focused on indoctrinating and training local cadres who would grow into the role of the new intelligentsia and workers. In many lands Moscow consciously sought to control social power by redefining it. The state set forth to strip the old intellectuals of their status and redistribute that status among proven socialist cadres. Among Turkmen intellectuals this meant control over learning, literacy, and print culture.

In 1919 Moscow created the Council of National Minorities (Sovnatsmen) within the Commissariat of Enlightenment (Narkompros) and made it responsible for allocating more duties to locals. Sovnatsmen was further expected to foster development of local languages so that socialism could be communicated clearly in the local tongue. In addition to training local cadres, Bolsheviks believed that by encouraging "forms" of nationhood they could quicken the emergence of "class cleavages," encouraging the peasants and proletariat of the various ethnicities to join in the building of socialism.[21] That is, the national proletariat would realize they had more in common with workers of other nationalities than with the other classes within their nation and would choose to join forces with the workers of the world rather than remain tied to the bourgeoisie simply because of a shared language or national heritage. The Bolsheviks also thought that by taking control of nationalism they could keep it from becoming a site for reactionary elements against Moscow. The state allocated considerable resources to institutionalizing national identities through the demarcation of territories, writing official histories, building up cultures, and standardizing and codifying languages.[22]

This policy of nationalization (*natsionalizatsiia*), for example, Turkmenification or Uzbekification, or nation building (*natsionalnoe stroitelstvo*) after the Twelfth Party Congress in 1923 came to be known as *korenizatsiia* (indigenization).[23] During the 1920s this program emphasized equality among national cultures. It endorsed national languages over Russian in the workplace, so as to replace those Europeans who had been part of the Russian imperial government with indigenous leaders literate in the local vernacular in order to develop national cadres.[24] Thus, Moscow envisioned local administrators as vessels through whom central organs would convey socialist ideology in the local language; information would be national in form, but socialist in content. While Bolsheviks generally viewed korenizatsiia as a temporary measure, they also expected that with the right policies and institutional structures "the greater historical process of the 'convergence' [*sblizhenie*] and 'merger' [*sliianie*] of nationalities" would advance toward one proletarian culture.[25]

The Struggle against Illiteracy

The harrowing conditions brought on by war and the revolutionary spirit of the Bolsheviks let to a militarization of language and everyday life. Culture became the "third front" after the war and the economy.[26] It remained an important "front" for decades with "cultural soldiers" or the "culture army" in the vanguard.[27] On that front, Lenin declared that "the fight against illiteracy was the single most important cultural task."[28] Alphabet became identified as an armament in the "struggle against illiteracy." *Sowatlyk ugrunda göreş* (Struggle for literacy) was a Turkmen-language newspaper dedicated to this question that reveals the combative language used to describe the situation. The revolutionaries' militaristic attitude encouraged an aggressive approach toward the role of culture in Soviet society. The Bolsheviks created the All-Union Extraordinary Commission for the Liquidation of Illiteracy (*likvidatsiia bezgramotnosti* [*likbez*]), a unionwide institution that undertook a campaign to eradicate illiteracy from Russia and the former imperial lands.[29] Extending the language of mobilization, the short form of this commission's title was gramCheka; conjuring up the siege mentality of a military campaign it combined the acronym for the secret police, *Cheka*, with the abbreviation for "literacy"—"*gram*" (*gramotnost'*).[30] The Bolsheviks were not afraid of sending signals that they were willing to use coercion.[31] The language of Bolshevism was an aggressive revolutionary speech. *Likbez* became an adjective to describe the new network of literacy schools; "Liquidation of Illiteracy!" became a cultural war cry.[32]

The Anti-Illiteracy Commission was responsible for generating activities to stir public interest in literacy skills. To assist, in 1918 printing and education departments were created within the Commissariat of Nationalities (Narkomnats) to supply local language materials to non-Russian peoples.[33] In December 1919 the Soviet People's Commissariat (Sovnarkom) issued a directive to national leaders to begin work on the eradication of illiteracy as a fundamental step in bringing revolutionary culture to the masses in the shortest time possible.[34] Permission, funding, and ideological guidance arrived from Moscow, but the Party expected local representatives to oversee the intricacies of reform: alphabet reform, teacher training, publishing textbooks and newspapers in vernacular languages, opening schools, and offering short courses.[35] The literacy campaign was itself a platform for the greater plan of modernizing citizens so as to create a socialist state; it also supported such immediate goals as educating the local populace in order to move them into the workforce.[36] The education of children was not ignored, but for the first several years the Soviet government focused its efforts on adult literacy as the state sought to quickly educate cadres.[37] The Commissariat of Enlightenment of the Turkmenistan Soviet Socialist Republic (TSSR) made local cadres responsible for conveying literacy to the people via book clubs, red teahouses, red clubs, red yurts, libraries, and reading rooms where they could read newspapers and other official literature.[38] Workers would also be offered night courses. Despite the enthusiasm of cultural workers, during the Civil War the struggle against illiteracy was fought primarily on paper, in decrees, and little of it actually touched people's lives.[39] The situation turned when Lenin's wife, Nadezhda Krupskaia, called for the creation of a network of small literacy schools or *likpunkty* (liquidation points) where a person would study for one or two hours a week in crash courses.[40] Running from six weeks to four months, these short courses for adults (over age fifteen) could be designed to teach functional literacy to the illiterate or political literacy to the semiliterate.[41]

During the Civil War, the role of the Red Army among Turkmen had been especially important on the Transcaspian cultural front, where men could be organized and brought together for regular classes. Soon after winning Transcaspia from the Social Revolutionaries (and British "interventionists"), Moscow created an oblast-level Narkompros office in the capital city Poltoratsk (Aşgabat).[42] Within this office was a commission that organized three-month courses for students, registered those who were studying and assigned them to a school, organized night classes for workers, oversaw the library and museums, and was responsible for a conservatory. Although it was difficult to organize schools and libraries, and of course to train more teachers, between 1919 and 1920 the Red Army managed to open 108 likbez schools for illiterate adults, 53 schools for the semiliterate, and 16 schools for literate adults in Transcaspia.[43] In the fall of 1920, the Red Army even established schools for local minorities so that there were likbez institutions for Uzbeks, Kazakhs, Tajiks, Tatars, and others in Transcaspia. Still, there were never enough books or supplies for any of the schools. In the 1920/1921 school year, there were only thirty thousand readers in Turkmen published for children, ten thousand math textbooks, and twenty-five thousand geography textbooks, for a population of one million.[44] There were simply not enough books—for children or adults.

In line with central directives and decrees from Narkompros, the first *likpunkty* (short course) was a two-month course on general education in Turkmen including basic math, geography, political literacy, methods of teaching literacy, familiarization with the fundamental principles of dialectical materialism, and the basic ideas for organizing elementary schools. The first sixty graduates were sent out into the regions of Poltoratsk, Tejen, and Mary *uezd*s to help the local Party representatives, the soviets, and Red Army representatives organize Soviet schools. In the fall of 1919, after the "liberation" of Poltoratsk, the *dayhans* (farmers/peasants) began organizing Soviet schools in *aul*s (villages) for children and a school for adults in the vicinity of Poltoratsk.[45] By the end of the 1919/1920 school year there were eighty schools with year-long courses for children serving thirty-five hundred students throughout Transcaspia. In addition, forty likpunkty were created to teach literacy to adults.[46] In the summer of 1920 there were in Poltoratsk one hundred students in the summer course.[47]

In 1921 Stalin, in his role as Commissar of Nationalities, gave a speech in which he suggested that the Party leadership should focus on "backward regions to [help them] develop their own press, schools, theaters, clubs, and cultural and educational institutions generally, functioning in the native languages."[48] The state endorsed its partnership with local cadres, making them responsible for such local entities. At their philosophical essence, these institutions overlapped with local Turkmen efforts to reform the literary language and spread literacy. In 1921 the Turkmen oblast was home to three hundred new schools.[49] For taking in socialist culture and improving literacy skills, there were fourteen clubs, sixteen libraries, seventeen readers' yurts, and eight movie theaters in addition to the Railroad Workers' Cultural Institute.[50] The newspaper *Türkmenistan* began publishing in 1920, and *Türkmen Ili* began in 1922. The Soviet state expected print culture to aid people in their trek along the "path to literacy."

Progressives and Bolsheviks Become Partners on the Cultural Front

In attaining local partners and gaining cooperation, the program of korenizatsiia was an area where, as Adeeb Khalid writes, "the grounds for cooperation between Moscow and the Jadids were substantial."[51] Korenizatsiia allowed Turkmen intellectuals who had been active reformers or who had been educated in new method mekdeps to continue their efforts toward modernity through literacy, starting with the "perfection" of the Turkmen writing system. Central Asians were interested in access to education and opportunities, while Moscow hoped that "facilitating education for the poorest classes would promote participation by those groups in the population upon whom the new leaders counted most for support."[52] Although all efforts eventually fell under the central administration, Turkmen alphabet reformers continued to believe that *Türkmençeleşdirmek*, or "Turkmenification," of the lexicon and script to accurately reflect the speech would increase literacy. Schools were key sites in reform.

Despite budgetary concerns, representatives to the First Turkmen Congress of Workers, Peasants and Red Army Deputies encouraged "speeding up the question [of literacy] and undertaking all measures to develop village schools for children and to eradicate adult illiteracy."[53] For example, in the first half of the 1920s, the degree of cooperation on both sides was such that the Anti-Illiteracy Commission agreed to allow mollas to teach Islam in Soviet schools, despite the Party's continuing fears about the influence of "dogmatic teachings in mosques."[54] The number of new-style mekdeps had continued to grow, and in 1925 even Gaýgasyz Atabaýew, chairman of the Turkmen republic's Council of People's Commissars, maintained that the state should not ban Muslim mekdeps "but should encourage them to teach scientific subjects and employ Soviet-trained teachers."[55] The Bolsheviks would "liquidate the world order" by "gradually undermining it," rather than "smashing" it.[56] As one Turkmen explained at a meeting of the Turkmen Congress:

> When I was in Kerki, I heard rumors that the Soviet power will forbid and destroy old schools [mekdeps] and arrest the mollas. We do not support this solution of destroying old schools. We strive to spread literacy among the people. Of course, in comparison with old schools, new, Soviet schools give students greater knowledge, but we do not have enough new schools for the population. The solution is not to close old schools and arrest teachers, but to erect new Soviet schools alongside them. And, only that path—without arrests—will win sympathy for the Soviet schools.[57]

At the same meeting, another Turkmen speaker addressed the influence of the remaining mekdeps and identified ways to bring class warfare into the schools, especially to working-class children:

> We do not have exact calculations of how many confessional schools exist . . . but they are in decline . . . this means that they cannot spread, yet the presence of them (in the indicated districts) explains the absence of Soviet schools[;] . . . in Lenin oblast there remain around forty, in Kerki around fifty. . . . We are not preparing to undertake repressive measures against confessional schools. We will advise them and gradually train the instructors.
>
> [City schools] serve, primarily, children of service providers and workers. According to statistics, children of the non-worker element make up 8 to 12 percent of students; those of workers equal 90 percent. In these schools we have undertaken the principle of tuition payments. Tuition is a temporary measure, which will be employed while we have weak local budgets . . . [eventually] we need to free at least 50 percent of the workers' children from tuition payments.[58]

Bolshevik aspirations to propel the revolution into the realms of culture, science, education, and ideology drew attention to local languages.[59] The faster languages were standardized, books were printed, and people became literate, the more quickly citizens could acquire the knowledge necessary for building socialism. Central policies provided locals with the right to use their language in finance and administration, and for the development of their press and publications, cultural organizations, and educational establishments.[60] Language was representative of political objectives as well as a medium for carrying out policy.

In 1925 the Turkmen Revolutionary Committee declared Turkmen and Russian to be the TSSR's state languages; central party organs were to conduct all correspondence in both state languages, "in parallel."[61] But there were rules beyond this edict, and it created a hierarchy of language use. For example, such large urban centers as Merv and Poltoratsk (Aşgabat) were to correspond with central Party organs in both Turkmen and Russian but were to communicate with lower apparatuses in the language of the native population. Kerki, Chärjew, and Daşoguz oblasts were to conduct all official correspondence in Turkmen only. Records in villages and districts were to be in the language of the predominant population, such as Kurdish, Baluç, and Jemşid. A region with an Uzbek majority was to keep records in Uzbek; regions with a European population would accordingly keep records in their language.[62] As the Bolsheviks erected the institutions that formed the state, they deemed legitimate so many official languages—and corresponding alphabets—that it made the complexity of administration unwieldy. Today one can see in archival holdings the manifestation of this policy as documents reflect the multitude of languages and alphabets. Indeed, the question of which alphabet Turkic peoples should write in occupied the intelligentsia for years.

Alphabet

Historians credit Azerbaijani cultural leaders with having been the "pioneers" of Latinization, as they were among the first Turks to identify the Western script as a tool for becoming modern.[63] Just as Jadid-inspired Turkmen reformers had done earlier, Turkmen Latinizers located their issue within a larger global experience. They placed Central Asia firmly within the Muslim world and within the emerging socialist world but also situated it within the larger modernizing world. In the end, the arguments reveal similarities, each encouraging a respective alphabet change as a means of finding accord with a modern world community. This is one of the striking intellectual continuities between pre- and post-1917 eras.

As early as 1917, Soviet Azerbaijanis had supported Latinization, and they eventually formed the Azerbaijani Committee for the New Turkic Alphabet (AzKNTA). The Azerbaijani revolutionary Samedaga Agamalyoglu led its members in a five-year-long campaign for a meeting at which they could address the issue formally.[64] He sought official support for Latinization, bringing the issue to Lenin directly in 1922. Agamalyoglu, who later became chair of the All-Union Central Executive Committee of the New Turkic Alphabet (VTsIK NTA), was a tireless advocate of Latinization, denouncing the Arabic alphabet as "an instrument of the old Muslim culture, while the Latin alphabet was a tool of the new socialist one."[65]

Prominent Azerbaijani intellectuals addressed the importance of alphabet both as a political issue and as one of great human interest. Nariman Narimanov, the chairman of the Council of People's Commissars of the Azerbaijani SSR, and Mamed Aga Shakhtatinskii, editor of the Azerbaijani newspaper *Şarqi Rus*, were two notable Azerbaijanis who published their views against the Arabic script in *Zhizn' Natsional'nostei* (Life of the nationalities), the official organ of Narkomnats.[66]

Shakhtatinski, who was a member of the original AzKNTA, wrote a manuscript titled "On the Light of the Latin Alphabet," in which he illuminates the orientation of Latinizers of the time:

> The Muslim world needs an international alphabet. The Latin alphabet is not only international; but it is pananthropic. It is known [even] to those peoples, like Russians, which do not use it. The Latin alphabet is known even by educated Muslims in Asia and Africa.[67]
>
> What needs to be done? It is very simple, it is necessary to replace the Arabic alphabet with the Latin, because it is agreeable for us Muslims as it is for the whole world . . . Latin writing [should become the basis for the] daily alphabet.[68]

The Russian language was written in the Cyrillic script, but imposing Cyrillic on non-Russian regions did not yet seem feasible or desirable in these early years, as resistance to all things Russian lingered among some peoples who had been under Russian imperial rule. Yet the powerful symbolism of alphabets led the Soviet leaders to pursue some form of change. The importance of the alphabet question drew political involvement from all corners of the USSR. Moscow viewed the Arabic script as synonymous with pan-Turkist and pan-Islamic sentiment and a potential threat to the advancement of socialism. Latinists viewed Arabic scripts as "backward" and the Latin script as a marker of modernity and progress.[69]

Newspaper articles and conference records supported these positions, complaining not only that there was a lack of vowel representation but also that the Arabic script was written from right to left while the numerals were written from left to right, making their simultaneous use cumbersome.[70] There were also arguments that the Arabic script was difficult to learn and that this was the largest factor in widespread illiteracy among the "eastern peoples."[71] Those Latinists who supported a change from the Arabic script to a Latin one repeatedly noted the superiority of the Latin script's "international" character.[72] This was more than perception and also showed serious bias against Muslim culture. Written from right to left, in the opposite direction of Cyrillic or Latin scripts, the Arabic script marked Muslims as literally backward in the eyes of Soviets. Nevertheless, Turkmen worked on reforming their Arabic writing system.

At the end of 1921, Turkmen intellectuals—with Moscow's money—formed the Turkmen Academic Commission (Türkmen Bilim Heýaty) to oversee language development. Its tasks included the design of a reformed Arabic alphabet that would reflect the peculiarities of a standardized Turkmen language, the codification of orthography and grammar, the development of terminology, the broadening of the Turkmen language's social functions through the expansion of the press, and the general advancement of literacy.[73] In its pursuit of modernity the state identified language standardization as the first necessary precursor to eradicating illiteracy, and it advocated the phonetic method of teaching literacy (as had Ismail Bey Gasprinskii and reform-minded Turkmen in the tsarist era). In order to teach with the phonetic method, the writing system needed to reflect the sounds of the language. In a continuation of the Jadid-inspired emphasis on accurate representation of Turkmen speech, the Turkmen Academic Commission set out to design an alphabet and produce materials for teaching with the phonetic method.

This commission was the type of state organ in which nationals could work to use the state's power to bring about change in local society. They likely envisioned this "strategic alliance" as a temporary situation, as did the Communists.[74] The goals of the commission reflected Moscow's aims while allowing locals the latitude to explore cultural questions with a fair amount of independence. The commission wrote textbooks and began its work toward language enrichment.

There were problems along the path to modernity, though. The commission had trouble getting books published in Turkmen. Muhammed Geldiýew, a member of the commission, expressed frustration in an article that most Turkmen did not even know the commission existed. Its location in Tashkent, to be nearer publishers, rather than in the Turkmen oblast made it more difficult to get the word out to Turkmen. The commission published the journal *Türkmen Ili*, but few issues ever came out. The commission even changed its name from *Heýat* to *Komissiýa* perhaps in an effort to make its title more comprehensible to citizens of the Soviet Union. It is not clear that either of these terms would have been familiar to the average Turkmen; the former term is Arabic and the latter Russian. Probably the very concept of such an entity was foreign to most.

Nevertheless, the Turkmen Academic Commission undertook its duties with vigor. Between 1923 and 1925, the commission refined the Turkmen Arabic script, grammar, and spelling rules.[75] Muhammed Geldiýew, the most active member of the commission, undertook the bulk of Turkmen language standardization. In 1923 and 1925 he standardized spelling and grammar and addressed the issue of distinctive long vowel sounds in Turkmen by adding diacritics to build more vowel graphemes. He created a categorically Turkmen, reformed Arabic alphabet.[76] That is, he designed it to serve the needs of the spoken Turkmen language, based primarily on the Teke dialect with some Ýomut characteristics.

Reformed Arabic Script, 1923

As a member of the Turkmen Academic Commission, Geldiýew published numerous textbooks and grammars; he designed the 1923 reformed Arabic script and generally personified the larger processes that were taking place between the Turkmen intellectuals and Moscow. A graduate of the Jadid medrese Galiya, in Ufa, Geldiýew provides in his work an example of the continuation of forward-thinking ideals into the Soviet period.[77] Ufa was an important tsarist provincial center where leaders such as Zeki Velidi Togan, Mir-Said Sultangaliev, and Lenin visited and made speeches. Geldiýew and the other students at Galiya lived at the intersection of Islamic, Turkic, and Russian worlds, and their education reflected these intersections. Yet the Soviet system challenged this intersection and dared Turkmen to locate themselves culturally and intellectually in the new socialist state. Geldiýew used his position to accommodate Soviet central policy with Turkmen cultural reform as well as to make Soviet policy serve what he saw as the needs of the Turkmen.[78]

The Turkmen Academic Commission's first step was to codify the Turkmen Arabic alphabet and orthography. For this they called on the experience of other Turkic groups.[79] Representatives from different Turkic areas assisted the Turkmen, but the influence of Tatar and Başkurt linguists seems to have been predominant.[80] Gibad (Gabat) Habibullovič Alparov (1888–1936), a schoolmate of Geldiýew's from the Galiya medrese, was the most involved and influential. He assisted the Turkmen Academic Commission from 1922 to 1924 and continued thereafter to play a significant role in Turkmen orthographic reform, collaborating with Geldiýew on more than ten language textbooks.[81]

One of Geldiýew's steadfast convictions was that Turkmen should be viewed as a language possessing peculiarities that set it apart from other Turkic languages. Based on his belief that speech could be represented in writing, his 1923 proposal was designed to distinguish vowel graphemes to a degree not found in earlier Turkmen alphabets. In this alphabet, most phonemes were signified by a different symbol, created by combinations of letters and diacritics, unlike the original Arabic alphabet, which used individual graphemes to represent multiple phonemes. Geldiýew's reform also addressed the controversial long vowels by increasing their number. In his capacity as a member of the Turkmen Academic Council (Döwlet alymlar geňeşi; or Gosudarstvennoi Uchennoi Sovet [GUS] in Russian, as the commission was renamed in 1924), Geldiýew also worked to codify spelling and grammar by creating or borrowing linguistic terminology.

Geldiýew's Feud with Garahanow

For about six months in 1924, the Turkmen Allaguly Garahanow was a member of GUS. It was then that a dispute began between Garahanow and Geldiýew over whether the Turkmen reformed Arabic script should be brought closer to or made more distinct from other Turkic scripts.[82] The original problem with the existing alphabet had been the perceived lack of symbols to accurately represent spoken Turkmen. Now, choices in alphabet construction became directly tied to issues of official national identity. Two small conferences were held to work out the alphabet issues where Geldiẏew and Garahanow put forth their views. Geldiẏew, who was still working closely with Gibad Alparov, kept an eye on the Tatar reforms and linguistic principles as he advocated for each vowel sound to be represented by a separate sign. Garahanow, who was working closely with Uzbek language reformers, wanted to have only four characters, even though Turkmen possessed nine different vowels sounds: [a], [e], [ä], [i], [ẏ], [o], [ö], [u], [ü], plus five long vowels. After these two meetings, Geldiẏew's alphabet continued to be used in textbooks, but Garahanow's was used in newspapers and journals.[83] This underscores the lack of standardization in language use at the time.

The two men essentially fought over influences on the Turkmen literary language, Uzbek versus Tatar, and over which of these two men should hold the authority to choose the legitimate form of the official language of Turkmenistan. Bourdieu's work on "Authorized Language" illustrates how such a commission could represent the institution in which the authority to legitimize speech resided—or in this case the symbolic representation of that speech in writing.[84] Uzbeks and Tatars were also each working to standardize their own language at this time, so who held authority was a significant cultural question.

Concerns over external influence on the Turkmen language persisted over the decades. In the 1920s, in conjunction with questions about script loomed the question of how to go about building a standardized literary language that would be understood by all Turkmen. Geldiẏew argued that the Turkmen language should develop based on its own innate richness. If a new term was needed it should be borrowed from other Soviet Turkic languages and not from "outside" languages (such as Russian). If these were not sufficient, then Turkmen should look to "Chagataẏ or Uyghur (old Turkic)." Only if these sources could not provide a term should Turkmen turn to European sources. He pointedly advocated borrowing from European sources rather than Persian or Arabic sources, noting that European culture would be the foundation for the future.[85] However, there were some Turkmen who argued that to be understood by the greatest number possible, the language should incorporate more Persian and Arabic and not turn to Russian or European languages, since few Turkmen knew Russian.[86]

Wepaẏ oglu (who now went by the Russian form of his name, Wepaẏew) wrote his thoughts on language in his poem "On Language-Dialect," which was published in *Tokmak,* a satirical Türkmen-language journal. In it he expressed his frustration with the difficulties of language reform. He argued that Turkmen should be proud of their language and should work to refine it, but he also advised that European languages (perhaps Russian)—not Persian or Arabic—should be considered when building vocabulary.[87] Questions of language purity are age-old and analogous histories of when a culture should borrow from another are found worldwide.

Delimitation of the Turkmen Soviet Socialist Republic

On 27 October 1924 the Turkmen oblast became the Turkmen Soviet Socialist Republic (TSSR). In part due to this synchronization of Turkmen identity with territory, along with accompanying political changes, the pace of work related to literacy and language accelerated.[88] It was just around this time that some Turkmen began to express an interest in creating a new writing system based on the Latin script.[89] Still, GUS pressed on with the Arabic alphabet reform. Their reasoning was not very complicated. Turkmen were ethnic Turks, and Turks had been using the Arabic script for a thousand years. They had been educated in it and they viewed it as a basic element of their Turkic culture. Their decision to alter and Turkify the Arabic alphabet did not mean that they were rejecting any part of that revered heritage. Even taking reform a step further to Turkmenify the alphabet by highlighting local peculiarities through the addition of letters was not in their view a rejection of the past but, rather, staking a claim on the future. They presumed that this future would still be Muslim, but also modern and nationally oriented as well as socialist—Turkmen were still working out the meanings of all of these.

Despite agitation for adoption of a Latin-based script, as had taken place in Azerbaijan, in 1925 the GUS announced another reform of the Arabic alphabet. This one was to accommodate sounds found in Russian words, which were becoming prevalent in Turkmen.[90] Turkmen intellectuals still had little interest in Latinization, however, and therein lay a divergence between central and local interests. Turkmen were willing to work within socialist parameters, but using their own script. Nevertheless, local and central aims were not antagonistic, and the central government kept sending money to fund the Turkmen's work.

As is often the case with language reform, the movement for Latinization was shaped by political goals as much as by cultural ones.[91] Letters became the mortar for building a socialist cultural edifice. However, the Turkmen intellectuals continued to pursue language standardization and codification in the Arabic script. They were not yet ready to "internationalize."[92]

Latinization and the 1926 Turcological Congress

In the years up until 1926, Turkmen intellectuals pursued codification of their language and worked on establishing a form of the Arabic script they believed would accurately represent that language in writing. Most Turkic intellectuals had just begun to make headway with their reformed Arabic scripts and had no interest in abandoning those efforts—until the central government made the adoption of a Latin alphabet mandatory. In 1926 Moscow, along with leaders in Azerbaijan, organized the First All-Union Turcological Congress in order to work out the Turks' adoption of a Latin-based script.[93] As central Party organs sought ways to foster cohesion among the Soviet peoples, they determined that a unified international Latin script would help smooth the process. The Party created the Commission for Reform of the Arabic Script within Narkomnats with aims divergent from those of GUS; this unionwide commission was to oversee the move away from the Arabic script not the restyling of it.[94] Activities on the cultural front were a chaotic mix of central policy and many layers of bureaucracy and academia.

Moscow's decision to pursue Latinization illustrates a direct relationship between political and social power and the role of alphabets and literacy. The center was stabilizing by the mid-1920s and the push for internationalization persisted. Archival documents and Michael Smith's analysis show that the central government continued to view influence over writing and literacy, both symbolic and material, as a valuable arrow to have in its quiver.[95]

As the Azerbaijanis undertook Latinization, a debate ensued in the unionwide papers *Novyi vostok* and *Zhizn' natsional'nostei* over whether the adoption of Latin script should be considered more widely and if so, how and when.[96] In the battles to build socialism, newspapers and journals were important weapons in the Soviet arsenal. In the flurry of opinions, the All-Union Scientific Association of Oriental Studies (Vsesoiuznoi nauchnoi assotsiatsiei vostokovedeniia [VNAV]) suggested that an "unofficial" All-Union Turcology conference should be organized.[97] From 26 February through 5 March 1926 linguists and Turcologists from around the Turkic world and Russia met in Baku, Azerbaijan, to discuss the possibility of replacing the Arabic writing system with a Latin-based script.[98] The conference proceedings reveal lively debates about issues of alphabet, language, and potential threats to literary tradition from serious sociocultural and linguistic perspectives, implying that individuals felt free to express their opinions, although, as with any language or alphabet history, its aims could not be divorced from politics.[99]

The 1926 Turcological congress was the turning point in Latinization as it inaugurated the formal and very public unionwide Latinization project.[100] Most in attendance, including Turkmen, advocated Latinization. Why would Turkmen advocate for Latinization when they had been so engaged with alteration of the Arabic script? The Turkmen participants had come around to the idea of Latinization with prodding from the state, but they insisted on using it "in parallel" with the Arabic script. Only a handful of Tatars, defensive of their long-established print tradition, were anti-Latin.[101] The decision to adopt a Latin-based script went much more smoothly than the actual implementation of it. The next thirteen years saw multiple conferences, struggles for linguistic control and political power, shortages of such materials as paper and typeset letters and symbols, and political purges. Latinization involved far more than the representation of speech in text; language reform mirrored the political situation and the effort to push society forward as quickly as possible.

Geldiẏew and the GUS were still at work on their reform of the Turkmen writing system and orthography when this new conduit to modernity—Latinization—confronted them. Geldiẏew, Bekki E. Berdiẏew, Bäşim Perengliẏew, and Ş. Şamuradow attended the 1926 Baku congress as representatives of Turkmenistan's Narkompros. Bäşim Kul'beşerow was there as a representative of the TSSR Central Executive Committee. When asked about their "mood" regarding Latinization the Turkmen representatives explained that they "had come to Baku without hesitation," but they anticipated shifting to the Latin alphabet slowly, "in stages." As they explained, Turkmen would begin by using Latin "in parallel" with the Arabic script.[102]

Orthography was a major secondary topic at the 1926 congress, occupying half of the sessions. The discussions show the overlap between Russian and Turkic scholars in their desire to implement a phonetically based writing system. The Russian linguist from St. Petersburg, Lev Shcherba, asserted that "words should be written as pronounced." He also made a distinction between "script" (a writing system) and "alphabet" (letters used in a writing system) to underscore the difference between a writing system and a spelling system (orthography).[103] It was the spelling of a word, the choice of letters in combination, that would allow readers to recognize a word based on their knowledge of the spoken language, he argued. Lev Zhirkov, professor of Oriental Studies at VNAV in Moscow, concurred, advocating for the phonetic principle, especially to accommodate words of Persian and Arabic origin.[104] Farhad Agazade, from the Azerbaijani Central Executive Committee, added that European words also needed to be addressed, arguing that they ought to "nationalize according to the rules of Turkic [languages]."[105] These points continued to occupy language reformers for decades and in fact were the impetus for a number of later such conferences in 1928, 1929, 1931, 1932, and 1935.

Individual Turkic groups, especially Tatars, who feared for their long literary heritage and printing tradition, and Kazakhs, who felt they had made great progress with their reform of Arabic script, preferred to continue with the reforms to the traditional writing system. But there was no overt resistance to Latinization among Turkmen.[106] In fact, Turkmen intellectuals embodied the degree of cooperation exhibited by Central Asian Turks more generally. While Geldiẏew and others likely believed that the Arabic alphabet was still an important marker of Turco-Muslim identity, they did not object during the conference the way Tatars did. In fact, the 1926 Baku conference records Bekki Berdiẏew's attempt to be cooperative with a succinct point as meeting with unfortunate timing. Berdiẏew used a sartorial metaphor to clarify his position on script change. Implying support for Latinization in a conciliatory manner that suggested Turkmen would still recognize their language even if it were written in new letters, Berdiẏew stood, explaining, "Yesterday I was dressed differently. Today I am wearing a hat. But do you not recognize me?"[107] His speech had little impact on the debate, because as soon as he got the words out the moderator abruptly told him that the conference had already determined the alphabet question. Apologizing, Berdiýew moved on to the question of literary language.

Literary Language

At the two-week-long congress, the main question of whether a Latin script should be adopted in place of the Arabic scripts was accompanied by a host of other pressing linguistic questions.[108] Representatives from a variety of regions identified other points of immediate practical importance, such as the question of terminology development, liquidation of illiteracy, instruction in schools in the native tongue, and translation of textbooks into local languages. An overriding theoretical as well as practical question became not simply whether they would Latinize but how they would do it uniformly. And the question of whether Turkic languages should unify was still open for debate.[109]

"Unification" of a Turkic literary language had been a point of interest among some Turks since Ismail Bey Gasprinskii had first suggested it in the 1880s. Turkic languages are historically mutually intelligible. However, wide geographic distances between groups and varied historical experiences led to the evolution of distinct vocabularies and pronunciations. The issue was not whether Turks could understand one another but how they should represent these distinct speech patterns in official writing. More important was the question of whether they would be able to understand one another in writing. If they were going to use different alphabets, it would impede mutual written intelligibility. In developing literary languages and in codifying modern forms of speech, Turks had to decide on the spellings and terms to include in dictionaries. Newspapers, textbooks, and official documents needed to depict a standardized language in order to facilitate literacy. In devising a Latin-based alphabet, the Turkic groups had to choose whether they would all use the same letters in a "unified" or "common" (Turkmen—*umumy*) script. Bekki Berdiýew argued that local peculiarities must be represented in literary languages. Thus, there could be no one unified literary language, despite the degree of mutual intelligibility between all Turkic "dialects." He underscored the importance of local peculiarities to the identity of a speech community and a nation, noting that a literary language is not the same as the local patois, and that "there could not be a common language among Turkic peoples."[110]

Two underlying principles were consistent throughout the fourteen years of the Latinization process. Primary was the belief that, as the key to modernity, mass literacy would automatically engender a responsible, enlightened citizen through access to universal education; this required an alphabet suitable to the "masses."[111] The second point was that the standard method of Latinization was to be based on the "phonetic principle": one phoneme to be represented by one grapheme.[112]

These points coincided with efforts of Turkmen reformers as seen in *Ruznama-i Mawera-i Bahr-i Hazar*, the newspaper in which Jadid-inspired Turkmen published their thoughts.

"Latinists" did not represent a singular interpretation of alphabet reform. For example, there were initially two basic views regarding how to choose the letters for the new Latin alphabet. One proposed creating an alphabet based on the International Phonetic Alphabet (itself based on the Latin of the French School of Phonetics). The second suggested distilling the many marks and letters of all Latin alphabets down to one. In the end, they opted for a third alternative: the alphabet was to be designed from a combination of the common Latin alphabet, Latin letters with "marks" (cedillas, diacritics), Cyrillic ("Russian") letters, and newly created letters, based on Latin.[113]

In February 1927 Agamalyoglu became chairman of the All-Union Committee of the New Turkic Alphabet (VTsIK NTA). Of the thirty-nine members, four were from Turkmenistan: Kumuşaly Böriýew, Muhammed Geldiýew, Bekki E. Berdiýew, and Bäşim Perengliýew.[114]

Latinization in Turkmenistan

At the second conference of the Turkmen SSR, in 1927, representatives discussed how the development of socialist culture among the Turkmen population depended on "building a socialized state" and that language was an essential aspect of socialism.[115] Not long afterward, the chairman of Turkmenistan's Central Executive Committee (TsIK), Nedirbaý Aýtakow, created Turkmenistan's Central Committee for the New Turkic Alphabet (TsK NTA TSSR) and made it responsible for Latinization.[116] Throughout Central Asia, such local institutes were created to handle the script reform. In Turkmenistan, the State Academic Council (GUS) within the Turkmen Commissariat of Enlightenment oversaw language planning more generally, including lexical enrichment and the development of a standardized literary language and orthography.[117]

The New Turkic Alphabet Committee published an alphabet chart proposing a unified script, but Turkmen intellectuals still found this insufficient for representing spoken Turkmen. Overall, Turkmen did not resist Latinization, but neither were they willing to forgo their linguistic identity. They accepted the idea of script change, as long as it did not interfere with the development of the Turkmen language or the spread of literacy or challenge the distinctiveness of Turkmen identity. Even for long-term dividends, the committee was not willing to withstand short-term loss. They engaged in this struggle, recognizing the power of language in the "symbolic conflicts of everyday life."[118] As a result, the formal steps toward Latinization began in Turkmenistan only in the summer of 1927, just a few weeks after the 1927 All-Union linguistic conference.

At this second Turcological congress (1927), which took place again in Baku, the question of creating one "unified" Latin alphabet for all the Turkic peoples persisted as a major topic. Geldiẏew maintained that it would be impossible for Turkmen to use such a script, because they could not possibly represent their language without all of their exceptional long vowels. He insisted that representation of the Turkmen language in writing was necessarily going to differentiate it from the other Turkic languages; Gasprinskii's unified Turkic script had never been realized due to just such arguments.

Participants queried Turkmen how they might reconcile a unified Turkic alphabet with the Turkmen long vowels. Geldiẏew gave them three options for indicating the Turkmen long vowel sounds in a word, such as in "My name": 1. write a dash over the vowel (*ādym*), 2. place a colon after each vowel (*a:dym*), 3. double the vowels (*aadym*). He then advocated the third option. He asserted that there was no reason even to discuss the difficulties associated with the first option because even the Arabic alphabet had not been able to handle such use of diacritics for Turkmen. The second option, he argued, was unsatisfactory because a colon was already in use as punctuation and would create confusion.[119] Geldiẏew's suggestion was accepted. In that year, Turkmen adopted a system of two consecutive vowels to indicate long vowels such as *adaalat* (justice), *shaahyyr* (poet), *kiise* (pocket). With this the issue was closed, and Turkmen turned their attention to questions of orthography (*ẏazuw düzgünler*).

GUS formulated new spelling rules, and the newspaper *Türkmenistan* announced it would begin to provide lessons.[120] Although Turkmen participated in the 1927 conference and subsequent linguistic conferences, they did not want the peculiarities of the Turkmen language (*osobennost' zvukov turkmenskogo iazyka*) obscured by the common orthography of "unification." Their objections, not to Latinization but to unification, were so strong that at the 1927 conference Kumuşaly Böriẏew said he would not even speak about what the Turkmen had accomplished at that point, because they had "accomplished nothing" regarding a unified Latin alphabet.[121] He simply put forth his ideas about the introduction of the Latin script being handled at the local level. He argued that the organization of printing machinery, publishing, and the preparation of courses for teachers should be concentrated locally—in the republics—while Moscow and Baku should continue to act merely as guides and should decide on only the broad questions.[122] However, because Turkmenistan was "behind" and had difficulties, for example, in publishing textbooks in the Turkmen language, it should, Böriẏew conceded, rely on the experiences of others such as Azerbaijan. After his comments on the general situation, Böriẏew took the opportunity to underscore the question that he considered of greater importance than whether one or multiple alphabets might be used by Turks: that of which orthography should be selected. Reflecting the persistent concern over pronunciation and spelling of localisms, Böriẏew was interested primarily in codifying a spelling system that would reflect a standardized Turkmen language.[123]

Orthographic Unification

Other aims of the 1927 Second Turcological Congress included questions of capital letters and print versus handwritten script; each bore influence on questions of unification. Among Soviet alphabet and language reformers, there were divergent views on the topic of capital letters and on the principle of one shape or letter to represent one meaning. The authors of a similar language project in Kyrgyzstan determined that the introduction of capital letters complicated reading and writing. Since the Kyrgyz group was focused on children's literacy and the development of the alphabet in pedagogical works, they chose what they deemed the simplest path: they were against capital letters. However, the authors of the Turkmen project disagreed; they found that "capital letters introduced the greatest technological advantage to facilitating reading and speediness in [a reader's] comprehension of a text."[124] This concern to advance literacy as quickly as possible represented a notable continuity with the former era. Even before encountering the Soviet drive for speed, reformers had felt that the need to develop universal literacy among their peoples was immediate. But now it was more than a concern; speed was a reality. Within Soviet structures the tempo with which change would take place increased.

The question of the degree to which other Turks should follow the Azerbaijani lead, especially in the effort to unify the alphabets, was constant through 1927 when Turkmen adopted their own version of a Latin alphabet. A problem arose at one point with respect to unification of alphabets because Azerbaijanis had begun using capital letters. Uzbeks were torn; some argued that literacy could be acquired more quickly if illiterates had fewer forms of letters to learn. Fierman suggests that it was Azerbaijani influence that swayed the Uzbeks to choose capitalization, for while they wished to simplify they hoped to keep their writing in line with other Turkic alphabets.[125] Turkmenistan's GUS saw an advantage to capital letters especially in math and science. While acknowledging that capital letters would result in shapes very close to that of lowercase letters and the limits of typographical technology had to be taken into consideration, GUS did not wish "to deprive the new Turkmen alphabet of the great technological advantage [capital letters could provide] in the relationship between reading and handling a text."[126] Thus, GUS explained that it would adopt capital letters as a means of expediting literacy.[127] Turkmen language planners expected swift alphabet acquisition among Turkmen, because the majority of the population was not fully literate. That is, most of the populace would acquire the ability to read and write in the Latin alphabet. Planners believed that if people were illiterate they would adapt to a script more quickly than if they possessed the skill to read and write in a previous alphabet that they had to then give up. This meant that Latinization would coincide with the spread of literacy.[128] The assumption that low literacy would allow Latinization to proceed at a "rapid tempo" was due to the perception that few individuals were invested in the Arabic script.[129] Still, the question of a unified alphabet remained unsettled.

Muhammed Geldiýew attended the 1927 conference, even though he was not a member of the official committee. He took umbrage at comments by the Crimean Tatar Çobanzade and the Uzbek Tynystanov about vowel harmony and a unified script. "We could follow Çobanzade's suggestion to organize a commission to create a scientific transcription system, but would one system be sufficient? Would one morphological system [be enough]?" Geldiýew asked from the audience.[130] He then challenged Çobanzade to clarify his position on vowel harmony (*singarmonizm*). This is a quality of Turkic languages which demands that only compatible vowels appeared in a word. Front vowels [a], [o], [y], and [u] appear in *oturmak* (to plant) whereas back vowels [ä], [e], [i], [ö], and [ü] appear in *ösdürmek* (to cultivate; to develop). The question, Geldiýew asserted, was not on which basis unification of the "languages" would be most convenient but, rather, whether the alphabet project should be based on the phonetic principle, a morphological principle, or both together. "Turkmen and Kyrgyz, unlike Kazakh, have properly preserved the rules of vowel harmony, how do we preserve this principle in a unified system?"[131] At the suggestions made by Çobanzade and Tynystanov that the Turkmen language might not have preserved this characteristic, Geldiýew responded adamantly, "Never say that Turkmen has not preserved vowel harmony."[132] He accused Çobanzade of spouting "nonsense" about orthography, then asserted his own opinion that the most pressing issue was in fact vowels. He focused on the fact that Turkmen possesses sixteen vowels. "Twelve," Agazade objected. "No," interrupted Geldiýew. "Not twelve. I maintain that there are sixteen. If we are to go ahead with unification according to Çobanzade's plan then the Turkmen language needs sixteen vowels. Without these additions, there can be no unification. Moreover, we must adhere to the phonetic principle. Morphology will not do. I repeat, no one can argue with the details of our alphabet, or the vowels appearing in it."[133] Although Geldiýew was blunt in his statements, he was not politically off course. In that same year, discussions of teaching methodologies in Narkomnats reaffirmed that local languages were the primary means for teaching. "Every national school was obliged to base its teaching methodologies and textbooks on the specific internal 'peculiarities' of the national languages."[134] Geldiýew fought for the symbolic capital imbued in a language or in this case an orthography.

The Russian linguist E. D. Polivanov, who had been involved in language planning from the beginning, used the Turkmen case to demonstrate that the idea of "unification" did not mean every alphabet would be identical. Some systems, he explained, would need to have special symbols to represent variation.[135] Agazade sought compromise for all, suggesting that they choose nine common vowels and make room for five more special vowels. It would seem that Geldiýew had made intellectual headway. Still, he was not making friends. Agazade took a moment to share that the Turkmen had been arguing with the Kazakh representative, Şonanov, about this question of extra letters for some time. He expounded on linguistic details, squeezing in a jab at Geldiýew that while there were varying numbers of vowels, "there have never been sixteen."[136] Before wrapping up, Agazade took the opportunity to deride GUS and remind the audience that it had submitted a cumbersome proposal that employed diacritics—a major faux pas at a time when unification sought to simplify alphabets as markers of the peculiarities of local speech.[137]

By 1928 the frustration with unification was apparent. Representatives at the 1928 Turcological Conference remarked that "anarchy" reigned in the question of unification.[138] Polivanov agreed, explaining that the dilemma with unification was that it had been proposed on the basis of vowel harmony.[139] Moreover, unification was not limited to an alphabet. It also included language development, such as legal terminology, in the Turkic languages.[140] Upon explaining how Turkmen had relied on the examples of other Turkic groups, who were more developed in their teaching reforms and language planning, Böriýew expressed irritation with the larger experience. He mentioned the question of unification specifically, underscoring that while Azerbaijan had become a regional leader in these areas, the fact that there was no movement one way or another was frustrating. Exasperated, he exclaimed, "We in Turkmenistan wish that Azerbaijan would just transition to the unified alphabet soon or let none of us transition at all."[141] Still debate continued.

The December 1928 VTsK NTA meeting in Kazan was a preparatory step for intensification of language planning that reflected the frenetic pace of Sovietization.[142] At that meeting, the members debated speediness versus realistic goals. Korkmasov suggested the slogan "Speed! On Time!" encouraging members to reach set targets. Alimjan argued for an "increased tempo," suggesting the completion of Latinization by 1 January 1930.[143] Others argued that targets had been set too high and should be modified. Efendiev, from Armenia, suggested that a sluggishness among Central Asians was keeping the project from reaching fruition, asking coarsely whether these were "people living in these territories or camels."[144] The categorization of Central Asians as "backward" and "uncultured" persisted. The 1928 plenum resolved to "accelerate" the adoption of the new alphabet. The resolution specific to Turkmenistan declared that it should speed up its translation of paperwork to the Latin alphabet, take care of the need for typewriters, hasten the tempo of printing in the new alphabet, and create conditions so the new Turkmen writing system could be in place within two years.[145]

Several more conferences took place in the following years, suggesting that the central Soviet agreed with the Baku-based Scientific Soviet, which found that alphabets and writing should be deliberated "not once, not twice, [but in] periodic check-ups." Without regular language maintenance, the members warned, there would be disagreements between language pronunciations and writing systems. To avoid divergences, they noted, it was necessary periodically to "repair" the writing system or, as Shcherba said, "sharpen it" like a pencil.[146]

As part of the path to socialism, the Party leadership intended to erase national identity over time; the Turkmen intelligentsia were adamant about retaining theirs. Each side must have been fully aware of the other's position. Nevertheless, each continued to work as if their goal was undoubtedly obtainable.

Cultural Revolution (Medeni ynkylap)

While the precise dates of the First Five Year Plan (1928–1932) did not shape language activity to the degree it did economic activity, a "considerable" influence can be traced.[147] As Latinization got under way, Sovnats TsIK SSSR called for courses to train teachers in the new alphabet as well as to support the political literacy of workers.[148] The state demanded that workers take responsibility for their role in the "Cultural Revolution," and it set mandates for literacy. In the years between 1926 and 1930, the movement to replace the Arabic script with a Latin-based script paralleled larger political changes within the Soviet system. "Progress" was accelerated, and centralization began to take precedence over local peculiarities. The campaign for Latinization reflected the Soviet state's increasingly centralized control over culture and aim to standardize life as well as language.

The first Five Year Plan certainly affected the atmosphere in which language politics were taking place.[149] Turkmenistan's Central Executive Committee demanded an increased tempo in education work in keeping with the surge of the Cultural Revolution.[150] In 1927 the Party called for factory workers to be literate in one year's time, and all collective and state farmers within two years. In May 1928 the Komsomol announced a kul'tpokhod or "cultural campaign" against "illiteracy [as well as] against the educational bureaucracy that had so far failed to cope with the problem."[151] Compulsion turned into coercion in the early 1930s with the beginnings of purges. The purges reached even into the secondary schools as old experts were being identified with sluggishness in the acquisition of literacy.[152]

One feature on the language front that shifted as the NEP ended and the Cultural Revolution began was the transition in emphasis from adult literacy to the education of children. The Central Committee made four-year schooling compulsory for all children effective in the fall of 1931 after the Sixteenth Party Congress called for both full adult literacy and universal primary schooling. By the late 1930s, classrooms for the young were the main sites for transmitting script change.[153]

Literacy became the focus of an extraordinary campaign, which evoked a sense of militarization on the cultural front where party members were soldiers in a cultural army and illiteracy was the enemy. There was also a shift in tenor when "courses" became "campaigns" (kul'tpokhod). The kul'tpokhod was manned by kul'tar-

meitsy (cultural soldiers) who organized into *kul'tbrigady* (cultural brigades). "The largest campaign for literacy (and Latinization) came in the fall and winter of 1929, thus coinciding with some of the great chaos of forced collectivization."[154]

At the next VTsIK NTA meeting, in January 1928, Böriẏew explained the Turkmen intellectuals' response to Latinization. "We began [to Latinize] in May 1927 when we received the resolution from the higher directive organs. . . . [B]efore that, there were some sympathizers among us, generally speaking though, now, in Turkmenistan there are no more strong Arabists and [we] are proper Latinists . . . we retain [the Arabic script] only while we transition to the Latin alphabet."[155] Böriẏew discussed the lack of resistance to the changes among Turkmen intellectuals, explaining at the 1928 meeting that Turkmen had held no formal debates about converting. Records do not discuss any drawbacks to Latinization, pointing out only the advantages over the Arabic script.

There was likely resistance of all sorts, both passive and active, among the people, but it went unrecorded—in all likelihood because it would have reflected as failure on the local Party representatives. Passive resistance could have been perceived as part of the learning process and never connected to political matters but thought of as the "natives'" inability to handle classroom material due to their need to acquire "culturedness" (*kul'turnost*), an important theme of the 1920s and 1930s. Böriẏew did mention more than once that "incidents" had occurred, for example in Çärjew, when they tried to convert village schools to the Latin alphabet. But he did not provide any detail about who protested or resisted, simply assuring the New Turkic Alphabet Committee that these events had been "contained."[156] Turkmen Party representatives remained largely unconcerned with a popular or clerical resistance to the assault against the Muslim religious identity bound up in the Arabic script. With such low literacy still, they argued, few people's daily lives would be disrupted. Indeed, the Party applauded the fact that the change in alphabet would have its greatest impact on the lives of the clergy, who, Aẏtakow presumed, "were afraid of losing their selfish, exploitive monopoly on literacy." In fact, Chairman Aẏtakow assured the VTsIK NTA that he did not expect clerics to seriously hamper Party efforts, writing, "There is no great clerical influence in Turkmenia."[157]

In any case, other problems arose, specifically surrounding the question of unification, both because of the struggle among various Turkic groups to assert cultural influence and because of the local Turkmen representatives' insistence on reflecting the linguistic peculiarities of their written language. The Turkmen remained particularly vocal about their desire to preserve in writing the distinctiveness of their speech. The long vowels of Turkmen were of particular concern, but also frequently mentioned in conference proceedings was the Turkmen proclivity for pronouncing the graphemes "s" [s] and "z" [z] with sounds "th" [θ] and "th" [ð].

The Turkmen were not the only group to frustrate the unification process. The Azerbaijani chairman Agamalyoglu was exasperated by the length to which some

FIGURE 1. Turkmenkul't imprint

academics theorized about unification. His words exemplified the revolutionary language of the "third front" when he exploded at the 1928 meeting, decrying that "[Professor] Polivanov keeps talking about unification, but he doesn't realize that we are on a battlefront where we need to *fire and fire* not just aim. . . . [U]nification will be created from the will [*volia*] of life, *not* from the will of scholarly invention."[158]

GUS/Turkmenkul't

In Turkmenistan GUS, the successor to the Türkmen Bilim Komissiýa, within the Turkmen Commissariat of Education oversaw language planning more generally, including lexical enrichment and development of a standardized literary language and orthography.[159] One practical undertaking that assisted alphabet reform was ethnographic and linguistic expeditions that the GUS oversaw. During this work the council's members spent several years working on standardizing the Turkmen language and preparing a dictionary.[160] Kumuşaly Böriýew, the director Muhammed Geldiýew, A. N. Samoilovich, and A. P. Potseluevskii were the most actively involved. In 1927 they began collecting vocabulary from books (both contemporary and ancient). Then in order to access the dialects of the workers, they undertook expeditions throughout Turkmenistan. The largest, in 1928, involved twenty-two male and two female researchers. The men collected vocabulary from the Ýomut, Ahal Teke, and Gökleň tribes, three of the largest, while the women collected proverbs, sayings, and songs.[161] Work on a dictionary began in the second half of 1928.[162] After their 1929 publications GUS expanded its terminology collecting to include all regions. They focused first on the Kalapyn and Ärsary in the

FIGURE 2. Front page from the journal *Türkmen Medeniẏeti*

Amu Darya region, and then Mary Teke, Saryk, and Sary tribes. Finally, they went to the smallest tribes: Igdir, Chowdur, Ali-eli, Änawli, and Nohur. There were also expeditions focused on music, tribal identity, and local customs.[163]

In 1928 GUS was renamed the Turkmen Cultural Commission (Institut Turkmenskoi Kul'tur, or Turkmenkul't).[164] From 1928 to 1932, the section for language and literature at the Institute of Turkmen Culture (Turkmenkul't) with Kumuşaly Böriẏew at its helm assumed responsibility of language planning and development. (This reorganized in 1932 to the Turkmen State Scientific-Research Institute).[165] Turkmenkul't and the Turkmen People's Publishing Commission (Turkgosizdat) were charged with the task of solving academic questions tied to the New (Latin-based) Alphabet.[166] Turkmenkul't used print media to communicate with the general public (see figure 1). The Russian-language journal *Turkmenovedenie* (Turkmenology) and the Turkmen-language journal *Türkmen medeniẏeti* (Turkmen culture) contained articles by Böriẏew, Geldiẏew, Garahanow, Gelenow, Potseluevskii, and others on alphabet reform, literary language development, Turkmen history, ethnography, and socialist culture more generally (see figure 2).

Geldiẏew Becomes Partner

In 1928 Muhammed Geldiẏew stopped work on the reformed Arabic script and shifted his attention full-time to creating orthography and grammar rules for a Latin-based alphabet. He argued that written language reflected spoken language and that language marked identity; literacy was imperative and a phonetic alphabet facilitated literacy. Geldiẏew worked within Party parameters but did not abandon his principles in depicting Turkmen language peculiarities or in teaching with the phonetic method. In 1929 he published another *Grammar* with Alparov as co-author. Largely aimed at codifying grammatical terminology such as a Turkmen term for "phonetics" (*ses bilimi,* or "study of sound"), it underscored long-vowel representation in the first chapter, which focused on phonetics.[167] Geldiẏew also pursued development of terminology, reinvigorating old terms found in poetry and literature to help create a socialist lexicon that could reflect the Turkic-ness of the language. This was very much in harmony with Soviet strategies of language development, and as the authors explained, new words needed to be introduced into the language because if the written word did not grow and evolve along with the spoken language, changing with the experience of its speakers, then the written language would reflect a "dead" language.[168] Geldiẏew had not forsaken the issue of long vowels and insisted that the Turkmen alphabet accommodate their expression. As early as 1928 Turkmen had worked out a system for expressing long vowels by writing double vowels in words. At the time Moscow accommodated such local details, and the VTsIK NTA accepted the Turkmen solution for expressing their literary language. Kamchin-bek even used it as an example to illustrate why there would not be 100 percent correlation between Turkic alphabets, despite efforts to unify, "because every national alphabet had to reflect local peculiarities."[169]

Issues of local peculiarities and identity persisted. At the 1928 VTsK NTA plenum Turkmen, Uzbek, and Kazakh representatives requested a return to discussion of capital letters. They proposed that every republic have the right (*pravo*) to adopt or not adopt capital letters. An argument ensued with unidentified voices from the audience quibbling over procedure until the chairman shouted at them.[170] He went on to clarify that the question should remain open and in the hands of Turkmenkul't. Geldiẏew responded, "Fine, many questions remain open, but there is no question about the 'right.'"[171] Geldiẏew seems to have been arguing that most issues should be decided in local committees. Geldiẏew's name does not appear anywhere else in the stenographic record, so it is not obvious how large a role he played at this conference.[172] What is obvious is that he had made himself known to the other

members and some did not like his ideas—or perhaps him. An unidentified voice
from the audience objected specifically to Geldiýew's suggestion. Although Latinization had eliminated the opportunity for their altered Arabic script, Turkmen still
intended to develop the Turkmen language, defeat illiteracy, spread enlightenment,
and make modern what was becoming a nation.

Turkmen did not protest against Latinization, but they also made it clear that
they were not interested in working on it until the central government issued a directive forcing them to do so. Turkmen intellectuals were asserting their national
identity through language. Muhammed Geldiýew and Gibad Alparov, authors of
an early Latin script textbook titled *Türkmen diliň grammatykasy* (Turkmen language grammar), wrote, "For every national group there is one marker that is the
most important—language. Throughout the world, every people has its own mother tongue. Our mother tongue is the Turkmen language."[173] Turkmen had evolved
in a short time from individual tribes to a nation with an identity growing increasingly determined by language.

Transition to Latin

On the eve of the tenth anniversary of the 1917 Revolution, at its second session
Turkmenistan's TsIK decreed that the Latin-based new Turkmen alphabet would
replace the old script in the TSSR. On 3 January 1928, TSSR TsIK and TSSR
Sovnarkom confirmed it as the official alphabet.[174] A few months later, the Turkmen committee for the new alphabet passed resolutions that confirmed the plan to
transition to the Latin alphabet. Official paperwork was to be written exclusively in
the Turkmen language and the new script by 1 October 1929 "keeping in line with
the korenizatsiia of the state apparatus."[175] The state required the administration to
prepare its employees and all publications to be written solely in the Latin alphabet
by 1 January 1929.[176] The new writing system was to be firmly established by 1 January 1930.[177]

As chairman of the TsIK, Aýtakow was responsible for the transition to the new
script in Turkmenistan, but as head of Turkmenkul't Böriýew was responsible for
textbooks, literature, and schools.[178] Aýtakow assigned the preparation of school
syllabi and courses to Geldiýew. Böriýew and Geldiýew were also obliged by their
positions in Turkmenkul't to prepare a textbook in Turkmen and Russian explaining the new alphabet. Finally, along with Artykow and Garypow (chair) the two
of them constituted a commission responsible for presenting material on the New
Turkic Alphabet to the TSSR TsIK.[179]

Turkmen newspapers and journals had begun printing sections with the new
Latin letters in the 1927/1928 school year. Other material in the new alphabet soon
began to appear. Narkompros started classes designed to instruct teachers and other

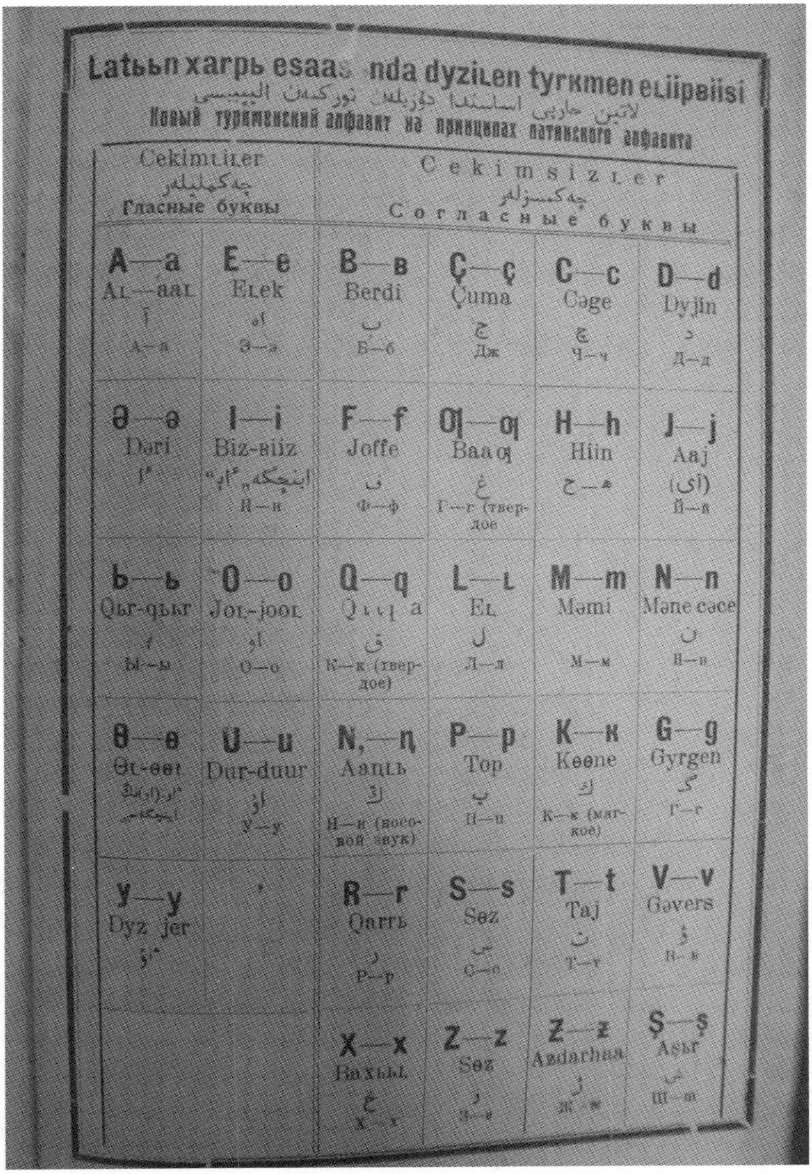

FIGURE 3. Turkmen Latin alphabet 1929

professionals in the new alphabet. Moscow assisted local budgets with financial infusions as well as with courses to help republican representatives prepare themselves as instructors of the new Latin alphabet (see figure 3).[180] By 1928 Narkompros was organizing courses for the "reeducation" of teachers. Teachers would be the first to gain cultural capital through their knowledge of the new alphabet and their ability to teach it to others. The state expected all village teachers to learn the new alphabet well enough to teach it in the likbez schools, kindergartens, and first grade classes beginning in the 1928/1929 academic year.

TSSR's Narkompros, Turkmenkul't, and Turkmengosizdat were all responsible for managing a five-year publishing plan to Latinize textbooks, study aids, and literature.[181] Sovnarkom instructed Narkompros not to send any textbooks written in the Arabic alphabet to the republics in the 1928/1929 school year. In addition to the script change, the Turkmen New Turkic Alphabet Committee assigned to Turkmengosizdat the task of publishing a new Turkmen language journal, *Gyzyl ýol* (Red path), specifically to run articles about the question of writing, the duty of teachers with respect to the new script, and news of regional happenings regarding literacy and learning.[182] Azerbaijan had earlier published a similar organ titled *Yeni Yol*. Thereafter other similar papers came out in local languages to support Latinization as well as korenizatsiia.[183]

The Arabic script was officially phased out by 1930, which was the same year that the local VTsK NA committee "self-liquidated." After 1930 Narkompros handled all issues concerning Latinization within the framework of education.[184] Although the alphabet change meant a shift in resources and the need for new books in the short-term, the long-term goals were still literacy and creating an alphabet that would support learning. Rather than dwelling on the loss of the Arabic script and the heritage symbolized by it, the members of Turkmenkul't, who were responsible for cultural development, focused on the social advances they thought Turkmen would gain. Here we see a clear coincidence of the goals of the Turkmen intellectuals and the central Party.

Conclusion

The Soviet campaign to eliminate illiteracy was a cultural means to attaining the greater and more specific political goal of Sovietization. Each proposal for a writing reform reflected the Soviet desire to use culture to stimulate social and/or political change, and each proposal operated variously as a point of intellectual debate (Arabic script was backward, Latin was modern), a symbol of identity (national, Soviet, or Muslim), and a practical means of facilitating literacy (functional and political). From 1917 to 1930, the roles of intellectuals, linguistics, and local identity shifted several times. The Soviet era began with attempts at political and intellectual compromise and aspirations to engender general enlightenment in Turkic communities.

The legacies of Jadidism were not suppressed. Instead they blended and eventually faded into state-led campaigns to build a Soviet society.

Turkmen language planners became involved in Latinization as part of the phenomenon of script reform that swept across the USSR. In the 1920s Turkmen intellectuals had not been limited by a simple, diachronic relationship between the central power and a local group. Rather, they had seen their initiatives in education and language merge with Bolshevik cultural endeavors. Alphabet reform transformed from a project designed by Turkmen to advance the Muslim community (as in the 1910s) to a project led by Moscow aimed at promoting international socialism. Yet there was remarkable continuity in Turkmen goals to ensure that a Latin script would reflect Turkmen linguistic specificities and in consequence define the Turkmen as a distinct people in the larger Turco-Islamic community within the USSR. While the campaign to Latinize Turkic alphabets began with a high degree of willingness to compromise on the part of most Turkmen academics, Moscow began tightening its oversight in the late 1920s.

Soon after these events, preparations for a conference began in 1930. It involved the members of Turkmenkul't, and it carried on the work to codify a standardized Turkmen language that was intelligible to the greatest number of people in Turkmenistan. The subsequent conference about Turkmen language, in 1936, would involve an entirely different group of people and would take on a completely different tone. Those who had been partners with the state in the 1920s found themselves persecuted by that same state in the 1930s.

Chapter 3

From the ABCs to the ABCs of Communism, 1930–1953

The question of Latinization was never limited only to that of alphabet.

The 16 May 1930 issue of *Türkmenistan* printed a front-page announcement in the Latin alphabet that read, "Pave the Way for the New Alphabet! [*Täze elipbiýi jol berin!*]." With the Latin script in place, the next step was to develop the literary language.[1] This task entailed the standardization of the lexicon, the codification of grammar and dictionaries, and the expansion of the vocabulary to support industrialization and socialization.[2] The new alphabet signaled a turn in the politics of language. The goals were nothing short of social transformation through the politicization of culture, especially language.

Two language conferences reflected Turkmen efforts to become a modern nation through language. In 1930 the Turkmen Cultural Institute (Turkmenkul't) organized a conference on language, grammar, and terminology. The aim was for Turkmen to take language reform into their own hands. Yet the 1930s were also years of creeping Russification and purges. Turkmen ultimately lost a great deal of control over their culture, language, and education while Moscow gained at their expense. The cultural intelligentsia in particular suffered during the purges. In 1936 a second language conference was organized at which the participants of the 1930 seminar were denounced as "bourgeois nationalists." The chief message of the 1936 conference was that Moscow was transferring power from local elites to the center—or local representatives of the center. The late 1930s witnessed an increase in the status of the Russian language in the Soviet Union, which decreased the status of most national languages and cultures. The history of alphabet reform illustrates a shift in the relationship between center and periphery as linguistic Russification reflected a tighter centralization of power more generally throughout the USSR.

Alphabet was imbued with the power to situate a people in the world. In the 1920s the transnational Latin alphabet was chosen specifically so as to modernize and internationalize Turkic peoples. By 1940, on the other hand, Turkmenistan's use of a Cyrillic-based writing system was emblematic of the *sliianie* (merging) of the Soviet peoples; Cyrillicization illustrated Russification of culture more broadly. The new Soviet person (*sovetskii chelovek/täze sowet adamy*) spoke at least some Russian and wrote his or her native language in the Russian script.

Traditional Western scholarship supposed that Cyrillicization was part of a deliberate Soviet effort to fragment language groups such as Turks in order to weaken cultural affinity.[3] But there is in fact a different and more complicated story: the Soviet state was hardly uniform in its policies and approaches, and there remained room for non-state actors to affect the direction of policy. This chapter illustrates the tumult of the levels of bureaucracy and the number of institutions involved in Cyrillicization, as well as the varied contributions of individual citizens. The opening of Soviet archives has assisted in scholars' ability to see the chaos and confusion of the Stalin period where we once thought that a totalitarian state held firm control over state policy. Examination of alphabet, language, and education policies in Turkmenistan reveals various forms of power that actors throughout society held in the first half of the twentieth century. This power related to language symbolism even during the years of industrialization, World War II, and the death of Stalin in 1953. These years also confirm the important role of the general populace in education and language policy. Sources show that teachers played an increasingly prominent role in substantiating the enduring connection between education, culture, and political policy, for example.

There are two different visions of the future of Turkmen identity. The first is the Jadid-inspired story of creating a modern Turkmen nation within the larger, modern, Muslim and Turkic worlds. This story continued more or less through 1930. The second is the Soviet-inspired vision of creating a population of Soviet Turkmen (and placing them in the socialist variant of modernity), embedded within the Soviet Union, and linked inextricably to Russians. Both stories are about forging a Turkmen identity, but each identity involves a very different type of Turkmen-ness and Turkmen future.

Turkmenistan's First Scientific Conference, 1930

Language conferences represent endeavors in language corpus planning and status planning. They reveal "efforts to purify, enrich, and/or standardize the language itself, on the one hand, and efforts to protect, foster and require the language on the other hand."[4] Such undertakings support national identity through language building: a literary language—a singular, uniform language—encourages a people to speak alike and fosters a sense of national consciousness.[5] At this time in Turkmenistan's history the overwhelming dominance of tribal dialects was such that there was an urgent need both for standardization and for the creation of a literary language if there was going to be a uniform state or nation. This 1930 language conference was a major step toward both.

Turkmenkul't organized Turkmenistan's first local conference on standardization of the literary language, terminology, and grammar to run from 19 to 23 May 1930 in Aşgabat.[6] There were 150 delegates in attendance, from around the

Turkic world and Russia, including B. Kerbabaýew, Abdülhakim Gulmuhamme-dow, H. Derýaýew, H. Baýlyýew, and A. Öwezow.[7] The purpose of the conference was to establish norms for the Turkmen literary language and to save the language from "anarchy." This push for language standardization amounted to cleaning up where there was perceived linguistic chaos. It corresponded with the final years of korenizatsiia and the need to provide workers with a language that could cogent-ly transmit socialist ideas. While functional literacy was still an important con-cern, political literacy would continue to define "literacy" in the USSR for years to come.[8] As Semen Dimanshtein, one of the directors of Moscow's campaign of language modernization, wrote: "By the term literacy we mean not simply alpha-betic literacy. This is not enough anymore. Today we demand political and techni-cal literacy in the broadest sense of the term."[9] Definition of the term "literacy" was expanding in politically important ways to reveal how this universal concern was being addressed at the local level. The conceptualization of literacy over the years was remarkably fluid. Its meaning was not constant but, rather, adjusted according to political exigencies.

The 1930 conference covered the intricacies of language reform in Turkmeni-stan: the basis for the literary language would be the language of the press, especial-ly the newspaper *Türkmenistan*; presses would standardize all words and grammar (there was to be no vacillation between tribal dialects); vowel-consonant harmony would be observed; the full forms of words would be used, not vernacular short forms, e.g., *alamok* (do not take) would be written *alanym ýok*; foreign verbs would be accompanied by Turkmen helping verbs (*mälim etmek, habar etmek*) or could be made into Turkmen verbs (*mälimlemek, habarlamak*). And it was the responsibil-ity of Turkmenkul't and the state publishing house (Turkmengosizdat) to oversee these usages in the Turkmen literary language (*Türkmen edebi dil*).[10] Thus, the liter-ary language would take precedence over any one dialect and would aid the people in becoming the Turkmen nation.

In advance of the conference, Turkmenkul't published articles about prepara-tions and what the participants would debate. Its chair, Böriýew, explained that in order to develop the Turkmen language, Turkmenkul't would borrow words from all other languages, including other Turkic and European languages, Russian, Persian, and Arabic.[11] As the conference declaration reveals, in order to make the written language intelligible to the greatest number of people, Turkmenkul't of-fered four basic rules for spelling borrowed words: (1) if a foreign word could be spelled with Turkmen sounds (phonemes as represented by the graphemes in the latest alphabet) it should follow Turkmen phonology; (2) foreign words should be Turkmenified (suffixes, plurals, and so on would come from Turkmen);[12] (3) in a word with long vowels, only one vowel grapheme would be written;[13] (4) foreign words that were brought into Turkmen to express wholly new concepts could be written according to Russian rules (*marksist, marksizm, komunist, komunizm*).[14]

At this point, in an attempt to "simplify and clarify the language," Turkmenkul't engaged in fashioning the literary language. To this end, it eliminated multiple forms of words in an effort to legitimize just one precise usage. Other words would have to be found or created in order to express the other meanings. The dictionary would be the acknowledged authority in this. Censorship was an essential tool in this endeavor. If authorities disapproved of a term, they cropped it out of the language. An important point of the conference that would reappear in later discussions about the validity of this work was the idea that Turkmen would retain commonly used words deriving from Arabic and Persian, so as not to lose their heritage.[15] Not only would the language be enriched with borrowings from Russian and European languages but many long-standing Arabic and Persian influences would also be preserved, for example, in words such as *ynkylap* (revolution), *ylmy* (scientific), *edebi* (literary). Language content would be as eclectic as Turkmen history.

In developing the literary language, Turkmenkul't continued to adhere to the phonetic principle. This was perhaps the most salient point at the conference, because it reiterated that Turkmen words would be spelled as they sounded rather than made to conform to any unified Turkic literary language. Based on this principle, the work done in preparation for the conference, especially the expeditions undertaken, had determined that some tribal pronunciations would be reflected in the written language. Because the members of Turkmenkul't firmly desired a written language that represented the sounds of spoken Turkmen, Böriýew, Geldiýew, and the other members amassed words and speech patterns from *all* Turkmen regions in order to derive a standardized language that was understood by the greatest number of people. Böriýew had argued for the Turkmenification of foreign words so that the people would be able to understand them.[16] "When we take an originally French word we should not use it in its Russian or French form, but should adapt the root to Turkmen forms, corresponding to the rules of the Turkmen language, so that these words will be understandable to the working people."[17] They would Turkmenify foreign terms as they entered the language.

Finally, the conference determined that the Turkmen alphabet would employ nine vowel graphemes: [a], [ä], [o], [ö], [u], [ü], [e], [i], [i].[18] Conference members would use the fewest number of letters possible. At long last, the issue of the long vowels was resolved. Turkmen would not mark them at all.[19]

In his report to the Turkmengosizdat, Böriýew, the conference chairman, acknowledged Samoilovich, Çobanzade, Alparow, and Geldiýew as having been instrumental in Turkmen linguistic work and the conference.[20] Why would the center have allowed for such a conference? At the time, the whole of the Soviet Union was still becoming literate. Turkmen, like so many across the USSR, were still "unformed, raw recruits, anxious to establish a place for themselves in the apparatuses of power."[21] In order to breathe life into the slogans of the day, to grow into the citizens the Soviet state envisioned, and to become modern, the people of

Turkmenistan needed to attain literacy. A literary language—with uniform spelling—would help to facilitate that.

Language versus Dialects

One of the focal points of the 1930 conference was the unification of the assorted Turkmen dialects into one literary language.[22] This was not an easy question as there were a number of tribes, each of which spoke a distinct vernacular. Although these vernaculars were mutually comprehensible, the intertribal variations have always been a tricky subject, specifically because of the efforts made to create a unified Turkmen national identity. The question of whether any one tribe would dominate occupied the 1930 conference and the ideas of the language planners for years after it.

Reflecting a consensus on the question of the written language, Böriýew wrote that the conference participants would not favor any single spoken dialect but would merge the various attributes.[23] The literary language would take on aspects of the many vernaculars so as to unite the tribes linguistically. In a newspaper article about the conference, Böriýew explained that the dialectical features would progressively fade and the literary language would be a common point of communication that was comprehensible to all tribes.[24] The creation of the literary language was a crucial step on the path to becoming the Turkmen nation.

Despite language planners' acknowledgment of tribal dialects and efforts to incorporate their peculiarities, the Teke linguist Garahanow accused Böriýew and Geldiýew (who was Ýomut) of using the Ýomut dialect as the foundation for the Turkmen literary language.[25] Böriýew addressed this issue, writing that the written literary language being constructed at the time was centered primarily on Teke and western Ýomut dialects, because most officials, educators, and journalists came from the related tribes. He noted that dialects from the eastern region near the Amu Darya were not as well represented as the dialects from the center of Transcaspia and there were few eastern tribal representatives (Ersary or Salyr, for example) involved in publishing newspapers and writing textbooks.[26]

The linguists who undertook this task were themselves from a diverse tribal heritage and did not reflect the fact that the Teke tribe was the most numerous in the republic. With numbers on their side and their centralized position in the republic's capital city, the Teke could have dominated language politics, but instead, Böriýew defended the language planners, explaining that Teke linguistic primacy would be the equivalent of Teke tribal dominance.[27] The ascendancy of any one tribe would not serve the goal of becoming a modern Turkmen nation. Some Turkmen saw the language planners' determination to bring dialectical variations into the literary language as successful. Others did not.[28] Garahanow even went so far as to publish a grammar textbook that contradicted the conference resolutions.[29] This presaged accusations of chaos and anarchy in the language that would arise. While Teke never did overtake the literary language, Garahanow's views on language construction would matter a great deal in the mid-1930s during the purges.

Centralization of Power

As the name of the All-Union Central Executive Committee for the New Turkic Alphabet reflected, Turkic languages had been the original targets for Latinization. However, the program soon expanded to include Chechen, Kurdish, Mongolian, and other non-Turkic languages. When the New Alphabet Committee met later in 1930, a total of thirty-six nationalities had adopted the Latin script. After the non-Turkic peoples joined in the Latinization movement, the name was changed from the Committee for the New Turkic Alphabet to that of the "New Alphabet."[30] VTsK NTA became VTsK NA ("Turkic" was removed). The center asserted material and administrative control in 1930, when VTsK NA moved its headquarters from Baku, Azerbaijan, to Moscow.[31] Moscow began to consolidate its control over the institutions of language and began to replace the old experts and take power away from the local elites.[32] Bolsheviks had planned for the substitution of the old Tsarist-era intelligentsia and specialists with a new generation of Moscow-loyal "cadres and specialists" who had been trained by the Party under the eye of Moscow.[33] When Moscow deemed the training of new specialists to be complete, it would be time for the old intelligentsia to move (or be moved) aside.[34] A symptom of this was the purge of Turkmen intellectuals and bureaucrats in the 1930s.

One of the clearest signs of change came in the form of an article published in *Turkmenovedenie* in the fall of 1931. It was especially significant that the letter appeared in this particular journal—the organ of Turkmenkul't—because it maligned the reputation of Turkmenkul't, its main writers, and intellectuals associated with writing about Turkmen culture. The impetus for the article was Stalin's piece in the magazine *Proletarskaia Revoliutsiia* (Proletarian revolution), which called for "purification for all the members of our daily work, the theoretical and the practical." The author, Veselkov, apparently took Stalin's writing as a signal that it was time to come down hard on nationalists, chauvinists, and those promoting "counterrevolutionary" ideals. He called for revision in "history, economic, science and literature, and in textbooks and periodicals" in Turkmenistan.[35]

Veselkov claimed that Turkmengosizdat and Turkmenkul't had "opened the largest possible field of action for agents of the class enemy and preachers of alien ideology. That is why the historical work of the offices of Turkmenkul't and published works by Turkmengosizdat [had to] be checked in a most rigorous way." He accused those working in the fields of cultural history and literature (Böriýew, Gulmuhammedow, Wepaýew, Geldiýew, Potseluevskii, and so on) of being guilty of using the press to present ideology that was "hostile" to "socialist construction and socialist culture."[36]

According to Veselkov, *Turkmenovedenie*'s editor, Böriẏew, was guilty not only of allowing all of this to take place in the pages of the journal he was editing but also for his weak attendance to it when he did acknowledge it. Veselkov wrote that over the years Böriẏew said nothing about Gulmuhammedow's keenness to use "Chagatay archaisms," which diverted him from the creation of a modern Turkmen literary language. Instead, Veselkov charged, Böriẏew published Gulmuhammedow in "mass quantities" creating "Gulmuhammedowian trends" in the language that tended toward a resurrection of the historical Turkmen language. He wrote similarly about Böriẏew, accusing him of failing to hold a clear position regarding other authors, whom he "helped smuggle in a hostile ideology in the Soviet press."[37] Veselkov's advice to readers was that "we must with intransigence eradicate everything alien and hostile to Marxist-Leninist theory, we must put the ideological front, especially the field of press and schools, under close and continuous supervision of the Party's organizations and the Soviet public."[38] A few months after the second part of Veselkov's two-part article, shocking news surfaced about the very men he had been vilifying.

Purges—Turkmen Azatlygy

In May 1932 the OGPU announced the discovery of Türkmen Azatlygy (Turkmen Freedom), a "counterrevolutionary nationalist" group that from 1922 to 1931 purportedly had been plotting to rise against the Soviet government, with the help of Turkmen emigrants in Persia, who were members of the White Army.[39] Their aim was ostensibly to establish an independent Turkmen state under the protection of British "imperialistic predators."[40] On 11 April 1932, at a session of the Central Committee TSSR, the chair of the Aşgabat city soviet, Atakurzov,[41] "unmasked" this series of crimes, resulting in a period of *atakurzovshhina*, or "prosecution by Atakurzov," during which he accused this "nationalistic counterrevolution" of "harming the ideological front and public education."[42] Although there was a complete lack of evidence that this Turkmen group ever existed, dozens of people and their family members were harassed and arrested.[43]

Those accused of being members of Türkmen Azatlygy fell into two general categories: intellectuals were purged in 1932 and bureaucrats were purged in 1937.[44] The intellectuals included the authors of Turkmenistan's 1920s language reforms and several individuals who held positions related to culture. The cultural purge began in 1932 when dozens of officials working in such institutions as the press, education, and Turkmenkul't were convicted of membership in Türkmen Azatlygy and sentenced to five years in jail.[45] These included Kumuşaly Böriẏew, the head of Turkmenkul't who had been a former commissar of education and head of the Turkmen state publishing house; Muhammed Geldiẏew, linguist and member of Turkmenkul't (though he had died of natural causes in 1931);[46] Begjan Nazarow, head of the korenizatsiia commission and deputy chair of TsIK; Ak-Murad Orázow, commissar of supplies; Bäşim Perengliýew, also a former education commissar and principal of the Central-Asia Zoo-Veterinary Institute; Seidmyrad Öwezbaýew, a member of the presidium of Gosplan; the poets Kümüşaly Burunow and Orazmämmet Wepaýew; Abdülhäkim Gulmuhammedow, former deputy editor of *Türkmenistan*, assistant editor of the journals *Tokmak* and *Daýhan*, and delegate to the 1925 First All-Turkmen Congress; Berdi Kerbabaýew, the writer and editor of *Tokmak*; and Ata Geldiýew, head of Narkomzem (the Ministry of Agriculture and Food) TSSR.[47]

In the mid-1930s Muhammed Geldiýew and other well-known intellectuals were branded "bourgeois nationalists" for the work they had accomplished just a decade earlier.[48] Where korenizatsiia had once encouraged Turkmen language development as being foundational to the creation of the Turkmen nation, now cultural capital was being invested in Russian. Where there had once been the threat of Great Russian chauvinism, there was now the "Friendship of the Peoples" and an impetus to introduce such Russian words as *traktor* (tractor), *sovet* (soviet), and *kolkhoz* (collective farm) into the Turkmen vocabulary.[49]

The issue of terminology had never really been settled, and in posthumous attacks on Geldiýew the issue was raised again. Geldiýew's desire to rely on existing Turkic vocabulary, found in other Turkic languages or in ancient literature, made him a target for those seeking to discredit "nationalists." Staunch Soviets objected to Geldiýew's approach, calling those who had used Arabic and Persian words in creating terminology "pan-Islamists" and considering those who translated Soviet-international words like "proletariat as *ýoksul*, or imperialism as *ýurtbasar*" (as opposed to the Russian *proletariat* and *imperializm*) to be nationalists.[50] Denunciations built on the work of Garahanow and continued to represent Geldiýew's works as those of an anti-Soviet national chauvinist who was trying to separate Turkmen from Russian and the socialist path. Work on the unified Turkic literary language came under special attack: "The language Geldiýew used in his 1929 articles continues his own pan-Turkist and nationalistic path. He was trying to build a literary language, which was shallow, that is, without taking from other languages and without becoming closer to Russian."[51] Purges were designed to rid the system of wreckers and counterrevolutionaries but also to cleanse the elite of the old specialists from the former generation. The attack on Geldiýew took place despite the fact that by 1929 he had come to support the idea of borrowing words from Russian, having stated at the Third All-Turkmen Congress of Soviets, "We feel that our poor language should fill itself with international words primarily from Russian on account of the closeness of Russian culture."[52] The Turkmen linguist Gurban Sopiýew denounced Geldiýew, Böriýew, Garahanow, and Wepaýew as class enemies who had tried to retain the influences of the old-Turkic language Chagatay. Accusations of "pan-Turkism" focused on Geldiýew's attempt to bring written Turkmen closer to the other written Turkic languages through the alignment of particular letters.

By the early 1930s the local Party had purged the men who had worked to build a Turkmen literary language and Turkmen national identity. A. Gulmuhammedow took his own life; B. Kerbabayew, the author and poet was imprisoned; Kümüşaly Böriyew was jailed in 1932.[53] Allaguly Garahanow, who had been a member of the Turkmen Academic Commission for just a few months in 1924, was on the attack. He had publicly disagreed with Geldiyew's 1923 alphabet proposal, and in 1932 he engaged in criticism of Geldiyew and the other members of the Turkmenkul't for their methods of language reform.[54] Garahanow's attack was an example of the ways in which personal jealousies and differences in opinion could become swept up in the changing political fortunes of the country. People like him used the changing political reality to push their visions for language and alphabet reform after their visions had lost out in earlier debates; sometimes out of simple opportunism. Europeans were not spared. Potseluevskii was "accused of being simultaneously a pan-Turkist, a great-Russian chauvinist, and a supporter of feudalism."[55]

As the leading members of Turkmenkul't ended up either dead or in jail, the organization disbanded and the periodicals *Turkmenovedenie* and *Turkmen medeniyeti* stopped publishing. As Edgar notes, the purges of 1932–1937 "eliminated most of the Turkmen communists who had been in power since 1924, and who had ideas of their own about nationhood and socialism in Turkmenistan." The purges also eliminated the intellectuals who had been working to create a modern, socialist Turkmen language and education system. The purges erased from the scene any vestiges of power that remained among the Jadid-inspired generation. Wepayew, Burunow, and Geldiyew were jailed or buried.[56] Their reputations were besmirched, and when the next linguistic conference took place the works of the 1920s and early 1930s were used in juxtaposition with a new era of language reform. Plans for a 1936 linguistic conference in Aşgabat aimed to right the "wrongs" of the linguistic past.

Later, in 1937–1938, Stalin's Great Purges took more of the Turkmen elite. Turkmen historian Bibijan Pal'vanova writes that in Turkmenistan during the "Great Terror" of the 1930s the state arrested over nine thousand people and repressed an estimated twenty thousand.[57] Gaýgasyz Atabaýew, Nedirbaý Aýtakow, Gurban Sähedow, and Allaguly Garahanow (who ironically had attacked others) were stigmatized as "enemies of the people" (*halk düşmany*) and were "eliminated;" that is, they were either jailed or executed.[58] The number of Turkmen intellectuals suffering humiliating or tragic fates created a rupture in the fields of language and education. It was also a break in continuity with the Jadids. The basic themes of progress, cultural transformation, and the creation of a modern Turkmen identity persisted, but there was a shift around the late 1930s that colored the type of Turkmen-ness and Turkmen future that people were working toward.

Marrist Language Theory

The rise of prominent philologist and ethnographer Nikolai Iakovlevich Marr (1864–1934) forced scholars across a wide variety of disciplines to conform to the ideological authority of his new school of linguistics.[59] During the Cultural Revolution, Marr argued, embedding his thesis in Marxism, that language was part of the superstructure and owed its inevitable evolution to changes in the economic base. That is, language was a reflection of class interests; it was a social construction and not related to race or language families.[60]

With the support of Stalin, Marr promoted the idea that the languages of the USSR were evolving, in accordance with *sliianie* (merger) toward unity (*edinstvo*). "In principle, no matter what their stage of development, Marr considered the Soviet languages equal; in practice, one language (Russian) was more equal than others. . . . If the 'nativizing' non-Russian languages of the east were to participate in the Stalin revolution and the march of progress, by necessity they had to adopt its Russian concepts and terms."[61] Although Marr argued that all languages were related and equal, he promoted the adoption of Russian vocabulary for non-Russian languages.

By 1934, as Marr's ideas gained primacy in the connection between intellectual ideas and socialist construction, individual scholars fell into clear pro- or anti-Marrist camps. "Older, 'bourgeois' linguists were criticized as 'Indo-Europeanists' and 'elitists' for neglecting non-Indo-European languages and for privileging the speech of the dominant classes and cultural elites over the speech of the masses."[62] Debate lasted until 1950, when Stalin weighed in on the subjects of linguistics, ethnogenesis, and class in a 9 May 1950 article in *Pravda*, beginning a linguistics campaign in which Stalin himself participated. In the intervening years, academic purges were based on the linguistic theory of Marxist-Leninist dogma: fierce conflicts among scholars and scientists pitted student against teacher and led to calls for "military measures . . . to purge bourgeois elements from academia."[63] The general trend toward the centralization of power, the end of korenizatsiia, and the rise of Marrism contributed to changes in language and educational policy across the USSR, and Turkmenistan was no exception.[64]

In 1936, at the First Turkmen Linguistic Conference, some of these Marrist notions such as *sliannie,* or the merger of languages, were promoted. In particular, Medina Iskanderovna Bogdanova (1908–1962), the head of the conference, and Döwlet Mamedow, the TSSR's Commissar of Enlightenment, advocated the *sliianie* of languages even as they worked to "perfect" Turkmen.[65]

The "First" Turkmen Linguistic Conference, 1936

Muting and eliminating the Turkmen intelligentsia in the early purges brought language planning to a temporary halt. However, within only a year's time the TSSR

Central Executive Committee had reorganized and restaffed a Turkmen alphabet committee with the intent of focusing on further standardization of Turkmen orthography and the use of foreign terminology.[66] In 1932 Turkmenistan's party created the Turkmen State Scientific Research Institute (Turkmenskii Gosudarstvenyi Nauchno-Issledovatel'skii Institut [TGNII]) as a successor to Turkmenkul't.[67] TGNII members planned to create terminological dictionaries for specific subjects such as "math, physics, anatomy, military science, language and literature, biology, and political economy."[68] The work of the past language reformers was to be reexamined closely so as to eliminate traces of their bourgeois nationalism. To this end, entholinguistic expeditions to the rural areas continued, now under the auspices of TGNII.[69]

In 1935 the Soviet Central Alphabet Committee sent Bogdanova from Moscow to Turkmenistan to evaluate the state of language work. She stayed on for more than twenty years to become the lead official in Turkmen language planning. Becoming head of TGNII in 1936, she worked with Potseluevskii to bring in specialists from Moscow and Leningrad, in the process both marginalizing the Turkmen members of her committee and Europeanizing language planning in Turkmenistan.

The mid- to late 1930s witnessed a mounting level of central Party control over the details of language construction in Turkmenistan and the other non-Russian peripheries. The transformation in Turkmen language planning was both symbolic and material. Earlier policies were reversed and the names of the men who initiated them were dragged through the mud. Bogdanova, a human embodiment of the Soviet state, represented double symbolism, first in her person and second in her last name, which in Russian means "God given." This transformation from Turkmen to Russian came to appear in language content and alphabet.

Bogdanova was technically and ideologically qualified to oversee work on Turkmen language development as she had graduated from the Central Asian State University in Tashkent (SAGU) having studied Turkish and Persian.[70] She handled the Turkmen language with skill and demonstrated in her correspondence with Moscow as well as in her publications that she was fluent in Turkmen.[71] Her ideology was appropriate for the times as she espoused Marrist theory.

At the 1936 linguistic conference, the main papers were delivered by Bogdanova, Potseluevskii, and Mamedow. Précis of the papers were published in the newspapers *Türkmenistan* and *Turkmenskaia Iskra*. The papers reflected the change that had taken place not only in Turkmenistan but around the USSR regarding culture and the shift in emphasis from local initiative to close central oversight of cultural activities. There had been a Unionwide shift from an accent on local cultures to one on Soviet or Russian.[72]

In his opening remarks, the chairman of the Council of People's Commissars Gaýgasyz Atabaýew noted that between 1930 and 1936 life in Turkmenistan had developed both materially and culturally. He explained that "to build socialism such words as soviet, communist, kolkhoz, Bolshevik, and tractor would have to enter the Turkmen language and be mastered by the majority of the people." Atabaýew underscored that taking "these types of words" (Russian) into the literary language would successfully develop and standardize the lexicon.[73]

Mamedow spoke first about how the "improvement in the well-being and the cultural level of the working masses was tightly connected with the success of the Communist Party" and, most especially, with material advancement. "Progress" was still about overcoming backwardness and now more than ever was directly connected to the economic situation. Schools were an area where the Party was able to demonstrate developments. Whereas, before, the educational sphere had been "saturated with mollas," Mamedow now counted more than four hundred thousand people studying in Soviet schools and measured the level of literacy at 62 percent. The "army of the proletarian intelligentsia" had increased to where the TSSR boasted forty-six hundred teachers and "hundreds of technicians and engineers that are all Turkmen"—a nod to the success of korenizatsiia. He proudly announced that a seven-year school system was functioning even in the villages. "The army of new people has grown to include kolkhoz chairmen, brigade-leaders, tractor drivers and Stakhanovites, who have enriched their native language with new international and Soviet vocabulary, liberating the language from the meanings and superstitions of the feudal epoch."[74]

Still, Mamedow argued, Turkmen people remained backward, and he identified language as the number one culprit in that crime. Here he shared the same basic idea with the Turkmen from the pre-Soviet times: that progress and modernity would arise only as a result of mass literacy. Mamedow wrote: "We are behind because we lack the rules of orthography, syntax and terminology. As a result, the language of our newspapers, textbooks, and other literature is not fully understood by the majority of the population, making it difficult to study the basics of science in our schools and creating obstacles to studying Party and state planning. All of this retards the rapid blossoming of culture, national in form, socialist in content." In direct opposition to what Böriýew wrote about the 1930 conference, Mamedow accused the planners of that 1930 conference of being responsible for "all the language problems" in Turkmenistan. He went on about how "the nationalist counter-revolutionaries, as well as chauvinists tried their best during the Soviet years to abort the formation of a unified, national standardized language which would have been understood by and available to the majority of the population."[75]

He directly accused "the nationalists" Geldiýew (posthumously) and Böriýew of having concealed their treacherous activities behind "masks." Having charged Böriýew and Geldiýew of favoring the Ýomut tribal dialect in early reforms, Mamedow accused Garahanow of trying to shift the rules of orthography such that they favored the Teke dialect, his work stemming from a desire to "ignite the wars between tribal dialects." For these reasons, Garahanow elicited "special attention";

most especially because of his attempts to bring to the Turkmen literary language "a grammar characteristic of the Turkish caliphate."[76]

In his conclusion, Mamedow cited five basic directives that the 1936 conference was instructing intellectuals to follow in their further work on language development. The most important was that "the basis for forming the united, national standard Turkmen language must be the living, spoken folk language, established by the Great October Revolution, based on the concentration of tribal dialects." This is, ironically, almost word for word what Böriýew and Geldiýew had called for over and over again: "a literary language that was as close as possible to the spoken language of the widest number of tribal dialects."[77] Only now, the Great October Revolution was the foundation for all cultural development, not the "innate richness" of the local language or the local culture for which Geldiýew had called.[78]

Ending with a quotation from Stalin, the "Leader of Nations," Mamedow wrote, "We have to give national cultures a chance to develop and grow to reveal all their potentials, in order to create conditions of merging [*sliianie*] them into one common culture, with one common language."[79] With this he revealed the main point of the conference itself and of language development as it would carry on into the 1980s.

In his report to the 1936 conference, the linguist Potseluevskii stated that the orthographic system of the Turkmen language was based mainly on resolutions of the 1930 Turkmen linguistic congress. He specified, "That congress was led by the counter-revolutionary nationalists Böriýew and Geldiýew . . . methodologically its resolutions were dangerous and damaging." The main disadvantages of that congress's work were the following: "a lack of tracking development of the living spoken language of Turkmen proletariat and progressive kolkhoz workers; insufficient tracking of phonetic trends of the living language and in particular complete removal of short labial vowels from all syllables except the first one; allowing confusing spelling and a lack of solutions for basic word spelling; a lack of solutions for the questions of conveying the meaning of Turkmen international words, Soviet words, and suffixes; and not relying on the experience of brethren republics."[80]

Bogdanova's own presentation did not mention anyone by name, but she leveled her accusations more generally at "panturkists," whom she accused of having oriented the Turkmen literary language to "the dead language Chagatay and even the ancient Uyghur language."[81] Instead, she explained, Turkmen would follow the "universal mold" in spelling (going from *kamynyyst* to *kommunist*, from *melissa* to *militsia*) and would employ readily available international-Soviet terms in place of "Arabo-Iranian elements" (going from *ýoksyllar* to *proletariat*, from *birleşik* to *sojuz*).[82]

Several Latin-based letters were changed in interesting ways. The Turkmen alphabet had contained both the graphemes "h" and "x," the former to represent the sound found mostly in native Turkmen words that has its equivalent in German, and the latter to represent the phoneme [kh] in Russian words. This was deemed confusing and the letter "h" was eliminated: *pahta* became *paxta* (cotton), *tahta* became *tagta* (wood); *kolhoz* became *kolxoz* (collective farm). In connection with this question was the spelling of words with the letters "s" and "z," which in the Turkmen literary language are the equivalent of the unvoiced and voiced phoneme [th].[83] These would be replaced with the Russian graphemes "c" and "з."[84] Besides, as Professor Potseluevskii pointed out, on the road to *sliianie*, "they [would] eventually be replaced by Russian sounds."[85]

Bogdanova's report focused on terminology and a set of tasks in linguistic work in the "epoch of building socialism." Perhaps her most salient point was to underscore the influence of the Revolution on the potential for the future *sliianie* of languages. She wrote, "New meanings, new revolutionary ideas are common for all nations of the Soviet Union. They determine common content for all languages of the Soviet Union in all their diversity and differences in appearance. Nowadays the language of selected nationalities of the USSR, no matter the form, all, without exception, are expressions of united class consciousness of the working masses." She explained, "One of the major tasks of the second five-year plan [is] to build a classless society and to destroy the vestiges of capitalism."[86] In other words, Soviet, socialist Turkmenistan required a new language to reflect the economic "advancements" and the spate of new ideas that had emerged as a result of the Revolution. Proper terminological development would be the foundation for this. Bogdanova identified the problems with the development of the Turkmen vocabulary as stemming from the biases of the 1930 conference. These included:

1. A pan-Islamic orientation to Arabic and Iranian elements.

2. A nationalistic bias, expressed mostly in the sphere of terminology and the efforts to Turkmenify all [borrowed] words, e.g. *ýoksyllar* instead of *proletariat*, *arkalaşykly hojalyk* instead of *kholhoz*. And in an unbelievable distortion of loan words trying to pass it off as if it would sound closer to the pronunciation of the local people: *kamynyyst* instead of *kommunist*, *kamyntyrna* instead of *komintern*, and *melissa* instead of *militsiia*. This was done purposefully, ignoring the experience of terminological work in brethren republics in order to isolate Turkmen literary language and Turkmen culture from the unifying stream of socialism building. . . . This could be seen in such words as *birleşik* [union] instead of *soýuz*, and *enelik* [matriarch] instead of *matriarhat*. . . . This nationalist bias only intensified the inter-tribal struggle for dominance of this or that dialect in the newly constructed [literary] language.

3. A pan-Turkist bias that denied the independent value of Turkmen . . . adopting the language of one of the economically strong Turkic nations (usually Azerbaijani or Anatolian Turkish) . . . [or] the use of dead Chagatay or old Uyghur languages as the base . . . as exemplified by such terms as *ynkylap* [revolution], *jemhuriýet* [society], *wagyt* [time], and *nesihat* [advice].[87]

Somehow, at the same time, the 1930 conference had also managed to emit a fourth point: "Great-power Russian chauvinist bias expressed by ignoring Turkmen language or uncritically introducing Russian words and terms into Turkmen. For example, *zalovaniýa, sredstvo, prepodavat etmek.* This bias was often used to isolate Turkmen Soviet literary language from the language of the masses."[88]

Bogdanova noted that other basic violations of "common sense" were seen in a lack of standardized spelling, which led to such irregularities as both *komunist* and *kommunist* or *kolektiv* and *kollektiv* being used; no standard way of representing the Russian letter ц [ts], which was written both as "ts" and "s"; along with щ, which was written as both "sc" and "şş." Even worse, she reported, there were no rules for representing letters, *я, ё,* and *ю.* The resolution of the 1936 conference would fix all of this. Moreover, Soviet-international terms that had an equivalent meaning would be expressed in the Turkmen: *борба* (struggle) would now be *göreş, выборы* (elections) would be *saýlar, выставка* (exhibition) would be *sergi, оборона* (defense) would be *gorama.* Those Arabic and Persian words that the majority of the masses had fully acquired and that were not distinguished from Turkmen terms would remain in use: *täsir* (influence), *hereket* (movement), *daýhan* (peasant), *halk* (people, nation), *ylym* (science), and *senagat* (industry). Soviet-international words that did not have an exact meaning in Turkmen were to be adopted in their natural forms: *agent* (agent), *aktiv* (group of activists), *analiz* (analysis), and *bolşevik* (Bolshevik). She went on to clarify the verbal forms of adjectives, suffixes, methods for writing all loan words, orthography, and pages of other linguistic considerations.[89]

A memo from the Soviet of Nationalities on 17 February 1937 assured the Central Executive Committee of the USSR that the 1936 conference had "stabilized" the Turkmen alphabet.[90] G. Musabekov, chair of the VTsK NA, in early 1937, wrote that the 1936 First All-Turkmen Linguistic Conference had cleared up the "muddle" in Turkmen orthography and terminology.[91] The 1936 conference decided that "international" words were to be used whenever an equivalent could not be found in Turkmen. It underscored a growing closer to Russian in its statement that these "international" words should be kept in their original Russian form. In reality, the main linguistic difference between the 1936 and the 1930 conferences was the privileging of international forms of words that had no equivalent in Turkmen.[92] Otherwise, international concepts that were absent from the existing Turkmen lexicon would be written in their original forms (*ideolog, imperialism*) or in Russian (*krizis* [crisis], *aktiv* [active]) if they had arrived via Russian, even if they violated the vowel harmony of Turkmen.[93] The main results of the 1936 conference were to mirror the transfer of power from native Turkmen elites to Moscow or its representatives and to eliminate the "nationalistic slant" from the Turkmen language.[94]

Cyrillicization

The newspaper *Sowatlylyk ugrunda göreş* (Struggle for literacy) began to publish in 1936. Its specific aim was to examine questions of literacy during this new era of cultural change. One thing the pages of the newspaper made clear was that, despite all the years of work toward "cultivating" the Turkmen people and bringing them out of their "backward darkness," Turkmen still had serious concerns about literacy and the system of likbez schools.[95] Also in 1936, the Central Committee's Orgbiuro began reevaluating the use of Latin scripts in the RSFSR. It formed the Central Scientific Institute of Languages and Alphabets (TsNIIIaP) to oversee subsequent "language construction" or Cyrillicization and began changing the North Caucasian and Northern Siberian writing systems to Cyrillic in 1937. By the end of 1938, all languages in the RSFSR officially employed the Cyrillic alphabet.[96]

Simultaneously, yet in marked contrast, in March 1937, the All-Union Central Committee for the New (Latin) Alphabet and the Central Institute of Languages and Writing of the People of the USSR reasserted use of the Latin alphabet in Turkmenistan and the other Turkic regions.[97] The Presidium of the Central Executive Committee of the USSR also passed a resolution confirming the place of Latin.[98] These two committees appeared to be working in direct opposition to TsNIIIaP. The fluctuation in central policy between alphabets was probably a sign that language policy was suffering from a lack of streamlined organization. In the late 1930s, the effects of the purges were seen not only in the personnel changeover in specific positions but also in the shift in ability and knowledge about official work. With the fear and the turnover of personnel running throughout Soviet administration, it follows that the bureaucratic work would take time to become organized.

As early as January 1939, Turkmenistan's citizens became involved in the implementation of Cyrillicization. It began with a letter from teachers in the town of Baýramaly, near Aşgabat, which called for adoption of the script in place of the Latin one.[99] Teachers, state employees, and scholars came out in support of the idea.[100] Such popular involvement in the decision gave a patina of popular approval to script reform. While there may indeed have been individuals who sincerely wished to change writing systems in order to be more Soviet, it is less clear where the ultimate decision came from. It was likely Stalin himself who drove the campaign.[101]

The Soviet government had spent more than ten years and an enormous amount of money implementing the Latin script. The decision to convert the writing of non-Russian groups in Russia to Cyrillic took place even as the All-Union Central Committee for the New Alphabet (VTsIK NA) still existed—the New Alphabet Committee in Moscow disbanded in December 1937. VTsIK NA even became involved in approving some Caucasian languages' adoption of Cyrillic. By April 1939, thirty-five languages had shifted to Cyrillic-based alphabets. The underlying reason for the widespread implementation of the Latin alphabet was its "international" character. However, in the late 1930s the meaning of the word "international" changed. Instead of global or wide-reaching, "international" had come to refer to things Russian, "the most revolutionary and progressive world language."[102] Political considerations such as the "bourgeois" nature of the Latin alphabet combined with linguistic arguments that the Latin-based system was an "obstacle to the mastery of Russian."[103]

Just as print media had been used to communicate to the public the details of the reformed Arabic script and then the Latin alphabet, journals and newspapers printed examples and explanations of the new Cyrillic script. In the late 1930s and early 1940s, the newspaper *Sowatlylyk ugrunda göreş* reported on schools, enrollment numbers, budgetary matters, literacy statistics, policies related to literacy, and advice to teachers on lessons and teaching methods.[104] One article published in *Sowatlylyk ugrunda göreş* indicated the types of concerns Turkmen expressed over Cyrillicization:

> Now more than twenty Soviet nations have transferred over to the Russian alphabet. This fact demonstrates that for all of our country's [*yurt*] nationalities learning the Russian language is a great pleasure. The USSR's people's great friendship [*beýik dostlygyny*] runs deep and is still secure.
>
> And in our Turkmenistan we school teachers feel it is the perfect time to settle the question of changing from the Latin to the Russian alphabet. It would be very useful for the development of the Turkmen people's culture and would serve to strengthen relations between Turkmen and Russians in brotherhood as they battle for a socialist culture.
>
> The changeover of Turkmen letters to Russian would eliminate the confusion and difficulties that exist because we are using two alphabets in Turkmenistan. Being able to read the Russian letters would make it easier for Turkmen to increase their level of skills and qualifications and would make it easier for Russians to learn Turkmen language and literature. Continuing with the two scripts creates confusion for Turkmen schoolchildren, and even worse, makes it difficult for Turkmen to read even their own language in newspapers and journals.
>
> Turkmen's conversion from Latin to Russian would doubtless increase Turkmen schoolchildren's successes. And, make it easier to translate Marxism-Leninism classes and literature into Turkmen, and for Turkmen workers to learn the books of Lenin and Stalin.
>
> The people's enemies and fascism's bourgeois-nationalist and Trotsky-Bukharin agents tried very hard to keep Turkmen people distanced from Russian people, and they are against the change in script. But under the leadership of the Turkmen people's BK(b)P TsKs and Comrade Stalin, their work and battle to destroy the enemies' nests and poisonous intentions have been eliminated. . . . The Russian alphabet offers the greatest possibilities on the cultural front in eliminating these poisonous intentions.[105]

Switching to the Russian writing system would eliminate confusion among Turkmenistan's students and make it easier for them to learn Russian. Knowledge of the lingua franca (*iazyk mezhnatsional'nogo obshchenia*) would lend itself to the friendship of the peoples.

Laying some groundwork for the "Friendship of the Peoples," on 13 March 1938, the Central Executive Committee issued its decree "On the Obligatory Study of the Russian Language in National Republic and Regional Schools."[106] Promising to increase the number of teachers and classes in the Russian language in schools and offering to provide courses for its own staff, the Soviet Orgbiuro, in coordination with local education ministries, organized a campaign to develop universal Russian language standards throughout the USSR.[107] Still, the 1938 decree continued to underscore the importance of the non-Russian languages.[108] Literature, textbooks, and ideology appeared both in Russian and in local languages at a cost borne by the central government. Turkmenistan's Ministry of Education had actually introduced Russian-language study in the schools a year earlier, adding Russian language as a subject in all Turkmen primary and middle schools in 1937.[109] This development in language education was in part due to the fact that by the mid-1930s the korenizatsiia policy had begun to wane. There was no announcement of the policy's decline; it was instead, as Donald Carlisle has written, a case of "benign neglect."[110] It was, however, signaled by a greater role for Russian as evinced by the 1938 law.

This new language policy reflected the extent to which Moscow held political control. These reforms were not merely linguistic but were dependent on extra-code factors. That is, such decisions had little to nothing to do with the way a language was spoken or was developing organically and had everything to do with political factors and political control over the way language was used. This was all strongly related to the dramatic changes that occurred with the purges of the 1930s. With former language planners out of the way, after the purges, the state had little with which to contend. Non-Russian languages became vulnerable to Russian influences and largely closed to all others.[111]

Literacy Fulfilled?

In 1939 Stalin announced that the people of Turkmenistan had attained a 90 percent literacy rate. Sources do not discuss whether he was taking script into consideration here when evaluating literacy.[112] He declared the Cultural Revolution a resounding success and that the people of Turkmenistan had "surpassed even a European country"; the people of Turkmenistan had "achieved a great success on the cultural front" as well as universal literacy.[113] Only one year earlier the state had advised citizens that the definition of "literate" was when one had completed an entire kolkhoz likbez course.[114] Stalin's announcement did not negate that definition, but it certainly allowed for a great many who had not taken the course to slip through as it would have been physically impossible for enough people to have graduated in one year's time so that the statistics could jump so dramatically. Newly literate adults represented 261,927 villagers (59.5 percent literate) and 119,052 urbanites (89.3 percent literate) in 1938 for a total of 66.4 percent literate throughout Turkmenistan in 1938. This denoted a 7 percent increase from 1937. Even with the influx of funds that went into likbez studies in 1938, it seems improbable that the number of people completing a likbez course would allow the statistics to jump to 90 percent. The numbers of literate adults even in archival records are inconsistent. It would appear that approximately one hundred thousand adults a year entered likbez and mekdeps for the semiliterate.[115] However, records also show that only 50–60 percent of those students graduated.[116]

Despite the pressing nature of international events in the late 1930s and early 1940s, on 11 May 1940, TSSR's Sovnarkom decreed the use of a Cyrillic alphabet for the Turkmen language. Three days later TSSR's Central Committee passed a law in accord with that decree.[117] The state scheduled all first and second grades of elementary schools to transfer to Cyrillic within the year. Turkmenistan's Publishing Commission agreed to change over textbooks by 10 May 1940 and to sponsor courses to aid in adult instruction. The Ministry of Education changed over all official writing concerning schools by 1 September 1940.[118] All state offices' and social organizations' stamps, seals, letterheads, and signage were also to be in the new alphabet. City, district, and town soviets had the duty to reissue street signs and those for public squares within two months' time.[119] Turkmenistan's Central Committee issued a public decree demanding all print in Turkmenistan be in Cyrillic by 1 May 1941.[120] The new alphabet had thirty-eight graphemes. Unlike in the Latin-based-script reform, this time the Turkmen linguists did not add supplementary graphemes to mark long vowel phonemes, because Turkmen dialects differ in their long vowel usage. Language planners did not want to create "complications" in Turkmen orthography.[121]

The newspaper *Turkmenskaia Iskra* explained that the change in script would facilitate literacy because the Russian language was growing increasingly important in schools, and students around the Soviet Union were learning the Cyrillic alphabet. The Turkmen Party leadership underscored that it made more sense to change the Turkmen language over to the Cyrillic alphabet than to waste time teaching students two separate scripts. By instituting the Cyrillic script, it argued, the Party would make it easier for Turkmen to learn Russian, as well as for other language groups to study Turkmen.[122] Proponents avowed, despite the political considerations connected to this script change, that "no harm" would come of it because the peculiarities of the sounds of Turkmen were being taken into consideration. Moreover, with arguments similar to those made about the Arabic script during Latinization, published articles complained that the Latin script did not fully represent all of the sounds of the Turkmen language and thus was wholly "inconvenient."[123] For the most part, though, it was argued, this was a change for the better; Cyrillicization was progressive. It was true that Russian and international words borrowed into the Turkmen language would be written according to the rules of Russian—rather than according to Turkmen—but this was a necessary aspect of the universalizing nature of this reform.[124] This approach to foreign words would make the words more similar to terms in other Soviet languages, enhancing the friendship among the Soviet peoples.

Throughout the 1930s and 1940s, state statistics-gathering agencies, schools, and newspapers kept track of the number of schools and students—adult and children. TSSR Narkompros was responsible for preparing 4,070 teachers by 15 July 1940, but as of August they had prepared only 2,946. The cities of Aşgabat and Krasnovodsk were singled out as being wholly unprepared.[125] Glowing praise for individual teachers, who assisted the processes of universal education and mass literacy, and special students, who reflected the success of the Cyrillicization and Russification campaigns, appeared in the press.[126]

In 1940 there were ten-day seminars on the new alphabet for hundreds of teachers in the oblasts. Those teachers were then slated to go out into the regions and teach the new alphabet to other teachers. Seminars at the *raýon* level were designed for elementary school teachers as well as those who worked with adults. The teachers participating in these seminars would then teach the new alphabet to elementary students in the first and second grades. TSSR had already ordered the books from TSSR Sovnarkom's press—though they were not delivered before the first seminars got underway.[127]

In 1940, to support the transition from Latin to Cyrillic, the state published new books in the Turkmen language in Cyrillic such as *A Primer for Children* (fifty thousand copies), *The Mother Tongue I & II*, *Grammar I & II* (sixty-five thousand copies each), and *Arithmetic I & II* (thirty-five thousand copies each). Books for adults also appeared in the new script. The linguist G. Sopyýew authored three books for "semi-literate" adults, including a primer, a grammar, and a general textbook. In summer and fall 1940, the newspapers *Sowet Türkmenistany* (formerly *Türkmenistan*) and *Mugallymlar kömek* (Teachers' aide) carried lessons for learning the new alphabet. At the same time, newspapers announced successes such as five hundred teachers enrolling in courses to prepare to introduce the new alphabet in schools.[128] There was a shift in cultural capital as Latin-based literature fell by the wayside and the state produced material in Cyrillic. In 1940, for example, the state publishing house printed 538,000 copies of Lenin's works in Turkmen in Cyrillic.[129]

The likbez schools introduced the new Cyrillic script, the state funded new libraries, and literacy workers continued to open clubs and teahouses. The Soviet state pressed adults to take advantage of the opportunities for cultural growth. Stories of personal success were shared in the newspapers. In Aşgabat, Haýrulla

Myradow, the supervisor of a meat combine—a *stakhanovite*—shared his personal story in the newspaper *Sowatlylyk ugrunda göreş*.

> I am fifty-five years old. I have spent most of my life working in a factory. If I were illiterate, working would be difficult because I wouldn't be able to calculate my work [and] I would be ignorant of news in the daily press.
>
> I thought about attending school to become literate, but I couldn't study because my factory did not offer classes. Every day my own son Ismail advised me, "Dad, you too should study, become literate." I listened and began studying at home immediately.
>
> Every day, my son Ismail taught me how to write the easiest words. It finally sunk in and in a little while I knew the letters. I guess that literacy is tied to diligence. So, then I was literate. I was reading newspapers and journals and every day I was calculating my own output [in the factory].
>
> Now I am a supervisor at the factory. I surpass the norms and that work earns me 600 manats. Our life has become joyous and happy.[130]

While there were such stories of *stakhanovism*, it would appear from most reports in *Sowatlylyk ugrunda göreş* that there was actually little interest among the Turkmen to learn Cyrillic and a great deal of avoidance especially among low-level bureaucrats. There was resistance to the new script. Articles even complained of teachers who remained "illiterate" because they had not bothered to educate themselves in the new writing system. The names of people who were "not paying attention" to the demands of culture, especially those working in kolkhozes and those in the education sector, were singled out and their names published in the newspaper. *Sowatlylyk ugrunda göreş* is full of articles listing the names of people who did not support the campaign to make people literate.

One revealing article about the problems with literacy at this time reported not only a dearth of participants in likbez courses but also a lack of action on the part of city bureaucrats. The article publicly named collective farm representative Annamurat Durdy oglu (it is interesting that the paper did not use the Russian form of his name) as being not only irresponsible but also illiterate:

> In Köşe village there are fourteen open spaces in the likbez. There should be 1,410 illiterate men and women vying for these spaces but instead, each day only four or five arrive; on some days it is only one or two. The city's Enlightenment sector's instructor held just one meeting. No one from the educational sector did or is doing anything. In order to build the culture of the likbez workers they dumped everything on the shoulders of Annamurat Durdy oglu who only works in the reading room.
>
> In Sverdlov kolkhoz there are five likbez schools. 452 people should join [because they have been identified as illiterate] but every day not more than two or three people join. The kolkhoz party organization representative Orazmämmet Annagylyç oglu should first tend to his own illiteracy—better yet join a school.[131]

The definition of literacy was changing again. We began with the shift from Islamic literacy to secular and then swung to Socialist literacy. These accompanied a shift from no ability to read to the ability to read in Arabic script, then to Latin script, and to Cyrillic script. Now people who could read in the Latin-based script had become "illiterate" (even if they could read "socialist" in the Latin-based script).

To familiarize readers with the new alphabet, *Sowatlylyk ugrunda göreş* published examples of it. It explained to readers that Stalin's concern grew daily, as did the responsibility of the people. "The Soviet government has a duty to develop the society's culture and is putting a lot of money toward this. Culture will develop the most if we teach kolkhoz workers and Turkmen workers the Russian alphabet and the Turkmen people's learning Russian will be made easier."[132] Turkmen newspapers addressed cultural change directly by asserting that script reform would bring the Turkmen language closer to Russian.[133]

> The past uncultured peoples will be replaced by cultured, healthy, and happy people living a free life. The current Latin alphabet could not satisfy this growth. In order to build this culture and work to our greatest abilities first we should know Soviet science and education. The new [Cyrillic] alphabet will help the Turkmen people and be a powerful tool in learning the language of our fraternal Russians [*doganlyk rus halkynyň dilini*].
>
> We will learn Russian with great pleasure. And our people's transferring to the new, Russian alphabet will be the greatest help in our cultural development. Reading rooms, clubs, libraries, and houses of culture will provide endless support to the people's literacy and culturedness.[134]

Sowatlylyk ugrunda göreş linked the Cyrillic alphabet closely to learning the Russian language and becoming cultured, similar to ways that the state in the 1920s had associated use of the Latin alphabet with being modern and international. Turkmen changed their writing system again, and as a result literacy shifted. Under korenizatsiia the state promoted the Turkmen language, and even that of such smaller language communities as Kurds. By the late 1930s linguistic Russification was unapologetically the goal of the day, and this attitude would persist through the 1980s.

Conclusion

Both the language development and definition of literacy in 1930s Turkmenistan and the implicit goals of literacy and culturedness in the 1940s were about creating a modern Turkmen national identity. Two conferences, in 1930 and 1936, aimed to make Turkmen language more uniform and contributed to the construction of the Turkmen nation. By the mid-1930s the centralization of power led to the purge of intellectuals who had worked on the 1930 language conference and left a combination of new actors in charge of Turkmen language reform: natives with very little authority and a new set of Europeanized Turkmen or actual Europeans, who set out to Sovietize the language, which meant adding Russian vocabulary. Russification was also in line with promotion of the concept of "Friendship of the Peoples" of the USSR, the campaign that began in earnest in these years.

The arrest of the Turkmen elite and the denunciation of their work and then the 1936 First Turkmen Language Conference paralleled political and cultural shifts taking place throughout the Soviet Union. By bringing language planners from Moscow and Leningrad to take over the work of the Turkmen linguists, the center demonstrated that it was moving away from korenizatsiia. The later adoption of the Cyrillic script in place of the Latin alphabet starkly symbolized the shift of cultural power from the peripheries to the center, and the Russification of Soviet Turkmenistan.

As the pages of the newspaper *Sowatlylyk ugrunda göreş* reveal, the 1930s and 1940s were not without their problems in liquidating illiteracy among the people. While there were stories of stakhanovites who delighted in learning to read and write, there were far more published news articles devoted to the struggle of literacy—about likbez schools with empty seats. Despite the shortcomings addressed in the press, in 1939 Stalin declared Turkmenistan 90 percent literate. Opinions differed over what percentage of Turkmenistan's population was literate, however, and even over the definition of literacy. The salient point is that literacy was center stage with even Stalin commenting on it, indicating literacy's perceived significance to the future of the Turkmen people.

Cyrillicization was perhaps the most significant symbolic act of the Stalin period, one that underscored the Russifying tendencies of the post-purge years. State and party organs preached that the use of Cyrillic would help to facilitate learning Russian, which would support literacy and "culturedness." The Russian alphabet and the Russian culture would help expedite Turkmens' acculturation into the Soviet system. Cultural capital shifted as Russian was elevated above other languages de facto, if not de jure.[135]

Chapter 4

Speaking Soviet, 1954–1984

The aim of Soviet policy has always been to teach the people of the Kirghiz steppe, the small Uzbek cotton grower and the Turkmen gardener to accept the ideals of the Leningrad worker.

Cyrillicization stabilized the Turkmen alphabet for several decades, allowing Turkmen scholars to turn their attention to other language issues. The main issues in the 1950s were those of language standardization and Sovietization. The former concerned scholars' desire to eliminate synonyms, reduce tribal dialectical variances, and trim the vernacular so the nation would speak a uniform official language. The latter involved the infusion of the Turkmen language with Soviet-international terms. Turkmen linguists believed that the way to solidify the nation was to foster literacy through the refinement of the literary language.

In 1951 a news article reported that "chaos reigned" in Turkmenistan with respect to language, referring specifically to issues related to terminology where multiple words were used to describe a single object.[1] Sovietization concerned the introduction of terms via Russian. New concepts (especially technical ones) were entering the language, and although some would be expressed with neologisms many more would be introduced through Russian vocabulary. These two considerations were important aspects of building "happy socialism" in Turkmenistan.[2]

Language planning and education reform after de-Stalinization were far less dramatic and intense compared to the first half of Soviet history. There were no "language fronts, no mass literacy or *korenizatsiia* campaigns, no upbeat statistics in recently alphabetized languages, or in the number of students receiving instruction in their mother tongue."[3] In the post-Stalin era, language planners were not occupied with new rules about alphabet or orthography. Instead, at language conferences and congresses they discussed the role of Russian and the teaching of Russian in non-Russian schools.[4] Scholars still paid attention to the local languages, but by the second half of the twentieth century publications were primarily occupied with the stabilization and enrichment of the Turkmen language.[5] Nevertheless, language policy in these years remained concerned with power and cultural capital.

Sovietization of Turkmen Vocabulary

In 1951 a member of the newly founded Turkmenistan Academy of Sciences, J. Amansaryýew, warned of complications with synonyms on the cultural front. To describe "linguistics," the various terms *dil bilimi*, *dil ylmy*, and *dilçilik bilimi* were all in use.[6] To refer to a kindergarten, in the 1920s *bakja* and *balalar bakjasy*, and the Russian *detskii sad*, were accepted, but then in the 1950s *çagalar bagy* came into use.[7] Language content warranted reexamination, because linguists such as Amansaryýew thought that for a language to flourish it should be streamlined. They wanted to reduce the variety of words in order to create a literary language even if that meant limiting the richness of the language.

Published articles explained a second but even greater concern, that anachronistic words of Arabic and Persian origin in the Turkmen lexicon should be replaced with "Soviet-international" words so as to support industrialization, the theories of the Marxist-Leninist revolution, and aspects of the new (Soviet) life. Words like *medjit*, *medrese*, *işan*, *molla*, and *bismilla* (mosque, Islamic college, cleric, clerical teacher, and call to God) should be taken out, and such words as *partiýa*, *komsomol*, *pioneer*, and *traktor* (party, komsomol, pioneer, tractor) should enter.[8] This did not mean that Moscow wanted to see publishing in Turkmen come to a halt or even slow down—just the opposite. As in earlier political eras, the idea of bringing information to a people in their native language persisted. It was important that Soviet citizens learn Russian, but it was even more important that they understand the party line, and the vernacular facilitated their comprehension. The problem identified by the Academy of Sciences and its representatives in the 1950s was that local languages needed to reflect more Soviet (Russian) influence.

It was not only in Turkmenistan that "chaos" was identified. Michael Smith relates that internal school, government, and Party reports between 1941 and 1950 reveal that the Russian language was in "peril." In 1949 "the Council of Ministers of the USSR was so frustrated with the 'drift' and 'chaos' on the spelling issue that it appealed directly to Executive Committee Secretary Beria to publish a recently compiled definitive set of spelling rules."[9] It was not only the Turkmen language that needed to be standardized. In 1950 Stalin revealed that language standardization continued to be a problem throughout the USSR. It was in this year that Stalin began the linguistic campaign against the linguist Nikolai Marr and his followers.

In an article published 9 May 1950, Stalin severely rebuked the school of linguistics led by the Marrists. He continued to opine on linguistics with leading *Pravda* articles (20 June, 4 July, and 2 August 1950).[10] These formed part of a flurry of activity on the language front that took place that year as Marrism was killed off by linguists, sixteen years after Marr himself had died. Stalin established himself as the Soviet Union's leading linguist. In "Marxism and the Problems of Linguistics," Stalin's article published on 20 June 1950, he wrote that teachers must "inculcate a love and a political conscious attitude for Russian." He wanted them to "teach students how to read intelligently, properly, easily and expressively; to write literately; to expound their thoughts in speech and print both freely and correctly."[11]

As Smith explains, the main lesson to take from the linguistic campaign of 1950 is that it revealed just how "vulnerable and unsteady" the Soviet state was on the cultural front. The state struggled to teach Russian across the USSR, and when it did manage to get Russian into a classroom it also had to acknowledge the national languages, both for practical reasons of communication and for reasons of respect. Even Stalin taught that people should master both Russian and their local language. "In a parable from his own life, he taught them that the national frontier was something they could only conquer in themselves, by maintaining the language of home, but especially by learning the language of the state." That Russian would become a second mother tongue was one of the predictions of the 1954 Linguistic Conference held in Turkmenistan.[12]

Second Linguistic Conference, 1954

Despite the work that took place in the 1920s and 1930s, even after Stalin's death in 1953 Party members saw the Turkmen language as "unstable." This time the issue was not so much a question of script but, rather, one of spelling and terminology. The Turkmen historian Annagurdow writes that authors, editors, and publishers had not fully adhered to the decisions of the First Linguistic Conference in 1936. Such linguists as Pigam Azymow began providing analyses of the Turkmen lexicon by counting the number of "Soviet-international words."[13] The TSSR central state became involved, as early as 1950 determining the need for a scholarly conference on terminology and announcing this to the public in 1951.[14] The Academy of Sciences organized a linguistic conference in 1954 so as to address the questions of writing Turkmen.

On 6–9 October 1954 Turkmenistan's Academy of Sciences hosted the Second Linguistic Conference on the Turkmen Language at its Institute of Turkmen Language and Literature in Aşgabat. The conference organizers reported that the need for this meeting lay in the "failings" of the First All-Turkmen Language Conference that had met in 1936. They underscored the faults of "traitors" and "wreckers" in the 1920s and 1930s who failed to light the politically correct path for Soviet Turkmen.

In his preparatory materials the conference organizer, J. Amansaryýew, accused the planners of the 1930 conference of having created problems in the Turkmen language with their "ideological leanings"; scholars who had been purged in the 1930s were easy targets. The lexical content of the Turkmen language remained a special sociopolitical concern in part, Amansaryýew argued, because those "counterrevolutionaries had tried to interject Arabic and Persian terms into the Turkmen vocabulary." A few years before the 1954 conference, Amansaryýew had already labeled Böriýew, Geldiýew, Wepaýew, and Ferid Efendi as "pan-Turkists and pan-Iranists." He accused them of "striving to interfere with the organization of Turkmen terminology" and trying to replace the Turkmen language with Anatolian Turkish and to allow the "untamed influences" of Arabic and Persian. Amansaryýew insisted that they could have found help in the "great" Russian language, but instead "they turned their faces away like someone without a homeland [*biwatanlar*]," preferring the internal resources of Turkmen.[15]

This 1954 conference appears to have been much smaller in scope than previous meetings. Its three announced foci were terminology, orthography, and punctuation. However, the conference materials make clear that the "order of the day" was to discuss issues of Turkmen terminology.[16] In earlier conferences alphabet, orthography, grammar, and more had to be worked out. In the 1950s language content was the main focus. The TSSR Academy of Sciences created a steering committee, which assigned to J. Amansaryýew the task of leading the discussion on linguistic terminology. To M. Annagurdow the committee assigned a presentation on translating Russian literature into Turkmen, and to Z. B. Muhammedow a paper on linguistic terminology. B. Şahmyradow addressed literary terminology, A. P. Lavrov addressed geographic terminology, Ö. N. and Mämetnyýazow dealt with the vocabulary of chemistry, while N. Geldiýew and B. A. Serebrinnikov discussed the substitution of Arabo-Persian words with Russian terms.[17] The state published the prepared papers the following year.

With their focus on standardizing terminology, the participants agreed that the first step was to eliminate "superfluous, parallel" terms. Just a few years earlier J. Amansaryýew had declared synonyms to be the main obstacle in the Turkmen's realization of "happy socialism."[18] Scholars complained that there was a lack of regularity in the Turkmen language, even in the use of grammatical terms. For example, in describing the "rules" of language two distinct terms were employed: *düzgün* (order, system) and *kada* (rule, custom). These synonyms, this "chaos," they argued, made it impossible to elucidate the meaning of one word. Moreover, there were different usages for basic terms such as "infinitive." Elementary schools used a Turco-Persian compound *nämälim işlik*, while higher education employed the Russian *infinitiv*. These sorts of "parallelisms" in school and scholarly terminology caused great consternation in 1954. Pigam Azymow wrote, "If the meaning of one word is shown through parallel terminology the students' thoughts will be discombobulated. Stalin himself had said so in his own works."[19] Azymow added to this, explaining that some authors' use of a Turkmen word, such as *adalga* (terminology), and others' use of a Russian equivalent, such as *termin*, created an insurmountable confusion. Moreover, the protocol for eliminating synonyms was not always to introduce Soviet-international terms in Russian but just as often to create neologisms in Turkmen. This created words with which the population was wholly unfamiliar.

At first blush it would appear that such comments on "parallelisms" and "chaos" were hypercritical nitpicking. Languages naturally absorb words from other languages. However, in the Soviet case, Sovietisms and "international" terminology were introduced in a deliberate way. There were some neologisms, but most terms were calques from Russian.[20] Language policy demanded that non-Russian languages be Sovietized as part of the effort to build a socialist lexicon. Language would facilitate the cohesion of the Soviet peoples. Thus, the Turkmen language was infused with Russian vocabulary.

At this Second Linguistic Conference, Professor M. N. Hydyrow delivered the paper on punctuation, identifying its role as aiding in the creation of a scientific system of writing and with improving reading in schools.[21] P. Azymow reviewed the resolution on orthography. He began by pointing out that, despite the number of earlier conferences, problems in writing and spelling persisted. Aside from rules for hyphenating proper nouns and spelling complicated suffixes, Azymow addressed the issue of phonetic spelling. In a shift from earlier endeavors to accurately reflect the spoken word in writing, the 1954 proposal suggested that some words would deviate from popular pronunciation. For example, in the case of a word having two parts, it should be written fully, not according to the vernacular: not *Almata*, but *Almaata*; not *Könürgenç*, but *Köneürgenç*.[22] The one rule quite specific to Turkmen was the spelling of letters "z," "l," "n," and "s" after a letter "d." These consonants are swallowed in the vernacular, softening the pronunciation: *bizde* becomes *bizze*, *ýoldaş* is pronounced *yollash*, and *destan* is *dessan*. Azymow and the other participants determined that the words should be spelled out in their fullest configuration, regardless of the spoken form.[23]

The 1954 congress pushed for standardization, formalization, and space for Russian influences. The conference records indicate that linguistic minutiae were far less important than the larger development of a socialist lexicon to support the new concepts that the Turkmen language was facing. And absorption of Soviet-international terminology lent itself to the cohesion of the Soviet people. Annagurdow stated clearly that words of Arabo-Persian origin and archaisms should be eliminated from the literary language. G. Ataýew seconded this, saying that the conference needed to build up the Soviet-international content of the language.[24] To this end, the participants provided lists of Russian words that were to be adopted wholesale into Turkmen: for example, *palto, kino, institut,* and *samolët* (words for "coat," "cinema," "institute," and "airplane").[25] The participants argued that Russian could greatly enhance discussion of technology in Turkmen. However, Russian could also contribute to building a socialist vocabulary for everyday life. An example of change in the Turkmen language, perhaps as a result of the 1954 conference, was a shift from using the Turkmen word *otly* ("train") to the Russian *poezd,* at least in the high-ranking newspaper *Sovet Turkmenistany.*[26] The Party would assist with courses and schools. It would target both visual and audio skills via the radio, cinema, newspapers, and journals. In this way, Turkmen and Russian would coexist and buttress each other.

The conference resolutions wavered between a greater prominence of and reliance on Russian and the continued nationalization of borrowed words.[27] This reflected the sociopolitical situation more broadly at a time when concern over strengthening the cohesion of the Soviet peoples was on the rise. In support of standardization and a solidification of socialist lexicon, the conference resolved that the TSSR Academy of Science staff be assigned the work of developing socialist terminology and producing technical dictionaries. The resolutions provided specific examples of the type of development expected by the conference participants: Foreign terms should enter Turkmen via Russian. Annagurdow offered as an example *l'humanité,* which would translate into Russian as *chelovechestvo* and then into Turkmen as *adamzat.*[28] Russian terms were to be written with Turkmen suffixes and reference to gender (despite Turkic languages being ungendered). For example, a female, communal-farm worker in Russian, *kolkhoznitsa,* would become *kolhozçy ayýal* in Turkmen. R. Esenow and G. D. Sanjeýew asserted that words such as *radiofikatsiia* and *kinofikatsia* should be written *radiolaşdyrmak* and *kinolaşdyrmak.*[29] However, prefixes, especially those from foreign languages, should derive from Russian: *antifaşistik, kontrrevoliutsion.* Acronyms would be rendered according to the Turkmen translation. "Central Committee," for example, would appear not in the Russian, TsK (*Tsentral'nyi Komitet*), but the Turkmen, MK (*Merkezi Komitet*).[30]

The 1954 conference led to greater Turkmenification through standardization of the literary language, even if it was still heavily Russified, in that it contributed to the cohesion of the nation. It aimed to bring together the language being taught in schools and the language of the press. The greatest contribution made to Turkmen identity, however, was in teaching the Turkmen to "speak Soviet."[31] In resolving to introduce more Soviet-international terms into the language, the conference was preparing the Turkmen language to become thoroughly Sovietized.

Post 1954

The 1954 Second Linguist Conference resolved that its participants would produce not only dictionaries (Russian-Turkmen and Turkmen-Russian) but also terminological glossaries addressing the economy, agriculture, science, and technology, and one that was to be illustrated. The TSSR's Academy of Sciences resolved to create a terminological commission that would supervise the language and propagandize the terminology accepted by the conference.[32] The Academy of Sciences assumed oversight of language in Turkmenistan, and its Institute of Languages and Literature remained responsible for carrying out regular reform throughout the Soviet years.

The 1954 conference was not the final word on orthography or language composition, but there were no other major language conferences in Turkmenistan during the Soviet era. Still, linguists and writers of pedagogical books continued to work on standardizing the literary language over the following decades.[33] Linguists continued to write about the issues and use the 1954 conference as a point of reference. In 1959 Pigam Azymow wrote an interesting booklet that brought together many of the issues concerning spelling. First he indicated that, although the earlier conferences in 1930 and 1936 had addressed issues of spelling, the rules were still being applied "incorrectly" or ignored. He gave examples of variant spellings he found in print: *statistik/statistiki* (statistic), *ylmyň/ylymyň* (scientific/academic), *dostluk/dostlyk* (friendship). His greatest concern was that there was variation between schoolbooks and the press. He therefore called for fundamental reform.[34] Variation between the languages of the press and of the schools was problematic in that these were the language sources from which the majority of the people would be learning. And since there was a link between literacy, identity, and modernity, the lack of a standardized literary language would slow down the nation's cultural transformation.

One issue Azymow addressed in his booklet that would come up again with great intensity after independence in 1991 was the issue of "Russian" letters in the Turkmen alphabet. A 1951 article in *Bol'shevik* by A. Mordinova and G. Sanjeeva called for the removal of Russian letters that do not appear in Turkmen words: я, ё, ю, щ, ц, ь, and ъ.[35] Azymow politely explained that this suggestion was a mistake because the letters were needed for those words that had entered Turkmen from Russian and moreover because Turkmen could not "withdraw into a national shell." He further noted that such comments undermined the ideas of their "drawing together and uniting in the common war toward the victory of communism."[36]

These debates illustrate the role of language in politics. Standardization of the Turkmen language was designed to facilitate the unification of the Turkmen peoples. The many dialects had been distilled down to a single literary language, and this was an important marker of the Turkmen nation. Perhaps an even more salient point is that such articles demonstrate the role of politics in language. The Turkmen language was standardized, codified, and was using a stable alphabet; now what remained was the enrichment of the vocabulary from Russian to enhance its Soviet qualities. The Turkmen language was a tool for the Sovietization of the Turkmen people.

Turkmenistan's Ministry of Culture focused on propagandizing the Turkmen-Soviet culture through print. To this end the 1950s witnessed a growth spurt in libraries, cultural clubs, and teahouses, where reading could take place individually and communally. Intellectuals, especially those at the Turkmen Language and Literature Institute of the TSSR Academy of Sciences, continued to discuss these issues, especially the spelling of acronyms, foreign words, new concepts, and the role of Russian.[37] In the post-Stalin era, Russification intensified.

What Did Russification Really Mean?

Jacob Ornstein writes that there was little difference in language policy before and after Stalin's death. He writes further that "linguistic drift [was] overwhelmingly toward Russian." Isabelle Kreindler writes similarly that "most national languages were narrowing in function."[38] Although I agree with Ornstein and Kreindler on much, here I must disagree. There was a slowing down in language policy after the death of Stalin, a focus on consolidation rather than on development. This meant a real difference between language policy under Stalin and later under Nikita Khrushchev and his successors. That is, languages were formulated, codified, and intensely debated up until the 1950s. But after the "thaw" we see efforts to secure what had been accomplished up until that point and to reinforce undertakings in language planning and development. In fact, with Krushchev's rise to power, Soviet language planning under Stalin was subject to noticeable criticism.[39]

In the post-Stalin era Russification of non-Russian languages was very real and occupied most of the time of language planners. Teaching was developed to help transcend "national barriers," and the main thrust in the post-Stalin era was to explain Sovietisms, which in many cases were taken directly from Russian. At the Turkmen SSR's Fifth Republican Teachers' Conference such borrowings were highlighted and applauded. Some such calques, called in Turkmen *internatsional-ismler* (internationalisms), included *býulletin*, *kartofel*,' *fantastik*, *şowenistik*, and *ýuridik* (bulletin, potato, fantastic, chauvinistic, and juridical).[40]

The intensification of "Soviet-internationalist terms" did not mean that all of the non-Russian languages were diminished, however. There were indeed some languages of smaller speech communities, especially within Russia, that contracted and even disappeared. Kurdish, for example, is almost never heard in Turkmenistan today, even though there are pockets of people who still identify as Kurds. Yet many languages held their own.[41] Titular republican languages did not weaken under the influence of Russian, as the numbers of speakers of those languages attest. Therefore, when considering the many studies of Soviet language policy, especially in the period after 1953, it is necessary to reflect carefully about which language group a writer is reporting—titular languages like Turkmen and Uzbek, which survived as languages of everyday interaction (certainly in the private sphere), or such minority languages as Kurdish or Abkhazian, which the state chose not to "mobilize" for broad sociopolitical communication.[42] For example, when Kreindler writes about linguistic Russification to the exclusion of other languages she is referring to minority languages such as Yiddish, Kurdish, and many in the Far North, whereas Gail Lapidus writes about the titular languages that the "durability of national languages has been little affected by the spread of Russian as a second language."[43] With this in mind, we should realize that Soviet policy toward languages was selective. The Party and the state promoted some (the titular languages) in elementary schools, films, and newspapers, while others (the languages of ethnic minorities without political territory or status) were allowed to wither away without any state support.

It is for this reason that Barbara Anderson and Brian Silver argue that we should think in terms of "asymmetry" in Soviet language policy. They write that "school-language policy has differentiated among the non-Russian nationalities either on the basis of their population size, their geographic concentration, or their political status." They further argue that we should think of post-Stalinist language policy as one of "bilingualism" rather than as one that suppressed local languages across the board.[44] Here they disagree with Kreindler and others' suggestions that the goal of Soviet policy was the eradication of non-Russian languages.[45] The bottom line is that the Turkmen language did not suffer the same fate as some languages in the Far North and the Caucasus, or Yiddish, for example. Turkmen was taught in schools, even Russian-language schools, and the majority of the population used the Turkmen language in their private lives.

According to the 1959 census, less than 1 percent of Turkmen considered Russian a native tongue.[46] And, whereas in the 1926/1927 academic year 82.7 percent of Turkmen students attended Russian-language schools, by the 1938/1939 academic year 61.5 percent attended Turkmen-language schools, only 13.2 percent attended Russian-language schools, and only 12.1 percent attended bilingual schools.[47] It is true that the capital, Aşgabat, looked different from the rest of the country. The proportion of non-Russian students attending Russian schools was higher in urban areas. By 1959 twenty-one of its twenty-four schools were Russian-language, despite the fact that 96.7 percent of Turkmen people considered Turkmen to be their native language.[48]

However, this study is concerned with the relationship of language to social power and cultural capital. In the Turkmen SSR, as in most other SSRs, Russian was in fact the language of power and upward social mobility. Anderson and Silver refer to this situation as one of "economic efficiency." That is, it is an "inefficient investment of personal resources to study in a language that has limited utility in the job market."[49] With this statement the authors refer to the non-Russian languages and the hegemony of Russian.

It is worth taking space here to reflect on the arguments of scholars of Soviet nationalities policy and language policy. Although there was no official language in the USSR, Lapidus writes, "Upward mobility—especially in scientific and political arenas—depends on local elites' mastery of the Russian language and cultural norms, while Russians experience little pressure to master the languages of the republics in which they live and work." Moreover, Ornstein tells us, "[parents] may merely realize, quite realistically, that Russian rather than the local language affords the best, and sometimes the only, means of access to the power structure and to elite status, since the higher one goes on the educational and vocational ladder, the more important is a command of Russian." Yaroslav Bilinsky asserts that "some parents want their children simply to pass for Russians, and some send them to Russian-language schools in order to prepare them for college."[50] When it came to the official sphere—that of higher education, science and technology, and bureaucracy—the Russian language ruled.

Cultural Policy under Khrushchev

After Stalin's death the next leader of consequence, Nikita Khrushchev, took hold of the reins of power as he ascended to the position of First Secretary of the Communist Party. It was under Khrushchev that the Soviet Union proclaimed "to have 'solved its nationality problem' and declared [itself] to be a country possessing 'an unprecedented unity of peoples,' with Russian as its 'language of interethnic communication.'" This was then articulated through the new principle that conceptualized the peoples of the Soviet Union as "The Soviet People: A New Historical Community" with "the Russian language as one of its fundamental 'hallmarks.'"[51]

The linguists Azymow and Kurbanow wrote about such issues in 1957. Drawing attention to the recently published *Russian-Turkmen Dictionary* by N. A. Baskakov and M. Khamsaev published in Moscow in 1956, they asserted that this dictionary had played an important role in the "stabilizing of Turkmenian [sic] terminology and in the further development of the literary language." Certainly dictionaries do stabilize languages, but what of the role of Russian? On that point the authors were clear, lauding its richness and citing it as having "immense significance as an important means of cultural contact" between the Russian and Turkmen peoples.[52] The 1960s also saw such publications as *The Turkmen Language in Our Time*, *The Turkmen Language Dictionary*, and *The Turkmen Orthographic Dictionary*, which were designed to stabilize the Turkmen language and integrate the Soviet-international terms into the vocabulary. Publication of the definitive Turkmen dictionary in 1962 contributed to the solidification of the standardized Turkmen literary language that is spoken today as the official language. Despite this progress, as the country entered a new sociopolitical era in the 1960s, language remained intricately linked to identity. While language was a critical barometer in measuring changes in Soviet nationalities policy, the education system was perhaps the most important institution.

Departure from Leninist Policy?

By the late 1950s and early 1960s, Soviet authorities had begun to emphasize Russification—largely via educational reforms—and the education reform of 1958–1959 was pivotal in Soviet nationalities policy. On 12 November 1958, the Central Committee ratified a set of "theses" outlining coming school reform. The Supreme

Soviet debated these theses on 24 December 1958 and the next day the set was ratified by the republics. This 25 December reform was titled "On Strengthening the Ties of Schools with Life and the Continued Development of the System of Public Education."[53] Thesis 19 concerned language policy. It declared that education in native languages would no longer be compulsory and offered parents the opportunity to choose the language of instruction for their children.[54] With this "free choice" an ostensible "juridical equality" was restored to languages.[55] Parents were to decide on the language of instruction for their children and even to choose whether students would study their own national language, a departure from the 1938 policy that made Russian compulsory. Families were to choose whether they would send their children to Russian schools, where Turkmen was still taught, though only for a limited class period, or Turkmen schools, where Russian was simply a foreign language. Kreindler determined that this was a "thrust of Russian into the center and [was] a major setback for the non-Russian languages." Kirkwood writes that this "caused much alarm among intellectuals and others who realized that such a measure, while it appeared to be progressive in a democratic sense, would clearly undermine the position of national languages." Yet Kirkwood acknowledges that some languages expanded despite such policies; Turkmen was one of them. Moreover, Bilinsky has noted that there was opposition to this reform in Transcaucasia, Moldova, Ukraine, and the Baltic states, but in Central Asia, including Turkmenistan, there was a positive reaction to the idea of the compulsory study of Russian.[56] This positive attitude among educated Turkmen is reflected in the news articles and scholarship of the day. The newspapers *Mugallymlar gazeti*, *Edebiýat we Sungat*, *Turkmenskaia iskra*, and *Sowet Türkmenistany* contain articles written in support by teachers, students, scholars, medical personnel, and people associated with kolkhozes, to name a few. Even though many were still speaking Turkmen at home, they recognized that the Russian language possessed greater cultural capital in the official sphere.

While a large majority of Turkmen spoke their native language, it was not the language of upward social mobility. Michael Rywkin writes, "Better educated Muslims learn Russian as an indispensable tool for their own advancement." Additionally, besides acting as the lingua franca of the SSSR and "forming a collective link between the numerous ethnic units of the Soviet Union, [Russian was] the bridge between the individual national cultures and 'world culture.'" Turkmen found Russian to be a critical world language that should enrich their own.[57]

In the 1960s early language policy was cited as one of the reasons for the fact that the Turkmen people had evolved into a "cultured republic." Linguists cited not only the development of the Turkmen language but also the fact that the study of Russian—facilitated by the adoption of Cyrillic for the Turkmen language—had enhanced the Turkmen's Leninist, socialist experience. A professor of Turkmen language, G. Sopyýew, published a lengthy article on the history of Turkmen alphabet reform that culminated in a glowing commentary on Turkmen literacy and culture:

> [After 1940] writing Turkmen in Russian letters became a national ambition and the Russian language burned like a great flame, enhancing literacy—actually helping to eliminate illiteracy completely—and putting an end to linguistic difficulties in schools.
>
> [Adoption of Cyrillic] helped to ensure that not only language but also culture was gained. Based on the influence of Russian culture, we [Turkmen] had the opportunity to develop our own culture. Russian enhanced the Turkmen literary language and orthography—it bettered them. Turkmen people moved from an illiterate, backward people to a proper Leninist and national political life—a widely literate nation with a socialist content and a cultured republic.[58]

Such articles demonstrated that although Turkmen still felt the need to justify language policies of the past, they found contemporary reasons for doing so. Even though Stalin was repudiated under Khrushchev, such linguistic achievements as the adoption of Cyrillic and the positive influence of Russian were hailed as great successes. Eradication of illiteracy had been central to the Turkmens' modern, socialist experience.[59]

Khrushchev's Language Policy

In July 1960 Khrushchev discussed language policy in connection with nationalities policy, harking back to Lenin to legitimize conditions:

> With the victory of Communism in the USSR, the nations will draw still closer together, their economic and ideological unity will increase, and the Communist traits common to their spiritual make-up will develop. However, the obliteration of national distinctions, and especially of language distinctions, is a considerably longer process than the obliteration of class distinctions. The Party approaches all questions of nationality relationships arising in the course of Communist construction from the standpoint of proletarian internationalism and firm pursuance of the Leninist nationality policy.[60]

Khrushchev was not alone in recalling Lenin's influence on language policy (see figure 4).[61] On the anniversary of Lenin's birth several Turkmen-language articles on language and nationalities related how the policies of the day still reflected the great leader's (*Beýik Serdar/Beýik Adam*) philosophies.[62]

Khrushchev went on to refer to language policy specifically, illustrating the concepts that held sway in these years: "The Party will continue promoting the free development of the languages of the peoples of the USSR, and the complete freedom for every citizen of the USSR to speak, educate, and teach his children in any language, with no special privileges, restrictions, or compulsions in the use of this or

FIGURE 4. Monument to Lenin, with Arabic, Latin and Cyrillic scripts

that language. By virtue of the fraternal friendship and mutual trust of peoples, national languages are developing on the basis of equality and mutual enrichment." He continued, commenting on the weighty question of the role of Russian: "The voluntary study of Russian, in addition to the native language, is of positive significance, since it facilitates reciprocal exchanges of experience and access of every nation and nationality to the cultural accomplishments of all the other peoples of the USSR and to world culture. The Russian language has, in effect, become the common medium of intercourse and cooperation between all the peoples of the USSR."[63]

Khrushchev's plan required that the Stalinist slogan of "friendship of the peoples" intersect with more recent ideas of "internationalism." The former required that the Soviet peoples cooperate, the latter involved "a mutual enrichment, elimination of barriers separating them and, furthermore, a development of common characteristics."[64] Turkmen news articles reported that study of both Turkmen and Russian in schools "fosters friendship."[65] Remarks on the "enrichment" of the Turkmen lexicon through Russian were common during these years. Not only would Turkmen and other native languages absorb Russian terms, they would take on international terms by way of Russian, which had "gained international importance."[66]

Khrushchev was not the only one writing about the "voluntary" study of Russian in the Soviet Union. Turkmen news articles echoed his enthusiasm, reflecting the power held by the Russian language and culture. Even the Turkmen language newspaper *Mugallymlar gazeti* published the occasional page in Russian about teaching Russian in Turkmen schools. Articles appearing in this section discussed the role of Russian and ways that its history helped Turkmen deal with difficulties in the 1960s, with one such article reporting that "Voluntary study of Russian dates back to the Russian Empire when the Turkmen realized that speaking Russian was necessary for them to advance their interests and modernize."[67]

As part of the plan to complete the construction of the Soviet Union through "one common language, culture, and other common characteristics," Khrushchev promoted the fusion (*sliianie*) of nations.[68] Two key terms heard during the second half of the twentieth century were *sliianie* (fusion or merger) and *sblizhenie* (rapprochement). *Sliianie* was to be achieved through the "voluntary" adoption of Russian as "the common medium of intercourse and cooperation." This merger of Soviet nations was to be achieved through "the elimination of national differences, the loss by people of national peculiarities." This would mean the adoption of Russian. Bilingualism would be an intermediate stage. Not only was Russian "the *lingua franca* for communication between diverse Soviet nationalities . . . but it [was] also the language of the bureaucratic and military machinery and industrial management. From accounting to train schedules, from technical specifications to copies in triplicate, the Russian language [was] the one used." Bilingualism was therefore "regarded as a necessary characteristic of the modern Soviet man." In the Turkmen language this was expressed as *täze Sowet adamy* (new Soviet man).[69]

Russian, for the peoples of the Soviet Union, was not a "foreign language" but, as Khrushchev advanced at the Twenty-Second Party Congress in 1961, the "second mother tongue." This notion was repeated frequently in the Turkmen language press as "*ikinji ene dili* [second mother tongue]."[70] Turkmen linguists predicted that by the 1962 school year "Russian language writing and dictation would be perfected" in schools.[71] School reform commented on nationalities policy by offering parents the opportunity to choose the language of instruction in which students would be taught. The study of Russian would be "voluntary." Yet at the same time, there was extensive recognition of the primary place of Russian in society. The Russian language was "a mighty instrument of transnational [*mezhnatsionalnyi*] relations, of strengthening the friendship of the peoples of the Soviet Union and in bringing them the riches of the Russian and world culture."[72]

It is in this context that we see in Turkmen newspapers calls for recognition that the Turkmen speech community was borrowing vocabulary from Russian on a regular basis. For example, in 1963, a PhD candidate in philology, Amanmyrat Annanurow, responded to a newspaper article by Berdi Kerbabaýew, Turkmenistan's most popular novelist. Kerbabaýew wrote about the history of language scholarship, praising the scientific study of language and crediting commissions and conferences with the development of the Turkmen language. Kerbabaýew posited that "it was with the concern, skill, and energy of linguists that our simple language was transformed into a literary language." He further asserted that he was against the one-to-one borrowing from other languages into Turkmen and said he was glad the commissions had not engaged in this practice.[73] In fact, language commissions had engaged in such borrowing, but his larger point about the development of the language was what elicited Annanurow's response.

Annanurow was energized, but straightforward.[74] He argued that "linguists do not create language, people create language." Languages were alive—or at least the Turkmen one was—and being "transformed daily." Turkmen was a "social phenomenon," not simply the result of linguists "working out of grammatical and orthographic rules." He then focused specifically on the influence of Russian on the Turkmen language:

> Every language is enriched by other languages. How? Two ways: The first, words are taken directly. The second, words are borrowed conforming to the morphology of the borrowing language. No language can grow without doing this. . . . Turkmen borrows words from Russian, words that are taken into all Soviet languages, and it is in this way that the Turkmen language is enriched. There are hundreds of such examples: *Sotsialistik Zähmetiň Gahrymany* [Hero of the Socialist Worker], *bäşýyllyk plan* [five-year plan], *çepçi* [leftist], *sagçy* [right winger]. We can even use such calques as the word *pisatel'* [author] in place of *ýazyjy*. Berdi Kerbabaýew's article was full of calques! But he argues against word-for-word translation. . . . [However], I say when necessary the living language takes what it needs from Russian.[75]

A year later, "scientific workers" at Turkmenistan's sole university, named for Magtumguly, wrote in another newspaper about these same ideas. They conceptualized Russian as the language that would "enrich" the other Soviet languages and as the linguistic conduit to such complex spheres of knowledge as science and technology:

> The Russian literary language is the secondary language of all fraternal peoples. The Russian language plays a significant role in the enrichment of the native languages' lexicons. Native languages, including the Turkmen language, relate to science, technology, [and] culture as well as various sectors of national economy only through Russian. A great many terms in the Russian language have gained international importance. Therefore, interest in studying and mastering the Russian language grows daily. This language is intensively studied at the national schools of the Soviet Union; the fraternal peoples of the democratic states are interested in learning Russian.[76]

These articles demonstrate that in the post-Stalin era Turkmen remained passionate about language reform and development. It was just that now, when the Turkmen language was a developed and fully functional literary language, the focus had turned from language development and codification to the enrichment of the vocabulary—via Russian. The Turkmen language, like all other Soviet languages, borrowed vocabulary from Russian—or more precisely was infused with Russian vocabulary at the behest of policy makers. This is part of the linguistic Russification that took place during the twentieth century. However, it was not the "enrichment" of the Turkmen language that presented social complexities but, rather, the use of the Russian language itself in the official sphere.

Brezhnev's "Cement"

Nikita Khrushchev left office in 1964, and Leonid Brezhnev took over as leader of the USSR until 1982. The eighteen years of Brezhnev's rule only deepened the prominence of the Russian language. Under Brezhnev, the Russian language was labeled the political "cement" of the Union, and these years witnessed a glorification of the Russian language, which Kreindler argues "surpassed that of Stalin's last years," with Russian "proclaimed as inherently superior to all other languages."[77] "Beyond its role as the medium of interethnic communication and as the chief language of science, technology, and culture, Russian was now endowed with unique attributes as the language of October, of Lenin and of the communist future."[78]

In his 1972 address on the fiftieth anniversary of the Soviet Union, Brezhnev reiterated Khrushchev's ideas, declaring that the nationalities question had been "resolved completely, resolved definitely and irrevocably." He went on to echo the Party's position that "in the process of socialist construction 'a new historic community—the Soviet people—has emerged' out of many nationalities comprising the USSR."[79] Brezhnev continued his comments on the nationalities question, stating, "The Party regards as impermissible any attempt whatsoever to hold back this process of drawing together of nations, to obstruct it on any pretext or artificially to reinforce national isolation, because this would be at variance with the general direction of development of our society."[80] For the most part, the rapprochement or drawing together (*sblizhenie*) of Soviet nations superceded the *sliianie* by the early 1970s. Brezhnev still wanted to integrate people but expectations were lowered.[81]

In 1972 Professor Pigam Azymow and other linguists participated in a conference in Aşgabat on "Trends in the Development of National Languages in Relation to the Development of Socialist Nationalities." Azymow published a report on the conference in which he discussed the necessity of Russian as a second language: "The intensive process over the last fifty years or so of learning Russian alongside the vernacular in all Soviet Republics has led to the situation where bilingualism acquires not only linguistic but also increased social significance. Knowledge of Russian as the common (major) language makes it possible for all Soviet Nations to communicate freely with one another."[82] Bilingualism was not merely a linguistic issue but deeply relevant to social relations. Russian held a privileged position.

In a Turkmen newspaper article, one young man told of his experiences with Russian as the language of interethnic communication. "During my military service, I befriended Russians, Ukrainians and Belorussians and such peoples. With the Russian language we became close friends. By means of the Russian language I have become familiar with the world's classic works: Pushkin, Lermontov, Chernyshevsky, and Dostoevsky. . . . Truly, we consider the Russian language to be our second mother tongue [*ikinji ene dilimiz*]."[83] Russian was no longer a "foreign language" but was "the common language of all Soviet citizens."[84]

The Soviet Constitutions of 1936 and 1977 declared that no language in the Soviet Union had official status. Whereas the Constitution of 1936, Article 121, explicitly declared the right to education "in one's native tongue," the Constitution of 1977, Article 45, offered merely "the possibility for instruction in one's native tongue."[85] Despite this juridical recognition of local languages, Soviet authorities still promoted Russian as the first among equals, "the language of the Revolution, of Lenin, of the 'great Russian people,' of Pushkin."[86] In addition to being recognized as the much vaunted "second mother tongue," Russian was the language of interethnic communications (*iazyk mezhnatsional'nogo obshcheniia*). That is, it was the language of communication or lingua franca among the many Soviet peoples.[87] Early commitments to national languages as an "essential means of socialist construction in a multinational state" were not abandoned,[88] but local languages were marginalized with second-tier status; or in the case of some minorities, third-tier.[89] The increasing permeation of Russian into school curricula strengthened with the recommendations of all-union conferences held in Tashkent, Uzbekistan, in 1975 and 1979, which suggested a multitude of ways that the study of Russian language could be increased and enhanced, and teacher training improved. In light of this situation, the language conference of 1979, held in Tashkent, is here worth consideration.

Tashkent Language Conference, 1979

The second Tashkent conference met on 22–24 May 1979 in Tashkent for the All-Union Scientific Theoretical Conference on "The Russian Language—the Language of Friendship and Cooperation of the Peoples of the USSR."[90] This conference is worthy of note because, as Roman Solchanyk suggests, it may have been the "most ambitious Soviet attempt at language planning since the education reforms of the late 1950s."[91] Yaroslav Bilinsky noted its "political importance" as underscored by the number of high-level bureaucrats who were in attendance. M. M. Mollaeva, Turkmenistan's ideological secretary, represented that republic. Solchanyk adds that this conference represented "a major landmark in the current campaign to promote the Russian language in the national republics."[92] Brezhnev did not attend, but he sent a message, which read in part:

> Under the conditions of developed Socialism, when the economy of our country has turned into a single economic complex [and] when there has emerged a new historical entity—the Soviet People, there is objectively growing the role of the Russian language as the language of international communication in the building of Communism, in the education of New Man. Together with that of one's own native language, fluent command of Russian, which has been voluntarily accepted as a common historical heritage by all Soviet people, facilitates the further stabilization of the political, economic and spiritual unity of the Soviet people.[93]

With these words Brezhnev highlighted all the main concepts regarding language and identity at this time: Russian was the language of "international" or interethnic communication, Russian had been "voluntarily" adopted by the Soviet citizens, who made up the "Soviet People."

The conference's keynote speaker was Sharaf Rashidov, First Secretary of the Communist Party of Uzbekistan, the host republic. He delivered remarks that also underscored major concepts of the day, saying, "The Russian language is the language of the great Lenin, the language of a great people, with extremely rich democratic and revolutionary customs and a well-developed culture." He also talked about "bilingualism," and the "rapprochement [*sblizhenie*] of nations."[94]

The thrust of the recommendations made by the Tashkent conference included an exhortation to Soviet officials to intensify the teaching of Russian in non-Russian schools and universities and to expand the teaching of Russian to include kindergartens. Moreover, the conference suggested that more teachers of Russian be trained and more textbooks be published in Russian. Upon the suggestions of Prokofiev, the USSR's Minister of Education, the conference recommendations included the proposals that social studies, general education, and specialized disciplines in higher education institutions be taught in Russian and that university students write their coursework and diploma projects in Russian.[95] Russian would come to occupy an even greater segment of the official sphere. Soon after the 1979 Tashkent conference, the USSR Ministry of Education undertook to realize its recommendations. In addition to several other declarations and practical steps, at the end of June 1979 the USSR Council of Ministers decreed that Russian would be taught in kindergartens and preparatory classes of non-Russian schools by 1 September 1980.[96]

At the conference Prokofiev mentioned Turkmenistan specifically in his speech, which focused on the rapprochement (*sblizhenie*) of the Soviet people. He noted that, along with the students in a handful of other republics, 80 percent of Turkmen students were studying in native-language schools.[97] Professor Bilinsky suggests that the number of students studying Turkmen was so high because, according to the 1979 census, only 12.6 percent of Turkmenistan's citizens (adults and children) were Russian.[98] That is, the majority of people were Turkmen speakers. The 1970 and 1979 censuses revealed the high retention rates for mother tongues among the titular nationalities. In Turkmenistan, where the total population was 1,525,284 and 2,027,913 in 1970 and 1979 respectively, 98 percent declared Turkmen as their native language, with only 15.4 percent and 24.9 percent claiming Russian as a second mother tongue.[99]

Demographics played a role in each of the republics, and in the USSR more generally. After the 1979 census, it became obvious that while Russians constituted over 50 percent of the Soviet population, by the end of the century a high birthrate in Central Asia and the Caucasus was going to reduce the Russian population to just over 40 percent.[100] In 1959 European nationalities represented 79.6 percent of the Soviet population. With the high birthrate in such regions as Central Asia and low birthrates among Europeans, the number of Europeans was predicted to fall precipitously. Soviet authorities reportedly referred to this demographic trend as the "yellowing [ozheltenie]" of the country.[101]

It was within this context that concerns over improving the teaching of Russian such as those heard in Tashkent were voiced. Fedot Filin, director of the Russian Language Institute of the USSR Academy of Sciences, was one to comment on the place of Russian as the "second native tongue" and the realization of bilingualism in the country. He made clear the relationship between demographic trends and the role of the Russian language:

> Whereas on the whole the Russians constitute more than half of the population of our country, in connection with the decelerated growth of population in those areas inhabited by the great bulk of Russians and the considerable increase in population in the Turkic-speaking republics, the correlation along nationality lines of children in the pre-school age group (and also in the school age group) is shifting substantially in favour of the Turkic-speaking population. In this connection, knowledge of the Russian language as the language of inter-nationality discourse is becoming particularly urgent [osobenno aktual'nym].[102]

Under Brezhnev, Russian remained the language of power, upward social mobility, and cultural capital. The militaristic language of the Revolution even resurfaced when the inspector of the USSR Ministry of Education called teachers of the Russian language "front line soldiers on the ideological front."[103]

Language Planning after Brezhnev

In December 1982 the Politburo member and future general secretary Konstantin Chernenko talked about "the problem of the relationship between the two leading trends in the development of nations under socialism: their all-sided development and flowering [rastvet] on the one hand and their steady rapprochement [sblizhenie] on the other."[104] Meanwhile, bilingualism remained a key component of educational laws. These undertakings were followed by the decree of June 1983 "On Further Measures for Improving the Study of the Russian Language." Then, in 1984, the Central Committee of the CPSU and the Supreme Soviet of the USSR approved reforms of schools that Michael Kirkwood has suggested were the most important since the 1920s.[105] One significant point of this school reform was that it deemed as its goal "the full mastery of Russian for every graduate of the secondary schools."[106]

This school reform also lowered the age of first graders from seven to six, at which age they would begin to study the Russian language. Russian lessons had been introduced on a trial basis in non-Russian kindergartens in 1973, and by the 1980s this program had grown to include nursery schools.[107] In addition, the number of extracurricular activities and elective courses for upper levels in the Russian language increased. Turkmen reports of song and dance groups and language and literature circles for girls and boys indicate that Russian language and culture occupied students in their extracurricular activities as well.[108]

Konstantin Chernenko and Yuri Andropov continued to use the terms *sblizhenie* and "friendship of peoples" liberally. Occasionally *sliianie* too made an appearance. But, the "spectre of Russification" was softened in these years, privileging the policy of bilingualism.[109] The national question never was solved despite the proclamations of the leadership. The lack of a solution became clear in the Gorbachev era.

Conclusion

Although not much time had passed since the 1936 conference, in 1954 Turkmen language planners held a second linguistic conference in Aşgabat. This time the focus was on writing, with special attention paid to literacy in schools. The 1954 conference thoroughly repudiated the 1936 conference and all who had participated in it as "wreckers." The establishment of the Academy of Sciences in 1951 gave language and education reform a home. The academy's scholars would oversee reform for the remainder of the Soviet years. Even though the 1950s saw more Soviet-international vocabulary introduced into the Turkmen language, reform in the mid-twentieth century actually fostered cohesion of the Turkmen nation by encouraging the standardization of the literary language. This was formalized with the 1962 publication of the Turkmen dictionary, which was a model of language use.

While some Western scholars have argued that post-Stalinist language policy was one of Russification with the goal of assimilating other languages to the point of nonexistence, Soviet scholars argued that the policy was an egalitarian one, offering equality of the language in the Constitutions of 1936 and 1977. Others still argue that we should think in terms of "bilingual education policy."[110] The Turkmen case demonstrates that policy fell between these extremes; that is, the Turkmen language, being a titular republican language, did not diminish in its capacity as an everyday, household language. However, because Russian was the language of upward social mobility and power, Russian held sway in official arenas and public spaces. Cultural capital was vested in Russian as the lingua franca and the "second mother tongue." Russian was the language of interethnic communication and, by the Brezhnev era, the "cement" that bound the Soviet peoples together.

The level of literacy in Turkmenistan cannot be considered without recognition that the knowledge of Russian pervaded society. As Desheriev and other Soviet linguists argued, bilingualism did not occur by chance and certainly did not take place in a vacuum. Official language policy did preserve Turkmen, but it also increasingly privileged Russian. As the language of higher education, science, law, medicine, and bureaucracy, Russian was the language one needed to know to get on within the system. Yet ethnic Russians were not obliged to learn non-Russian languages even when they lived and worked in the republics. The Party ordered languages so that Russian was on top and held more currency than local languages. Over time the Russian language gained in value. Language policy was permissive of many national languages, but Russification was real both as national languages were enriched with Russian vocabulary and as there was a steady expansion of the teaching of Russian. Russification did not overshadow the Turkmen language completely, but the Soviet state did signal that it sanctioned the imbalance between the Russian language and the national languages.

Chapter 5

From Happy Socialism to Independence, 1985–1996

Culture Is Strongly Tied to Literacy

The basic themes of progress, cultural transformation, and the creation of a modern Turkmen identity persisted into the post-Soviet period, yet changes in political realities and the details of everyday life shifted dramatically. Not unlike in the 1910s, when notable social shifts occurred among Muslims, the 1980s and 1990s created a changing world order in which the Soviet nationalities would redefine themselves. In the 1910s Muslims sought to preserve their heritage in a world where modern concepts challenged identity and traditions. Similarly, in the late twentieth century, Muslim peoples in the same region witnessed a declining Soviet Union and ultimately a powerful change in their everyday lives. Although Central Asians had not sought independence, many citizens welcomed the opportunity to express cultural autonomy. It is worth exploring the early years of that expression of cultural autonomy and the reconceptualization of the Turkmen nation and underscoring the roles played by language and script.

Fluid conditions during glasnost (late 1980s) and then independence (1991) made space for greater efforts at experimentation with new expressions of national identity and of self. Language was one important form of those expressions. It is worth noting that glasnost never took hold in Turkmenistan to the degree it did elsewhere in the USSR; consequently, discussion of it remained rather circumscribed. There were, however, unprecedented shifts in social power. Throughout the Soviet Union, Russian language and culture lost currency while national languages and cultures gained at its expense. Moreover, the Turkmen, like several other national groups, decided to abandon the colloquially named "Russian alphabet" in a symbolic act of shedding their Soviet skin; in 1993, Turkmenistan's government passed a law adopting a Latin-based alphabet. Cultural capital was shifting. Turkmen were again moving "forward" but now instead of surging ahead at an accelerated rate toward a socialist utopian future, they were moving away from their Soviet past.

The decision to abandon the Cyrillic script reflected more than a change in letters, and the 1990s represented a new era in power relations; that is, those who knew Turkmen and could write in the new Latin-based script would soon hold the technical, scientific, and managerial positions that had once been held by Russian speakers. They would become the country's doctors, teachers, and engineers. Additionally, in 1993, in an aim to Turkmenify education, Aşgabat redesigned its educational (*bilim*) program, removing Russian as a language of instruction. The country was leaving behind the bilingualism of the USSR and asserting a strong Turkmen identity.

Intellectuals and state officials played important roles during this transformative era. However, the people (*halk*) had strong feelings about the changes. A variety of Turkmen voices participated in the discourse on identity during the early years of independence as society once again debated education, literacy, and cultural power. It is interesting to examine how symbolic power manifested itself once again and to relate this era to earlier ones through an examination of power more generally.

In the post-Soviet era, Turkmen were concerned with maintaining literacy even as they embarked upon a new era of language planning and alphabet reform. In 1991, at independence, the percentage of Turkmen claiming "good knowledge" of their native language and literacy was figured to be in the high 90s.[1] When President Saparmurat Nyýazow noted that he expected the new Latin-based Turkmen alphabet to raise literacy, he referred to the alphabet's ability to facilitate Turkmen's joining the international community rather than to its ability to raise functional literacy. In fact, "literacy" came in part to refer to learning about information technology, and later English and Turkish, in addition to the ability to read and write. President Nyýazow and several academics perceived a direct link between the Latin script and the English language, which they recognized as possessing international currency. Nyýazow wrote, "just as the Cyrillic alphabet had aided in Turkmen's learning Russian, the new [Latin] alphabet will assist the populace in their learning English." The new "international" script would support other endeavors to situate the country within the international community. Despite the strong desire to join the international community, there was not the same need for haste as there had been in the 1910s when literacy rates were under 10 percent. Still, reformers were aware that any changes to the language might negatively affect mass literacy. The president called for the development of new textbooks, identifying it as Turkmen linguists' primary consideration, for "they must not allow mass literacy in the mother tongue to fall during the alphabet transition."[2]

In 1991, when the USSR dissolved and the Soviet republics became sovereign countries, the former republics acquired new political status, cultural independence, and ownership of a great deal of natural and energy resources. However, they also inherited crumbling Soviet infrastructures, a dysfunctional political system, and scant technological, industrial, or scientific means of supporting themselves. With so many immediate concerns, it is remarkable that Turkmenistan chose to focus on script reform, language purity, and language status as early endeavors.

Language has been seen as an intermediary to power. However, would a change in language status, diminishing the role of Russian language or removing the Cyrillic writing system, actually strengthen the new state? What was the advantage to the state or the population in socially marginalizing citizens who did not speak Turkmen by pushing Russian out of public spaces?[3] Why put the population's literacy at risk by adopting an entirely new Latin-based writing system? What was the relationship between the new script and Turkmen identity? Unpacking the finer details of language and education reform during these early years of independence will help explore these questions within the broader sociopolitical context of Turkmenistan's early years of independence.

Gorbachev in Moscow, Nyýazow in Aşgabat

In 1985 Mikhail Gorbachev gained the most powerful position in the USSR as general secretary of the Communist Party. Nevertheless, he faced opposition that only intensified as his liberalizing reforms stripped power from the more conservative Communists. His methods weakened his own power base since "liberal" intellectuals and the general populace were left with little to fill the void when his administrative and social reforms perestroika (restructuring) and glasnost (openness) dispossessed the Soviet system of its legitimacy. Gorbachev had offered a three-pronged solution to the decaying Soviet system: marketization, an attack on the command economy (that provided the people with no immediate alternatives); democratization, which confronted traditional party power and attacked corruption; and decolonization, a proposal to allow fragmentation of the Union and devolution of power to the republics.[4] Gorbachev aimed to soften, or at least neutralize, the conservative "hard-liners" within the Soviet administration, mobilize the intelligentsia in a critique of the traditional system, and stimulate popular support for his reforms.

Such Soviet policies as *korenizatsiia* laid the foundation for the rise of nationalism in the 1990s, allowing some nationalist movements to grow out of Soviet-era identity policies while others rebelled against the policies that had defined them.[5] Some Turkmen, like other nationalities, took advantage of glasnost to assert their national identity, announcing cultural, political, and even ecological demands.[6] In many cases, questions of language came to symbolize the general atmosphere in which Soviet "hard-liners" and ethnic Russians opposed "reformers" and "radicals" who threatened Moscow's central authority. The pro-Russian-language/anti-Russian-language arguments reflected the broad-based cultural rejuvenation and national reassertion that was taking place throughout the Soviet Union. In Turkmenistan, Turkmen speakers called for the elimination of Russian toponyms and began building mosques, while Islamic texts began to appear in bazaars and traditional belief systems and such practices as folk healing flourished alongside formal religious rituals.[7] Larger concerns about power, sovereignty, and access to economic resources began to manifest as environmental protests, religious assertions, and demands for language reform throughout the Soviet Union—with the

Baltic republics in the vanguard.[8] Intellectuals targeted the iconography of everyday life to symbolize the freedoms of the new era and the pride that had never diminished during the previous period. As had so many communities throughout history, the Soviet peoples saw language and alphabet as emblematic of the society they envisioned.[9]

Glasnost and Language

In 1986 the Twenty-Seventh Party Congress reaffirmed that the nationality problem had been "solved" and asserted that there was a "free choice" in language.[10] However, with the introduction of glasnost there was a new freedom in discourse about language. In 1987 the USSR Academy of Sciences and the journal *Istoriia SSSR* held a "roundtable" where the nationalities question and issues surrounding language were discussed.[11] Such entities as Party Congresses, the Central Committee, and the USSR Writers' Union continued to address these issues, although not evenly. In the late 1980s the Party declared the importance of Russian in "business-like tones," declaring plainly that it "widens access to the achievement of science, technology, and of native and world culture."[12] On 24 April 1990, the Central Party passed "The Law on Languages of the Peoples of the Soviet Union" in what Fierman describes as "a last-ditch effort to preserve the common Russian linguistic space."[13] This law made Russian the official language throughout the Soviet Union for the first time, but its status was fleeting. There was a growing tension between central and local demands on culture. At the same time, several republics, including Turkmenistan, declared their titular language the official language. Already by the early 1990s, such terms as "second mother tongue," "harmonious bilingualism," and "friendship of the peoples" were reported to "set people's teeth on edge" and were considered to be not only "unrealistic" but even "insulting."[14] The era of glasnost would soon progress into one where the question of language and identity was not just one of many but was the central question.

Declarations of cultural autonomy in the USSR did not wait for full political sovereignty. In the late 1980s various republican representatives and "reformed" communists asserted themselves in policy areas and even more firmly in cultural arenas.[15] Glasnost allowed for public critique of the Soviet system and its legacy. This soon translated into national and popular fronts that clamored for cultural reforms. In 1988 Estonia and Lithuania established popular fronts, and Estonia declared itself a sovereign republic. The Baltic peoples sought both symbolism and legitimacy by declaring their respective national languages as the state language. Similar undertakings in Georgia and other republics followed, with varied success. Non-Russians had resented the role of Russian as the lingua franca (*iazyk mezhnatsional'nogo obshchenia*) of the USSR. Glasnost offered the opportunity to discuss the role of local languages and the possibilities of reducing Russian's role as a language of instruction in schools. By May 1990, all republics were following Estonia's initiative, adopting laws that raised the status of the titular nationality's language to the level of the state language.[16]

In Turkmenistan in 1985 the Communist Party's Central Executive Committee elected the chairman of the TSSR's Communist Party, Saparmurat Atayýewiç Nyýazow, to be the First Secretary of the TSSR's Central Committee. Nyýazow would hold the leadership position in Turkmenistan—answerable to Moscow—until Aşgabat declared its sovereignty on 22 August 1990. He then oversaw the election of unopposed candidates to Turkmenistan's Supreme Soviet, which in turn elected him the country's first president in November 1990. In the huge sociopolitical shift that took place in the years following Gorbachev's rise to power, Nyýazow would play the key role in the way language and education became politicized in Turkmenistan.

Turkmenistan's Language Status and Social Power

In the final years of the Soviet Union, language's increasing topicality illustrated how Soviet power was dissolving, giving way to the influences of nationalism. In 1988 an All-Union Conference of the Soviet Union Communist Party mentioned language policy in its resolution, and unionwide debates began to intensify, especially in Moldova and the Baltic States. Nyýazow, like Gorbachev, was faithful to the Party, however, and showed no interest in seeing the USSR break up. Throughout the years of glasnost and perestroika he continued to deliver speeches in support of the Soviet Union as a whole. For example, in 1988 Nyýazow addressed the economic situation: "While advocating a rational expansion of the republics' rights, we believe that it is necessary for this to be combined with the strengthening of our Union's unity. We Turkmenians have had an opportunity to become convinced from our own experience that the republics need a strong center, as M. S. Gorbachev said."[17] At this time, Nyýazow was still advocating for a strong centralized system.

In September 1989 the CPSU Central Committee heard Gorbachev's position on the nationalities question, specifically on the question of local control over resources. In response national representatives from around the USSR conveyed their frustrations over a lack of political autonomy, fair economic relations with the center and other regions, and even military autonomy. Iu. N. Prokofiev, First Secretary of the Iakut Province Party Committee, raised the question of transforming autonomous republics into Union republics especially as it would facilitate clarity in ownership and administration of land, mineral wealth, and other natural resources. President Nazarbayev of Kazakhstan named mineral wealth, timber, and water rights as considerations but, more emphatically, demanded an end to the testing of nuclear weapons in Kazakhstan so the "people could breathe clean air." He also cautioned against any singular exuberant "ethnic purity" or "national priority" that could destabilize the central Soviet government—a prophesy of what would come. R. Kh. Khabibullin, First Secretary of the Bashkir Province Party Committee, also complained about the lack of access to natural resources, focusing on "profound social and cultural" inequalities and noting that "in Estonia, with a population only forty percent that of Bashkiria, one-hundred five magazines and other periodicals are published. We," he exhorted, "publish only ten periodicals, and in the publication of books per capita our Estonian comrades publish twenty-eight times more than in Bashkira." He also noted that Bashkirs had only three hours of television per day in their mother tongue. Nyýazow was the final speaker:

> Our republic has still not adopted, and is not discussing, a draft law on giving the national language the status of state language. We are doing this not because our language has not been infringed upon but because we believe that one must not skip stages. The republic today is not ready to adopt a state language, although people are coming to us from a number of regions and trying to persuade our scholars and intelligentsia to do so immediately. We have decided to adopt a state program to develop the functioning of both the Turkmenian language and the languages of all the peoples that populate our republic. Eventually, after a certain amount of preparation, we too will adopt a state language. Practice shows that in the republics that have adopted a state language problems have arisen between nationalities. Therefore . . . we must make preparations so as not to infringe the interests of any nation. Today this question cannot be resolved by slogans alone. On the other hand, the adoption of Russian as the state language for the whole country would relieve tension.[18]

It is fascinating to view Nyýazow's attitude toward language at this time in contrast with his later policies. This speech was quite conservative coming from a man who would later become fervently nationalistic—when he thought he could capitalize on it at home. Yet here, as the Soviet Union's very foundation was shaking, Nyýazow hoped that it would not crumble and held fast to his Russified upbringing, ultimately suggesting Russian as the solution to "relieve tension." He was sticking with the history he knew, advocating for Russian as the lingua franca for all the nationalities of Turkmenistan. Aşgabat was taking note of events in the Baltic States and Caucasus, where the people sought both symbolic and real political legitimacy through the declaration of their respective national languages as the state language. Nyýazow played it safe, waiting cautiously to see which way the political winds would blow.

In the late 1980s in Turkmenistan there were some who took advantage of glasnost to express a desire for a "cultural renaissance."[19] The group Agzybirlik (Unity), which some referred to as a popular front (*narodnyi front*), was most vocal on the question of language. Led by Nurberdy Nurmamedow, who was later arrested, it advocated for a resurgence of the Turkmen language in place of Russian. On 8

September 1989, nearly thirty intellectuals (writers, artists, and educated people) gathered for two hours to speak "energetically" about various topics:

1. The lack of education of the national language.
2. The lack of education of the history of the nation.
3. The lack of education of art.
4. The poor standards of education in the medical field.
5. The horrible state of the environment.[20]

The famous Turkmen author Rahim Esenow had expressed similar concerns in a 1988 newspaper interview. He argued that people should not be divided into categories of "big and little brother" and that Turkmen should be learned especially in the cities where Russian dominated, saying, "Language is the key to many hidden secrets to a people's culture and history."[21] Agzybirlik proposed a solution to some of these problems. And though the group was not officially recognized by the state as a legal entity, its proposals were openly discussed in the newspaper *Komsomolets Turkmenistana*. It recommended

> instituting Turkmen as the official language of government, but [said] this cannot be done immediately because our city is 41 percent Turkmen, 41 percent Russian and 18 percent are made up of other ethnicities who all speak Russian. We will not forget that half of the Turkmen people cannot speak the Turkmen language. This is the same situation in other parts of the republic. Do you think we can just get rid of the Russian language? So if we do make Turkmen the official language, what's next? Isn't it better to prepare before we make a swift change to allow the majority of the people in Turkmenistan to adjust? The way we see it, Turkmen people want to study the language.[22]

Popular fronts and other similar undertakings in Georgia and other republics also saw varied success.[23]

The legal dissolution of the USSR began in the Baltics when, in March 1990, Lithuania voted to secede from the Soviet Union; Estonia and Latvia followed. Three months later, in June, Russia declared its sovereignty. As political winds shifted the USSR was disintegrating. The republics held presidential elections and First Secretaries began taking on the title "President." On 27 October 1990, Nyýazow became Turkmenistan's first president when official organs announced that 98 percent of the electorate had voted for him.[24]

Nationalist eruptions and economic protests compounded the effects of failed Soviet policies, causing Gorbachev to lose his hold on power in a coup in August 1991. The USSR disintegrated as Moscow recognized declarations of independence announced republic by republic. Nyýazow retained his position during the country's transition to an independent state. During the summer coup attempt against Gorbachev, Nyýazow waited silently, denouncing it only after its failure was unmistakable.[25] Turkmenistan declared its independence on 27 October 1991.

The Language of Sovereignty

Language was highly visible in claims of autonomy throughout the former Soviet Union.[26] By spring 1990, following Estonia's example, ten republics had adopted laws raising the status of the titular nationality's language to the level of the state language. Turkmenistan's Central Executive Committee passed "The Law on Language" on 24 May 1990. A special commission on language designed the law in order to raise the status of Turkmen to the official language of the state. The law read: "Turkmen is the state language of Turkmenistan." Then it cryptically added, "All citizens will be guaranteed the right to use their mother tongue."[27] Despite the ambiguity with respect to such ethnic minorities as Kurds and Baluchi, as of that day the official status of Russian in Turkmenistan began to wane and the social capital of Turkmen language speakers began to rise. A great many ethnic Turkmen welcomed this law on language. Like their new flag and anthem, language would reflect the social shifts taking place under their newly minted president.

Language and subsequent cultural policies not only symbolized the importance of the national language, they concurrently provided ethnic Turkmen with opportunity and encouragement to seize a form of power that had long been beyond their reach. Instead of Russian, the Turkmen language became the conduit to political, economic, and social power. Turkmen speakers began to occupy the positions in state service once held by Russian speakers.

Citizens who spoke only Russian were to become disadvantaged and divested of the social power the Soviet system had afforded them. During the Soviet years Russian speakers had possessed Bourdieu's linguistic capital and had access to both sociocultural and material power due to their social capital. Now linguistic capital was vested in the Turkmen language, and language policy conferred social power on speakers of that language. Such intellectuals as Professor Tagangeldi Täçmyradow credited (or blamed, depending on their perspective) Gorbachev for the very possibility of such a rise in the Turkmen language's status.[28] Language was emblematic of the social shifts beginning to take place. A wide variety of ethnic Turkmen welcomed this situation.[29]

Some citizens, however, were concerned about the change in Turkmen language status going so far that the country might abandon Russian altogether. Scholars trained in Russian under the Soviet system often advocated bilingualism as a practical measure that reinforced national claims rather than threatened them. They did not want to lose a valuable resource.[30] Some did not want to lose the only language they knew. In Aşgabat, the former included Täçmyradow, doctor of philology, whose research did much to promote the history of Turkmen language development. He was cautious about post-Soviet linguistic nationalism. While he championed the study of Turkmen and the language history, he still saw the Russian language as a useful tool. In the 1980s he had responded to the broader discussion among academicians, questioning whether the state language should be that of the titular nation. At that time, he noted that Germans, Baluchi, Uzbeks, Kazakhs, and Russians each represented a notable minority and unique language community within Turkmenistan. He called for the state to keep these minorities in mind as the question of language status and a possible state language came under discussion.[31] His articles continued to promote the usefulness of bilingualism, even after the Law on Language was adopted in 1990. In fact, he went so far as to suggest that the Commission on Language, which had adopted the Law on Language, should consider an "alternative program."[32] He strongly advocated for both Turkmen and Russian to be official languages, citing Russian as the language of relations among national groups and suggesting that Turkmen be specified as the language of literature, science, and technology.

Professor Myratgeldi Söýegow was also pragmatic about the community's maintaining Russian, even as he led the Turkmenification of the alphabet and authored numerous articles about Turkmen language reformers in the 1910s and 1920s.[33] Professor Rejep Berdiýew, another Turkmen linguist, encouraged Turkmen not to lose their ability in Russian, writing, "knowledge of two or even ten languages means greater resourcefulness."[34] None of these writers meant to undermine the development of Turkmen as a language of instruction or state, but they viewed Russian as a useful, international language. They asserted the idea that Turkmenistan's people could maintain their national identity even while using the Russian language to their advantage. In fact, Russian was not the only language of influence Turkmen considered. The roles of Turkish and English also came under consideration.

As in many instances of script or language reform throughout history, the state sanctioned the Law on Language, but intellectuals carried out the associated tasks. In Turkmenistan, even before the government made any formal announcements, scholars were exploring the possibility of changing the country's writing system. One major question facing all the Turks of the former Soviet Union was how to define their relationship with Turkey. Turkey, motivated by cultural and linguistic ties with Turks in Central Asia, the Caucasus, and Russia, sought to position itself as a bridge between East and West.[35] Such visions inspired the concept of a "Turkish model" that promoted Turkey as a counterbalance to Russia's legacy and a Western envoy that would stave off Iranian or radical Islamist influences.[36] In the late 1980s Turkey's president, Turgut Özal, visited Central Asia, and later, in the early 1990s, the Turkish prime minister Mesut Yilmaz made several public statements stating Turkey's readiness to provide social and economic support to their cultural brethren. Turkish scholars began focusing on the history, culture, and language of the former Soviet Muslims. President Özal led summits focusing on economic and trade relations, legislative matters, and regional security issues. Language and education received special attention at linguistic conferences. Ultimately, each Turkic group determined their individual relationship with Turkey, Russia, the United States of America, Iran, and China, and they located themselves within the new post-Soviet world as their local leadership saw fit.[37]

In November 1991 Marmara University in Istanbul hosted the first international symposium on alphabet reform among former Soviet Turks. Turcologists from Turkey and the former Soviet Union proposed and discussed drafts of Latin-based alphabets. The participants engaged in detailed debates over which alphabet would be useful and whether all Turks—including those in Turkey—should perhaps consider adopting one unified Turkic script that would build on the alphabet used in the Turkish Republic.[38] The conference participants considered the suggestion of a pan-Turkic alphabet, and at least one Uzbek publication on the topic circulated, but it received very little attention otherwise.[39] The Turkmen scholars did not consider it a viable path, especially as they sought ways to underscore the particulars of their language rather than blur them by sharing the symbols with other languages.

Independence, 1991

Prior to stepping down from his position, in March 1991 Gorbachev organized a Unionwide referendum on the unity of the USSR. Turkmenistan's government reported that 97 percent of eligible voters had voted to maintain the Soviet Union. These results represented not only an unambiguous decision but also a dumbfounding turnout.[40] The particularly high results became most awkward for the Turkmen leadership when Gorbachev was ousted. Turkmenistan's leadership had never supported the dissolution of the Union and had even signed an economic agreement as late as 18 October 1991, presumably with the expectation that no such great change would occur.[41]

On 26 October 1991 Turkmenistan held a second referendum on the question of independence. Aşgabat reported that 97 percent of eligible voters turned out to vote on the two-question ballot. The first question was about independence, and the second sought approval for President Nyýazow's proposed political and economic program. The state provided ballots in both Russian and Turkmen. The official tally came to 94 percent in favor of independence.[42] This was an astonishing turnaround in popular opinion and casts suspicions on both referenda.

Representatives from the Commission on Security and Cooperation in Europe who monitored the elections surmised that the numbers implied that the government possessed the power to sway popular opinion and obtain any vote that suited it. Political scientist Mark Beissinger also notes the persuasive role of Turkmenistan's government in its populace's decision making, underscoring that it was the state—in the person of Nyýazow—and not a popular front or separatist movement that decided the timing of independence.[43] With the knowledge of hindsight, having observed Nyýazow's oversight of voting in later years, we now know that these referenda foretold how Nyýazow would handle "democracy."[44] None of the referenda were real in any sense. There were no opposition candidates in elections, there was no verifiable count of the votes, state supervisors told their employees who to vote for, and Nyýazow always won by a statistically improbable margin.

The initial vote to stay in the USSR represented the greater common outlook. The people of Turkmenistan did possess a great deal of natural resources, but their standard of living was low, they were heavily dependent on Russia for logistics and securities that affected Turkmenistan's place in the world and everyday life, and it was disconcerting to think about becoming an independent country for the first time in history. Turkmenistan did not so much win its sovereignty as it saw its former station in the world evaporate out from underneath it.

In later referenda (1992 and 1995), in which Nyýazow ran for president uncontested, he again won over 90 percent of the vote. Despite harsh criticism from the CSCE for holding irregular elections, Nyýazow's political standing remained secure, and in 1993 he signaled this by taking the title Türkmenbaşy, or Leader of the Turkmen, alluding to Mustafa Kemal in Turkey who had taken the surname Atatürk (Father of Turks).[45] Other Central Asian states held referenda similar to those in Turkmenistan after gaining sovereignty in 1991, but no other leader would match Nyýazow in garnering expressions of support—official and popular, simulated or heartfelt.

Turkmenistan began a new journey on the path to fitting in with the international community.[46] Only, this time, the history of forging a modern nation was behind it. There was a Turkmen nation in place. What was about to change was the conceptualization of that nation and how language was an emblem of the nation.

Emblems of the State and Nation

In December 1991 Aşgabat hosted the initial meeting of Central Asian leaders to discuss forming the Commonwealth of Independent States in which they would all hold equal status. The meeting was indicative of the anxiety of all Central Asian leaders in the face of political upheaval. The newspaper *Izvestiia* recorded Nyýazow's opening words:

> The idea of bringing together here all the leaders of the Central Asian republics and Kazakhstan has been dominating my thoughts for the past two days. After all, we ought to size up the situation together, not separately, adopt a decision and, most important, coordinate our positions for getting out of this political impasse. In principle, to be frank, there is little cause for any special joy in the fact that we have wound up outside the boundaries of the Union of Slavic republics. Confrontation must not be allowed. On Wednesday afternoon, I decided to sit down at the telephone and start to call the Presidents. "Are you in agreement?" I asked Nazarbayev first. "There simply is

no other way," he answered. "We are at such a point now that if we procrastinate, we could end up with unpredictable consequences." That's what each of them said.[47]

For the first time in history Turkmen possessed a sovereign polity. But there were no blueprints, and even Nyýazow was unsure about how much of the old Soviet political infrastructure should stay in place. In the 1990s Turkmen were no longer struggling toward modernity in the same way they had in earlier eras. Although there remained a great need for development and growth throughout Central Asia, the Soviet system had provided them with access to the basic facets of modern life: universal literacy and education, modern medicine, technology, and industrialization. However, many citizens worried about the country's future in its new international context and especially how their children would fare in the new world that was opening to them. It was within the context of new relationships and questions about the political status of culture in geopolitics and international relations that questions of language and identity arose again.

Culture was one important tool that Nyýazow used to maintain his power. He did not simply retain his leadership position after the dissolution of the USSR; he mastered methods of continuously increasing his personal power. In one notable speech Nyýazow explicitly mixed politics with culture, underscoring that "the Turkmen people demand to know their history."[48] He went on to announce his intention to develop programs on Turkmen culture and language. His support for national pride and a culture that could buttress that pride began with programs designed to put a spotlight on Turkmen language and culture. Nyýazow created the Miras Institut (Heritage Institute) to oversee the mining of uncontroversial Turkmen national culture from its repositories. Archeology, for example, was officially sanctioned as a politically safe field for digging up and displaying ancient Turkmen history. The Golýazmalar Institut (Manuscript Institute) was founded to explore ancient texts and translate them from the old Turkmen in the Arabic script into modern Turkmen in the new alphabet. While Turkmenistan already possessed its sovereignty, Nyýazow was looking for ways to shore up his own authority. To this end, Nyýazow broke up the Academy of Sciences into such independent institutions as the Institute of Turkmen Language and Literature, which he reestablished as an independent institute directly involved in alphabet reform and language development.[49]

In independent Turkmenistan, public debate about bilingualism and national pride in language arose not only among linguists and educators but also among the general public, as they explored independence with a reinvigorated interest in national identity.[50] Academic studies provided linguistic or cultural advice in order to promote increased use of Turkmen. Change did not take place overnight, but by the second half of the 1990s, Turkmen would become the primary language in higher education and government.

Popular Opinion about Language and Alphabet Purity

The new status of the Turkmen language led to discussions of further sociocultural reforms, including a script change.[51] Indeed, throughout Soviet space, ethnic groups began to discuss renouncing the Cyrillic script they had used since 1940.[52] While the state led language and alphabet reform, Turkmenistan's populace participated in shaping reforms by joining in public debates over whether the script should change, and if so, how. Men and women representing diverse fields wrote articles for newspapers about language, alphabets, literacy, and national identity. Opinion articles on education reform appeared in newspapers and in teachers' journals.[53] These published observations were an expression of agency found in debates that took place among Turkmen in the earliest years of their independence—a small window of time when the government allowed a certain latitude for expression of opinion in the press on a limited number of topics. Unfortunately, even that degree of free speech would not survive the decade.[54] No equivalent is found in the second half of the 1990s in Turkmenistan. The early 1990s offer a unique insight into Turkmen popular opinion about their national identity and the symbolic power of language and culture in their society.

While published sources indicate that a number of citizens actively supported language and alphabet reform, there was also resistance to alphabet reform and the change in language status. People wrote articles arguing explicitly against changing the script. Even greater opinion was likely expressed at the individual level, verbally or through forms of passive resistance.[55] For example, at times in everyday life, questions of national identity became secondary to ease and performance, and so even individuals who had learned the new Latin alphabet would write in Cyrillic from time to time. Why not? They were accustomed to writing in it; it was the script they had learned in school. More than twenty years after independence, when you asked someone to write their name or address, most adults still scribbled in the "Russian alphabet."[56] While people used the new Latin alphabet in official materials and public forums, for years after the reform many continued to write personal materials in Cyrillic.[57] It is not surprising that reform did not take immediate hold especially considering that in the early twenty-first century a larger-than-life photo of President Nyýazow drafting his new book *Ruhnama* loomed over Aşgabat—displaying his pages written in the Cyrillic script![58]

It is probable that a great many more people conversed about reform rather than wrote about it, and most did not express their opinion in the press. My analysis does not try to prove that a majority of the population necessarily favored reform. Instead, I will demonstrate that a significant portion of the citizenry expressed their opinions in a constructive manner that was overlooked by outsiders, likely because few saw the value in investigating the Turkmen press. These articles went unnoticed because they are in Turkmen language newspapers, and foreign analysts likely expected to find little beyond state-sanctioned filler in the news. Plus, Turkmen language materials were not widely available to scholars. But there are gems to be found among these articles. Discourse analysis of newspaper and journal articles allows me to trace patterns of thought regarding national identity and the role that ethnic Turkmen saw their language playing in the new country. These articles help us to understand the nuances of Turkmen's reach for linguistic and social power more generally.

Turkmen were aware that similar reforms were being undertaken in other former republics. For example, an interview with the Moldovan education minister in the Turkmen newspaper *Mugallymlar gazeti* underscored that his community was already working on education reform, making Moldovan the language of instruction, and adopting a Latin-based script.[59] The news article underscored that Moldovans offered a great example. This was significant because the Moldovans were also a small nationality who had a language and alphabet quite different from Russian. That they were emerging from the Soviet experience and emphasizing language encouraged Turkmen efforts to do the same. The same newspaper ran a short article about progress being made at a Turkmen elementary school when the director delivered a speech "in his native tongue" during "Turkmen Language Week."[60] It was newsworthy that a school principal would make a speech in his native language rather than in Russian. In these years language laws elevated the official status of all titular languages so that their status in everyday usage would rise as well. As for Turkmen, it was slowly being adopted in venues where Russian or another minority language had once dominated. For example, the Kazakh-language elementary school near Mary changed its language of instruction from Kazakh to Turkmen because, as the principal told me, "This is Turkmenistan," and Turkmen was the native language.[61]

As the status of Turkmen language rose, ordinary Turkmen began to comment publicly on the importance of knowing Turkmen in order to be considered a "true Turkmen." In interviews with citizens outside a meeting of the Mejlis (Parliament), one reporter praised a man's abilities in Turkmen. The man, Ýusup Nurhan, a "cultural worker" responded with some pique, saying, "A man who does not know his own mother tongue cannot be considered a real man. In my opinion," he continued, "one is Turkmen, the state language is Turkmen, and the Law on Language has been passed. Knowing this, we are all enriched." The article also mentioned that Turkmenistan was poised and ready to join the world order with enthusiasm. It ended with a poem:

> The People's [*Halk*] wishes will come to fruition in the end.
> I waited for today for many centuries.
> Today I am the poet of an independent country
> Turkmenistan—my ancient country, you are independent![62]

Turkmen would speak their own language and they would once again write it in the Latin script, the international alphabet of the West. They would join the international community or the new world order that was emerging as the Soviet Union faded away.

Another particularly pointed issue discussed in the newspapers and journals was the desire to purify the Turkmen language. As the Turkmen language attained official status, people began to talk about its content. They questioned the use of Russian loan words where Turkmen words were available—*klas* (class), *ulitsa* (street), *biblioteka* (library), *student* (student) instead of *sapak, koçe, kitaphana*, and *talyp*. For some Turkmen, it was not enough to elevate the Turkmen language to a higher social status—now they wanted the language cleansed of Russian terms. These issues mushroomed to combine with questions of alphabet and the signs used to represent the sounds of Turkmen. Newspapers and journals contain fascinating exchanges of ideas that inform our understanding of how Turkmen viewed language as vital to their national identity, both in reconceptualizing that identity under the new circumstances of independence and in viewing it as a means of connecting that identity to a heritage in which they took pride.

The debates diverged into two related but distinct topics: that of language purity and that of alphabet purity. Journal and newspaper articles began debating the merits of divesting the alphabet of letters that were used only in foreign words. These exchanges were fueled by one particularly academic question that had made its way into the popular press. The question was "Why should the Turkmen alphabet contain the [Cyrillic] letters Ш [sh], щ [shch], ж [zh] and signs, ь and ъ?"[63] The authors, Turkmen linguists P. Azymow and B. Çaryýarow, contended (erroneously) that these letters had no significance for the Turkmen language, were used only in foreign words, and thus should be eliminated. Their argument elicited a great deal of public response.[64] In the original scholarly article, which was reprinted in the popular *Mugallymlar gazeti*, Professors Azymow and Çaryýarow suggested that in addition to the five graphemes listed above the sounds represented by Cyrillic letters ё [yo], ю [yu], я [ya], ц [ts], and ч [ch] should be eliminated from Turkmen. They insisted, as had their early twentieth-century forefathers, that "every phoneme [sound] should be represented by *one* grapheme [letter]."[65] Some felt that it was not the best time in Turkmenistan's history to bother with alphabet reform. One writer stressed that he felt the issue should not be determined by academics alone. Hoping to see a larger cross-section of the citizenry participate he asked, "Don't others have the right?"[66] Each writer addressed Azymow and Çaryýarow by name and often responded directly to other citizens who had published their opinions.

The question of alphabet purity led to debate about language purity. Articles, for example, asked why people even bothered using Russian words when perfectly acceptable Turkmen words were available. One argued that the language in textbooks should be "cleaned up." That is, teachers wanted an end to translations from

Russian, which they said felt "heavy to them" and created "confusion among the students."[67] They insisted that books be written in Turkmen rather than translated from Russian. Joining this debate, a middle school teacher from Gyzylarbat equated language purification with horse or cattle breeding, pointing out that Turkmen would never dream of mucking up the Ahal Teke horses' genes with those of an English breed. So why, he asked, would they think about "polluting" a Turkmen textbook with translation from Russian?[68] The very manner in which the teacher, Meredgeldiýew, conceptualized language reveals much about Turkmen identity, which is steeped in a nomadic heritage and a history of dependence on animals.[69] Letters in newspapers and journals echoed the demands of Meredgeldiýew in that they wanted Turkmen life and values reflected in textbooks. They not only wanted to stop "feeling a sense of translation" when they opened a textbook but also wanted to be able to teach subjects that were genuinely Turkmen and with an authentic vocabulary.[70]

Teachers insisted that in light of the 1990 Law on Language, textbooks should be "completely rewritten according to the exigencies of local conditions."[71] A husband-and-wife team of instructors wrote that they wanted to bring local nuances to the framework of global topics such as biology and medicine. All ethnolinguistic groups accumulate their own cultural, historical, environmental, spiritual, and socioeconomic worldviews.[72] Among the Turkmen, not only their nomadic heritage and unique history but also their relationship with the environment differed from that of other Turks because of the extensive expanse of desert as well as the long coast of the Caspian Sea upon which they live. Turkmenistan's territory consists of 90 percent desert; it fosters a distinct breed of horse; it is a littoral state on the Caspian with a history of fishing; and it suffers specific ecological concerns because of the cotton industry and irresponsible modern irrigation methods, such as in the Garagum canal. The teachers thought that Turkmen language required precise terminology to express these complexities and idiosyncrasies.[73]

Citizens, especially teachers, wrote newspaper articles sharing their opinions, fears, and hopes for the country and its future. They wrote about democratization, the role of the party, and the political outlook. A special section titled "Political Themes" in the paper *Edebiýat we sungat* reveals a number of thoughtful pieces about the direction the new country would take.[74] Language was only one issue on the minds of the people, but it remained a significant point in public discourse. Turkmen stressed the importance of language in locating oneself in the new global order as well as the need for local language development: "For Turkmen national culture to be a part of the collective world culture, our people's development should synthesize the characteristics of general humanity.... [Thus] as part of a classroom's work to develop well-bred, cultured children, Turkmen words [should be] taught in the place of Russian words.... Literacy [in one's mother tongue] develops the state internally and allows for relations with the outside world."[75] Although the country had achieved full literacy during the Soviet years, literacy reemerged as a topic of concern. Soon the country would be focusing on language enrichment and the development of terminology as major points of national pride.

While in the earliest years of independence, some newspaper and journal articles argued that Turkmenistan should promote Turkmen as the official language and abandon the Cyrillic script; others argued that it was not the best time in Turkmenistan's history to bother with alphabet reform. The 1990s were a time of "shock therapy" in which the whole former Soviet Union was suddenly faced with the breakdown of the command economy and the demands of the free market. The country was experiencing uncertainty in every sphere of life. Turkmenistan was suffering from scarcity of foods and consumer goods just as in Russia, where Moscow had instituted a system of *talony* or ration cards for certain foods beginning in 1989. In Turkmenistan a teacher wrote a news article about the beginning of summer camp for children and openly discussed the lack of food. He wrote, "Our country is facing real political difficulties . . . [here] we have to run around looking for food for the children's camps."[76] Another article linked the issue of scarcity specifically to the question of writing and alphabet reform: "While we have a paper shortage, why should we waste time, waste pencils, and use up the paper we do have, just to get on people's nerves [with alphabet change]?"[77] Just over a year after this article was published (February 1991) it would no longer be possible to express dissatisfaction with language policy in the press.

Latinization II

Within the first year of independence Turkmenistan's government determined that the country would adopt a Latin-based script in place of Cyrillic and that this new alphabet would be distinctive. At a press conference for the May 1992 "Aşgabat Summit of the Former Soviet Central Asian Republics, Turkey, Iran and Pakistan," a journalist asked President Nyýazow, "What can you tell us about the transition to a new Latin-based alphabet? When will it happen?" The president responded, "Our scholars are working on this. However, to address the matter fully will take a minimum of three years."[78] Scholars agreed with the president that the issue should not be rushed.[79] Literacy was the greatest consideration, as it had been with the first Latin-based script.

At the recommendation of the linguist Dr. Pigam Azymow the state formed a six-man committee with professors Myratgeldi Söýegow and Aşyr Orazow as the cochairs. The committee drafted an alphabet, which they presented to scholars from the institute of language named for Hojamyrat Baýlyýew and the institute of literature named for Magtumguly, and all the scholars endorsed the new writing system. The new alphabet had twenty-three basic letters and seven letters created through the use of diacritics. "The committee agreed that these diacritics would signify distinctly different phonemes. The use of a distinctive mark to create one single sound or phoneme was to help with literacy, specifically such concerns as reading, writing, and saying the word as it is written."[80] The committee introduced the new alphabet to the public by way of the newspapers *Türkmenistan* on 19 August 1992 and *Mugallymlar gazeti* on 21 August 1992. They did this in the same fashion the scholars had introduced the first Latin alphabet in 1928: in a chart that showed both the current writing system (Cyrillic) and the newly proposed system (Latin), with examples of how to employ the letters in spelling specific words, and how to replace the Cyrillic letters with Latin equivalents. This method of introduction was designed to maximize the comfort level of the populace, making learning to read and write the new letters as easy as possible.[81]

In September 1992 Turkmen linguists Pigam Azymow and Myratgeldi Söÿegow, members of the Academy of Science, participated in the International Turkic Language Congress held in Ankara, Turkey.[82] These men were scholars of renown in Turkmenistan and had published at length on language issues. In their presentation at the congress, they announced Aşgabat's official position on script and language reform and explained the decision to undertake Latinization, which included a desire "to buttress the country's newly attained independence, to be recognized as a member of the world community, to take membership in the United Nations . . . and to develop the [country's] sense of sovereignty." They discussed the manner in which they intended to present the new Turkmen national alphabet to the public. "During the past fifty to sixty years, the Turkmen language and Turkmen linguistics have grown and developed. The Turkmen language has been declared the state language and Turkmenistan is [ready] to take its place in the world union of nations which has changed fundamentally [since the fall of the USSR]."[83] Language and script were infused with great cultural capital during these years as they became linked with sovereignty. The very idea of an alphabet marking the international status of the nation was one that led these scholars to look back and examine the history of the earlier alphabet reforms.[84]

At the Ankara gathering in a forum of linguistic specialists, these Turkmen professors approached reform to include the finer points of language about their concerns over the shape of letters and children's ability to acquire facility in the new script. They even mentioned how they were distinguishing this new Latin alphabet from the 1928 alphabet:

> We are all aware after centuries of experience that the shape of the printed letter has a great effect on the shape of its cursive version. To preserve the demands of the handwritten (cursive) letter and the printed letter equally is difficult. Despite elementary schoolchildren's repeatedly being taught cursive they so often revert to the printed letter. With an eye to this, in our draft of the alphabet the letters' cursive form closely resembles the printed form. Capital letters are another similar concern. The way a

capital letter is written distinguishes it from its lower-case form. These must be taught just right in the classroom. In the Latin alphabet of the 1920s the capital letters were too difficult.[85]

Once again literacy or facility in the Turkmen language was paramount in determining language policy more broadly.

The scholars were primarily concerned with children's ability to learn the new alphabet. The entire population would be expected to learn the new alphabet, and while everyone would have a few years to do so, the Alphabet Committee felt particularly concerned with the population's aptitude. Azymow and Söÿegow also discussed why they were distancing themselves from the 1928 Latin alphabet. They felt it was inappropriate to revert wholesale to the 1928 Latin-based script because that had been designed by the "colonial" Soviet power.[86] They believed that historical circumstances demanded that they create an alphabet that was in some way distinguishable from the one Turkmen introduced in 1928. This new Latin-based alphabet was going to "distance" the Turkmen from their Soviet heritage—a desirable result in the view of these scholars. Nonetheless, they admitted taking lessons from the history of earlier reforms so as to avoid unnecessary mistakes. Why, after all, reinvent the wheel when Turkmen had a century of language reform to call upon? In many respects it was exemplary of the ways in which cultural capital was revalued more generally.

Attention to language and alphabet also led to questions of relations between Turkmen and other Turkic groups. Professors Azymow and Söÿegow explained that they agreed in theory with the pan-Turkic aims expressed in the unified Turkic script proposed at the 1991 Istanbul conference (the symposium held on 18–20 November 1991 by Mamara University), conceding that it could indeed be beneficial to carry out Turkmen alphabet reform in coordination with other Turkic groups, as some conference participants proposed. (Turkmen soon decided to step away from that idea.) Moreover, it would not hurt, they said, to bear in mind Turkey's long and "rich" experience with a Latin-based alphabet.[87] They considered the possibilities of borrowing from Turkey's alphabet, but they also took care to look at the German alphabet, which they noted possesses sounds similar to those in Turkic languages when marked with diacritics (umlauts).[88] After all, the "New Turkmen National Alphabet" was designed in part to signify Turkmenistan's independence as a Turkic nation and country in the new world order. The language reformers took seriously the concepts available from all languages; this may have foreshadowed the distinctive approach the alphabet ultimately took.[89]

In October 1992 there was a follow-up conference in Turkey called the Ankara Summit, which Turkmen scholars attended.[90] In this same year, Turkey provided aid in the form of scholarships for Central Asian students, publication of thousands of books in the new alphabet, funding for a Turkish section in the Turkmenistan State Library, and two schools in Aşgabat.[91] Despite Turkish scholars' and the Turkish government's support, Turkmen scholars undertook alphabet and language reform largely on their own. In the end, Aşgabat pursued an alphabet "based on its own unique letters in order to mark every single [Turkmen] phoneme" of the literary language. The alphabet and the still evolving literary language were to reflect the language of the people even while they shaped the language of the people and their identities as independent Turkmen.

Ideas about literacy were still connected to accurate representation of the sounds of the language. To mark every phoneme with an individual grapheme, scholars believed, would facilitate learning to read—that is, the one-sound-one-signifier approach would ease learning to read and write and would aid in reading words as they were in the spoken language.[92] The reasons for the adherence to phonemic representation of language were based on an approach to maintaining high levels of literacy that had been attained during the Soviet period (and especially after the Second World War).[93] The phonetic method that had dominated early twentieth-century alphabet reform remained important to literacy at the end of the twentieth century.

Implementation

In his 18 January 1993 presentation to the Academy of Sciences, President Nyýazow elaborated on the methods of Turkmen alphabet reform, underscoring that the state was responsible materially and intellectually and that the best approach to implementation was a measured pace.[94] Backed by Azymow and Söýegow, Nyýazow framed the question of the national alphabet as being significant to economic as well as to political issues in the newly independent country.[95] He noted, for example, his hope that the national currency, the manat, and Turkmen citizens' passports would soon be printed in the new Turkmen alphabet.[96] Scholars stressed that this was logical because the development of the Turkmen language, popular press, national culture, and other such things are tied to economics and politics.

Finally, on 12 April 1993, President Nyýazow announced publicly with at least nominal support from the academic community that over a three-year period Turkmenistan would adopt a Latin-based "Turkmen National Alphabet" in place of their Cyrillic alphabet. On the same day the Mejlis (Parliament) passed a resolution in support of Nyýazow's decision. The transition would further the aims of the 1990 Law on Language and the reforms planned in the 1993 education reform.[97] The president explained that the Cabinet of Ministers, in cooperation with the Institute of Language and Literature and regional officials, would oversee the creation and implementation of a new alphabet for the Turkmen language.[98]

The question remained about how to implement a Latin-based alphabet. The "Turkmen Language's New Alphabet State Advisory Commission" (a combination of state officials and academics) created a thirty-letter alphabet.[99] The Cyrillic vowels [ө], [ё], [ю], [я] were Latinized as [ö], [ẏo], [ẏu], [ẏa], but the letters ц, щ, ь, ъ were not reconstituted in the Latin alphabet. And, despite earlier objections against relying too heavily on the 1928 alphabet, the committee based twenty-six of the thirty new letters on the previous alphabet, implying that they were indeed avail-ing themselves of the historical experience of their predecessors—again revealing a continuity between eras and in the strategic cultural choices being made regarding language and script.

The commission then recommended the reform to the public via the press, stressing that it was imperative to change from the Cyrillic to the Latin script in a manner that preserved comprehension. Certain scholars stressed that, although the move from Cyrillic made sense, they could not ignore the fact that popular literacy was vested in that script. This was one reason for the state's decision to undertake alphabet reform in an unhurried manner. Aşgabat did not follow Mustafa Kemal Atatürk's 1928 example of Latinization in the Turkish Republic, which allowed for transition in only a three-month period.[100] Azymow and Söẏegow agreed with Nyẏazow about the pace of implementing reform over a number of years: "devel-opment of the Turkmen language, national education and enlightenment, nation-al culture, and such issues that are tied to economics and politics should not be hurried. These multi-faceted issues should be pondered and worked over slowly."[101] There was a state-driven program using newspapers, journals, radio, and television to announce all information regarding the alphabet reform. The Alphabet Com-mission began displaying the new alphabet in newspaper mastheads and television spots, broadening slowly from there. The schools began with the first grades and each subsequent year expanded the focus to include the upcoming class, keeping pace between classroom instruction, teacher training, and the development of new textbooks.[102] Government offices were the final targets for reform.

The new Turkmen alphabet acted as a symbol of Turkmenification, simultane-ously asserting a separate and distinct national identity, even while moving Turk-menistan one symbolic step closer toward its Turkic brethren. In eradicating Cy-rillic, Aşgabat signaled participation in an anti-Russian cultural stance that was moving swiftly throughout the former Soviet Union. Muslims throughout Central Asia, the Caucasus, and even the Tatars in Russia were discussing adoption of a Latin-based alphabet.[103] Voices within the ethnic Turkmen community supported reform as a means for underscoring the distinction of their nation's newly acquired sovereignty and power.

Literacy and Information Technology

In June 1993 President Nyẏazow delivered a speech communicating his rationale for script reform and his expectations in the "State Program for the Implementa-tion of the New Turkmen Alphabet in Turkmenistan, 1993–1995."[104] These expectations included enhancing Turkmenistan's cultural revival, its ability to communicate with other countries, and citizens' access to information technology and computers. At a theoretical level, the concept of literacy in Turkmenistan came to be discussed in the context of the idea of computer literacy. It was with this speech that Nyýazow began to impose himself so manifestly on the reform process.

Nyýazow declared that the first goal of Latinization was to express Turkmen identity. His second goal, access to global computer technology, did not clash with the former, but it challenged the alphabet reformers to devise one system that would be suitable to both goals. The president made a presentation to the Mejlis in which he discussed the highlights of Latinization. He devoted a third of that speech to access to information technology and the idea that a Latin script would facilitate the use of computers.[105] To that end, President Nyýazow himself insisted that all letters in the new alphabet be taken from signs found on computer keyboards.[106]

In that same year Nyýazow demanded that every classroom house a computer—much as he had once exulted that every garage would soon house a Mercedes—not just Herbert Hoover's "chicken in every pot and a car in every garage."[107] An article in *Mugallymlar gazeti* discussed the expectation that every classroom would soon offer computer classes.[108] However ,"computer literacy" was something that only a few citizens would gain in the early years of independence even after classes were established and internet cafes began sprouting up around urban areas.[109]

Nyýazow first called for awareness of information technology in Turkmenistan. Then he demanded that the new alphabet be compatible with computers and keyboards. He went so far as to insert himself into the alphabet-designing activities. All of this occurred despite the lack of access to information technology in Turkmenistan and the small number of computers per capita. And later, most illogically, when the circumstances finally did arise to allow for information technology infrastructure to be built in Turkmenistan, the president not only did nothing to aid it but was active in blocking it. His regime's restrictions on internet access created a formal block to implementing the new alphabet and communicating with the international community. Nyýazow claimed to want to join the world community and placed the emphasis on computer literacy, yet he himself was the greatest obstacle to Turkmenistan's achievement of those goals. The new Latin-based Turkmen letters were distinctive, but odd and did not lend themselves to literacy of any kind.

Instead of borrowing letters directly from Turkish, English, or German, the 1993 New Turkmen National Alphabet Committee introduced "universally recognized signs": $, ¢ [sh], £, ƒ [zh], ¥, ÿ [ŭ], Ñ, ŋ [ng], reflecting President Nyýazow's insistence that the new alphabet accord with "aspects of Western technology."[110] However these signs were awkward, not well received by the public, and could only be created through manipulation of Microsoft Word Latin-I. In 1995 the committee refined the letters, and Professor Söýegow was compelled to explain in a newspaper article that the alphabet commission had decided to modify the 1993 alphabet.

The sign $ would no longer represent [sh]. Instead, the committee chose Ş because, Söýegow explained, "not all keyboards in Turkmenistan possessed the '$' symbol," but all computers could create the ş sign. Along with Professor Öwezow, Söýegow wrote articles stressing that the language planners wanted this alphabet to correspond with all keyboards.[111]

By 1996 the commission implemented further modifications, replacing £, ¥, and Ñ with ž, ÿ, and ñ. Not long after that it changed ÿ to ý. It is understandable that a new country faced for the first time with the responsibilities of managing a new system would accomplish some tasks in fits and starts. But it cost time and money to modify the alphabet. Books printed in the 1993 version became obsolete in just two years' time. Public signage, purchased from a company in Moscow, changed again and again. Teachers had to keep up and ensure that students were learning the new letters. The state had to reprint packages and labels for products in the new alphabet. In the case of a local brand of sugar cubes the packaging had been printed according to the 1993 alphabet. The letter ñ appeared in the word *Türkmenistanyñ*. However, after the 1996 reforms the letter ñ replaced ñ. The factory had to correct thousands of boxes of sugar—by hand—covering the old ñ with tiny stickers showing the letter ñ to spell: *Türkmenistanyñ Altyn Asyr önümi* (Turkmenistan's Golden Era product). The symbols of independence did not come easily.

Implementation of the New Turkmen National Alphabet symbolized not only de-Sovietization but also very serious concerns about how to mark the nation as it joined the "countries of world civilization." Once the government decided on a final form for the writing system it turned its attention to education. Questions of the national language continued to resurface as Turkey persisted in its proposals to unify all Turkic scripts, and the ethnic Russian community, along with many Soviet-educated Turkmen, grumbled about the hardships of language reform. Non-Turkmen parents thought it bad enough that they had to deal with new language and alphabet in the workplace, but they were thoroughly disgruntled that their Russian-speaking children faced an increased use of Turkmen in the schools.[112] Meanwhile, because for many classes the language of instruction had changed from Russian to Turkmen, the state had to quickly train more teachers in literary Turkmen. Beginning in 1993, educational reforms upset the system dramatically. In the following years, language and education would be the greatest social concerns among Turkmenistan's citizenry and among the state's most ruinous social undertakings. Education as a whole suffered during the Nyýazow era.

Conclusion

The years 1985–1996 were as tumultuous as any in modern Turkmen history. In 1996 the official language and alphabet were not those of 1985. For Turkmen the locus of formal political power had also shifted, from Moscow to Aşgabat, and social capital more generally was retracting from Moscow as each nationality explored cultural reforms and techniques for signifying their new post-Soviet identities. Many language communities began expressing their grievances openly as Gorbachev's new policy allowed for expression of discontent. By the 1990s, such phrases as "second mother tongue" and "friendship of the peoples" were too much to swallow any longer. Even though as late as 1990 the Soviet Union declared Russian the official language, by that time the republics, including Turkmenistan, were announcing their titular languages as the official languages of the republics. Language policy would soon be turned on its head. Social and cultural domains reflected some of the earliest efforts of national groups breaking from their Soviet past. Throughout the former Soviet Union language was perhaps the most illustrative domain for expression of national identity.

Alongside so much change, there remained continuity in considerations over language symbolism. Turkmen, like several other groups, decided to design an alphabet that would refer to their Turkic-ness without subsuming themselves within the Turkic world. Just as Jadid-inspired Turkmen had several positions by which to orient themselves, independent Turkmenistan had several historical identities in which to locate themselves within the new world order. Professors Azymow and Söÿegow explained: "Turkmenistan's decision to make the Turkmen language the official state language marked the fundamental change in Turkmenistan's positioning in the global order."[113] By this they meant that Turkmenistan was moving away from Russia and taking a more westerly stance. They chose a locally oriented, world alphabet over one such as the Unified Turkic script, which could have underscored their membership in the Turkic cultural continuum. The same symbolism and perceptions of power that had driven alphabet reform among early twentieth-century progressives held currency in the post-Soviet period: modernity, literacy, identity, and position in the world community.

Anti-Russian, cautiously pro-Turkish, and intrigued by international power, Turkmenistan experimented with globalization, foreign relations, and the international market. In 1995 it joined the United Nations and declared a position of permanent neutrality.[114] Aşgabat referred to the new status as "a real factor of stability, good neighborliness and mutual confidence in Central Asia," employing it to strategically distinguish the manner in which Turkmenistan "joined the world dialogue."[115]

Changes that Turkmen made to language and script after 1991 reflected a very deliberate break with the Soviet past—what Laura Adams would call a "fracture" with the past.[116] Yet we see retention of many of the Soviet institutions that were charged with implementing these reforms. As in earlier eras, Turkmen elites were concerned about levels of literacy and the pace at which Turkmenistan engaged the larger world. The decisions to make the Turkmen language the official language and to replace Cyrillic with a Latin-based alphabet were clear responses to decades of Soviet control. But reform was undertaken slowly, scholars ensured that the populace had access to various forms of the two alphabets in newspapers and primers, and at every step the connections between the writing system and literacy were noted. Despite the inherent challenges faced by the change of script, the scholars involved in Turkmenistan's alphabet reform attempted to reduce the amount of trauma the people would experience. The linguists' firm belief in the usefulness of alphabet reform propelled them in their work. The idea that the Latin-based script would move Turkmenistan forward in the world, make information technology more accessible, facilitate the learning of English, and provide a symbolic break from Russian power, all contributed to the beliefs that the country should leave the Russian script behind.

Chapter 6

Altyn Asyr Nesli

Nyýazow's Golden Generation, 1996–2006

Alphabet reform was an aspect of the new Turkmen country's joining in the "world community."

Anyone who complains about going without sausage or bread for a day is not a Turkmen.
I admit it, there are too many portraits, pictures and monuments. I don't find any pleasure
in it, but the people demand it because of their mentality.

President Saparmurat "Türkmenbaşy" Nyýazow was the leading agent of transformation in post-Soviet Turkmenistan. He had the final word on strategies to be employed in remaking Turkmenistan's society and thus in determining who possessed forms of power. Under Nyýazow, the Turkmen leadership continued to define social or cultural capital by ethnolinguistic nationalism that said Turkmen-speaking ethnic Turkmen had the right to socioeconomic power. But to these policies of Turkmenification were added significant new educational programs. Nyýazow sought to use education to teach the nation's people to become independent Turkmen rather than Soviets. There was continuity in using literacy and education to build a nation and to centralize power. Yet there was discontinuity in terms of what the Turkmen nation was to look like. This discontinuity was intensified by change in the content of education and in the definition of literacy—that is, Nyýazow was able to build upon all of the literacy, alphabet, and educational work of the twentieth century, but he used this as a counterpoise, and anti-Soviet policies were at the core of his Turkmenification programs.

Nyýazow strove to marshal the people into reconceptualizing the Turkmen nation, and through coercion when necessary. Whereas nationalism has the ability to create cohesion between peoples and overcome differences between ethnic groups, it can also accentuate distinctions. Nyýazow's cultural programs underscored differences. The new Turkmenistan was a country being designed for ethnic Turkmen. Nyýazow labeled this period the "Golden Era" (*Altyn Asyr*) and set out to create new citizens much like the Soviets had sought to stimulate the New Soviet person (*sovetskii chelovek/täze sowet adamy*).[1] Indeed, part of Nyýazow's aim was to mold what he labeled the "Golden Generation" (*Altyn nesli*) into loyal ranks of citizens for the new country. He envisioned a generation uncontaminated by nostalgia for Soviet days, one that would be ideologically reliable: faithful to the nation and loyal to him.

In Nyýazow's Turkmenistan, the citizenry contributed to the processes of cultural production even while they were the targets of the state's cultural products.[2] They were at once the audience of discourse even as they were the authors of it, singing songs, reciting poetry, writing articles to newspapers, and generally paying homage to Türkmenbaşy. A study of the importance of cult and education as tools of state power will elucidate the ways in which national identity was constructed and articulated in post-Soviet Turkmenistan under President Nyýazow, and the methods through which Nyýazow legitimized his authoritarian leadership, first to co-opt Turkmen citizens to support his regime and then to coerce them as participants in his personality cult.

Post-1991 political sovereignty placed many former Soviet ethnic groups in a position to assert themselves culturally. Language was one of the most prominent sites for such affirmations of national identity. While language and education had long been sites for social reform and political expression, President Nyýazow's policies in Turkmenistan politicized each of these social spheres to the degree that non-Turkmen ethnic groups became socially and economically marginalized. It is valuable to discuss policy uses of alphabet, language, and literacy from 1996 to 2006, when there was a shift from nation building, or Turkmenification, to what I call Nyýazowization. This shift included a change in popular opinion around the year 2000, when even previously supportive Turkmen began to reject Nyýazow's policies. Why did Aşgabat want to marginalize Russian speakers? With the rise of Turkmenification, was it enough to be ethnic Turkmen? What of those Turkmen who did not speak the native language? Examples of language and education policy in twenty-first-century Turkmenistan will illustrate that Nyýazow's exaggerated cult of personality did not bolster his administration but, rather, served to undermine it.

The National Revival Movement

During much of the Soviet era, Russian dominated as the lingua franca. It gave access to political or social power in technical or professional fields and higher education—denying power to those who did not speak it. Turkmenistan's National Revival Movement (Türkmenistanyň Umumy Milli Galkynyş Hereketi) reversed this situation in Turkmenistan, promoting the Turkmen language at the expense of Russian, repositioning the vernacular, and empowering the Turkmen language community in new ways. Turkmen language politics were foundational to the National Revival Movement.

The National Revival Movement was President Nyýazow's official program aimed at building a state based on a national Turkmen identity and culture. National Revival began on 17 January 1994 at the convocation of the fifth assembly of the Halk Maslahaty (the People's Council), which was, until 2008, the highest representative body in Turkmenistan.[3] "Revival" of the national culture ranged from broad programs reintegrating Islam into daily life, such as state sponsorship of mosque building, to specific decrees requiring traditional Turkmen dress in schools. Revival built on cultural antecedents, fostering a fusion between Turkmen ethnicity, an Islamic heritage, and the secular state. Even before the onset of independence, Aşgabat had begun initiating political and social reforms so as to move away from Soviet-era practices. Tensions over the choice of Turkmen versus Russian, especially in the field of education, had persisted throughout the Soviet period. It was, therefore, understandable when post-Soviet reforms targeted language and education in tandem, locating them at the center of a program of Turkmenification.

In 1990, when Turkmen was declared the official language of Turkmenistan, it ascended to the language of state, business, administration, and education, reorienting the relationship between Turkmen and Russian languages as a means for balancing social and economic power. A Turkmen national identity was asserted through language as most Russian-language spheres began to shift to Turkmen usage. Although Russian was still heard as the language of interethnic communication, its public use began to decrease dramatically even at the highest levels.[4] Intellectuals and state administrators trained during the Soviet era were forced to reformulate public interactions; society found itself surrounded by television, radio, and signage that reflected Turkmen cultural values, expressed in the Turkmen language, and ultimately written in the new Latin-based alphabet.[5] Russian language speakers, who did not know Turkmen, found themselves outmoded and out of work. Not only were the criteria for social status reversed but Russian speakers found themselves unskilled for a labor market that Aşgabat was redesigning to emphasize Turkmen language.

Western reports focused on the brain drain, but what these reports missed was that there had been a base of popular support for the president's initial cultural policies in the early 1990s. What was unacceptable to Western analysts was tolerable to a substantial number of ethnic Turkmen. Only 28 percent of Turkmen had claimed Russian as their second language in the 1989 Soviet census.[6] With the Turkmenification of the social structures, a portion of the population felt they were not losing out as much as they were gaining a country they could claim as their own.[7] The new language policy not only gave Turkmen a sense of justice, after decades of Russian language hegemony, it promoted the sort of self-respect that nationalism encourages. Villagers who were once sneered at on city buses for speaking the "provincial tongue" suddenly found themselves sought out for state positions that were previously obtainable only by the Soviet elite.[8]

Punctuating the language issue was the change in alphabet that had been instituted in 1993, which deliberately distanced the people from Russia and oriented the country toward Turkey and the West. Most important, it was another symbolic break with the Soviet past. Aşgabat's rhetoric aimed to create cohesion among Turkmen, as defined by the state, and to keep non-Turkmen out of that collective. The post-Soviet Turkmen nationalism not only excluded non-Turkmen from the nation, it also kept "Russians" from being a part of the elite and prosperous in the newly designed state.[9] Turkmen who could speak the Turkmen language felt justified in becoming the new elite.[10] Turkmen speakers began to take over the most prestigious jobs and positions of responsibility, while Russian-speaking professors, scientists, doctors, and lawyers found themselves relegated to working as taxi drivers.

I do not argue that all ethnic Turkmen found the post-Soviet system to their benefit. Indeed, Turkmenistan had become a highly politicized country where everything fell under the umbrella of Nyýazow's National Revival Movement. The regime fired academics who wrote histories contrary to Nyýazow's writings; books that disagreed with Nyýazow's perpective were burned; publications began including quotes from the president's book, *Ruhnama*, to demonstrate that an author was intellectually indebted to Nyýazow; and widespread use of the title "Türkmenbaşy" underscored Nyýazow's supreme place in the society and emphasized the hierarchical Turkmen heritage in which ancestors are revered and authority figures are rarely questioned. No space was left unpoliticized. Still, there was a period of popular support for linguistic policies, and Nyýazow initially was able to consolidate power in a largely favorable atmosphere.

To further underscore Nyýazow's own position of power, in 1999 at a meeting of Turkmenistan's Halk Maslahaty, Foreign Minister Boris O. Shikhmuradow proposed that Nyýazow be named president for life.[11] At the time Nyýazow "modestly" maintained he should not accept, insisting that the presidential election scheduled for 2002 should go ahead as planned. A day later, when citizens gathered ostensibly of their own will at the great hall of the Halk Maslahaty chanting *"Halk! Watan! Türkmenbaşy!* [The People! The Fatherland! Turkmenbashy!]," Nyýazow made an emotional display: "I thank you very much. I am a little overwhelmed. . . . Dear friends, I would not say I am afraid of this task. Your desire is [equal to] the law. . . . I want to say, honestly, that in Turkmenistan the people respect me so much I cannot sleep. Respected people, I am so grateful to you, it is difficult for me to speak."[12] After expressing his hesitancy to accept the honor, he consented. This step required a change to the constitution. So the Halk Maslahaty amended the constitution that day, naming Nyýazow "President for Life" (*birinji omürlük prezidenti*).

In less than a decade, comrade Saparmurat Ataýewiç had evolved from a Russian-speaking, Party-loyal atheist to Türkmenbaşy, or "head of the Turkmen." He was now a Turkmen-speaking Muslim leader of a nation-state—he even made the pilgrimage to Mecca in 1992. Nyýazow's personal transformation mirrored (or perhaps prefigured) the transformation he hoped to bring upon the entire Turkmen nation. During his conversion, he became the architect of a nationalization program that highlighted language, religion, and ethnicity, which he used to legitimize his role as the new country's authoritarian leader. His program was a new variant of the different nation-building programs that have characterized the history of the Turkmen people from the early twentieth century onward. That Nyýazow was successful in styling himself as the country's founding father during glasnost was ironic because he allowed so little of it to be experienced in Turkmenistan.

The National Revival Movement was an overarching theme for reform that shaped such social spheres as language, education, and labor. Language and education would become foundational to the Revival Movement. The term "movement" has a very formal sound to it, and while it appeared in news articles and speeches, it was not a commonly used slogan in every day speech. Instead, the catchphrase that embodied the ideals of the discourse was *Altyn Asyr,* or golden century, the metonym for all that the state promoted as good about independent Turkmenistan. This was the phrase that appeared in the names of shopping centers and hotels, in descriptors of products made in Turkmenistan such as bottled water and yogurt, and as the moniker for the generation that never had known Soviet life—*Altyn Nesli* (the Golden Generation). As the "termless chairman" of the National Revival Movement's committee, Nyýazow himself greatly influenced access to social and economic power within the Turkmen population. His singular hold on power, along with his ubiquitous portraits and statues, encouraged interpretations of his presidency as a dictatorship propped up by a cult of personality.

President Nyýazow used discursive programs including visual images, physical ritual, and transformation of public space that garnered power and lent a sense of legitimacy to his new role as president.[13] He gained formal power, but his cultural policy concurrently provided Turkmen speakers with the opportunity to grab political, economic, and social power. Communicated through public signage linking *Halk* (People) with *Watan* (Nation) and *Türkmenbaşy,* the discourse implied a symbiotic relationship between the three. It also referenced the agency of Turkmen in noting their responsibility toward the new nation. The state appropriated power (Watan/Türkmenbaşy) while ethnic Turkmen-speaking Turkmen asserted a national identity. "*Halk! Watan! Türkmenbaşy!*" was chanted at parades, holidays, and other spectacles.

Popular participation was crucial to the success of the National Revival Movement; language reform requires readers, writers, and speakers. All of the symbolism related to education, parades, theater, music, dress codes, and the public accolades heaped on President Nyýazow needed a participatory audience. Yet only certain sectors of the society participated. The population was divided by into "Turkmen" and "non-Turkmen." This was not simply an ethnic question but a linguistic one as well. The Soviet elite who had advanced socially or economically as Russian-speaking were denied status in twenty-first-century Turkmenistan. Doctors, lawyers, professors and other professionals began losing their jobs. This included ethnic Turkmen. A Turkmen person who did not know his or her mother tongue was not considered a "true" Turkmen.[14] Revival movement programs were implicitly designed for the consumption of true Turkmen.

The Power of Public Texts

Nyýazow took control of the power of public texts in post-Soviet Turkmenistan by asserting the primacy of the Turkmen language as language planners began work to create a categorically Turkmen lexicon. A section in the Turkmen Language and Literature Institute (formerly part of the Academy of Sciences) became devoted full-time to language development. It undertook one subject at a time, creating lists of new words or suggesting the revival of ancient Turkmen terms to supplant Russian and some international vocabulary. The army received new terms for everything from canteens to epaulets. In some cases old words were assigned new meanings, as with the word *mülkdar*, which originally meant "landowner" but was assigned the meaning "farmer."[15] In this situation all Turkmen-language speakers had equal access to the cultural capital, as the information was not only published but was also announced over television and radio. One did not even have to be literate to absorb the new vocabulary.

Neologisms were created for the burgeoning new market of goods made in Turkmenistan. For example, a Turkmen word was designed to replace *ketchup*. Bottles of ketchup came to feature the word *öwrümeç* on their labels.[16] Rather than use the internationally recognized term that the country had employed for decades, the Language and Literature Institute created this completely new word. Apparently, "ground-up tomatoes" sounded more Turkmen. Bottled water, soda, and milk products packaged throughout the country reflected the National Revival Movement via the Turkmen names and terms on their labels as "Altyn Asyr" products. President Nyýazow officially headed this initiative, but some scholars claimed they had supported it and had in fact suggested to Nyýazow in 1999 that it was time they began seriously implementing the language policies they had been composing throughout the first decade of independence.[17] While it is true that Nyýazow relied heavily on linguists to carry out the reform and write books explaining the process to the population, it is difficult to determine the exact role the academics played in the decision-making process.

But we can see the role of academics more generally through their many textbooks, television appearances, and newspaper articles. On 1 January 2000, the Language and Literature Institute began publishing a newspaper devoted solely to the language question: *Turkmen Dili* (Turkmen language). The newspaper, offering etymological discussions in layman's terms aimed at the general public, was a vehicle for explaining new terms to the public. It reinforced the messages of signage that the state had used to transform public space from Soviet to Turkmen. Signs, posters, and placards literally spelled out the language reforms and brought the discourse of the National Revival Movement into the public eye. In that same year Nyýazow began to require officials to speak Turkmen in public.

While public texts put new phrases into context, television and radio taught pronunciation. Street signs, state documents, and textbooks bore the "New National Turkmen Alphabet." Street names were changed from those of Soviet figures to Turkmen heroes and literary figures, while slogans devoted to "Neutral, Independent Turkmenistan" replaced Soviet slogans. The names of Turkmen figures and heroes began to replace Russian toponyms. The state encoded public space with officially sponsored writing to support cultural policy. Despite the new names, people continued to use the Soviet names for theaters, streets, and public venues: Pervogo Maia Theater, Prospekt Svobody, Ulitsa Moskovskaia, and Prospekt Lenina rather than the Parahat Theater, Görogly köçesi, On ýyl abadançylyk, and Türkmenbaşy Şaýoly. This minor resistance to Revival indicated that, despite the overarching power of the regime, the people found ways to generally follow the "official transcript," in James C. Scott's parlance, while using a "hidden transcript" among themselves. The public simultaneously found ways to use the discourse to its advantage; conformity was an act of agency. Scott writes about such use of an official discourse to achieve one's personal aims, typifying it as a form of agency that one might use by participating in the official discourse just to survive within a restrictive system.[18] One might also manipulate the system to one's own aims, such as paying bribes to obtain a job or get into university. As one article reported, "[In Turkmenistan] everything can be bought and sold. For money you can not only enter any university, you can pass any examination, without spending a single day attending classes, and at the end still get a degree."[19] On 12 July 2004 even Nyýazow recognized the problems of bribery and nepotism in the university admission process.[20] Participation in the Nyýazowization of the country and culture was one way that people survived. Teachers, students, and intellectuals were most obviously caught up in this net of ostensible empowerment as they grappled with the daily homilies to the leader and the enslavement of the culture to support Nyýazow's policies.

A Second *Korenizatsiia?*

In addition to cultural reform, a general overhaul of various labor sectors resulted in a reduction of jobs, which then fell to people along ethnolinguistic lines. Former elites and many professionals were removed from their jobs for lack of knowledge of Turkmen. Nyýazow himself had politicized the language question by declaring in 2000 that he wanted to see "the complete and universal introduction" of the national language in public life. He underscored his seriousness in televised broadcasts criticizing officials who spoke Russian better than they did the national tongue. For example, he fired his foreign minister specifically for the latter's weak knowledge of Turkmen.[21] This allegedly protective attitude toward the Turkmen language actually became an act of national self-humiliation as officials were ordered to speak only Turkmen in public and many bumbled through the experience.[22]

In fall 2001 Nyýazow announced that each state sector would be responsible for ensuring their employees' proficiency in Turkmen. the medical institute, the law school, universities, and government offices slowly began to transition to Turkmen as the language of daily communication. The Language Institute stepped up its codification of Turkmen equivalents for Russian language terms one field at a time: medical, military, education, and so on. Implementation of this policy did not simply lead to abstract linguistic or cultural power but redefined access to economic power by denying work to non-Turkmen speakers. Government ministries offered their workers night classes in the Turkmen language, and schoolteachers were given language exams. However, over the next few years, those illiterate in Turkmen were removed from their work.[23] Professor Tagangeldi Täçmyradow suggested that the country had embarked upon a second era of *korenizatsiia* (nativization).[24]

The effect was most significant among teachers. Between 1999 and 2002, the state dismissed roughly up to twelve thousand teachers, largely representative of non-Turkmen ethnic groups such as Russians, Armenians, and Uzbeks, from their positions ostensibly due to budgetary concerns.[25] By 2002 the Ministry of Education completed the transition from a ten-year to a nine-year system of education. The reduction in course load was used to justify the cutback in teachers. These changes in education coincided with demands that all state employees demonstrate knowledge of Turkmen and *Ruhnama*. Education can be a unifier and a source of social cohesion, but it can also be divisive, excluding some from society.[26] In this case, those who did not speak Turkmen were excluded.

Language reform is not atypical of state building. However, the intensity of the Turkmen programs left non-Turkmen politically disenfranchised and economically marginalized. Western communities have found this brand of nationalism offensive, and some analysts have allowed the "strange[ness]" of the system to overshadow their analysis.[27] However, some Turkmen saw this as justice for decades of "oppression," and they supported a Turkmen-dominated independent Turkmenistan.[28] For them political independence and cultural exclusivity went hand in hand.

While speakers of the Turkmen language rapidly gained social or linguistic capital, those who did not know the language were left voiceless.[29] In closing the Russian-language theater, opera, and ballet, prohibiting the importation of foreign texts, and making Turkmen the language of instruction and administration, the state situated language at the core of the National Revival Movement.[30] State discourse implied that post-Soviet Turkmenistan provided only enough space for the empowerment of "true" Turkmen. This implication became a demographic reality with the exodus of Russian-speaking "others" who were weary of Turkmenification.[31] The nation took shape as a Turkmen one, but the loss of many specialists left the professional core, the economy, and society weakened.[32]

Turkmenification through Education

The post-Soviet reforms set in motion a decade of change in education to support broader national cultural programs that would not only assert an intense strategy of Turkmenification but also reverse Russification. The Russian language was not eliminated completely from newly independent Turkmen schools but was relegated from a language of instruction to a foreign language. While the demotion of Russian was part of the overall social reorientation of Turkmenistan, it was also part of a trilingual program that made the study of English compulsory along with Turkmen and Russian. This "three-language policy" (*üç dil siyýasaty*) seemed far-sighted when instituted in 1993, but it was on a scale that public schools could not support.[33] Due to the change in status of the Russian language, the study of English soared, and Turkmen citizens signed up for classes at private Turkish "Başkent" language centers, sought out Peace Corps volunteers, and paid for private tutors in order to learn English.[34] President Nyýazow encouraged the policy, declaring that knowledge of this international language would aid Turkmenistan in catching up to global standards. He even explained that one underlying reason for transition from the Cyrillic alphabet to a Latin-based one in the 1990s was that, "as usage of the Cyrillic alphabet had made it easier for Turkmen to learn Russian, so would a Latin script assist them in learning English, the international language of technology."[35] The shift away from Russian was an important point of discontinuity with the past.

Yet even as citizens and educators pursued study of English, President Nyýazow announced that the foreign-language curriculum would be seriously curtailed in public schools.[36] State sponsorship of the three-language policy was being abandoned in favor of emphasis on Turkmen. State-sponsored foreign languages would be taught only at specialized language schools or designated institutes of higher learning. The policy intended to focus schools more narrowly so that students would spend more time on fewer subjects and perfect their knowledge of specific topics, such as Turkmen history. Nyýazow's stated expectations that this narrowing of education focus would lead to better teaching and better learning was an opinion that many parents did not share.[37]

A year later Nyýazow again addressed the question of foreign languages when, in a 2002 televised meeting with university rectors, he formally delineated which institutes of higher learning would teach foreign languages.[38] In his view this reduction of state services did not eliminate the opportunity for individuals to study foreign languages. The president reminded viewers that if people wanted to learn foreign languages they could take advantage of *Dil*, or language centers that had been established around the country by locals and international representatives. At that time the state allowed twenty-one language centers around the country to run through the work of intermediaries.[39] Nyýazow was transferring responsibility for the study of foreign languages from the state to the individual. He explained that streamlining instruction within public schools would help to prevent a surplus of unnecessary specialists such as translators, if it was, in fact, engineers that were needed. Essentially this policy realigned the state's responsibility in education, transferring foreign languages to the private sector and announcing Nyýazow's intentions to organize higher learning with respect to market demands as he saw them.

Despite this restriction on language study, in the early 2000s a number of elementary schools were still teaching both Russian and English as foreign languages (see figure 5). State publications continued to emphasize that the long-term goal was "to perfect" the study of languages in schools. Thus, various languages, including Turkmen, Russian, and English, were to be taught as early as the preschool level. This is a perfect example of the endless internal contradictions that confounded analysts and continued the confusion surrounding the country. Nyýazow's pronouncement contradicted the state's educational practice.

Contributing to the inability of administrators to carry out actual orders were the president's predilection for firing of ministers after only short terms in office and the steady streams of changes that kept systems such as education and medicine in a constant state of crisis—and that perpetuated corruption.[40] Persistent corruption related to various grabs at forms of power. State employees took chances to win personal gain throughout the 2000s. Nyýazow then frequently took the opportunity to draw the public's attention to the corrupt behavior, remove the individual from his or her post, and characterize *himself* as the people's advocate. For example, at a televised April 2004 cabinet meeting, Nyýazow announced the removal of the education minister, two deputy ministers, and the deputy head of the education department of Aşgabat based on corruption charges. According to the president, every one of the capital's kindergartens had added "dead souls" to the number of employees for whom it drew salaries. The administrators allegedly pocketed this money even as they continued to assert that they did not have enough money to pay a living wage to their actual employees.

Presidential Popularity and *Ruhnama*

The National Revival Movement continued to capitalize on Turkmen heritage, revealing an increasingly Nyýazow-centered orientation. Adherence to a strict line of cultural policy and celebration of Nyýazow's Turkmenistan diluted the Turkmen people's role in the symbiotic relationship from vital supporters to coerced partic-

FIGURE 5. Turkmen elementary school students

ipants. The years 2001–2002 began to see a decline in popular support for Turk-menification as even the "true" Turkmen began to feel that Nyýazowization was overshadowing it.[41] The president's book, *Ruhnama*, played a significant role in this shift.

Ruhnama (The book of the soul) was President Nyýazow's two-volume historical-spiritual tome, which he wrote ostensibly in order to guide the Turkmen people in their newly found independence; in all likelihood it was actually ghostwritten. It offered Nyýazow's interpretation of Turkmen history, his autobiography, stories of Turkmen ancestors and their important deeds, and a moral code combining Turkmen and Islamic values. For example, it encouraged children to respect their elders and guided fathers in just discipline within the family. It also underscored the cults of personality Nyýazow created around his own mother and father. As *Ruhnama* became the official text of the National Revival Movement, its message intended to strengthen Nyýazow's position as leader during what he deemed to be the "Golden Era" in Turkmen history.

Nyýazowization through Education

Published in December 2001, the first volume of *Ruhnama* became a part of the educational curriculum in 2002; the second volume was introduced into the school curriculum in September 2004, "further reducing the time allotted to a traditional curriculum."[42] Much public discourse surrounded the book and was shaped by it as state workers were required to take weekly lessons and public speeches referenced it. Most citizens quietly went along with the public recitations, numb to the ubiquitous signage referencing it and grudgingly accepted it as part of the curriculum. Not only were there classes on *Ruhnama* itself but teachers were to integrate it into the curriculum more broadly. Except for *Ruhnama*, the history of Turkmenistan, and a short course in world history, Nyýazow ordered social subjects excised from school curricula. Aside from these three, he called social subjects "empty" and "unessential," deeming them inapplicable to life and unworthy of study.[43] In 2004 primary and secondary schools generally devoted between two and four hours a week to *Ruhnama*; universities and institutes from four to eight hours a week; additional time was devoted to Nyýazow's other texts. *Ruhnama* not only had a heavy presence in school curricula, it also played a role in shaping the discourse of twenty-first-century Turkmenistan. It colored physical, social, and cultural space throughout the country. For example, the state required every organization—including state-sponsored mosques—to make space for a *Ruhnama* room or a corner where the bright pink book was displayed and staff had to spend time reading it (see figure 6). This was little different from the Red Corner (*krasnyi ugol*) in Soviet homes where Soviet propaganda had been displayed. These had originally been places in the home for religious icons, but Soviet leaders commandeered and desacralized the space, creating one in every activity center, school, and organization. Such corners now supported the Nyýazowization of the country.

With the *Ruhnama* one was reminded of the long shadow cast by the *Short Course History of the Communist Party of Soviet Union* (1938), which also had been ubiquitous. While the subject of much quiet and discreet ridicule, at least by intellectuals, the *Short Course* was also enormously influential, especially in shaping

FIGURE 6. Ruhnama and statue of Nyýazow, Daşoguz

the popular culture of Stalinism.[44] While adults tolerated the *Ruhnama* and the Golden Era propaganda, schoolchildren were at its mercy. Parents were outraged at the dwindling state of education throughout the country. Every child was required to purchase a copy of *Ruhnama* and carry it to school daily. The book cost two dollars, representing a significant expense for families earning only fifty dollars a month. The state dissuaded teachers from offering contradictory ideas and limited their professional development.[45] Everywhere people looked for ways to send their children abroad or to enroll them in the network of private Turkish schools despite uncertainties of the role Islam played in them.[46]

Larger-than-life photos of Nyýazow had graced public buildings and city streets long before *Ruhnama* appeared. But it was with this text that Nyýazow finally pushed what had been nation building and Turkmenification beyond what many Turkmen found acceptable. Claiming this book to be an "inspired text," Nyýazow labeled it the "sacred book" and the "lighthouse for the people."[47] With this text, the president put into full effect the Nyýazowization of Turkmenistan.

Under Nyýazowization fewer and fewer people had access to cultural capital as less and less was made available. The parameters within which the people could function became increasingly tight. Language, religious practices, traditions, and customs, even lineage, all came under intense scrutiny. Nyýazow's programs and policies took over the public sphere, leaving no room for non-Turkmen. The state took control of education in ways that squeezed people to the point of discontent; resistance took both passive and active forms. The greatest act of resistance was to emigrate and join one of the opposition groups in exile; the most common act was to send one's child to school and complain about the system to friends. The option of sending one's child to schools in a foreign country was available to those with money or to those lucky students who won scholarships.

Teaching the Nation

In addition to complications created by the change to Turkmen as the primary language of instruction and the great number of state employees who lost their jobs due to lack of ability in Turkmen, ethnic issues played a role in the Turkmenification process. An employee from the Turkmen Education Ministry reported to US embassy representatives that, "under the terms of an unwritten order 'handed to us from above,' universities have been encouraged to reject applicants with non-Turkmen surnames, especially ethnic Russian."[48] While some teachers were fired because they did not know Turkmen, most of these claimed that they were let go simply for not being ethnic Turkmen. Although there was never any publicly stated official policy targeting non-Turkmen, they "were often the first targeted for dismissal when layoffs occurred. [And] there was societal discrimination against ethnic minorities, specifically Russians."[49] Language policy and the budget justified personnel changes.[50] One former Ministry of Education administrator reported that the ministry had offered teachers Turkmen-language lessons after school hours free of charge.[51] Several teachers confirmed this, although others complained that they were never offered such opportunities. These same teachers felt sure that even if they had learned Turkmen it would not have mattered, because ethnicity was as much an issue as language.[52]

Beginning in 2004 the state stopped recognizing diplomas from outside of Turkmenistan earned after 1993. This meant that state employees received a letter summarily dismissing them from their positions.[53] It also meant that students who tried to leave Turkmenistan to escape the Revival Movement would find their degree of limited value upon returning home. A graduate of a British or a Turkish university would be able to find work in a foreign company in Aşgabat, but that private market was not large enough to sustain everyone who was disgruntled with Turkmenistan's education system.

Under Nyýazow there were extraordinary crises in payments not only to teachers but also to other state employees. Some regions were as much as six months behind in receiving their salaries.[54] A general fatigue and frustration developed among educators. They felt unappreciated and underpaid by the state, especially as teaching hours were expanded from eighteen to thirty-six hours a week. Too many classroom hours compounded the perceived lack of opportunity for self-improvement or

FIGURE 7. Turkmen university students

paid preparation.[55] This was compounded by overcrowding in the classrooms due to a 2000 presidential decree that reduced the number of teachers.[56]

Ethnic tensions revealed themselves in education as well as in other spheres of life as de-Sovietization and cultural de-Russification went hand in hand.[57] In 1999 there were 99 Uzbek (in Dashoguz and Lebap), 55 Russian (mainly in Aşgabat and Mary), 49 Kazakh, and 138 mixed-language schools throughout Turkmenistan.[58] In 2003/2004, international news reports of the closure of all non-Turkmen schools created confusion over their status. Most of these schools did not close down but, rather, were reformed under the guidelines of the National Revival Movement. The schools were "Turkmenified"; that is, the language of instruction changed to Turkmen and other languages fell into unofficial use. The principal of one Kazakh school explained that these schools were still needed to serve the community, but with a wry tone he noted, "This is Turkmenistan, one should know Turkmen."[59]

Molding the Golden Generation

Turkmenistan's cultural policy increasingly reflected Nyýazow's authoritarian rule. Nyýazow's method of rule was to micromanage. As a result, his ideas, no matter how unscientific, were initiated. Ministers could not object because doing so would lead to their removal from office or even jail for the slightest offense. What follows are some of the major developments in Turkmenistan's education system during these years, including a focus on vocational training and the use of work as a pre-requisite to access education. They relate not so much to Turkmenification as to Nyýazowization and his attempts to mold the Golden Generation. They also illustrate why Nyýazow lost the support of the Turkmen people.

Two Years, Public Service to Qualify for Higher Learning

On 4 July 2003 the Cabinet of Ministers announced that, in order to gain practical experience, high school graduates would be required to have two years' work experience (*stazhirovka*) in their selected area of study before they could apply for admission to institutes of higher learning.[60] Thus, at age sixteen, children who wished to pursue higher education were expected to find an internship or a paid position in a country where unemployment was estimated to be between 30 percent in urban areas and 70 percent in rural areas.[61]

When the Ministry of Education announced that admission to universities and institutes would be based on an applicant's practical experience, urbanites lined up at state administration offices while rural youth sought work in areas concerning wheat and cotton in the hope of entering the agricultural university.[62] Students anticipating studying at the medical institute found themselves cleaning floors in hospitals.[63] Some argued that there was a certain logic to this program and it could, in theory, be beneficial both to the country and to students individually.[64] However, it was put into motion without much preparation and was poorly managed. Students did not gain the knowledge the concept intended.

Some citizens went so far as to label it free labor, as the students were expected to spend their two years' practicum within the department or ministry they would serve upon graduation. A fundamental problem with the program was that the state provided banks, hospitals, schools, and businesses with little guidance as to how to mentor these young people. For example, the students assigned to the banks were supposed to be engaged in daily banking activities and taught managerial skills. However, many reported that they were assigned simple tasks such as filing or running errands. They complained that they got little guidance or mentoring.[65]

Cleaning floors and filing papers did not prepare a student to pass a test related to the practice of medicine or law. Yet these were the jobs available to the inexperienced. Moreover, the general conditions around the country hampered the feasibility of even marginal success when high unemployment was keeping even well-qualified individuals from obtaining work.

Locals dubbed this the "two-plus-two program," referring to the fact that the two years of internship left students of four-year programs with only two years of formal learning.[66] The students received their stipends from the government, and criteria for the program were met on paper, but in reality it suffered from weakness in implementation. Educators were generally unhappy with this concept, but they had little opportunity to speak out or affect policy. Some educators quietly rebelled by reorganizing their programs so that the students received closer to three years of classroom study.[67] Since students were required to attend short seminars or classes every three months during the two years of work, some teachers intensified and lengthened the duration of these meetings, so that they would have more time with the students.[68]

The decree requiring two years of practical experience for admission to higher education took the country by surprise. Ironically, because the number of applicants dropped dramatically so did the cost of bribes.[69] The government addressed corruption unevenly. That is, President Nyýazow habitually called officials and administrators before him in televised meetings and berated those who had been found guilty, before dismissing them from their positions; summaries regularly appeared in newspapers the following day. Several school directors and education department officials were fired for providing false labor documents indicating that a high school graduate had two years of work experience.[70] In this way Nyýazow seemed to be taking advantage of the situation, presenting himself to the public as the singular official who was looking out for the people's best interests as he worked tirelessly to keep "dishonest" individuals out of the government. Several cases of false information on work experience, or forged experience documents, led to such a presidential display.

Quotas

In spring 2002 President Nyýazow announced in a television broadcast that he was reforming higher education so as to keep admission and graduation rates in line with market trends.[71] Independent of the issue of practical experience, he explained that he wanted to avoid a glut of interpreters, for example, if it was in fact agriculturalists that were needed. Spaces opened at the various institutes, based on estimated market demands determined by the Ministry of Education. Before independence, more than thirty thousand enrolled in higher education each year.[72] This number dropped precipitously in 2000.[73] State quotas made allowances for less than 10 percent of high school graduates to attend universities or institutes. Both Turkmen and international observers feared that Nyýazow was dumbing down the population so that he could control it. Naturally, the country was deeply concerned by what came next.[74]

Vocational Training

Almost in direct response to questions concerning practical training and his vision for the country, in winter 2003 the president underscored that he wanted schools to emphasize vocational training.[75] In December 2003, in a televised meeting with students and art workers, he told the audience that higher schools should abandon what he deemed to be "useless" lessons and instead concentrate on training skilled specialists.[76] He also admitted that there was a lack of financing in the education sphere and promised to provide one hundred thousand dollars in assistance.[77] While the president made clear that he did not intend the state to fund studies that were covered by the private sector, he did indicate that he was willing to increase state expenditure on vocational study as part of the National Revival Movement.[78] Academics who participated in the conceptualization and design of the long-term program explained that it was one of many paths that could have been taken, and although they were aware of the deficiencies they also recognized a certain logic for a young country that needed to meet basic infrastructural needs.[79]

In 1997 the state had placed vocational schools under the authority of related ministries, administrative offices, and *häkimliks* (governors or authorities in the five *wilaýets* and the city of Aşgabat) so that they could prepare workers in specific trades as necessary. For example, the Ministry of Agriculture or the Ministry of Foreign Affairs respectively would determine quotas, deciding how many students should be enrolled in courses in farming versus animal husbandry, or in international affairs versus German-language study. The schools were also linked to various factories and places of work that fell under the auspices of state administration. This would have allowed each sector to supply workers for itself. For example, the "State Cotton Concern" prepared students for the cotton industry, providing "trained" employees to the state cotton factory. The *State's Goals for 2010* recorded that training of specialists would be implemented to meet the requirements of the national economic sectors. The plan intended to ensure that school and higher education conformed with international standards, that the quality of the professional training at schools was improved, and the number of unemployed youth in the labor market was reduced. Particular attention was paid to the creation of the network of educational institutions to train specialists at high school level. Institutions might be state-owned or private.

Vocational and technical study was broadly defined to include internet training, language instruction, cultural events, and preventative health care. Nevertheless, as of spring 2003, the greatest problem with this scheme to develop technical studies was that there simply were not enough technical or vocational schools to meet the needs of the population.[80] An extension of vocational/technical training was formalized as part of Turkmenistan's military training.[81] So that conscripts could learn a skill during this period of service, President Nyýazow decreed in 2002 that enlisted men and women should engage in practical training.[82] It was with this decree that thousands of policemen, nurses, and laborers lost their positions. The state explained that these fields had been burdened with a surplus of unnecessary positions created during the Soviet era. Nyýazow intended to reduce the demands on the national budget by cutting down on numbers and placing military conscripts into some of the remaining positions. Conscripts, untrained in medical treatment, replaced fifteen thousand nurses and took over as traffic police and on construction projects and began farming on state lands. While the state regarded this as an opportunity for practical learning, the populace and the international community regarded it as free, unspecialized labor.[83] This program was not popular among Turkmenistan's people.[84]

The International Community's Contributions to Turkmen Education

Many Turkmen feared that if access remained so restricted, the country would lose generations of knowledge. In 1997 Nyýazow had dismantled the Academy of Sciences—the only institution that granted doctoral degrees. The various sections of the academy were hived off and made into independent institutes, such as the Institute for Language and Literature. Anyone who had been working on a higher degree was simply out of luck as the programs came to a halt. It appeared that the post-Soviet generation would be "lost." This was quite ironic since Nyýazow had gone so far as to call the children who were in school at the turn of the twenty-first century not only the "Golden Generation" but also the *Bilimli Nesil,* or the "Learned Generation."

While the limited quantity of educational opportunities was distressing, the greatest concern of parents and teachers was the quality of education in Turkmenistan, especially the perceived threat that ideology posed to knowledge and thinking skills. Parents were troubled over the excessive presence of national culture in curricula, including *Ruhnama,* and the reduction of schooling to nine years. An increasing number of families sent their children abroad for education, at their own expense. Since foreign embassies recognized and shared these concerns, several governments made education a priority in their relations with Turkmenistan. The embassies of the United States, Pakistan, Germany, India, Great Britain, and France each offered a type of study abroad program. The Peace Corps offered a handful of English-language classes.[85] An Iranian cultural center in Aşgabat promoted Persian language and culture. The case of Turkish influence and aid in Central Asia has been so extensive that it must be attended to individually.

The Turkish Government

Turkmenistan's endeavors to revamp its educational system were accompanied by extensive support and funding from the Turkish government, which in the early 1990s was eager to act as the "big brother" or model for the newly independent Turkic states of the former Soviet Union.[86] The United States and other Western powers favored this "Turkish Model," especially considering the proximity of potential Iranian influences. Turkey's then-president Turgut Özal visited Central Asia and later prime minister Mesut Yılmaz made several public statements about Turkey's readiness to provide social and economic support to their cultural brethren. This came in the form of scholarships for thousands of Central Asian students to study in Turkey, publication of thousands of books in the new Turkmen alphabet, funding for a Turkish section in Turkmenistan's State Library, and the establishment of Turkish government-sponsored schools in Aşgabat.[87]

The Turkish government established several institutes in Turkmenistan, including one primary school, İlk Öğretim Okulu, and a high school, the Anadolu Lisesi, in 1993; a Turkish Language Center (TÖMER) in 1993; and a Vocational Training Center (YAMEN) in 1996.[88] This training center offered courses in plumbing, electronics, weaving/embroidery, sewing, and textiles. Students receiving a certificate at the end of their study possessed "practical, marketable skills." The Turkish International Cooperation Agency (TICA/TIKA) oversaw many similar undertakings, such as the opening of Turkish cultural centers, student and teacher exchange programs, academic conferences, provision of scholarships for university students, the opening of the Turkish language schools (TÖMER), training of bank and management personnel, broadcasting to Eurasia, and training for public administrators and bureaucrats.[89] Perhaps the greatest assistance was in providing some small number of those who had graduated high school during the "Golden Era" with marketable skills.

Private Turkish Schools and the Başkent Foundation

In addition to the Turkish government's schools a private Turkish foundation, Başkent, undertook educational initiatives throughout Turkmenistan much as similar foundations had done throughout Central Asia and the Balkans.[90] Beginning in 1993, the private foundation, independent of the Turkish government, established English language classes for adults at a nominal fee, opened a university in Aşgabat (The International Turkmen-Turk University), and built fourteen primary and secondary schools around the country.[91] These were secular schools rooted in Muslim values, though no classes in religion were taught.[92]

Hundreds of "Turkish schools" around the world made up a loosely connected network in which teachers, administrators, and sponsors promoted the philosophies of the Turkish cleric Fethullah Gülen.[93] Gülen brought together members of the religious, educational, and business communities to establish centers of learning based on the teachings of Said Nursi (1873–1960). Adherents of the Nursi philosophy believed that through education it is possible to teach students to live a life deeply ingrained both in Islam and in the modern scientific world.[94] The aim of these schools—in addition to offering education—was not to teach religion per se but to impart discipline to the students by stressing Islamic values and ethics (*ahlak*), which were seen as "unifying factors between different religious, ethnic, and political orientations."[95] The underlying methodology was for the teachers to embody spiritual ideals and impart them through model living (*temsil*).[96] Students lived on campus in dormitories and were taught not to drink, smoke, gamble, lie, cheat, or steal, and generally to live a good life through the words and examples of their teachers. This high level of discipline appealed to Turkmenistan's parents.[97]

Başkent was arguably successful in Turkmenistan, in that the numbers of schools grew consistently. Under Nyýazow the local population recognized these schools as offering the best alternative form of education in Turkmenistan. Every year three to six hundred students took the entrance examination at each of the secondary schools, although there was space for only fifty to two hundred, depending on the size of the school.[98] They were also popular among parents, as the administration was known for being relatively honest—that is, they did not demand bribes for admitting students as other schools or universities did, and the entrance exam was both challenging and transparent.[99]

The modus operandi of the Turkish schools around the world was deference to local custom. Their policy was to work closely with ministries or departments of education, offering curricula approved by the local government. In Turkmenistan—and this was an extreme case—this meant that, although the curriculum was challenging, it also included *Ruhnama* and required the administration to send administrative representatives (but not students) to every state-sponsored celebration to affirm the Nyýazowization of the country.[100] Despite complying with these standards, by August 2011 the Turkmen government had nationalized the International Turkmen-Turkish University and closed down most of the schools. The government became concerned with what it perceived to be a missionary undertaking of the schools and the influence of the Gülen Movement or ("Nurjular" as they were colloquially called).[101]

The End of an Era

On 21 December 2006 Nyýazow died of a heart attack, ending twenty-one years of rule marked by authoritarianism and a mercurial cult of personality. Holiday decorations came down in Aşgabat as the city went into official mourning. While displaying Nyýazow's picture, state television played Chopin's Piano Sonata No. 2.[102] (Western European classical music was an odd choice in a country that had become so nationalistic.) His funeral was one of much open lamentation, as people wept. But it was likely that many adults shed tears for the country's uncertain future rather than for the sixty-six-year-old *Beýik Serdar* (Great Leader), a term that had also been used for Lenin and Stalin. Children, however, grew up knowing no other system or leader and were caught up to varying degrees in the legacy of Türkmenbaşy. Not only were many of their tears real but their suffering was multidimensional as they not only feared for their future but sincerely mourned the loss of the man Boris Shikhmuradow once described as the "consolidating factor" around which the country was creating "an atmosphere of social harmony."[103] Although there were critics who upon his death recalled that Nyýazow had acted in an increasingly authoritarian manner during his tenure, Shikhmuradow's statement indicates how Nyýazow also invigorated Turkmen national identity.

Conclusion

The role of culture in larger social experiences is considerable, demonstrating the power of language; the importance of history in nation-building programs—or in this case, the National Revival Movement; and the use of culture to garner political power. President Nyýazow capitalized on the importance of language in the Turkmen heritage. In addition to maintaining his leadership position since the late Soviet period, Nyýazow suggested cultural reforms that implicitly referenced the past and encouraged academic debate that relied on historical experience, in order to cultivate his position in the new nation. Nyýazow created an ethnolinguistic nationalism to solidify and legitimize his rule. This nationalism marginalized citizens who did not speak Turkmen restricting their access to social power and even employment. Questions of identity and the discourse of nation building are accordingly of more than theoretical interest. They go to the heart of how society, the economy, and ordinary people's lives were organized in the first twenty years after the end of the USSR. In this respect, Turkmenistan is not unique but is exemplary.

On the cusp of the twenty-first century, Turkmen state policies altered dramatically from Turkmenification to Nyýazowowization as President Nyýazow sought personally to shape Turkmen identity in his own image. Beginning with an approach like that of Mustafa Kemal Atatürk (Father of the Turks) in Turkey, he took the name Türkmenbaşy, but then much like the Shah of Iran he proposed himself as the nation's "savior."[104] Nyýazow personally decided how to define what it meant to be a "true" Turkmen, according to his own idiosyncratic definition. Turkmen language and education once again became politicized, as learning became a medium for socioeconomic discrimination when the state closed Russian-language schools and restricted higher education to ethnic Turkmen. State cultural policy divided socioeconomic life along linguistic lines when the state fired doctors, teachers, and state employees who did not speak Turkmen.[105] This cultural upheaval had material rather than merely symbolic consequences.[106]

Turkmenistan's parents and critics alike became increasingly worried by Nyýazow's education policies. The quota system, the emphasis on vocational studies, and a requirement that students have two years' practical experience before they could graduate all undermined the quality of education. The state reduced the number of years of schooling from ten to nine, making it impossible for students to apply to universities in other countries because they did not have enough years of education to fulfill transcript requirements. Finally, Nyýazow made his book

Ruhnama the central text in schools. Parents feared the ironically labeled *Bilimli Nesil* (Learned Generation) would be a lost generation.

The cult of personality that Nyýazow encouraged in fact limited his achievements rather than solidifying them. The symbiotic relationship between the people, the nation, and Nyýazow signaled in the phrase *"Halk! Watan! Türkmenbaşy!"* was gradually eroded by cultural policies that became so intrusive, so implausible, and so entangled in the practicalities of daily life that the average Turkmen underwent a transformation from "coproducer" and willing audience member to reluctant, coerced consumer. After *Ruhnama* entered schools in the early 2000s *Altyn Asyr* began to see a decline in popular support, as even the "true" Turkmen grew alienated from the regime, sensing that Nyýazowization was overshadowing Türkmenification.

Chapter 7

The Era of Might and Happiness, 2007–2014

Upon Nyýazow's death on 21 December 2006, a space opened for new authority. For the first time the opportunity arose for an individual who previously had not been a part of the Soviet system of government. Gurbanguly Mälikgulyýewiç Berdimuhamedow assumed the presidency two months after Nyýazow's death in a manner that revealed the persistence of Soviet methods. According to Turkmenistan's Constitution, upon Nyýazow's death the legal successor was the Speaker of the Parliament, Owezgeldi Ataýyew, and he should have become acting president. Instead, Ataýyew was arrested, and in late February the Supreme Court of Turkmenistan sentenced him to five years in prison for corruption and immoral behavior.[1] Berdimuhamedow, the vice president of the ministerial cabinet, assumed the role of acting president with the support of the parliament, which voted on Ataýyew's resignation.[2] On 11 February 2007, Berdimuhamedow ran in what was Turkmenistan's first multicandidate election, though in reality he faced no real opposition because the candidates were all from the Democratic Party of Turkmenistan (DPT), which had changed its name from the Communist Party in late 1991 and posed no real threat. According to the Central Electoral Commission turnout for the election was more than 98 percent and Berdimuhamedow won 89.7 percent of the vote.[3] The security services, in the person of Akmurat Rejepow, and a circle of presidential advisors gave Berdimuhamedow the support he needed to take power.[4] Berdimuhamedow was sworn in as president on 14 February 2007. Although the transfer of power was peaceful there had been a quiet struggle behind the scenes, revealing that Soviet-style devices were still in play.

The new president began instituting reform on several levels right away. He never openly renounced Nyýazow's legacy, but he repealed some of Nyýazow's key policies. He implemented educational reforms on his first full day in office, suggesting its importance. But it was not immediately clear whether these reforms were more symbolic than substantive. Do they hold promise for real change in a system that has long needed it, or are they little more than window dressing, designed to present the regime in a positive light to the international community? Is this regime as authoritarian as Nyýýazow's? Is Berdimuhamedow the reformer the Turkmen people have been waiting for? Although he has improved the education system, there remains room for further reform.

When Berdimuhamedow assumed office there was much speculation about the potential for a Khrushchevian thaw. No dramatic revolution came to bear, but Berdimuhamedow did reform the education sector with international standards in mind. From his earliest days in office, he made statements indicating that he expected to see change. At the 1 September 2007 cabinet meeting he was quoted as saying, "Today, the task of developing scientific and technological capacity is extremely urgent and appropriate organizational efforts and new thinking are needed for this. We have to keep up with the times and scientific and technological advancement."[5] Change did in fact follow and some of Nyýazow's key policies were repealed. Nyýazow's cult of personality was slowly taken apart, significant education reform offered new opportunities for students, and the regime began to allow greater access to the internet through internet cafes and the distribution of computers among students. All this took place despite the regime remaining authoritarian in nature. Why would Berdimuhamedow offer reform when the country remained opaque, secretive, and mostly closed to outsiders? In part, his reforms related to or established nominally democratic institutions offering window dressing that the president could point to as evidence of the country's democratic principles.[6] These undertakings are designed as much for global consumption as for an internal audience. Neither the West nor Turkmenistan's people bought the show put on by the government, even when it ran multiple candidates in presidential elections. However, such trappings allow Turkmenistan's government to assert that it was elected by the people and lay claim to legitimacy.

Early Reform

On his first day as president, Berdimuhamedow overturned President Nyýazow's most damaging educational policies, issuing a new law that reinstated ten years of education and that abolished the two-plus-two program that had required students to take on compulsory work upon graduation from secondary school. In keeping with this decree, beginning on 1 September of the 2007/2008 academic year, education was expanded to ten years in secondary schools, to five years in higher education institutions, and to six years in medical schools and some art institutions.[7] This growth from nine to ten years was accomplished by having the ninth grade students of the 2006/2007 school year continue into tenth grade in the 2007/2008 school year; there were no graduates in spring 2007. Berdimuhamedow pointed out that extension of schooling to ten years "complies with world practices," implying that Turkmenistan once again was considering its place in the world.[8] On his first full day in office, the president signed the decree "On Improving the Educational System in Turkmenistan," determined to develop "the educational system in Turkmenistan and [bring] it in line with the standards set forth by developed countries."[9] Turkmenistan was once again situating itself in the world through education policy.

Academy of Sciences

Work on postgraduate degrees resumed in June 2007 when President Berdimuhamedow reconstituted the Academy of Sciences via presidential decrees: "On the Activities of Turkmenistan's Academy of Sciences" and "On Improving the Scientific and Research System of Turkmenistan."[10] Berdimuhamedow explained that his undertakings would keep the country "in step with the times" and again hopes rose for normalization of cultural programs. People waited for a thaw.[11] In total, this meant that individuals possessing a higher degree who had five years' work experience and could "prove themselves capable of doing academic research in a chosen field" were eligible to compete for admission to postgraduate studies in Aşgabat.[12] The Academy allotted Candidates of Science no more than three years to complete their dissertations.[13] This window of time may not sound unreasonable, but in reality it makes completing dissertations a challenge as many candidates work a full-time job while writing their dissertation.

Another reform began on 1 September 2007 and was reflected in the decree "On Improvement of Work of Teaching and Educational Establishments." It reduced the maximum weekly work hours for schoolteachers of Turkmenistan from 30 to 24 and the annual work hours from 1,250 to 850. Classes and nursery school groups were limited to twenty-five students maximum, and physical education classes were reintroduced.[14] Additionally, in 2007 the average monthly salary was 507 manats (178 US dollars). Berdimuhamedow increased the salaries of state employees and by 2012 the average salary was 943 manats (331 dollars). These reforms encouraged hope among scholars and citizens as possible evidence of the new regime's fresh approach to social issues.[15]

On 24 September 2007, President Berdimuhamedow spoke at Columbia University in New York City, where he highlighted the innovations to be undertaken in education. He declared that "the development of education takes precedence over other aspects of my policies," saying, "Let me tell you frankly that the atmosphere today in Turkmenistan is just incredible. Our children feel such a strong and intense yearning for knowledge that we just can't fail and let them down." During the question-and-answer portion of the president's appearance he addressed the role of *Ruhnama*, stating that officials would continue to pay attention to it because "it is a critical text." He further asserted that the text would remain mandatory reading "in all educational institutions—from kindergarten through college. Why? Because it contains a lot of wisdom related to our heritage."[16] But by 2013, in a reversal of policy that had stood firm for over a decade, the state removed *Ruhnama* from curricula altogether. Classes on it were abandoned for other subjects: economics, environmental science, cultural legacy of turkmenistan, and world culture.[17] However, this new approach to texts did not immediately remove all information about *Ruhnama* since textbooks referenced it or included quotations from it. This began to change in 2014 when books written by President Berdimuhamedow or devoted to him began to supplant Türkmenbaşy's works in schools. In addition, the presidential resolution "On Improving the Performance of Educational Establishments" announced the removal, in May of that year, of portraits of President Nyýazow or symbols dedicated to him from elementary and secondary schools. By autumn of 2014, these had been replaced by likenesses of the new president. It seemed as if a new cult of personality was replacing that of the Golden Era.

National discourse reflects the change in leadership. President Berdimuhamedow has dropped references to the Golden Era and the Golden Generation and instead has been promoting the notion of a new "era": The Era of Might and Happiness. In one of the many books authored by Berdimuhamedow he explains that this new era was also the "epoch of happy people of the mighty state" and "the prosperous epoch of the powerful state."[18] In his writings and in newspaper articles he labeled the era one of renewal, implying that there would be major reform of Nyýazow's policies.

Cult of Personality?

As President Berdimuhamedow dismantled Nyýazow's cult of personality, he restored the calendar, removed Nyýazow's portaits, issued new currency without Nyýazow's image, eliminated Nyýazow's 19 February birthday as a holiday, and moved the Neutrality Arch, atop which rested the statue of Nyýazow that rotated according to the sun. Yet a new cult developed around the second president, demonstrating his desire to preserve his own power.[19] Nyýazow textbooks and his image slowly disappeared from public space. But new ones penned by Berdimuhamedow took their place while images of the second president came to decorate classrooms and state offices. Students were able to forget the passages from *Ruhnama*, only to see them replaced with quotations from the current president's speeches and statements.

While President Nyýazow had many titles, including *Serdar* (chief, or military leader), which was also applied to Stalin, President Berdimuhamedow goes primarily by "Esteemed [*Hormatly*]" president or "*Arkadag* [Patron]." The Council of Elders (*Ýaşulylar Gengeşi*) anointed the president with this honorific title in 2010, which is reminiscent of Nyýazow's nickname Türkmenbaşy.[20] And while not as striking as when Nyýazow's silhouette appeared in the corner of television broadcasts, Arkadag's photo soon began to appear on the front cover of every newspaper in Turkmenistan, as Nyýazow's once had done. It had appeared that ideology was going to be removed from the classroom, but there was only a substitution. Berdimu-

FIGURE 8. Berdimuhammedow's photo at conference in Daşoguz May 2007

hamedow's books on a wide variety of topics—more than one man could ever really hope to master—from music and horses to tea and natural medicine—became part of school curricula. Whereas students had previously participated in dancing and singing (*Çäre*) that praised Türkmenbaşy they soon came to laud Arkadag instead (see figure 8).

Nyýazow had instituted a loyalty oath, or pledge of allegiance, wherein citizens pledged their loyalty to the state and to Türkmenbaşy himself. Berdimuhamedow changed the oath, substituting "the people [*halk*]" in place of the mention of Nyýazow. While Nyýazow was still acknowledged as the first president of the country, his image as the savior and father of the nation was invoked less and less.[21] Berdimuhamedow can never take the title "first president," but his photos now hang in place of Nyýazow's in classrooms and state offices. And while the state stopped building statues to Nyýazow, it started to redesign the landscape, erecting a monument in the image of Berdimuhamedow. This tribute bears a striking resemblance to the one Catherine the Great erected in memory of Peter I in St. Petersburg. The unmistakable likeness depicts Berdimuhamedow on horseback set atop what appears to be a stone wave. Prominently located in Aşgabat, it was unveiled with much fanfare (see figure 9).

Like Nyýazow, Berdimuhamedow is of the Teke tribe. He is from the Gök Tepe (Ahal) region near Aşgabat. In a departure from Nyýazow's efforts to unify the

FIGURE 9. Monument to President Gurbanguly "Arkadag" Berdimuhamedow

Turkmen nation through Turkmenification and his own cult, Berdimuhamedow unapologetically favors the Ahal Teke. Although the second president has built up the infrastructure around the country as a whole, and presidential candidates have represented the five major regions, the Ahal Teke are favored when it comes to jobs and political power.[22] Ýomut intellectuals in Aşgabat complain of a "Teke mafia."[23] The government's proclivity for promoting fellow Teke, especially Berdimuhamedow's relatives, has alienated a significant portion of the country.

Corruption and the Youth Bulge

Except for the International University for the Humanities and Development, founded in 2014, where tuition is about thirteen hundred dollars per year, education in Turkmenistan is mostly free.[24] However, a pervasive culture of "gift giving" and bribery creates a substantial cost to families. Parents pay teachers to give students extra attention and for them to receive good grades, to enter universities, and to graduate. It is not unusual for students to pay between fifteen thousand and seventy-five thousand dollars for a university degree. It can take several thousand dollars just to gain entry into a university. Admittance "rates" vary according to the amount of money one can earn in a certain field. Therefore, the cost to enter the Academy of Arts is approximately fifteen hundred dollars, entrance to the police academy is about four thousand dollars, while law school costs nearly fifty thousand dollars.

Turkmenistan's chronic corruption led Transparency International to rank the country number 154 out of 176 countries in 2016.[25] Corruption became a persistent topic even at official levels in 2015/2016.[26] The phrases "serious shortcomings in work" and "step up the fight against corruption" began to appear frequently in state-run media.[27] President Berdimuhamedow continued President Nyýazow's tradition of addressing corruption by singling out individuals for public humiliation and dismissal. This method was frequently used to explain systemic shortcomings. In 2015/2016, Berdimuhamedow used it to explain the "economic malaise" that the country was suffering because of reduced energy revenues.[28]

In the first half of the twenty-first century, Turkmenistan is experiencing a youth bulge with 45 percent of the population under age twenty-four and 43 percent between ages twenty-five and fifty-four.[29] This high number of young people creates an opportunity for societal growth even while it indicates a need to invest more in schools. Despite the state's building new schools many older schools are in need of repair, and teachers are often expected to cover the costs themselves. The problem is not that there are too few schools but that there are too few resources directed to them. Taking in just over 7,000 first-year students in the 2014/2015 academic year, higher educational institutions were only able to accommodate around 7 percent of the 110,000 school graduates annually. There were approximately 24,000 students enrolled in higher educational institutions that year. However, the twenty-one civil and five military institutions (not including the Academy of Sciences, which only graduates PhDs) should have had capacity for many more. Costly educational reforms in Turkmenistan, ranging from introduction of internet access to supplying brand-new campuses for higher educational institutions, were made possible by the government's access to energy wealth.[30] With new schools and institutions, the government is working to increase space for more students. However, some citizens complained that these most recent efforts are focused more on "quantity than quality."[31]

Language and Literacy

In the post-Nyýazow era functional literacy is not studied. Citizens and officials alike believe that the country has reached full literacy. When I mentioned to people in Turkmenistan that my study of Turkmen history examined periods of illiteracy, I was met with the reaction "What illiteracy?" This was most notably from officials at the Ministry of Education in December 2012. They scoffed at the idea, seeing no relationship between literacy/illiteracy and comprehension. Comprehension suffers in the post-Soviet era as students are expected to recite memorized passages more than they are expected to engage in higher-order thinking or problem solving.

Yet unlike under Nyýazow such studies have been taking place in a wider variety of languages.

Under Berdimuhamedow, a new official stance toward Russian indicated that the language was regaining importance. In fall 2007 Russian was restored to the airwaves with the creation of the *Owaz* (Melody) radio channel, broadcasting in Turkmen, English, and Russian. Despite a more generous attitude toward the Russian language, Turkmen remained the state language and the official language of instruction. While most classes are taught in Turkmen there has been a persistent shortage of textbooks in the official language. Such courses as dramatic arts, law, and medicine had been unofficially taught primarily in Russian using Soviet-era books. For years, instructors in these courses had translated textbooks from Russian to Turkmen or spoken Russian in the classroom.[32]

The brochure for the Turkmen State Institute of Economics and Management highlights the Department of Foreign Languages. It explains: "In the Prosperous Epoch of [the] Powerful State the main purpose of study is to further improve knowledge of foreign languages: the development of communication skills; an understanding of the socio-political information, [and] based on mastery of specific terminology; and teaching to read and understand professional literature."[33] This institute's inclusion of English in its curriculum is indicative of a broader move throughout Turkmenistan to advance the study of English. Turkmenistan hosted the Asian Indoor and Martial Arts Games on 17–27 September 2017. The main language of this sporting event was English. In order to prepare the country to be a good host, President Berdimuhamedow strongly encouraged the study of English at all levels. The US embassy in Aşgabat believed that Berdimuhamedow was working "to bring international standards and international experience to Turkmen practices" and to "integrate into the international community"[34] But changes were happening slowly so as not to create instability.

Despite problems in the education system in the post-Soviet era, Nyýazow's three-language policy (*üç dil syýasaty*) was never repealed, and English maintained a presence in schools. Still, there were serious flaws in the teaching of English, as instructors had little access to the language in the original. The State News Agency of Turkmenistan wrote: "Particular attention is paid to the study of foreign languages as a key factor of training highly qualified specialists who have professional mobility in conditions of the information society. . . . It is obvious that the fact that specialists of different sectors know several languages facilitates the early integration of Turkmenistan into the world economic and humanitarian systems. International forums and events organized by the Ministry of Education and educational institutions of our country jointly with international organisations, diplomatic missions of different countries and educational centres are of particular importance in this context."[35] Interest in foreign languages went beyond English, but the emphasis on English persisted, undoubtedly in relation to the country's preparations for the

2017 Asian Games and perhaps more generally to the quest to meet international standards.

Qualified Professionals and International Standards

President Berdimuhamedow declared 2012 to be the "Year of Education, Science, and Technology." He wrote about the state having a broad vision and declared, "Henceforth, the state will devote intense attention to the development of the educational sphere and will look after creating conditions for this, so that the young can receive a modern education on par with international standards."[36] On 27 January 2012 he signed a decree designed to develop standards for the "comprehensive reform of the national education system and improving teaching methods."[37] This decree expanded elementary education from ten years to twelve, beginning in September 2013. The state's electronic news source, *Turkmenistan the Golden Age*, wrote, "The transition of secondary schools in the country to the 12-year term of study is an important step to bring the national education system to an international level."[38] In accordance with this decree, children would start schooling at age six, whereas they had previously begun at age seven. In September 2013, both six- and seven-year-old students entered elementary school in a double class; the first cohort to graduate under this system will do so in the year 2026. With this reform, the president undertook to bring Turkmen education into line with international standards and to give students the opportunity to apply to universities in other countries.[39] Leaked census information reveals that in 2012 there were over forty-two thousand Turkmenistani citizens studying abroad, indicating that the second president was not as worried about outside ideas as the first president had been.[40]

Still, in 2009, policy harked back to an earlier era when security personnel stopped at the border more than one hundred university students, who were returning to Kyrgyzstan and Bulgaria to resume study abroad. The Turkmen state forced them to turn back at the Aşgabat airport. No satisfactory explanation was ever offered. It has been speculated that Aşgabat became nervous about sending impressionable youth to Bishkek's American University of Central Asia, where there are opportunities for independent thinking.[41]

Despite this particularly notable setback, newspapers reflected Berdimuhamedow's declared interest in raising "deeply educated, broad-minded and talented individuals."[42] The president's attitude signaled change in policies toward study abroad and indicated that the government was becoming less apprehensive of international influences. It also reflected his alarm over a lack of qualified professionals in the country. It was at this time that the government began to build and renovate hundreds of new schools in rural as well as urban areas and allow better access to information technology.[43]

FIGURE 10. Çäre, students in Daşoguz, 2007

Information Technology

After Berdimuhamedow assumed the presidency, schools slowly began gaining internet access and computers. Berdimuhamedow stated that he intended to "connect all educational and scientific establishments, organizations and enterprises to the global web of internet."[44] Meager experience and training left Turkmenistan without much familiarity with technology but the number of people who access the internet via a computer at school or work or on their personal telephone is growing.[45] In the earliest years of his rule, Berdimuhamedow allowed for the state to establish internet centers in urban areas; about fifteen opened. These internet sites were expensive to access, charging near to four dollars per hour. Also, users were required to register with a passport, creating the possibility for the state to monitor users' web activity. State censorship remains in place with opposition websites such as *Gundogar* and *Chronicles of Turkmenistan* and some Western sites blocked.

In 2011 the state began supplying laptop or notebook computers to students in order to promote computer literacy. Reports estimate the number of computers as being in the hundreds of thousands. In fact, the word "notebook" entered the Turkmen lexicon as a reference to laptops. Still, it is not possible to know how many students were actually using the computers, because teachers limited students' use

FIGURE 11. Students at Aşgabat conference on education November 2015

of computers for fear that there would be damage for which the teachers would be accountable.[46] As a result, a number of students do have access to computers and even the internet officially but in actuality do not have many opportunities to use either.

In April 2011, in a real departure from Nyýazow's policies, the Ministry of Education instituted an exam on information technology in secondary schools in place of the final exam on the *Ruhnama*. The holiday known as the Day of Science, 12 June 2012, "became the main date of 2012 for perfecting [the] scientific sphere of Turkmenistan." On that day, the president made a real contribution to the sciences, allocating ten million US dollars to the budget of the Academy of Sciences for enhancing the country's scientific potential and to stimulate "creative activity" by increasing the salaries of "scientific workers" who earned degrees or titles.[47]

Holidays and Students

Turkmenistan's government is not alone in its use of public space for mass spectacles and festivals.[48] Throughout Central Asia, students participate in singing and dancing troupes on such holidays as Nowruz (spring equinox) or Independence Day. In Turkmenistan, though, there is a systemic problem whereby students, even in higher educational institutions, miss an inordinate amount of time in the classroom due to their preparation for and attendance of such large-scale events as mass parades and affairs aimed at praising the regime (referred to as *Çäre*). At these events youth chant patriotic phrases or extol the virtues of the president with shouts of *"Arkadag Shöhrat!* [Glory to the Protector]." Such occasions occur as often as weekly. Schoolchildren, teachers, students, and instructors join the employees of state-financed organizations in marching and singing panegyrics in honor of the president and at red-carpet welcomes.[49] Despite the fact that instructors and students loathe such activities, which can leave them outdoors in severe heat or cold for hours, the state persists in organizing mass celebrations and punishes anyone who refuses to participate. While Berdimuhamedow often speaks of training "highly qualified specialists," one instructor asked astutely: "Where are we supposed to get highly qualified specialists when teachers are endlessly being corralled into attending mass cultural events to mark national holidays . . . and students in higher education spend huge amounts of their time at all these events and senseless gatherings to show their support for Berdimuhamedow's policies[?]"[50] This has led one opposition website to designate the generation growing up under Berdimuhamedow as "Generation 'Ch'" recalling the sound of the first letter in the word *Çäre*.[51] While Berdimuhamedow proclaimed that the Era of Might and Happiness would witness a break from Nyýazow's policies and did institute some important reforms, much of everyday life carries on as before.

Conclusion

Naming his era one of "renewal," President Berdimuhamedow began reversing President Nyýazow's educational policies immediately upon taking office. While these accomplishments must be acknowledged as reforms, they were essentially recovery from Nyýazow's damaging policies more than social advancements. Berdimuhamedow's reform has been encouraging but also unpredictable. His extension of compulsory education from nine to twelve years meant that students became eligible to enter foreign universities without having to first complete high school abroad. International influences seem not to threaten this regime as they did the previous one. Indeed, it would appear from the president's statements that the state is using education to position itself globally. Internet access, though still not widely available, was expanded to some institutes and schools and a handful of internet cafes. Circumstances improved for instructors and students alike. These reforms contributed to the cultivation of "highly qualified specialists" and suggested that President Berdimuhamedow wanted to open up the country. In fact, his education policies have contributed to Turkmenistan's slow emergence from its self-imposed isolation under Nyýazow. However, this opening should not be mistaken for democratization. Even with more schools being built and more teachers being hired back to work, political content and such politically driven activities as using students as dancers at state affairs are a drain on education. Despite repealing some of Nyýazow's most damaging educational policies and dismantling his cult of personality, Berdimuhamedow's early reforms were promising but inconsistent.

There has been change in Turkmenistan under the second president. He repealed some of Nyýazow's key educational policies; he slowly dismantled Nyýazow's cult of personality; significant education reform offered new opportunities for students; and the regime began to allow greater access to the internet through internet cafes and the distribution of computers among students. These undertakings are designed as much for global consumption as for an internal audience. However, neither the international community nor Turkmenistan's people believe in the government's display of reform, even when it ran multiple candidates in presidential elections. Such trappings allow Turkmenistan's government to assert that it was elected by the people and lay claim to legitimacy, despite the regime's remaining authoritarian in nature.

In 2014 the Turkmen identity was not the same as in 1914. The Turkmen people had experienced four distinct alphabets and three different types of government and had become a unified nation with a literary language. Their century-long journey illustrates the evolution of Turkmen identity and the intersection of literacy, language, and power.

Conclusion

Literacy, language, and learning contributed centrally to the development of Turkmen national identity. Modern Turkmen culture evolved and developed from a set of strategic choices made partially in response to political circumstances and partly in an effort to situate Turkmen identity within the greater world. That is, a twenty-first-century Turkmen national identity and culture were not only constructed but also deliberately hewed in response to the specific circumstances in time and space of burgeoning global modernity. Turkmen made these choices in order to gain forms of power in society or social capital. Although political exigencies forced change upon the lives of the historical actors, the ideal of shaping society through learning persisted. One constant was the aim to transport Turkmen society to modernity via literacy, which led to calls for an alphabet that accurately reflected a refined, standardized language and an education system that would teach it. The aim of modernity through literacy was also an objective of colonizing powers, including Russia and the USSR. It relates closely to ideologies of empire that sought to elevate the colonized, civilize them through literacy and education, and raise them from their "inferior," or perhaps even "barbaric," status. Concepts of civilization and literacy were handmaidens to comparable efforts, aims, and objectives.

In this history, the first proponents of modernity were Jadids and those Turkmen they inspired. Convinced of the connection between reading for comprehension and learning, Jadid-inspired Turkmen redefined the meaning of literacy from rote memorization to functional reading and writing. They also began using a refined alphabet that allowed them to mark every vowel with diacritics, thus making reading easier. The contributions of the tsarist empire toward Turkmen education were not insignificant, but the Jadid-inspired discourse was important in the sociocultural history of the Turkmen of this time, and of Central Asia more broadly. This first study of Jadidism among Turkmen demonstrates that Turkmen were very much in accord with the rest of the Turkic world and were ready for reform in ways that were previously unrealized.

The Soviet era began with a partnership between Bolsheviks and locals who both aimed to transform the Turkmen community. Initially, the Turkmen reformers' ideas were not suppressed but combined with state-led campaigns to build a Soviet society. Local intellectuals worked on language reform within Soviet state organs, wrote textbooks, and began the standardization of the language. All of this allowed them to continue pursuing such ideals as the creation of modern citizens through universal education. The Liquidation of Illiteracy campaign, for example, was exemplary of the "grand transformation" that the Soviets pursued in their perfection of society.[1]

In 1926 Latinization was a modernization campaign that Soviets pursued in order to move forward. Moscow's decision to shift written Turkmen from the Arabic script to a Latin-based one was intended to mark the language as a "modern," international writing system, moving it away from its "backward," Arabic script. In short, for this brief time, the social goals of Turkmen reformers and the Soviet administration coincided. Both wished to bring Turkmenistan into modernity, and both the Turkmen and the Soviets viewed alphabet reform as a critical tool for transforming society from traditional to modern.

Records from the 1920s and early 1930s indicate that Central Asians were interested in defining their own futures. Turkmen intellectuals wanted to have a say in how their nation would be defined through language. The 1930 linguistic conference reveals the work they were willing to do toward that effort. The purges of the 1930s represent a major rupture, however—an undeniable act of destruction. Illiteracy had been an enemy of the state in the 1920s. In the 1930s the men who had worked to eradicate illiteracy themselves became enemies of the state. Yet these Stalinist purges did not wipe out the modernist strivings of the Soviet state, which still wanted to see a modern, literate Turkmen population that could contribute to the workforce and to the future. Scholars have written about the relationship between the Soviet state and modernity, noting "the modernizing goals that the Soviet leadership sought to achieve: industrialization, urbanization, secularization, universal education, and literacy."[2] Despite the brutality of the purges, the state continued to create a modern Turkmen nation, only now without the Jadid-inspired Turkmen.

During the 1940s linguistic capital in Turkmenistan shifted dramatically from the Latin script to Cyrillic and from the Turkmen language to Russian. Unlike earlier decisions to change writing or education, which involved locals and entailed numerous conferences, the decisions to adopt a Cyrillic alphabet and introduce the mandatory study of Russian was made at the highest levels of Soviet government. The decision locus moved from the local to the center, which reflects an important shift in political power. But, as with all policy, the central government relied on the many layers of bureaucracy and especially on local institutions for full implementation. Having the majority of the Soviet people adopt the Cyrillic alphabet was not simply a practical means of getting the country to use one pragmatic writing system; it was also a way of denoting people as "Soviet."

The decades of the 1950s–1970s were spent standardizing the language, with linguists focusing on stabilizing the literary language. The language conference of 1954 led to greater Turkmenification through the standardization of the Turkmen literary language—even if it was heavily Russified—in that it contributed to the cohesion of the nation. In the literary language the linguists aimed to bring together the language being taught in schools and the language of the press. The greatest contribution the conference of 1954 made to Turkmen identity, however, was in teaching the Turkmen people to "speak Soviet." Replete with Soviet-international terms (Russian) the Turkmen language now shared its modern vocabulary with the other Soviet languages.

Much of all this was reversed in the earliest years of independence (after 1991) when President Saparmurat Nyýazow changed the alphabet back from Cyrillic to a Latin-based script in part to move away from Russia and become closer with Turkey. Nyýazow, who took the name Türkmenbaşy (Leader of all Turkmen), sought to organize society according to ethnolinguistic criteria. Aşgabat also undertook nation building, which institutionalized the definitions of peoples. The state defined people as Turkmen or "Russian"—an imperfect definition, to be sure—as it sought to categorize people and to do it all for the convenience and benefit of the state.[3] Nyýazow politicized the language, declaring in 2000 that he wanted to see "the complete and universal introduction" of the Turkmen language in public life. The Russian language, which had held the higher status, was demoted as use of Turkmen in public spheres surged.

There were massive education reforms under Nyýazow, many of which drove parents to send their children abroad to study or to enroll them in Turkmenistan's "Turkish" schools. For example, by 2002 the Ministry of Education completed the transition from a ten-year to a nine-year system of education. Parents and teachers were distraught over what they believed was going to be a "lost generation" of uneducated students. Meanwhile, ironically, Nyýazow had labeled those same children the "Learned Generation [*Bilimli Nesil*]." These changes in education coincided with demands that all state employees demonstrate knowledge of Turkmen. An estimated twelve thousand teachers, largely representative of non-Turkmen ethnic groups such as Russians, Armenians, and Uzbeks, were dismissed from their positions between 1999 and 2002. By 2005 more than two hundred thousand ethnic Russians had left Turkmenistan.[4]

Although Turkmenistan's political leadership and intellectuals differed in composition and perspective over the years, they have projected a consistent interest in making their populace literate in order to become modern. Both of those terms—"literate" and "modern"—have meant different things to each of the different governments. Turkmen identified cultural transformation as the means by which they could become a modern, progressive society. Literacy was key to conveying those values. Throughout the decades, Turkmen intellectuals focused on alphabet reform and language development as foundational to developing a literary language, which would aid in spreading literacy.

Power

Pierre Bourdieu expanded upon the economic concept of capital to include nonmaterial matters such as "verbal facility, cultural awareness, scientific knowledge, and educational credentials" as forms of currency through which one could gain power.[5] Cultural power has adapted as access to it changed hands through possession of knowledge, language, or ethnicity in each era. In some decades it paid to be Turkmen, in others it was more profitable to be Russian—or at the very least a speaker of that language. During the mid-Soviet years there was currency in speaking Russian and knowing Party doctrine. Being literate meant both knowing how to read and write and knowing how to deploy Marxist-Leninist dogma. But by the time of independence, Turkmen gained status at Russians' expense, leaving those who did not speak Turkmen unable to work or get an education. As Türkmenbaşy put forth his new programs one needed to become literate in his *Ruhnama* ideology as well to survive the system. Once again literacy was tied tightly to political knowledge.

Over the century examined here, power appeared in a variety of guises. For progressive Turkmen in the 1910s, the Turkmen language and schools were the sites for struggle (*müjadele*) over ideological dominance. Jadid-inspired Turkmen fought their battles in the pages of newspapers and in classrooms, with poetry, polemics, and in literacy courses. In the 1930s Turkmen—as so many others throughout the USSR—were caught up in purges, some of which focused on the cultural intelligentsia and temporarily put a halt to language work. In the 1950s linguists debated spelling, grammar, and language content without the massive purges of the 1930s. After independence those who spoke Turkmen held social power and those who did not lost it—as well as their jobs.

Early twentieth-century progressives challenged the authority of traditional Islamic clerics by expanding the social meanings of literacy and transforming access to knowledge. In the late twentieth century, President Nyýazow likewise claimed legitimacy of his rule through the semiotics of sovereignty (flag, anthem, and alphabet), while some members of society resisted by avoiding the new Turkmen alphabet.[6] In the early post-Soviet years, language and education reform would be among the greatest social concerns of Turkmenistan's citizenry. Some were empowered and others were disempowered due to language skills or access to education.

Local dialects, regional languages, and Russian at times vied for dominance while at other times amicably coexisted, in Turkmenistan as well as throughout the USSR. This meant that the languages in which people learned to read and write gained or lost currency according to political standards. Identity too was closely linked to the politics of language. Local sentiment reflected frustration with the status of Russian, based less on the republicwide use of Russian and more on its dominance in official arenas. Calls for parity between national languages and Russian were focused more on language status and prestige than on actual daily usage.[7] Appeals for change in the status of Turkmen during glasnost and after 1991 bore witness to the fact that the symbolic place of language and alphabet was just as important as actual language usage.

Modernity

Turkmen strove to make their society "modern" over the decades. Yet as political circumstances fluctuated, the parameters by which "modern" was defined—as well as the concepts of learning, literacy, and the power connected to each—were ever changing. Then and now there is no single definition of modernity. Indeed, for Turkmen the considerations defining "modern" and "modernity" shifted sufficiently that the very idea of what it meant to symbolize the modern Turkmen nation was often in flux. These fluctuations were connected to recognition of changes in the world and a reconsideration of tradition, faith in progress, a burgeoning trust in reason, respect for science, and possibilities for societal growth.[8] In short, the frequent upheavals in Turkmen language and education resulted from a continuously changing notion of modernity.

Literacy

It is important to consider multiple "modernities," and to consider the value of "literacies" rather than a single definition of "literacy." As James Collins and Richard Blot note, among anthropologists there is a "social meaning of literacy."[9] To understand what "literacy" means, we must place the term in the context of everyday life. Thus, the definition of literacy takes on different meanings as various ideologies surface. One point that remains consistent is that literacy and progress became linked in Turkmenistan.

Jadid-inspired Turkmen comprehended literacy to mean reading and writing for broad comprehension in the native language rather than rote memorization in Arabic or Persian. They were also concerned with universal literacy, which meant advocating for the education of women. During the Soviet period there was at first a partnership between the local Turkmen and the Soviets who had been working on literacy and education. The Turkmen were brought into the Soviet administration and were able to continue their efforts even into 1930. The state sponsored a military-like campaign to eradicate illiteracy. Literacy was now not only about learning to read and write but also about being ideologically cultured.

In the early 1930s, when Moscow reoriented power from the periphery to the center and purged the local intelligentsia, there was also a revision in the under-

FIGURE 12. Wedding registry in Aşgabat

standing of literacy. To the mainstays of reading, writing, and the comprehension
of Soviet ideology was added the need to know Soviet-international terms. In terms
of literacy, the second half of the Soviet period was taken up with this agenda. In
many ways this meant Russification of non-Russian languages. It meant that Soviet
peoples needed to be ideologically literate as well as able to read and write.

In post-Soviet Turkmenistan, under Nyýazow and Berdimuhamedow, language
and script were saturated with cultural capital as they were tied to sovereignty. In
the twenty-first century, rather than spreading literacy as they had in earlier eras
Turkmen scholars were now concerned with maintaining it. Literacy still meant
learning to read and write. Yet computer literacy was on the state's agenda and was
paid much attention, as Nyýazow promised to put a computer in every home. But
computer literacy never came to mean much as the state itself blocked citizens' access to the internet and in reality most people could not afford a computer. The
dimension of knowledge or cultural literacy that overshadowed everything was
Nyýazow's book *Ruhnama*. Students memorized it, faceless voices recited passages
from it on television, scholars referenced it in their works, and entire conferences
were devoted to it. Being able to recite a passage from *Ruhnama* was part of being a good and "literate" Turkmen in the "Golden Age [*Altyn Asyr*]." Rejection of
Ruhnama is part of being a good Turkmen in the "epoch of happy people of the
mighty state."

President Berdimuhamedow dismantled Nyýazow's cult of personality, but there are signs that he is developing one of his own. This is reflected in school curricula and events involving students such as *Çäre*. Politics and policy continue to shape public space and culture as language and education develop under Berdimuhamedow.

The principal lesson from this history is that learning and literacy were not just important markers of modernity, they generated it as well.[10] As Turkmen learned to become a nation, they did so largely through reading and speaking about what it meant to be Turkmen. Language, which was not an important marker of identity in the nineteenth century, had by the twenty-first century become the fundamental criterion for national identity.

Notes

Introduction

Epigraph: Vansina, *Paths in the Rainforest*, 251.

1. Doctors without Borders, *Turkmenistan's Opaque Health System,* April 2010, retrieved from http://www.doctorswithoutborders.org/news-stories/special-report/turkmenistans-opaque-health-system/, accessed 20 August 2016; Bruce Pannier, "Neutral Turkmenistan Chooses a Side in Afghan Conflict," 23 June 2016, retrieved from http://www.rferl.org/content/turkmenistan-afghanistan-neutrality-policy-punctured/27815538.html/, accessed 20 August 2016; Institute for War and Peace Reporting (IWPR), "Turkmenistan: Niazov Playing Havoc Again," 20 November 2005, retrieved from https://www.iwpr.net/global-voices/turkmenistan-niazov-playing-havoc-again/, accessed 25 November 2005; Catherine Fitzpatrick, "German Foreign Minister in Turkmenistan: 'We Share an Approach in Life,'" *Eurasianet*, 23 November 2011, retrieved from http://www.eurasianet.org/node/64575/, accessed 20 August 2016.

2. Here "modern" refers to a complex of economic, political, and cultural changes evolving initially in Western Europe but which quickly reverberated throughout the rest of the world with European imperial domination. Its meaning is not constant among the Turkmen, as political and cultural exigencies changed the demands put upon them and altered their values. The most persistent components of becoming modern were optimism, a desire to progress, and the attempt to find one's place in the world. On modernity, see Kotkin, "Modern Times," 111–64; Hoffmann and Kotsonis, *Russian Modernity*; Giddens, *Consequences of Modernity*.

3. Bourdieu, *Field of Cultural Production*, 54, 68; Bourdieu, *Language and Symbolic Power*; Bourdieu and Passeron, *Reproduction in Education*; Bourdieu, "Systems of Education," 338–58.

4. Swartz, *Culture and Power*, 1. Some of the many examples that could be cited for comparison include Ansari, *Modern Iran since 1921*; Ascoli and von Henneberg, *Making and Remaking Italy*; Berdichevsky, *Nations, Language and Citizenship*; Brenner, *Controlling Knowledge*; Ciscel, *The Language of the Moldovans*; Chatterjee, *The Nation and Its*

Fragments; Chen, *Modern Chinese*; Haeri, *Sacred Language*; Jusdanis, *Belated Modernity*; Rorlich, *Volga Tatars*.

5. Peyrouse, *Turkmenistan*; Šir and Horak, *Dismantling Totalitarianism?*; Anceschi, *Turkmenistan's Foreign Policy*; Sabol, "Turkmenbashi," 48–57.

6. Landau and Kellner-Heinkele, *Language Politics*, ch. 6; Edgar, *Tribal Nation*, ch. 5.

7. Edgar, *Tribal Nation*; Edgar, "Fragmented Nation," 257–72.

8. "Oguz" was originally a political term referring to members of the sixth-to-eighth-century Gök Türk empire on the Chinese border, whose name is attributed to an eponymous leader Oguz. It is also the name modern scholars apply to the family of southwestern Turkic dialects. Oguz arrived in the West after disturbances in Mongolia set off a chain reaction that led Turkic tribes across the steppe in search of pasturage. See Golden, "Migrations of the Oguz," 47–81. On Oguz transformation into Seljuks, see Leiser, *History of the Seljuks*.

9. That is, people who speak a Turkic language found primarily in Turkey, Azerbaijan, Kazakhstan, Kyrgyzstan, Uzbekistan, Tatarstan, parts of Russia, and western China.

10. *Rodoslovnaia Turkmen*; Bregel, *Khorezmskie Turkmeny*; Geiss, *Pre-tsarist and Tsarist Central Asia*.

11. Edgar offers an interesting and well-thought-out introduction to early Turkmen history in which she emphasizes the genealogical claims to Turkmen-ness. Edgar, *Tribal Nation*, 20–25. Edgar, "Emancipation of the Unveiled," 132–49, also offers a rich source for understanding Turkmen identity.

12. Edgar, *Tribal Nation*, 20; Irons, *Yomut Speaking Turkmen*, 40; Golden, *History of the Turkic Peoples*, 207–19, 221–25, 307. Turkmen remain mindful of their tribal and clan affiliations and are still expected to know three generations of ancestors.

13. Tekin, *Orkhon Turkic*.

14. Due to certain vowel requirements, it is more appropriate to speak of the Turkmen as using a Perso-Arabic script, but for ease of language and familiarity I will use "Arabic script" here.

15. Edgar, "Genealogy," 266–88.

16. For the discussion about "modernity," see Jusdanis, *Belated Modernity*; Duara, *Rescuing History from the Nation*; Chatterjee, "Talking about Our Modernity," 263–85; Mingolo, *Local Histories/Global Designs*; Çinar, *Modernity, Islam, and Secularism*.

17. Täçmyradow, *Türkmen edebi diliniň leksikasynyň sowet döwründe normalanysy*; J. Hudaýbergenow, *Türkmen diliniň emreli dialekti* (Aşgabat: Ylym, 1977); A. Geldimuradow, *Türkmen edebi dilinde wariantlaşma* (Aşgabat: Ylym, 1983); G. Kul'manov, *Geoklenskii dialekt turkmenskogo iazyka* (Aşgabat: Ylym, 1991).

18. For a description of where in Turkmenistan dialects and corresponding tribal identities are located, see Clark, *Turkmen Reference Grammar*, 18.

19. Täçmyradow, *Türkmen Edebi Diliniñ Orfoepiýasy*, 22.

20. Clark, *Turkmen Reference Grammar*, 16; Telephone interview with Turkmen linguist Yusuf Azemoun, 11 February 2017 (notes in author's possession).

21. Potseluevskii, *Dialekty turkmenskogo iazyka*, 28–30. I thank Adrienne Edgar for sharing this source with me. See also Clark, *Turkmen Reference Grammar*, 21.

22. Edgar, *Tribal Nation*, 149.

23. On discursive formations, see Foucault, *Archaeology of Knowledge*, 32–33. See also Calhoun, *Nationalism*, 3.

24. Dirlik, "Revisioning Modernity," 284–305. See also Lee, "Reinventing Modernity," 355–68; Eisenstadt, *Multiple Modernities*; Eisenstadt, "Multiple Modernities," 1–29.

25. Giddens, *Consequences of Modernity*, 177. See also Taylor, *Modern Social Imaginaries*; Kamali, *Multiple Modernities*, 19; Kaya, "Modernity, Openness, Interpretation," 44.

26. Findley, *The Turks in World History*; Khalid, "Being Muslim in Soviet Central Asia," 123–43.

27. Kotkin, "Modern Times"; Krylova, "Soviet Modernity," 167–92.

28. Dirlik, *Revisioning Modernity*, 291.

29. Rappaport and Cummins, *Beyond the Lettered City*; Bermel, *Linguistic Authority*.

30. Clement, "Emblems of Independence," 171–85; Tekin, *Orkhon Turkic*.

31. Hezretguly Durdyýew, "Türkmen Milli elipbiýi: taryh we tejribe," *Türkmen Dili*, 4 March 2000, 2.

32. Graff, *Legacies of Literacy*; Houston, "Literacy Campaigns in Scotland," 49–64; Johansson, "Literacy Campaigns in Sweden," 65–98.

33. Graff, *Literacy and Social Development*, 3; Graff, "Assessing the History of Literacy," 259.

34. Graff, *Labyrinths of Literacy*, 308–9.

35. Fishman, *Writing Systems*; Fishman, Ferguson, and Das Gupta, *Language Problems of Developing Nations*; Jernudd and Shapiro, *Politics of Language Purism*, 113–41.

36. Charles A. Ferguson, "Language Development," in Fishman, Ferguson, and Das Gupta, *Language Problems of Developing Nations*, 27–36.

37. Carron and Bordia, "Introduction," in *Issues in Language Planning and Implementing National Literacy Programmes*, 23.

38. Brass, *Language, Religion and Politics*, 23–43.

39. Bourdieu, *Field of Cultural Production*, 165. See also Coulmas, "Language Adaptation," in Coulmas, *Language Adaptation*, 2.

40. Fishman, "Sociolinguistics," 10. For earlier studies of language as a form of "social

power" (though not so named), see Ferguson, "Diglossia," 325–40; Geertz, "Linguistic Etiquette," 286–90; Labov, "Phonological Correlates," 164–76.

41. Bourdieu, *Language and Symbolic Power*, 55.

42. Bourdieu, *Language and Symbolic Power*, 166, 170.

43. Bourdieu, *Field of Cultural Production*.

44. Bourdieu, *Language and Symbolic Power*, 170.

45. Bourdieu cited in Khalid, *Muslim Cultural Reform*, 6.

46. Clement, "Changes in Turkmen Alphabets," 266–80.

47. Comte, *System of Positive Polity*, 2:213, wrote "language forms a kind of wealth"; Bourdieu, *Language and Symbolic Power*, 43.

48. Khalid, *Muslim Cultural Reform*; Kırımlı, *National Movements and National Identity*.

49. Dunlop, *New Russian Nationalism*, 16; Siegelbaum and Sokolov, *Stalinism as a Way of Life*, 25; Hoffmann, *Stalinist Values*, 45–56; Dadabaev, *Identity and Memory*, 24–26.

50. In 1987 Täçmyradow welcomed a long-awaited Russian-Turkmen dictionary published for schoolchildren. It was needed because those who studied in Turkmen schools were severely deficient in their knowledge of Russian. T. Täçmyradow, "Söz manysy sözlükden gözlenýär," *Mugallymlar gazeti*, 25 September 1987, 2–3.

51. Paul Theroux, "The Golden Man: Saparmurat Niyazov's Reign of Insanity," *New Yorker*, 28 May 2007, retrieved from http://www.newyorker.com/magazine/2007/05/28/the-golden-man/, accessed 31 January 2017.

Chapter 1: Jadid-Inspired Paths to Modernity, 1914–1917

Epigraph: Muhammet Atabaý oglu, "Okuw we Turkmen mekdepleri," *Ruznama-i Mawera-i Bahr-i Hazar*, 9 January 1915, 2. (In Turkmen, "Ylymsyz hic bir one gitmez. Korluk bilen galar.")

1. Baldauf, "Jadidism in Central Asia," 73.

2. On these points more generally, see Kotkin, *Magnetic Mountain*, 7; Kotsonis, "Introduction," in Hoffmann and Kotsonis, *Russian Modernity*, 1–16.

3. Mugallym Muhammetguly Atabaý oglu, "Näjure bolup şkollar açylandyr Türkmenler aralarynda," *Ruznama-i Mawera-i Bahr-i Hazar*, 31 March 1915, 2.

4. Khalid, *Making Uzbekistan*, 46. See also Allworth, *Central Asia*; Hélène Carrère d'Encausse, *Islam and the Russian Empire: Reform and Revolution in Central Asia* (Berkeley: University of California, 1988); Roy, *New Central Asia*, 41; Ulugbek Dolimov, *Turkistonda Jadid Maktablari* (Tashkent: Universitet, 2006).

5. Kurbanov and Kuz'min, *Ocherki po istorii*, 10–11.

6. In Turkmen molla indicates a man or woman with an elementary education who can read or recite prayers; a graduate of a mekdep. An imam is a prayer leader. An *ahun* designates a person with a higher education, a graduate of a *medrese* who probably worked as an instructor at one.

7. Communication with Gözel Amanguliýewa, Golýazmalar Institut (Manuscript Institute), 20 March 2002, Aşgabat; Medlin et al., *Education and Development in Central Asia*, 27.

8. "Shkoly Turkmen'," *Zhurnal Ministerstva Narodnogo Prosveshcheniia (ZhMNP)* 32 (1911): 168–71.

9. Kurbanov and Kuz'min, *Ocherki po istorii*, 9, 13, 14; Medlin et al., *Education and Development in Central Asia*, 29. Bringing together the material and spiritual worlds, *waqfs* were religious endowments that defined a property in perpetuity for a purpose serving the Islamic community. A donor designated the purpose and conditions before death in a *waqfiyya* or *waqf* document. The *waqf ahli*, or family *waqf*, provided an inheritance for the donor's descendants. *Waqf khayri*, the charitable or public *waqf*, supported such social institutions as schools, mosques, gardens, the poor, orphans, or some other facet of society that embodied a donor's intentions to reach his or her salvation in the hereafter through a pious act in this world. A school supported by a *waqf* endowment linked education to larger social concerns, identifying it as an important community entity. See Coulson, *History of Islamic Law*; R. D. McChesney, *Waqf in Central Asia: Four Hundred Years in the History of a Muslim Shrine, 1480–1889* (Princeton, NJ: Princeton University Press, 1991). The *waqf* became a symbol of Soviet social change when it was eliminated as a source of funding for schools. Keller, *To Moscow, Not Mecca*.

10. "Shkoly Turkmen'," *ZhMNP* (1911): 168–71; Bendrikov, *Ocherkii po istorii*, 58.

11. Kurbanov and Kuz'min, *Ocherki po istorii*, 52; "Shkoly Turkmen'," *ZhMNP* 32 (1911): 161; Nikolai Petrovich Ostroumov, "Musul'manskie maktaby i russko-tuzemnye shkoly v Turkestanskom krae," *ZhMNP* 1 (1906): 148.

12. It is worth noting that administrators were not thinking of nongendered individuals, but specifically boys. I thank Marianne Kamp for her comments on this.

13. Geraci, "Russian Orientalism," 159; Crews, *For Prophet and Tsar*.

14. Cited in Geraci, "Russian Orientalism," 144–45. Buddhist regions were also targeted after 1905, but Tolstoi primarily aimed "to penetrate the solid Muslim mass that was estranged from European civilization." Kreindler, "Educational Policies," 164.

15. Khalid, *Muslim Cultural Reform*, 86–88, provides information on the state-sponsored Turkic-language periodical *Turkistan wilayatining gazeti* and its editor from 1881 to 1917, Nikolai Petrovich Ostroumov, who had been a student of Il'minskii. See also Khalid, "Muslim Printers," where he discusses the press in Turkestan, noting that "*Turkistan wilayatining gazeti* was the sole forum for public debate" at the turn of the twentieth century.

16. Edgar, *Tribal Nation*, 31, citing B. A. Khodjakulieva, "Russko-tuzemnye skholy v Zakaspiiskoi oblasti (konets XIX–nachalo XX v.)," *Izvestiia AN TSSR*, seria obshestv. Nauk, no. 4 (1995): 13. I thank Adrienne Edgar for sharing her notes on this source.

17. Kurbanov and Kuz'min, *Ocherki po istorii*, 42.

18. Kurbanov, "Obuchenie." (All translations from the original language are mine, unless otherwise noted.)

19. Kurbanov and Kuz'min, *Ocherki po istorii*, 28.

20. Edgar, *Tribal Nation*, 31; Kurbanov and Kuz'min, *Ocherki po istorii*, 27.

21. Hezretguly Durdyýew, *Ýigriminji Ýyllarda Türkmen Dil Biliminiň Ösüşi*, 29, 30. Khalid, *Muslim Cultural Reform*, 83, writes that the local population in Turkestan "steadfastly ignored the new institutions."

22. Türkmen Döwlet Milli Arhiwi (TDMA) TSSR, f. 1, op. 1, d. 14, l. 150.

23. *ZhMNP* 32 (1911): 188–89.

24. Annagurdow, *Sowet Türkmenistanynda Sowatsyzlygyň*, 8–9; Kurbanov, "Obuchenie." There were 179 mekdeps in 1893. Bendrikov, *Ocherki*, 309.

25. TsGA TSSR f. 1, op. 2, d. 2778, ll. 47–48.

26. Rorlich, *Volga Tatars*, 88; Khalid, *Muslim Cultural Reform*, 89.

27. Rorlich, *Volga Tatars*, 88. Gasprinskii founded his first school in 1884. And while several well-known individuals had come before him expressing foundational ideas, there was no coordinated effort until Gasprinskii endeavored to treat the Muslims' societal problems on a grand scale and across the many Turkic peoples of the Russian empire. Allworth, *Central Asia*, 172; Uli Shamiloglu, "Formation of Tatar Historical Consciousness: Şihabäddin Märcani and the Image of the Golden Horde," *Central Asian Survey* 9, no. 2 (1990): 39–49; Lazzerini, "Gasprinskii's *Perevodchik/Tercuman*," 151–66. On Gasprinskii's attempts to stretch the movement across many Muslim peoples, see Kuttner, "Russian Jadidism and the Islamic World."

28. Edgar, *Tribal Nation*, 33. Gasprinskii and some Ottoman Turks promoted the idea that the many Turkic peoples should employ a unified literary language. Turkmen did not agree. On Ottoman Turks, see M. Şükrü Hanioğlu, *The Young Turks in Opposition* (New York: Oxford University Press, 1995).

29. Khalid, "Backwardness," 250.

30. Edgar, *Tribal Nation*, 33.

31. Täçmyradow, *Türkmen edebi diliniň Sovet Döwründe*; Söýegow, "Türkmen edebiyatında ceditçilik dönemi"; Edgar, *Tribal Nation*.

32. See Khalid, *Making Uzbekistan*, 36; LåleCan, "Trans-imperial Trajectories: Pilgrimage, Pan-Islam, and the Development of Ottoman-Central Asian Relations, 1865–1914" (Ph.D. diss., New York University, 2012).

33. Kurzman, *Modernist Islam*.

34. Muhammetguly Atabaý oglu, "Hemme işlerde Türkmenler başka milletlerden geridir," *Ruznama-i Mawera-i Bahr-i Hazar*, 6 February 1915, 2–3.

35. Böriýew on occasion published under his original name, "Böri," without the Russian ending.

36. Muhammetguly Atabaý oglu, "Okuw işleri we Türkmen mekdepleri," and "Täze okuw düzgüni," in *Ruznama-i Mawera-i Bahr-i Hazar*, 14 December 1914, 2, and 6 February 1915, 2.

37. Myratgeldi Söýegow, "Collected Works" (unpublished manuscript), 155. Alişbeg Aliýew was author of the first Turkmen textbook.

38. Kurbanov and Kuz'min, *Ocherki po istorii*, 38–40.

39. Täçmyradow, *Türkmen edebi diliniñ Sowet döwründe ösüşi we normalanyşy*, 215–25.

40. Throughout the 1920s, his works were performed at the Turkmen State Theater along with those of Karaja Burunoglu, Şemseddin Kerimi, Berdi Kerbabaẏew, and Ẏaradankulu Baraẏoglu, graduates of the new method school in the Turkmen village of Kaka. Myratgeldi Söegov (Söẏegow), "Tek Dramıya Edebiyat Tarihine Girmiş Olan Yazar: Ayıcan Haldurdiyev," *Bülten Press* (2001): 34.

41. Transcribed in Söẏegow, "Türkmen edebiyatında ceditçilik dönemi," 118.

42. Söẏegow, "Türkmen edebiyatında ceditçilik dönemi," 113–14.

43. Khalid, *Muslim Cultural Reform*.

44. Berdiev, *Ocherki po istorii shkoly Turkmenskoi SSR*, 5. At this time in the Russian empire, literacy was measured by self-reporting and only the ability to read. It was not limited to the ability to read in Russian, but in any language. I thank Ben Eklof for his help with this information. Today's Turkmen scholars doubt this low statistic but do not have the resources or the time to build a case otherwise. They currently spend their time on projects mandated by the state in support of a particular brand of nationalism.

45. Kurbanov and Kuz'min, *Ocherki po istorii*, 15.

46. Under the Russian imperial system the Turkmen were legally defined as *inorodsty* (alien), a term used to designate non-Russians in the empire. However, within Central Asia the term *tuzemtsy* (native) was prevalent. See Khalid, *Muslim Cultural Reform*, 74; Khalid, "Backwardness," 236.

47. Söẏegow, "Türkmen edbiyatında ceditçilik dönemi," 112.

48. Muhammetgulu Atabaẏ oglu, *Ruznama-i Mawera-i Bahr-i Hazar*, 13 January 1915, 2. See also Myratgeldi Söẏegow, article in *Bülten Press* 26 (2000): 4.

49. Söẏegow, "Türkmen edebiyatında ceditçilik dönemi," 114. Such medicinal metaphors were common in these years.

50. Öwez Muhammetẏar oglu, "Ẏeni usul," *Ruznama-i Mawera-i Bahr-i Hazar*, 3 February 1915, 1.

51. Myratgeldi Söẏegow, "Ilk Türkmen Kıtabı Yazarı: Alışbek Aliev," *Bülten Press* 1 (1999): 9.

52. He specifically references Aliẏew's textbook, which taught with the phonetic method that reformers wanted to see used in schools.

53. Mugallym Muhammetguly Atabaẏ oglu, "Okuw we Turkmen mekdepleri," *Ruznama-i Mawera-i Bahr-i Hazar*, 9 January 1915, 2.

54. Mugallym Muhammetguly Atabaẏ oglu, "Okuw we Türkmen mekdepleri," *Ruznama-i Mawera-i Bahr-i Hazar*, 9 January 1915, 2.

55. For the Ottoman case, see Evered, *Empire and Education*, 276.

56. Kurbanov, *Obuchenie v konfessional'nykh*, 41–42.

57. Lazzerini, "Ismail Bey Gasprinskii and Muslim Modernism," 26–27.

58. Mugallym Muhammetguly Atabaẏ oglu, "Okuw we Türkmen mekdepleri," *Ruznama-i Mawera-i Bahr-i Hazar*, 9 January 1915, 2.

59. Öwez Muhammetýar oglu, "Ýeni usul," *Ruznama-i Mawera-i Bahr-i Hazar*, February 3, 1915, 1.

60. "Sorag/Jogap," *Ruznama-i Mawera-i Bahr-i Hazar*, 9 January 1915, 4. I am grateful to Touraj Atabaki for bringing this form of polemic to my attention.

61. Myratgeldi Söýegow, "Orazmammet Vepayev," *Bülten Press*, no. 20 (2001), 1–2. Kerbabaýew was a Turkmen poet and author, and Wepaý oglu uses the Turkmen—not Russian—form of his name.

62. On the Young Movements in the Russian empire, see Atabaki, *Modernity and Its Agencies*.

63. Öwez Muhammetýar oglu, "Ýeni usul," *Ruznama-i Mawera-i Bahr-i Hazar*, 3 February 1915, 1.

64. Lazzerini, "Ğadidism at the Turn of the Twentieth Century," 153.

65. A. M. "Türkmenler ders okaň," *Ruznama-i Mawera-i Bahr-i Hazar*, 10 February 1915, 2.

66. Öwez Muhammetýar oglu, "Hormatly atalarymyz," *Ruznama-i Mawera-i Bahr-i Hazar*, 6 February 1915, 2.

67. Khalid, *Muslim Cultural Reform*; Rorlich, *Volga Tatars*.

68. Mugallym Muhammet Atabaý oglu, "Türkmen aýallarynyň zehini," *Ruznama-i Mawera-i Bahr-i Hazar*, 17 March 1915, 3; Kamp, *New Uzbek Woman*, 34.

69. From the Arabic, *milla* originally referred to a religious group. In the Ottoman empire *millet* was a legal designation for non-Muslims. By the twentieth century, *millet* in its Turkic form had begun to take on a meaning closer to "nation" in some regions. "Millet," *Encyclopaedia Islam*, ed. C. E. Bosworth et al. (Leiden: E. J. Brill, 1993), 7:61–64; Braude, "Foundation Myths of the *Millet* System"; Kamp, *New Uzbek Woman*, 34; Khalid, "Nationalizing the Revolution," 156–59.

70. Mugallym Muhammetguly Atabaý oglu, "Türkmen halkyna," *Ruznama-i Mawera-i Bahr-i Hazar*, 14 December 1914, 2; Mugallym Muhammetguly Atabaý oglu, "Okuw we Türkmen mekdepleri," *Ruznama-i Mawera-i Bahr-i Hazar*, 9 January 1915, 2; Mäneli Seýit Ahmet Durdy Işan oglu, "Ýaşulylarymyza, *Ruznama-i Mawera-i Bahr-i Hazar*, 17 February 1915, 2. Sometimes an author referred to the Turkmen people as the "Muslim people [*musulman millet*]." See Seýit Ahmet Durdy Işan oglu, "Ruşça-Türkmença mekdepler üçin ýazaýlan hatdyr," *Ruznama-i Mawera-i Bahr-i Hazar*, 27 February 1915, 2.

71. Mugallym Muhammetgulu Atabaý oglu, "Galyň jähetinden ýagny ynsan söwdasy Türkmenler arasynda," *Ruznama-i Mawera-i Bahr-i Hazar*, 24 February 1915, 2; "Habarlary," *Ruznama-i Mawera-i Bahr-i Hazar*, 16 January 1915, 2.

72. Nizami cited in Söýegow, "Türkmen edebiyatında ceditçilik dönemi," 116.

73. On *millet* among Turks, see Edward Allworth, "The 'Nationality' Idea in Czarist Central Asia," in Goldhagen, *Ethnic Minorities in the Soviet Union*, 229–47.

74. Muhammetgulu Atabaý oglu, "Täze açylan Türkmen okulu," *Ruznama-i Mawera-i Bahr-i Hazar*, 23 January 1915, 2–3.

75. Mugallym Muhammetgulu Atabaý oglu, "Galyň jähetinden ýagny ynsan söwdasy Türkmenler arasynda," *Ruznama-i Mawera-i Bahr-i Hazar*, 24 February 1915, 3; Öwezgeldi Mämmetgurban oglu, "Täze ýagşy adat," *Ruznama-i Mawera-i Bahr-i Hazar*, 13 March 1915, 2. See also Myratgeldi Söýegow, "Şair we nesirji," *Mugallymlar gazeti*, 26 November 1997, 3.

76. Mugallym Muhammet Atabaý oglu, "Türkmen aýallarynyň zehini," *Ruznama-i Mawera-i Bahr-i Hazar*, 17 March 1915, 3.

77. Edgar, "Emancipation of the Unveiled"; Northrop, *Veiled Empire*; Kamp, *New Uzbek Woman*.

78. Molla Sabyr Söýün, "Galyň," *Ruznama-i Mawera-i Bahr-i Hazar*, 6 March 1915, 2.

79. Mämetgurban oglu, "Täze ýagşy adat," *Ruznama-i Mawera-i Bahr-i Hazar*, 13 March 1915, 2.

80. Touraj Atabaki, "Enlightening the People: The Practice of Modernity in Central Asia and Its Trans-Caspian Dependencies," in *Central Asia on Display: Proceedings of the VII. Conference of the European Society for Central Asian Studies,* ed. Gabriele Rasuly-Palesczek and Julia Katschnig (Vienna: Lit Verlag, 2004), 127.

81. Lazzerini, "Gasprinskii's *Perevodchik/Tercuman*," 145.

82. Lazzerini, "Gasprinskii and Muslim Modernism," 173–74.

83. I. A. Beliaev was the first editor, and when he left Transcaspia after the February 1917 Revolution, A. C. Aliev took over. A. Tsvetkov edited the Persian-language pages. The paper is also known by a Russian title, *Zakaspiiskaia Tuzemnaia,* although only tiny sections from the editor were printed in Russian.

84. Mugallym Muhammetguly Atabaý oglu, "Türkmen Halkyna," *Ruznama-i Mawera-i Bahr-i Hazar*, 14 December 1914, 2.

85. Alyşbeg Aliýew, "Sowatsyzlyk," *Ruznama-i Mawera-i Bahr-i Hazar*, 3 January 1915, 2.

86. See Austin Jersild, "Rethinking Russia from Zardob: Hasan Melikov Zardabi and the 'Native' Intelligentsia," *Nationalities Papers* 27, no. 3 (2010): 503–17.

87. Articles did not report on traditional mekdebs or medreses.

88. "Habarlary," *Ruznama-i Mawera-i Bahr-i Hazar*, 20 March 1915, 2.

89. "Habarlary," *Ruznama-i Mawera-i Bahr-i Hazar*, 16 January 1915, 2.

90. "Habarlary," *Ruznama-i Mawera-i Bahr-i Hazar*, 30 January 1915, 2.

91. "Habarlary," *Ruznama-i Mawera-i Bahr-i Hazar*, 13 February 1915, 2.

92. "Habarlary," *Ruznama-i Mawera-i Bahr-i Hazar*, 20 February 1915, 2.

93. Gibb, *Arab Conquests in Central Asia*.

94. Fierman, *Language Planning*, 58.

95. Poppe, *Altaic Linguistics*.

96. Täçmyradow, *Türkmen edebi diliniň Sovet*.

97. "Habarlary," *Ruznama-i Mawera-i Bahr-i Hazar*, 16 January 1915, 2.

98. "Türkmen Bilim Heýatynyň Türkmen imlasy hakyndaky karary," *Türkmen Ili* 5–6 (1923): 51–52. On the various Turkic groups, see Heyd, *Language Reform*; Rorlich, *Volga Tatars*; Fierman, *Language Planning*; Altstadt, *Azerbaijani Turks*; Lazzerini, "Gasprinskii's *Perevodchik/Tercuman*."

99. John W. Slocum, "Who and When Were the *Inorodsty*? The Evolution of the Category of 'Aliens' in Imperial Russia," *Russian Review* 57, no. 2 (1998): 173–90.

100. Khalid, *Muslim Cultural Reform*, 211.

101. See Khalid, *Muslim Cultural Reform*, especially 134–36.

Chapter 2: Partners in Progress

Epigraph: E. Jumayýew, "Türkmeniň edebi dilini kontrrevolutsion milletçileriň täsirinden arassalamaly," *Sowet Türkmenistany*, 5 October 1937, 2.

1. Iğmen, *Speaking Soviet with an Accent*, 147n3. See also Figes and Kolonitskii, *Interpreting the Russian Revolution*; Gorham, *Speaking in Soviet Tongues*; Kenez, *Propaganda State*; Rabinowitch, *Bolsheviks in Power*. I follow Sheila Fitzpatrick in her use of terms according to the group and period under discussion, which she explains in *The Cultural Front*, 1. She writes, "Until 1918 the Communists were known as Bolsheviks, but continued to use both terms throughout the 1920s and 1930s. Both terms were used in the 1920s, but in the 1930s the term 'Communist' was used in most contexts."

2. For documents on literacy among Turkmen in the Russian empire, see Rossiiski Gosudarstvennyi Arkhiv Sotsial'no-politicheskoi Istorii (RGASPI) f. 122, op. 1, d. 58, l. 131; Gosudarstvennyi Arkhiv Rossiisskoi Federatsii (GARF) f. 1235, op. 93, d. 583a, ll. 30, 30ob; f. 130, op. 3, d. 178, ll. 27, 27ob.

3. Slezkine, "USSR as a Communal Apartment." See also Suny, *Revenge of the Past*; Brubaker, *Nationalism Reframed*; Smith, *Bolsheviks and the National Question*; Simon, *Nationalism and Policy*; Martin, *Affirmative Action Empire*. Experts created a lexicon to define ethnic groups according to their perceived stage of historical development: *narodnost'* (people), *natsional'nost'* (nationality), and *natsiia* (nation). On this see Slezkine, *Artic Mirrors*; Hirsch, *Empire of Nations*.

4. Annagurdow, *Ocherki po istorii likvidatsii negramotnosti v sovetskom turkmenistane* (Aşgabat, 1961), 43.

5. As Martin, *Affirmative Action Empire*, 127, points out, the Party's label of certain ethnic groups as "culturally backward" corresponds perfectly with official 1926 literacy rates, which show Turkmen at only 2.3 percent literacy. This categorization of the Turkmen as among the "culturally backward" peoples was officially confirmed in 1932 when the Commissariat of Education listed them among ninety-seven culturally backward Soviet nationalities. See "Ob udarnom kul'obsluzhivanii otstalykh natsional'nostei," *Biulleten' narodnogo komissariata po prosveshcheniiu RSFSR* 5 (1932): 13–14.

6. Lenin from Kenez, "Liquidating Illiteracy," 173. Lenin is known to have underscored this point with his comment that "An illiterate person . . . [finds] himself outside of politics,

he needs first to learn the alphabet. There cannot be any politics without [literacy]. Without it there is only gossip, fairy-tales, and prejudices, but no politics." D. Korkmasov, "Ot alfavita—k literturnomy iazyku," *Revoliutsiia i natsional'nosti* 9 (1935): 34.

7. See Khalid, *Nationalizing the Revolution*, 145–62, for an overview of Jadidism and a powerful version of this argument, with emphasis on Jadids who lived in what is today's Uzbekistan. See also Hirsch, *Empire of Nations*, 5–60.

8. Khalid, "Backwardness," 232.

9. Altstadt, *Culture in Soviet Azerbaijan*, 63.

10. See Peterson, *Power of Words*; Wagner, *Literacy, Culture, and Development*; Hirshon with Butler, *Teach Them to Read*; Miller, *Between Struggle and Hope*.

11. *Istoriia Sovetskogo Turkmenistana: chast' pervaia (1917–1937)* (Aşgabat: Ylym, 1970), 12–139; Pipes, *Soviet Union*, 180–81; Tod, "Malleson Mission," 53.

12. With delimitation, Turkmenistan became a political entity on a par with Russia, Azerbaijan, and other Soviet Socialist Republics (SSRs). On the national delimitation, see Haugen, *National Republics*; Sabol, "Creation of Soviet Central Asia"; Vaidyanath, *Soviet Central Asian Republics*. On the drawing of borders, the role of local elites, and ethnicity, see Hirsch, *Empire of Nations*, esp. ch. 4. See also Keller, "Central Asian Bureau."

13. Numbers cited in Edgar, *Tribal Nation*, 66.

14. Edgar, "Genealogy," 279.

15. D'Encasse, *Decline of an Empire*, 24–25.

16. James Riordan, *Sport in Soviet Society: Development of Sport and Physical Education in Russia and the USSR*, 3rd ed. (Cambridge: Cambridge University Press, 1979), chs. 1–4; Goldman, *Women, the State and Revolution*; Gorham, *Speaking in Soviet Tongues*; Kelly, *Children's World*; Tricia Starks, *The Body Soviet: Propaganda, Hygiene, and the Revolutionary State* (Madison: University of Wisconsin Press, 2008); Vinokur, *Russian Language*.

17. Annagurdow, *Sowet Türkmenistanynda*, 9, 20, 34, 56; Grant, *Soviet Education*, 22.

18. Kenez, *Propaganda State*, 8.

19. Fitzpatrick, *Cultural Front*, 115.

20. Tagan Durdyýew, *Formirovanie*, 43, also 35–58; Fitzpatrick, *Russian Revolution*, 103; *Istoriia Sovetskovo Turkmenistana*, 215.

21. Martin, *Affirmative Action Empire*, 8–20; Slezkine, "USSR as a Communal Apartment."

22. Hirsch, *Empire of Nations*, 9. In 1923 the Twelfth Party Congress formally addressed questions concerning the numerous national minorities.

23. Simon, *Nationalism*, 13; Martin, *Affirmative Action Empire*, 12. "*Korenizatsiia* is best translated as indigenization. It is not derived directly from the stem *koren*- ('root' with the meaning 'rooting'), but from its adjectival form *korennoi*, as used in the phrase *korennoi narod* ('indigenous people')." Martin, *Affirmative Action Empire*, 10.

24. Korkmasov, "Ot alfavita," 34; Serdyuchenko, "The Eradication of Illiteracy," 28. See also Edgar, *Tribal Nation*, on korenizatsiia in Turkmenistan.

25. Smith, *Language and Power*, 3. For further discussion of these terms, see Pipes, *Soviet Union*; Rakowska-Harmstone, *Russia and Nationalism*; Simon, *Nationalism*; Suny, *Revenge of the Past*. Martin, *Affirmative Action Empire*, 5, translates *sliianie* as a fusion of nations, which Lenin said could be achieved only "through a transitional period of the complete freedom of all oppressed nations."

26. *Pervyi vseturkmenskii s'ezd*, 65; Eklof, "Russian Literacy Campaigns," 132. See Fitzpatrick, *Cultural Front*, 2, for definition of the "cultural front."

27. "1940-njy," *Sowatlyk ugrynda göreş*, 5 January 1940, 1. By 1940 the term "culture army" was written using the Russian word "armiia."

28. Kenez, *Propaganda State*, 75.

29. Eklof, "Russian Literacy Campaigns." The Bolsheviks assigned the responsibility of the liquidation of illiteracy to Narkompros; within Narkompros it was delegated to the Committee for Political Education (Politprosvet—Glavnyi politiko-prosvetitel'nyi komitet), created on 19 July 1920 and overseen by Lenin's wife, Nadezhda Krupskaia.

30. Eklof, "Russian Literacy Campaigns," 132. *Cheka likbez* from *likvidatsiia bezgramotnost'* was also used.

31. Terry Martin breaks down the Soviet institutions into those of soft and hard power. He categorizes those that were responsible for cultural production such as language and education as "soft" power entities. Hirsch, *Empire of Nations*, 12–15, uses "cultural technologies of rule" to describe mechanisms used by the state to strengthen state power through modern methods of centralization, to supplement coercive systems, and to advance the revolution. Examples of cultural technology would include the census, maps, museums, educational curricula, media, and language.

32. Serdyuchenko, "Eradication of Illiteracy," 24–28. Larry Holmes discusses the "assault on ignorance," in *Kremlin and the Schoolhouse*, 7.

33. The decree of the Soviet People's Commissariat (Sovnarkom) named "The Elimination of Illiteracy within the RSFSR population" announced that the commissariat was fighting illiteracy "for the purpose of allowing the entire population of the Republic to participate consciously in the political life of the country." Kenez, *Propaganda State*, 77. Furthermore, those citizens aged eight to fifty who could not read or write had a duty to become literate in either their mother tongue or Russian.

34. Serdyuchenko, "Eradication of Illiteracy," 23–24; Täçmyradow, *Türkmen edebi diliniň Sowet döwründe ösüşi we normalanyşy*, 155.

35. Annagurdow, *Sowet Türkmenistanynda*, 45; "Ot predstavitlia VTsK NA Iusupova to Kul'tprop TsK KP(b)T" (Materiýaly Ylymlar Akademiýasynyň Merkezi Ylmy Kitaphanesi, folder R, 176), 27.

36. Grenoble, *Language Policy*, 44–45. See also Edgar, *Tribal Nation*, 71–128.

37. Per the instructions of Lunacharsky, the focus on adult "*vospitanie*" (literally, "upbringing" but also referring to a general sense of knowledge and understanding of social norms) continued into the mid-1920s. *Pervyi vseturkmenskii s'ezd*, 65.

38. Annagurdow, *Sowet Türkmenistanynda*, 9; İğmen, *Speaking Soviet*; *Pervyi vseturkmenskii s'ezd*, 65–77; Turkmen State National Archive (Türkmen Döwlet Milli Arhiwi [TDMA]), f. 377, d. 1, op. 227, ll. 26–32.

39. Annagurdow, *Sowet Türkmenistanynda*, 44; Kenez, *Propaganda State*, 75.

40. *Direktivy VKP(b) i postanovleniia Sovetskogo pravitel'stva o narodnom obrazovanii, vypusk 2-i," Is-tvo Ak. Peknauk RSFSR* (Moscow, 1947), 118; Annagurdow, *Sowet Türkmenistanynda*, 13.

41. Ivanova, *Chto dala Sovetskaia vlast'*, 16.

42. From 17 July 1919 until 1926, Aşgabat (spelled Askhabad during the tsarist era) was called Poltoratsk after the Russian military leader P. G. Poltoratsk who fought in the Red Army on the Transcaspian Front during the Civil War. TDMA f. 377, op. 3, d. 49, l. 25; *Sovet Türkmenistanynyň medeniÿetiniň taryhy (1917–1970)*

43. Annagurdow, *Ocherki*, 49.

44. Annagurdow, *Ocherki*, 56.

45. *Nabat revoliutsii*, 15 February 1920, 2. The related news articles underscored that these citizens had consulted with the appropriate Soviet power and had submitted requests to provide the schools with teachers. In other words, these were officially sanctioned schools, and such successes suggested the power of the central state.

46. Twenty of the schools were located in cities or near semiurban areas (Poltoratsk, Mary, Tejen, Kranovodsk, Bairam-ali, Kaka), while the other sixty were founded in rural areas. Annagurdow, *Sowet Türkmenistanynda*, 49–51.

47. TDMA f. 377, op. 3, d. 49, l. 25; *Istoriia SovetskogoTurkmenistana*, 218.

48. Winner, *Kazaks of Russian Central Asia*, 140.

49. TDMA f. 8, op. 2, d. 100, l. 46; *Istoriia Sovetskogo Turkmenistana*, 216.

50. This was a far richer cultural array of cultural facilities than was available in the early post-Soviet years under President Nyÿazow. TDMA f. 25, op. 1, d. 161, l. 214; *Istoriia Sovetskaia Turkmenistana*, 220, citing TsGA UzSSR, f. 34, op. 1, d. 868, l. 14.

51. Fitzpatrick, *Cultural Front*, 133; Khalid, "Nationalizing the Revolution," 159. See also Edgar, *Tribal Nation*, 71, who comments that "*korennoi* [indigenous]" refers to the Soviets' efforts to use local languages and education to make Soviet power seem "homegrown and approachable."

52. Fierman, *Language Planning*, 59.

53. *Pervyi vseturkmenskii s'ezd*, 33.

54. GARF f. 1318, op. 1, d. 1698, ll. 1–7.

55. RGASPI f. 62, op. 3, d. 42, l. 24, cited in Edgar, *Tribal Nation*, 122.

56. *Pervyi vseturkmenskii s'ezd*, 37.

57. *Pervyi vseturkmenskii s'ezd*, 33.

58. *Pervyi vseturkmenskii s'ezd*, 70.

59. David-Fox, *Revolution of the Mind*, 3.

60. Smith, *Language and Power*, 46. GARF f. 1235, op. 118, d. 1, ll. 117, 131. Moscow

paid for translation of documents in Turkic republics in the local languages. GARF f. 130, op. 7, d. 147, ll. 234, 260.

61. *Zasedanie fraktsii tiurkologicheskogo s'ezd*, 1 March 1926, in GARF f. 5409, op. 1, d. 109, l. 49. Turkmen State National Archives sources reflect this parallelism as late as 1926, where documents were printed in the Turkmen language in the Arabic script and then translated in Russian in Cyrillic.

62. *Pervyi vseturkmenskii s'ezd*, 3–30.

63. The nineteenth-century Azeri playwright Mirza Fath 'Ali Ahundzadä (Akhundov) (1812–1878) proposed a reformed Arabic script, a Latin writing system, and finally a Cyrillic script as part of his modernity project. Ildeniz Kurtulan, "Azerbaycan'ın Abece Sorunu," *Defter* 15 (1990): 29–33; A. K. Rzaev, *Akhundov: Iz istorii politicheskoi i pravovoi mysli* (Moscow: Iuridicheskaia literatura, 1980), 29; *Stenograficheskii otchet vtorogo plenuma*, 80.

64. Altstadt, *Azerbaijani Turks*, 124; Smith, *Language and Power*, 126. The 1920s saw the first *formal* attempts to bring a Latin-based script to Soviet peoples, but this was not a new concept among Turks or Russians. As early as 1918, the Yakuts were the first to decide on a Latin-based script (introduced by Orthodox missionaries), but their geographic remoteness and religious differences prevented them from having much influence on other Turks. Bilal Şimşir, *Türk Yazı Devrimi*, 97–98.

65. *Pervyi vsesoiuznyi*, 254; Fierman, *Language Planning*, 213.

66. For example, Nariman Narimanov, *Zhizn' Natsional'nostei* 7, no. 1 (1922), 13.

67. Mamed Shakhtakinskii, "K reforme arabskogo alfavita," *Zhizn' natsionalnostei* 10, no. 4 (1922): 4; translation from Winner, *Oral Art and Literature*, 136.

68. From Shakhtakinskii's manuscript, "On Latinization," GARF f. 1318, op. 1, d. 1700, ll. 47–145.

69. Martin, *Affirmative Action Empire*, ch. 4, provides the best explanation and historical overview of "cultural backwardness" (*kul'turno-ostalost'*) as it applied to the Soviet "east" and "west." See also K. Sahatov, "Razvitie turkmenskogo iazyka," *Turkmenovedenie* 8–9 (1929): 80–81. The Latin script was at the time considered "international," and there were even discussions about shifting Russian to a Latin-based script. See Smith, *Language and Power*, ch. 5.

70. Mamed Shakhtakinskii, "K reforme arabskogo alfavita," *Zhizn' natsionalnostei* 10, no. 4 (1922): 4.

71. The Japanese experience refutes the validity of this propaganda and implies that literacy problems lay not with script but with social programs. Galantı, "Arap ve Japon Yazıları." One could also point to widespread literacy among Jewish men, who used a Hebrew script that shared many characteristics of the Arabic script. See Estraikh, *Soviet Yiddish*.

72. In the early 1920s the push for internationalism was strong, as the hope of spreading the Revolution beyond the former Russian empire continued. K. Boriev, "Latinizatsiia turkmenskogo alfavita," *Turkmenovedenie* 9 (1928): 13–14. In 1928 "international" and "Latinization" were synonymous with Westernization and did not necessarily mean Rus-

sification. However, just a year later, Europeanization did most definitely indicate both Russification and harmony between Turkmen and the language of the great October Revolution. See K. Sahatov, "Razvitie turkmenskovo iazyka," *Turkmenovedenie* 8–9 (1929): 80–81.

73. Muhammed Geldiýew, "Türkmen bilim komissiýasynyň düzülişi hem onyň eden işleri," *Türkmen Ili* 6–8 (1924): 70. Edgar, *Tribal Nation*, 73; Haugen, *Establishment*, 120. According to Edgar and Haugen the Turkmen Academic Commission began its work in 1922. I think the confusion comes from the fact that it gained permission to begin its work at the end of the year in 1921. Geldiýew always refers to 1921.

74. Khalid, "Nationalizing the Revolution," 151; Khalid is referring to a phrase used by the Turkestani Jadid reformer Fitrat in 1919.

75. "Türkmen bilim komissiýasynyň imla dogrusynda bolan kararynda göçürme," *Türkmen Ili* 6–8 (1924): 73–74.

76. Täçmyradow, *Türkmen edebi diliň Sowet döwründe ösüşi we normalanyşy*, 160.

77. Galiya medrese's records are well preserved and consequently we can know much about the education of Geldiýew and his generation of earlier Soviet reformers. The curriculum included history, mathematics, geography, ecology, chemistry, and physics. The library was reportedly rich and the students had access to newspapers in Russian, Tatar, and Arabic. Khasanov, *Galimjan Ibragimov*, 11–12, 90–123.

78. Muhammed Geldiýew, "Minnetdarlyk," *Türkmenistan*, 5 November 1926, 2.

79. M. Geldiýew, "Türkmen bilim komissiýaniň düzülişi hem onyň eden işleri," *Türkmen Ili* 6–8 (1924): 70.

80. Täçmyradow, *Türkmen edebi diliň Sowet döwründe ösüşi we normalanyşy*, 156; Hezretguly Durdyýew, *Ýigriminji Ýyllarda*, 24.

81. Täçmyradow, *Muhammet Geldiýewiň*, 8–9; Durdyýew, *Ýigriminji ýyllarda*. Neither the assistance of this Tatar nor the contributions of the Azeri Agabekov in any way diminishes the Turkmen nature of these reforms. Although not Turkmen themselves, and although Alparov encouraged reliance on the Tatar example, they clearly intended to aid in the Turkmenification of the language.

82. Garahanow had been a member of the Turkmen Academic Commission for about six months. *Türkmen Ili* 6–8 (1924).

83. Durdýew, *Ýigriminji ýyllarda*, 30–31.

84. Bourdieu, *Language and Symbolic Power*, 107–16.

85. M. Geldiýew, "Türkmenistan gazetiniň dili ýaky bizde adalga meselesi," *Türkmenistan*, 14 April 1925, 2; Edgar, *Tribal Nation*, 145.

86. A. Kh., "Edaralary ýerlesdirmek we termin meselesi," *Türkmenistan*, 31 October 1926, 3; Edgar, *Tribal Nation*, 145.

87. Balykçy, "Dil-Şiwe dogrusynda," *Tokmak*, January 1926, 3. Wepaýew published this poem under the pseudonym Balykçy.

88. See Edgar, *Tribal Nation*, ch. 5.

89. "Elifba meselesi," *Türkmenistan*, 12 January 1925, 2.

90. "Türkmenistan Respublikasynyň Halk Komissarlar Şurasynyň Karary," *Türkmenistan*, 1 July 1925, 1.

91. Fishman, *Advances in Language Planning*, introduction.

92. Kumuşaly Böriýew, "Türkmenistan ylmy konferentsiasyna degişli," *Türkmenistan*, 25 April 1925, 2.

93. GARF f. 5409, op. 1, d. 109; Şimşir, *Türk Yazı Devrimi*.

94. GARF f. 1318, op. 1, d. 1699, ll. 2, 6, 8, 9.

95. Smith, *Language and Power*, 124.

96. A. Samoilovich, "Novyi turetskii alfavit," *Novyi vostok* 5 (1924): 390. GARF f. 1318, op. 1, d. 1697, l. 11.

97. GARF f. 5402, op. 1, d.108; RGASPI f. 17, op. 113, d. 169, ll. 5, 180–85.

98. Martin uses the term "spontaneous" to describe Latinization, but records show that it was a years-long process with many influences. Martin, *Affirmative Action Empire*, 185. For example, see GARF f. 1318, op. 1, d. 1699, l. 2.

99. Şimşir, *Türk Yazı Devrimi*.

100. The Soviet Turks decided upon Latinization before those in the Turkish Republic did. Records from the congress show that the Soviets knew at this time, through the representative of the Turkish Ministry of Education who attended the 1926 congress, that Turkey was thinking about changing its writing from Arabic but that the government had not yet decided precisely which script it would choose. GARF f. 5409, op. 1, d. 109, l. 58.

101. *Zasedanie fraktsii tiurkologicheskogo s'ezd*, 1 March 1926, in GARF f. 5409, op. 1, d. 109, l. 49; *Pervyi vsesoiuznyi*, 277–80, 288–89, 305–9.

102. *Zasedanie fraktsii tiurkologicheskogo s'ezd*, 1 March 1926, in GARF f. 5409, op. 1, d. 109, l. 49.

103. L. B. Shcherba also took a patronizing tone, insisting that the example of the "cultured" Russian language could lead the Turks in the perfection of their languages. L. B. Shcherba, "Osnovnye printsipy orfografii i ikh sotsial'noe znachenie," *Pervyi vsesoiuznyi*, 176.

104. *Pervyi vsesoiuznyi*, 161–62.

105. *Pervyi vsesoiuznyi*, 166.

106. *Pervyi vsesoiuznyi*, 167–70.

107. *Pervyi vsesoiuznyi*, 327.

108. *Pervyi vsesoiuznyi*, 10.

109. M. Şahmyradow, "Dil hem imla gurultaý," *Türkmenistan*, 7 October 1925, 1.

110. *Polozhenie sovetov*, 12.

111. *Polozhenie sovetov*, 17. In addition to the speeches available from the stenographic records relating to the 1926 congress, there is a summary of the congress and the general aims of Latinization in a report made available to the Turkmen party leadership in the same year. This document also explains the Turkmen elite's understanding of linguistic points and the goals they identified as within the interest of Turkmen language development.

112. *Polozhenie sovetov*, 16, 26.

113. *Polozhenie sovetov*, 18–22; GARF f. 1318, op. 1, d. 1700, l. 92.

114. Bäşim Külbeşerow was there as a representative from Moscow; Şahamuradow's role is unclear. According to Smith, *Language and Power*, 125–35, Moscow allowed Baku to steer Turkic language planning in part because the central power saw the Azerbaijanis as an alternative influence to the Tatars among Turks. There is evidence suggesting that Moscow never intended Baku to become an autonomous source of policy or initiative, however. The central government nevertheless gave the Baku leaders a free rein in the days of Latinization. Agamalyoglu and the other planners attained significant influence over Muslim culture throughout the USSR.

115. *Vtoroi s'ezd Sovetov TSSR (26 marta–3 aprelia 1927). Stenograficheskii otchet* (Aşgabat: Turkmenskoe Gosudarstvennoe Izdatel'stvo, 1927), 4–13.

116. The Central Committee was responsible to Turkmenistan's lead political and governmental body, the Central Executive Committee (TSSR TsIK). Potseluevskii, *Dialekty turkmenskogo iazyka*, 17.

117. Potseluevskii, "Lingvisticheskaia ekspeitsiia GUS'a," 28; V.A. Uspenskii, "Muzykal'no-etnograficheskaia ekspeditsiia k iomudam i goklenam (dokladnaia zapiska Narodnomu Komissaru Prosveshch TSSR)," *Turkmenovedenie* 6, no. 2 (1928): 29.

118. "Harplar latynlaşdyrýarys," *Türkmenistan*, 29 June 1927, 1.

119. Muhammed Geldiýew, "Täze elipbiýiniň kä bir yazuw düzginleri dogrusynda düşündirme," *Gyzyl ýol* 1 (1928): 2–3. The committee did sanction the creation of one new letter, ə [ä], noting that it was used not only in the Turkmen but in all Turkic languages.

120. "Latyn esasynda kabul edilen Turkmen elifbasy," *Türkmenistan*, 30 June 1927, 1; Täçmyradow, *Türkmen edebi diliň Sowet döwründe ösüşi we normalanyşy*, 167.

121. *Stenograficheskii otchet pervogo plenuma*, 57.

122. *Stenograficheskii otchet pervogo plenuma*, 58.

123. *Stenograficheskii otchet pervogo plenuma*, 59.

124. *Polozhenie sovetov*, 29. GARF f. 1235, op. 123, d. 19, ll. 32–57.

125. Fierman, *Language Planning*, 84–85.

126. From the letter from the Turkmen Academic Council TSSR, 13 July 1926, no. 4574, cited in *Polozhenie sovetov*, 25.

127. GARF f. 3316, op. 19, d. 842, l. 33.

128. At the 1927 Turcological conference it was suggested that only 2–5 percent of the estimated population of one million Turkmen were literate. This estimate is far too low and was probably designed to make progress in the new script look like enormous growth. It is similarly asserted as the key to the success of Latinization in the Turkish Republic, 1928. Fierman, *Language Planning*, 97.

129. *Stenograficheskii otchet pervogo plenuma*, 57.

130. *Stenograficheskii otchet pervogo plenuma*, 146.

131. Kazakh actually did preserve vowel harmony.

132. *Stenograficheskii otchet pervogo plenuma*, 113, 127.

133. *Stenograficheskii otchet pervogo plenuma*, 128.

134. Smith, *Language and Power*, 72.

135. *Stenograficheskii otchet pervogo plenuma*, 144.

136. *Stenograficheskii otchet pervogo plenuma*, 147.

137. *Stenograficheskii otchet pervogo plenuma*, 149.

138. *Stenograficheskii otchet vtorogo plenuma*, 45.

139. *Stenograficheskii otchet vtorogo plenuma*, 47.

140. GARF f. 3316, op. 22, d. 62, ll. 3–5.

141. *Stenograficheskii otchet vtorogo plenuma*, 141.

142. Fierman, *Language Planning*, 98–110.

143. *Stenograficheskii otchet vtorogo plenuma*, 81.

144. *Stenograficheskii otchet vtorogo plenuma*, 39.

145. *Stenograficheskii otchet vtorogo plenuma*, 223–24. The 1928 plenum also demanded that the TSSR begin teaching its national minorities in the Latin script. The TsIK SSSR was, for example, responsible for ordering all medical personnel to adopt the Latin script, for ordering typeset letters and symbols and typewriters from abroad, and publishing laws in the new script. GARF f. 3316, op. 13, d. 11, ll. 197–98. Individual language reformers were concerned with daily, local successes. Böriýew announced that Turkmenistan wished that the "all-union committee would be concerned with securing typewriters for our republic. We have not a single typewriter but we soon will want our institutions to write outgoing papers in the Latin alphabet." *Stenograficheskii otchet vtorogo plenuma*, 55. See complaints about the delay in the use of typeface in state organs. "Vypusk alfavita nado uskorit,'" *Turkmenskaia iskra*, 19 January 1928, 3.

146. *Polozhenie sovetov*, 6–7, 8–9.

147. GARF f. 3316, op. 28, d. 769, l. 198.

148. GARF f. 3316, op. 42, d. 164, ll. 78–79; David-Fox, *Revolution of the Mind*, 4.

149. Fitzpatrick, *Cultural Revolution*, 8–40; David-Fox, "What Is Cultural Revolution?"; Hirsch, *Empire of Nations*, ch. 5.

150. *Postanovleniia 3-go vseturkmenskogo s'ezda sovetov*, 19.

151. Fitzpatrick, *Cultural Revolution*, 25.

152. Gail Warshofsky Lapidus writes that "the Cultural Revolution coincided with a dramatic shift in educational policy." See "Educational Strategies," 80.

153. Eklof, "Russian Literacy Campaigns," 139. *Sowatlylyk ugrunda göreş* contains articles related to this. See also Fierman, *Language Planning*, 143; and Arnove and Graff, *National Literacy Campaigns*, for other case studies.

154. Fierman, *Language Planning*, 108; Eklof, "Russian Literacy Campaigns," 139 (in this same volume see comparable brigades and militarized literacy campaigns in Cuba and Nicaragua).

155. *Stenograficheskii otchet vtorogo plenuma*, 139.

156. *Stenograficheskii otchet vtorogo plenuma*, 140–41.

157. ARAN f. 676, op. 1, d. 40, l. 8. This was especially true in comparison to Tatar and Uzbek communities, where the Party's resentment of clergy was intense. See also GARF f. 3316, op. 4, d. 151, ll. 9–31.

158. *Stenograficheskii otchet vtorogo plenuma*, 117.

159. Potseluevskii, "Lingvisticheskaia ekspeitsiia GUS'a," 28; V. A. Uspenskii, "Muzykal'no-etnograficheskaia ekspeditsiia k iomudam i goklenam (dokladnaia zapiska Narodnomu Komissaru Prosveshch TSSR)," *Turkmenovedenie* 6, no. 2 (1928): 29. GUS would later be renamed Turkmenkul't.

160. Potseluevskii, "Iazykovoe stroitel'stvo Turkmenii."

161. Blackwell, *Tradition and Society*, provides examples of songs and poetry.

162. Böriýew created nearly five thousand examples of terms and usage; Begjanow and Ýakuwyew collected works from fishermen and tribes on the west coast; all then turned his or her work over to Samoilovich who collected words for the Turkmen-Russian Dictionary.

163. Potseluevskii, "Dil we edebiýat ugrunda"; Potseluevskii, "Lingvisticheskaia ekspeditsiia GUS'a"; Potseluevskii, "Razvitie Turkmenskogo iazyka"; K. Sahatov, "Razvitie turkmenskogo iazyka," *Turkmenvodenie* 5–6 (1931): 17–18; and *Turkmenovedenie* throughout.

164. "1929 god Ianvar'–Fevral,'" *Dnevnik Turkmenkul'ta* (February–March 1930).

165. Materiýaly Ylymlar Akademiýasynyn Merkezi Ylmy Kitaphanesi, folder R, 176; Potseluevskii, "Iazykovoe stroitel'stvo Turkmenii," 44.

166. Azymow and Söýegow, "Türkmen Elipbiýi," 69–77.

167. Azymow and Söýegow, "Türkmen Elipbiýi," 18–50.

168. Geldiýew and Alparow, *Türkmen diliň grammatykasy*, 16–17.

169. *Zasedaniia VTsIK NTA, 22–24 July 1928*, in GARF f. 1235, op. 123, d. 19, l. 27.

170. *Zasedaniia VTsIK NTA*, 217, in GARF f. 1235, op. 123, d. 19, l. 27.

171. *Zasedaniia VTsIK NTA*, 217.

172. Perhaps the first unnamed voice from the audience is Geldiýew's.

173. Geldiýew and Alparow, *Türkmen diliň grammatykasy*, 11. The authors explain how a common Turkic language evolved into many because of the different historical experiences and the geographic spread of Turkmen.

174. ARAN f. 676, op. 1, d. 40, ll. 6–8.

175. ARAN f. 676, op. 1, d. 40, l. 26.

176. ARAN f. 676, op. 1, d. 40, l. 26.

177. Narkompros had special responsibilities to ensure the thoroughness of the transition by establishing summer courses to prepare village teachers and to oversee the transition among first and second grades, in village and city schools, by 1 September 1928 but for third and fourth grades by 1 January 1929. *Zasedania komiteta po provedeniiu novogoturkmenskogo alfavita ot 11 mart 1928 g.*, in ARAN f. 676, op. 1, d. 40, l. 26.

178. ARAN f. 676, op. 1, d. 40, l. 26ob.

179. ARAN f. 676, op. 1, d. 40, ll. 65–66.

180. GARF f. 5451, op. 13, d. 509, ll. 12–22, 52–53; Fierman, *Language Planning*, 99; Azymow and Söýegow, "Türkmen Elipbiýi," 70.

181. The central government sent monies to support these activities. See GARF f. 3316, op. 10, d. 22, l. 17. Literature was to change over by 1 October 1928, although newspapers had until 1 October 1929 to change scripts. *Postanovlennia TsIK* and *SNK SSSR 7 August 1929*, in GARF f. 3316, op. 22, d. 10, ll. 40–40ob; GARF f. 3316, op. 21, d. 902, ll. 1–2ob.

182. ARAN f. 676, op. 1, d. 40, l. 155–55ob.

183. GARF f. 3316, op. 42, d. 164, ll. 89–90; *Resolution of the Central Publishing House of the Peoples of the USSR, 20 January 1928*. On Ossetian language, Uzbek, and those of RSFSR, see ll. 91–103 (1927); on Moldovan ASSR see l. 80 (24 April 1928). All were resolutions of the Sovnats TsIK SSSR.

184. K. Iunusov, "Sostoianie latinizatsii v Turkmenii," *Revolutsiia i pis'mennost'* 4–5 (1932): 69–73.

Chapter 3: From the ABCs to the ABCs of Communism, 1930–1953

This chapter title comes from a passage in Smith, *Language and Power*, 151–52, which refers to the Soviet state's ideological shift that involved an emphasis not only on the political nature of literacy but also on its technical nature as modernization and industrialization set in. *Epigraph*: From a letter from Iusupova, member of VTsK NA, to TSSR's Kul'tprop TsK, in ARAN f. 676, op. 1, d. 1015, l. 27.

1. A literary language is one that differs from the vernacular in that it has been standardized by elites, usually scholars, and codified, usually with a dictionary. The concept was an important one in Turkmenistan at this time because the language was being used to link a formerly loosely connected and stateless group of tribes.

2. Potseluevskii, "Lingvisticheskaia ekspeditsiia GUS'a," 25–28; Potseluevskii, "Razvitie Turkmenskogo iazyka," 71–72; Sahatov, "Razvitie turkmenskogo iazyka," *Turkmenovedenie* 8–9 (1929): 80–81; E. Klemm, "V Institut Turkmenskoi kul'tury," *Turkmenovedenie* 5–6 (1931): 17–18; K. Sahatov, "Razvitie turkmenskogo iazyka. (V poriadke obsuzhdeniia)," *Turkmenskaia Iskra*, 29 May 1929, 2; Azimov and Desheriev, *Sovetskii opyt razvitiia natsinal'nykh kul'tur na baze rodnykh iazykov*, 11.

3. Paul B. Henze describes Cyrillicization as "devised [by Moscow] . . . deliberately made as different from each other as possible," in "Politics and Alphabets of Inner Asia," 382, 402. See also Ermolaev, *Censorship in Soviet Literature*.

4. Joshua Fishman, "Exploring an Overlooked Sociolinguistic Phenomenon," in *The Earliest State of Language Planning: The "First Congress" Phenomenon*, ed. Joshua Fishman (Berlin: Mouton de Gruyter, 1993), 2.

5. Spolsky explains that some critics see the standardized version of a language as a conspiracy of the established elite to maintain power. Spolsky, *Language Policy*, 27.

6. *Türkmenistan 1-inji ylmy konferentsiýasiniň edebi dil, adalga, hem imla dogrusynda çykaran karary* (Aşgabat: TSSR-TTEMK, 1930).

7. Söýegow, *On çynar*, 63–64. According to Edgar, *Tribal Nation*, 147, the Turkmen conference was scheduled to coincide with the fourth plenary meeting of the All-Union New Alphabet Committee in Almaty on 5 May 1930 so that the participants could move right on from Almaty to Aşgabat. See Gurban Gulyýew, "Birinji ylmy konferentsiasynyň ehemiýetli hyzmatlary nämeden ybarat?" *Türkmen medeniyeti* 6–7 (1930): 5; Kumuşaly Böriýew, "Türkmenistan ylmy konferentsiasynyň degişli," *Türkmenistan*, 20 April 1930, 2.

8. Smith, *Language and Power*, 141.

9. Smith, *Language and Power*, 151. Dimanshtein made such comments in 1933–1937.

10. *Türkmenistan 1-inji ylmy konferentsiýasynyň*, 8–10.

11. Kumuşaly Böriýew, "Türkmenistanyň birinji ylmy konferentsiýasy," *Türkmenistan*, 6 April 1930, 2–3.

12. See Medzhnun, "Turkmenskaia nauchnaia konferentsiia po voprosam literaturnogo iazyka, terminologii i orfografii," *Turkmenovedenie* 6–7 (1930): 7; Medzhnun, "Puti razvitiia turkmenskogo iazyka, *Turkmenskaia iskra*, 16 May 1930, 3.

13. Previously, in the Latin script, Turkmen had represented long vowels with two graphemes: *aat, latyyn*.

14. *Türkmenistan 1-inji ylmy konferentsiýasynyň*, 13.

15. *Türkmenistan 1-inji ylmy konferentsiýasynyň*, 13–15.

16. Böriýew, "Türkmenistanyň birinji ylmy konferentsiasy," 2–3.

17. Böriýew, "Türkmenistan ylmy konferentsiasynyň degişli," 2–3, translation from Edgar, *Tribal Nation*, 147.

18. *Türkmenistan 1-inji ylmy konferentsiýasynyň*, 16.

19. Since 1930 Turkmen has been written without markers of long vowels. This is to the disadvantage of newcomers to the language who have to guess where long vowels occur. Material from the period when long vowels were marked with two graphemes is perhaps the easiest material for a foreigner to read.

20. *Türkmenistan 1-inji ylmy konferentsiýasynyň*, 3–6.

21. Smith, *Language and Power*, 144.

22. Böriýew, "Türkmenistanyň ylmy konferentsiýasyna degişli," 2.

23. Böriýew, "Türkmenistanyň birinji ylmy konferentsiýasy," 2–3. See also Edgar, *Tribal Nation*, 148–53.

24. Böriýew, "Türkmenistanyň birinji ylmy konferentsiýasy," 2.

25. Täçmyradow, *Muhammet Geldiýewiň*, 31.

26. Edgar, *Tribal Nation*, 151; Böriýew, "Türkmenistanyň ylmy konferentsiýasyna degişli," 2.

27. K. Böriýew, "Türkmen dili," *Türkmen medeniýeti* 3–4 (1931): 40–44.

28. Gurban Gulyýew, "Birinji ylmy konferentsiýasynyň ähmiýetli hyzmatlary nämeden ybarat?" *Türkmen medeniýeti* 6–7 (1930): 5; A. Begjanow, "Garara garşy garar," *Türkmenistan*, 9 January 1931, 2.

29. Edgar, *Tribal Nation*, 153.

30. In 1929 G. Musabekov, chairman of the Central Executive Committee SSSR, edited by hand "On the new Latinization *of the Turco-Tatar alphabet*" to read "On the new Latinization of the *alphabet of the peoples of the Arabic script SSSR*." GARF f. 3316, d. 22, op. 10, ll. 17–17ob. Italics mine.

31. *Stenograficheskii otchet chetvertogo plenuma vsesoiuznogo komiteta novogo tiurkskogo alfavita* (1931), 251.

32. Fierman, *Language Planning*, 223; Smith, *Language and Power*, 138.

33. Fitzpatrick, *Russian Revolution*, 133–34, 158–59.

34. Durdyýew, *Formirovanie i razvitie*, 58.

35. Veselkov, "Pis'mo tov. Stalina," 44.

36. Veselkov, "Pis'mo tov. Stalina," 45.

37. Veselkov, "Pis'mo tov. Stalina," 46.

38. Veselkov, "Pis'mo tov. Stalina," 47.

39. Vorshev, "Osnovnye etapy," 79; Edgar, *Tribal Nation*, 124. OGPU became NKVD in 1934 and KGB in 1954.

40. S. Dimanstein, "Borba na ideologicheskom fronte v Srednei Azii," *Revoliutsiia i natsional'nosti* 12 (1934): 30.

41. Atakurzov had been a member of the Party since 1926. He had served in the Red Army. He was supported by Kuliev, who was a chair of the Regional Committee of Komsomol of Aşgabat City and a member of the CCCPT (Central Committee of Communistic Party of Turkmenistan) and a member of CCK TSSR (Central Committee of Komsomol of TSSR).

42. Vorshev, "Osnovnye etapy," 79. The epithet *Atakurzovshchina* parallels *Ezhovshchina*, a term referring to the terror wrought by Stalin's NKVD chair, Nikolai Ezhov, who led the Great Purges in 1937–1938.

43. Edgar, *Tribal Nation*, 127–28.

44. See Edgar, *Tribal Nation*, for a full discussion of the purges including the 1937 political purge of bureaucrats.

45. Bibijan Pal'vanova, *Tragicheskie 30-e*, 31. Edgar, *Tribal Nation*, 124, writes that intellectuals were arrested in May 1933.

46. Tagangeldi Täçmyradow, *Muhammet Geldiýewiň*, 10.

47. Edgar, *Tribal Nation*, 124–25 (Edgar gives further detail based on archival research); Vorshev, "Osnovnye etapy," 79; Pal'vanova, *Tragicheskie 30-e*, 31–32; Soegov, "Stranitsy iz istorii turkmenskoi," 133.

48. Söýegow, *On çynar*, 21–66.

49. Tillett, *Great Friendship*; ARAN f. 676, op. 1, d. 934, l. 49.

50. G. Gurtmyradow, "Türkmen dilinde terminologiýa işlemekligiň ýiti meseleri dogrusynda birnäçe söz," *Şuralar Türkmenistany*, 30 January 1930, 3; G. Gurtmyradow, "Dil we adagalarda arapçylyga we milletçilige garşy," *Şuralar Türkmenistany*, 5 April 1935, 2.

51. Täçmyradow, *Muhammet Geldiýewiň*, 46, citing K. Baýrammuradow, *Söwesýeň edebiýat ugrunda* (Aşgabat: Ylym, 1970).

52. "Rech Tov. Geldieva na tret'em vseturkmenskom s'ezde sovetov," *Turkmenskaia Iskra*, 12 May 1929, 1.

53. Söÿegow, *On çynar*, 55; Täçmyradow, *Muhammet Geldiÿewiň*, 30; Edgar, *Tribal Nation*, 156.

54. Allaguly Garahanow, "Nazariÿa meÿdanyna bol'şewiklik berkligi bilen göreşliň," *Medeni Ynkylap* 4–5 (1932); Täçmyradow, *Muhammet Geldiÿewiň*, 31.

55. Edgar, *Tribal Nation*, 155, refers to the attacks on A. Potseluevksii's *Rukovodstvo dlia izucheniia turkmenskogo iazyka* (Aşgabat: Turkmengosizdat, 1929). See also I.L-I, "Za bol'shevistskuiu podgotovku kadrov: ob odnom uchebnike turkmenskogo iazyka ego avtore," *Turkmenovedenie* 1–2 (1932): 44–50.

56. Edgar, *Tribal Nation*, 128; Söÿegow, *On çynar*, 82.

57. Pal'vanova, *Tragicheskie 30-e*, 106. See also Oleg Khlevniuk, "Les mécanismes de la 'grande terreur' des années 1937–1938 au Turkmenistan," *Cahiers du Monde Russe* 39, nos. 1–2 (1998): 197–208.

58. Söÿegow, *On çynar*, 54; Edgar, *Tribal Nation*, 127.

59. Unbegaun, "Some Recent Studies," 117.

60. Thomas, *Linguistic Theories*, 96, 94.

61. Smith, *Language and Power*, 88.

62. Edgar, *Tribal Nation*, 154. See also Smith, *Language and Power*, 80–120.

63. Smith, *Bolsheviks*, 97. For the debate, see page 1 of *Pravda*, 20 June, 4 July, 2 August 1950.

64. See Edgar, *Tribal Nation*, 153–58, on the influence of Marrism in Turkmenistan.

65. Even in archival documents Mamedow's name is spelled differently; sometimes as Mämmedow.

66. ARAN f. 676, op. 1, d. 1015, ll. 24–28.

67. Potseluevskii, *Izbrannye Trudy*, 79.

68. Edgar, *Tribal Nation*, 156.

69. Potseluevskii, *Izbrannye trudy*, 79.

70. Soegov, "Stranitsy iz istorii," 133.

71. ARAN f. 676, op. 1, d. 934, ll. 45–48, 74–88; M. I. Bogdanova, *Osnovnye voprosy terminologicheskoi raboty v Turkmenii* (Aşgabat: Turkmengosizdat, 1936).

72. Katerina Clark and Evgeny Dobrenko, eds., *Soviet Culture and Power: A History in Documents* (New Haven: Yale University Press, 2007), 249–50.

73. "TSSR Halk Komissarlar Sowetiniň başlygy ÿoldaş Atabaÿewiň Türkmenistanyň lingvistik Birinji gurultaÿ açylandaky aÿdan sözi," *Sowet Türkmenistany*, 21 May 1936, 1.

74. ARAN f. 676, op. 1, d. 934, l. 49.

75. ARAN f. 676, op. 1, d. 934, l. 50.

76. ARAN f. 676, op. 1, d. 934, l. 51. See also ARAN f. 676, op. 1, d. 934, ll. 48–54; Edgar, *Tribal Nation*, 161; Täçmyradow, *Türkmen edebi diliniň*, 64.

77. Kumuşaly Böriÿew, "Türkmenistaň birinji ylmy konferansiÿasy," 2; Geldiÿew, "Täze elipbiÿiniň kä bir yazaw düzgünleri dogrysynda düşündirme," *Gyzyl ÿol* 1 (1928): 2–3.

204 Notes to Pages 80–84

78. Muhammed Geldiýew, "Türkmenistan gazetiniň dili yaki bizde adalga (istilah) meselesi," *Türkmenistan*, 14 April 1925, 2.

79. ARAN f. 676, op. 1, d. 934, l. 54.

80. ARAN f. 676, op. 1, d. 934, l. 55.

81. ARAN f. 676, op. 1, d. 934, l. 77.

82. ARAN f. 676, op. 1, d. 934, l. 74–88.

83. As in the English "th" in "think" (unvoiced) and "these" (voiced). The letters "s" and "z" represent the unvoiced and voiced [th] in most Turkmen dialects.

84. ARAN f. 676, op. 1, d. 934, ll. 103–4.

85. Potseluevskii, *Fonetika*, 22–23.

86. ARAN f. 676, op. 1, d. 934, ll. 74, 75.

87. ARAN f. 676, op. 1, d. 934, ll. 74–78.

88. ARAN f. 676, op. 1, d. 934, l. 78.

89. ARAN f. 676, op. 1, d. 934, ll. 74–88.

90. ARAN f. 676, op. 1, d. 934, l. 121.

91. ARAN f. 676, op. 1, d. 934, ll. 45–48, 109–109ob.

92. Edgar, *Tribal Nation*, 163, 162.

93. ARAN f. 676, op. 1, d. 934, ll. 77–88.

94. Edgar, *Tribal Nation*, 161; ARAN f. 676, op. 1, d. 934, l. 76.

95. Gulnazarov, "Partiýanyň direktivini ýerini ýetermeýärler," *Sowatlylyk ugrunda göreş*, 17 August 1936, 2; Salyh Mämiýew, "Sowatly bolmaga uns bermeýär," *Sowatlylyk ugrunda göres*, 17 August 1936, 2; Nazar Esenow, "Okuçylary doly gatnaşdyrmaly," *Sowatlylyk ugrunda göres*, 17 September 1936, 3; H. M. Annaberdiýew, "Diňe 46 protsenti gatnaşýar," *Sowatlylyk ugrunda göreş*, 23 September 1936, 2.

96. Smith, *Language and Power*, 156–57.

97. ARAN f. 676, op. 1, d. 934, l. 101.

98. GARF f. 3316, op. 13, d. 27, l. 267.

99. "Türkmen hatyny latyn elipbiýinden rus elipbiýine geçirmeli (mugallymlaryň haty)," *Sowet Türkmenistany*, 6 January 1939, 1; "Türkmenistan SSR-niň hemme işçilerine, işçi aýallaryna, kolhozçylaryna we kolhozçy aýallaryna we intelligentsiýasyna Baýramaly rayon mugallymlarynyň ýüz tutma haty," *Sowet Türkmenistany*, 26 August 1939, 1.

100. H. Babaýew, "Türkmen elipbiýini täze elipbiýe geçirmek ösüşiň güýçli çäresidir," *Sowet Türkmenistany*, 22 August 1939, 2; P. Azymow, "Täze elipbiýe geçmek dili we edibiýaty has-da baýlaşdyrýar," *Sowet Türkmenistany*, 29 October 1939, 3; G. Sopyýew, "Rus elipbiýsi esasynda düzülen Türkmen elipbiýine geçmegiň ähmiýetli," *Ýaş kommunist*, 14 January 1939, 1. See also Täçmyradow, *Türkmen edebi diliniň*, 186–88.

101. Smith, *Language and Power*.

102. Fierman, *Language Planning*, 136.

103. Smith, *Language and Power*, 157. The change was accompanied by the refinement of spelling rules. Aman Berdiýew, "Täze elipbi okuw işini aňsatlaşdyrar," *Ýaş kommunist*, 14 April 1940, 2.

104. Annagurdow, *Sowet Türkmenistanynda*, 324–70.

105. Sähet Muradow, Bazar Gurbanow, Öweznaýazow, Hal Nepesow and Geldi Şukurow (all teachers), "Türkmen hatyny latin elipbisinden rus elipbiýsine geçirmeli (mugallymlar haty)," *Sowatlylyk ugrunda göreş*, 11 January 1939, 3.

106. Berdiýew, *Ocherki po istorii*, 117; Martin, *Affirmative Action Empire*, 307–8.

107. This is a theme common to literacy campaigns in a number of countries. See Arnove and Graff, *National Literacy Campaigns*.

108. Smith, *Language and Power*, 160.

109. *Programma po russkomu iazyku*, 3.

110. Carlisle, "Modernization," 224.

111. Kreindler, "Non-Russian Languages," 353.

112. Annagurdow tells us that in 1940 adult literacy in Turkmenistan was still estimated at only 75 percent. Annagurdow, *Sowet Türkmenistanynda*, 351.

113. Author's name illegible, "Medeni Revolýutsiýanyn Beýik Üstünligi," *Sowatlylyk ugrunda göreş*, 29 December 1939, 2–3.

114. A. A. "Haçan doly sowatly edersiňiz," *Sowatlylyk ugrunda göreş*, 5 January 1938, 2.

115. TMDA f. 377, op. 11, d. 375, ll. 8–10.

116. TMDA f. 377, op. 11, d.199, ll. 18–20; op. 11, d. 375, ll. 9–10.

117. GARF f. 5446, op. 1, d. 167, l. 87.

118. TürkmenTAG, "Türkmen hatynyň rus elipbiýsiniň grafigine geçirlmagine tayýarlyk," *Ýaş kommunist*, 10 April 1940, 4.

119. "Täze elipbiýe geçmek," *Sowatlylyk ugrunda göres*, 7 August 1940, 3.

120. "Türkmeniň täze elipbisini girizmäge tyýarlyk görmek baradaky çäreler hadynda. TK(b)P Merkezi Komitetiniň Býrosynyň 1940-njy ýyl 3-nji aprelde çykaran karary," *Sowet Türkmenistany*, 10 April 1940, 1.

121. Musaev, *Alfavity iazykov narodov SSSR*, 61. This made reading more difficult for foreigners, but native speakers were able to decipher meaning through context.

122. Berdiýew, *Ocherki po istorii*, 117. For details of the law on Cyrillicization and steps for implementation see *Chetvertaia sessia Verkhovnogo Soveta TCCP: 10–14 maia 1940 g.; Stenograficheskii otchet*.

123. Annagurdow, *Sowet Türkmenistanynda*, 319.

124. "Täze elipbiniň projekti dogrysynda düşündiriş," *Ýaş kommunist*, 4 April 1940, 3.

125. "Täze elipbiýie geçmek," *Sowatlylyk ugrunda göres*, 7 August 1940, 3.

126. Atanyjazow and Saparow, "Sowatsyzlygy ýok etmekige köp uns bermeli," *Sowet Türkmenistany*, 20 April 1940, 1.

127. A. Orazow (vice-editor of the newspaper), "Täze elipbiýi öwrenýärler," *Sowatlylyk ugrunda göreş*, 17 May 1940, 2.

128. Annagurdow, *Sowet Türkmenistanynda*, 350, 351.

129. *Istoriia kul'tury Sovetskogo Turkmenistana (1939–1970)* (Aşgabat: Ylym, 1975), 198; TürkmenTAG, "V.I. Leniniň eserleri Türkmen dilinde," *Sowet Türkmenistany*, 20 April 1940, 1.

130. "Stahanovit," 22 January 1939, *Sowatlylyk ugrunda göreş*, 3. Stakhanovites were exemplary Soviet workers who in the tradition of Comrade Stakhanov surpassed all quotas, working extra hard for the Soviet state.

131. "Likbezler opurlyşykda," *Sowatlylyk ugrunda göreş*, 28 May 1940, 1.

132. "Rus elibiýi Türkmen halkynyň medeniýeti has hem ösdirer," *Sowatlylyk ugrunda göreş*, 28 May 1940, 2.

133. Aman Kekilow, "Pikir alyşmak ýoly bilen. Türkmen täze elipbisiniň projekti hakynda," *Sowet Türkmenistany*, 11 April 1940, 1.

134. "Medeni ösüşde has öňe gideris," *Sowatlylyk ugrunda göreş*, 28 May 1940, 3.

135. Elissa Bemporad writes of a "straight-forward, rapid path to acculturation into the Soviet system," in *Becoming Soviet Jews: The Bolshevik Experiment in Minsk* (Bloomington: Indiana University Press, 2013), 4. See also Kirkwood, "Glasnost'," 63.

Chapter 4: Speaking Soviet

Epigraph: Conquest, *Nation Killers*, 129.

1. "Adalga meselese düzgune salmaly," *Sowet Türkmenistany*, 3 January 1951, 3; Täçmyradow, *Türkmen edebi diliniň*, 73.

2. Amansaryýew, *Türkmen diliniň lingvistik*, 11.

3. Kreindler, "Soviet Language Planning," 46.

4. To name a few, there were all-union conferences held in Tashkent in 1962, 1975, and 1979; in Baku in 1969; in Frunze in 1971; in Kishinev in 1972; in Alma-Ata in 1973; and in Yerevan in 1974. See "Türk dilleriniň dialektologiýasy boýunça bütinsoýuz maslahat," *Mugallymlar gazeti*, 12 June 1963, 2.

5. N. Altyýew, "Türkmen diliniň orfografiýasy we punktuatsiýasy hakynda," *Mugallymlar gazeti*, 24 August 1962, 4; A. Garryýew, "Türkmen alymlary hakynda ajaýp kitap," *Mugallymlar gazeti*, 21 December 1962, 3.

6. Amansaryýew, *Türkmen diliniň lingvistik*, 5–6; Täçmyradow, *Türkmen edebi diliniň*, 74.

7. Täçmyradow, *Türkmen edebi diliniň*, 72; A. Aliev and K. Böriýew, *Rusça-türkmença sözlük*, 253; Kh. Baýlyew, B. Garryýew, *Türkmençe-rusça sözlük*, 251.

8. G. Saryýew, "Türkmen täze elipbisi hakynda," *Ýaş kommunist*, 12 April 1940, 2.

9. Smith, *Language and Power*, 166.

10. Murra, Hankin, and Holling, *Soviet Linguistic Controversy*, 70, 86, 96.

11. Smith, *Language and Power*, 169–70.

12. Smith, *Language and Power*, 172. See also *Türkmen edebi diliniň terminologiýasy*, 5; Täçmyradow, *Türkmen edebi diliniň*, 86–87.

13. Azymow, "Türkmen dilçilik biliminiň käbir meseleleri," 4; "Adalga meselesini düzgüne salmaly," *Sovet Turkmenistany*, 3 January 1951, 2.

14. Täçmyradow, Türkmen edebi diliniň, 74; "Türkmenistan lingvistleriniň ikinji gurltaýyna taýýarlyk görülýär," *Sovet Turkmenistany*, 9 January 1951, 1.

15. Amansaryýew, *Türkmen diliniň lingvistik*, 5–6.

16. Amansaryýew, *Türkmen diliniň lingvistik*, 5.

17. Magtumguly adyndaky Dil we Edebiýat Institutynyň golýazmalar fondy, Aşgabat (Manuscript holdings of the Language and Literature Institute named after Magtumguly), no. 160, folder no. 10, 275–96, 300–318.

18. Amansaryýew, *Türkmen diliniň lingvistik*, 11; Azymow, "Türkmen diliniň käbir meseleleri hakynda," 11.

19. Azymow, "Türkmen diliniň käbir meseleleri hakynda," 9–10.

20. A calque is a word or phrase borrowed from another language by literal, word-for-word or root-for-root translation.

21. *Türkmen edebi diliniň punktuatsiýasy*.

22. *Türkmen edebi diliniň orfografiýasy*, 12–13.

23. *Türkmen edebi diliniň orfografiýasy*, 18.

24. M. Annakurdov, "Terminologia turkmenskogo iazyka i zadachi ee uluchsheniia," TSSR YA Magtymgyly adyndaky Dil we edebiýat insitutynyň golýazmalar fondy, no. 160, folder no. 10, 239, 300–305.

25. *Türkmen edebi diliniň orfografiýasy*, 11.

26. While there was a move back to Turkmen words in the post-glasnost era, linguist Professor Myratgeldi Söýegow explained that during the 1950s–1980s even commonplace words like "class" were written as *klas* instead of the Turkmen *sapak*.

27. Scholar N. A. Andreev discussed a similar concern regarding the Chuvash language. Because of simultaneous usage of Chuvash and Russian terms for international ideas, he suggested that the Chuvash literary language rely more heavily on Russian. Täçmyradow, *Türkmen edebi diliniň*, 87.

28. *Türkmen edebi diliniň terminologiýasy*, 12–13.

29. Magtumguly adyndaky Dil we Edebiýat Institutynyň golýazmalar fondy. Aşgabat, Turkmenistan (Manuscript holdings of the Language and Literature Institute named after Magtumguly), no. 160, folder no. 10, 300–305, 415–17.

30. *Türkmen edebi diliniň terminologiýasy*, 10–11.

31. This concept comes from Petrone, *Life Has Become More Joyous*, 1, stemming from "speaking Bolshevik" in Kotkin, *Magnetic Mountain*, ch. 5.

32. Amansaryýew, *Türkmen diliniň lingvistik*, 14. This was confirmed by the Presidium of the High Soviet of the TSSR on 2 April 1955.

33. Conversations with Dr. Bajan Çaryýarow, Turkmenistan's Manuscript Institute, Aşgabat, winter 2003 (notes in author's possession).

34. Azimov, *Orfografiia*, 6.

35. A. Mordinova and G. Sanjeeva, "Nekotorye voprosy razvitiia vladopis'mennykh iazykov narodov SSSR," *Bol'shevik* 8 (1951): 3.

36. Azimov, *Orfografiia*, 9.

37. T. Täçmyradow, M. Hudaýgulyew, and B. Hojaýew, "Türkmen Diliniň orfografik sözlük," *Sovet Turkmenistany*, 31 May 1963, 3. In 1958 there were 207 cinemas, 770 cultural clubs, and 932 libraries (with 2 million holdings). See Türkmenistan SSR-niň, 4.

38. Ornstein, "Soviet Language Policy," 125, 127; Kreindler, "Missed Opportunity," 262.

39. Kreindler, "Soviet Language Planning," 51; Bilinsky, "Education," 418; Yaroslav Bilinsky, *The Second Soviet Republic: The Ukraine after World War II* (New Brunswick, NJ: Rutgers University Press, 1964), 12.

40. Kreindler, "Soviet Language Planning," 55; Ýa. Tekäýew we O. Rejepow, "Rus dilinden Türkmen diline giren otnositel sypatlaryň we ahyrlarynda ýumşaklyk belgisi bolan atlaryň ýazlyşlary," *Mugallymlar gazeti*, 8 August 1958, 4; Nazarow, *Türkmen dilinde Rus alynma sözleri*.

41. William Fierman, "The View from Uzbekistan," *International Journal of the Sociology of Language* 33 (1982): 70–78. The town of Bagyr just outside of Aşgabat has a notable "Kurdish" community (author's field observations, 1997, 2001).

42. See Deutsch, *Nationalism and Social Communication*, 97–126.

43. Lapidus, "Educational Strategies," 105.

44. Anderson and Silver, "Equality, Efficiency," 1034. Bilingualism was defined as "knowledge of both one's own language and another, most often Russian." See Lewis, "Bilingualism as Language Planning," 76.

45. Kreindler, "Changing Status"; Carrère d'Encausse, *Decline of an Empire*.

46. Tsentral'noe statisticheskoe upravlenie pri Sovete ministrov SSSR, 181–201.

47. For 1926/1927, see Tsentral'noe statisticheskoe upravlenie SSSR, pt. 5, 134–43. For 1938/1939, see *Itogi vsesoiuznoi perepisi naseleniia 1959 goda*, 1962, 132. This dramatic increase in the number of students attending Turkmen-language schools was because, during korenizatsiia, there had been a program to build schools and promote the native language. This led to a growth of Turkmen language schools in these early years.

48. Tsentral'noe statisticheskoe upravlenie Turkmenskoi SSR, *Kul'turnoe stroitel'stvo Turkmenskoi SSR*, 76–77. In Aşgabat in 1980, 87 percent of the schools were Russian medium schools. See Lewis, "Bilingualism," 81.

49. Anderson and Silver, "Equality, Efficiency," 1022–23.

50. Lapidus, "Nationality Question," 103; Ornstein, "Soviet Language Policy," 135; Bilinsky, "Education," 425.

51. Kreindler, "Missed Opportunity," 261.

52. P. Azimov and A. Kurbanov, "Linguistics Work in Turkmenistan," *Turkmenskaya iskra*, 17 October 1957, 2–3, translated in the *Current Digest of the Russian Press* 9, no. 44 (11 December 1957): 30–31.

53. Bilinsky, "Soviet Education Laws"; Ornstein, "Soviet Language Policy," 126; Krushchev, *On Strengthening the Ties*.

54. Kirkwood, "Glasnost'," 64. Schools' choice was limited as it was essentially titular languages that were supported. In Turkmenistan this meant choosing primarily between Russian and Turkmen. However, there were a handful of schools in Uzbek and a few in Kazakh. In Turkmenistan there were no schools for such smaller minorities as Kurds, Armenians, Ukrainians, Baluchi, or Jews. This lack of support for some groups led to real grievances, which were expressed in the early 1990s.

55. Kreindler, "Non-Russian Languages," 355.

56. Kreindler, "Forging a Soviet People," 262; Kirkwood, "Glasnost'," 64; Bilinsky, "Soviet Education Laws."

57. Rywkin, "Religion, Modern Nationalism and Political Power," 276; Low, "Soviet Nationality Policy," 19; also Ýa. Tekäýew we M. Batyrow, "Ene diliniň we edebiýatyň okadylyşyny gowulandyrmaly," *Mugallymlar gazeti*, 21 August 1958, 2.

58. G. Sopyýew, "Türkmen elipbiýiniň kämilleşmegi," *Mugallymlar gazeti*, 23 September 1964, 2.

59. M. Annagurdow, "Tutuş sowatlylar respublikasy," *Mugallymlar gazeti*, 5 June 1964, 2–3.

60. "Programme of the Communist Party," *Pravda*, 30 July 1960, cited in Ornstein, "Soviet Language Policy," 129.

61. Lenin had asserted that no single language—and certainly not Russian—should hold the status of "state language." See V. I. Lenin, "Nuzhen li obiazatel'nyi gosudarstvennyi iazyk," in *Polnoe sobranie sochinenii*, 4:293–95.

62. Editorial, "Beýik Serdaryň doglan gününe," *Mugallymlar gazeti*, 17 April 1958, 2; Editorial, "Beýik Adam," *Mugallymlar gazeti*, 22 April 1958, 1; A. Rejepow, "V. I. Lenin eserleri Türkmen dilinde," *Mugallymlar gazeti*, 22 April 1958, 2.

63. Ornstein, "Soviet Language Policy," 129, 130

64. Vardys, "Soviet Nationality Policy," 325. For the differences between these slogans and concepts, see A. M. Abaeva, "Nekatorye voprosy razvitiia sotsialisticheskikh natsii v period razvernutogo stroitelstva kommunizma," *Izvestiia Akademii Nauk Turkmenskoi SSR* 6 (1963): 42.

65. R. Gubaýdulin, "Harplyk bilen hoşlaşyk baýramy," *Mugallymlar gazeti*, 3 February 1964, 3.

66. No author, "Rus we Türkmen dilleriň deňeşdirme grammatikasy," *Mugallymlar gazeti*, 21 October 1964, 4.

67. No author, "Iz istorii prepodavaniia russkogo iazyka turkmenskii shkole," *Mugallymlar gazeti*, 20 November 1964, 3.

68. Oleh S. Fedyshyn, "Khrushchev's 'Leap Forward': National Assimilation in the USSR after Stalin," *Southwestern Social Science Quarterly* 48, no. 1 (1967): 37. See also B. Gafurov, "Uspekhi natsionalnoi politiki KPSS i nekotorye voprosy internatsionalnogo vospitania," *Kommunist* 11 (1958): 10–24.

69. Vardys, "Soviet Nationality Policy," 325; Olcott, "Yuri Andropov," 111; Rywkin, "Religion, Modern Nationalism and Political Power," 275; Vardys, "Soviet Nationality Policy," 333.

70. N. S. Khrushchev, *O programme Kommunisticheskoi partii Sovetskogo Soiuza* (Moscow: Gospolitizdat, 1961), 90; Ç. Jumaýew, "Katalar Türkmen dilinde bolsady," *Mugallymlar gazeti*, 26 July 1962, 4.

71. O. Mürrikow and B. Akynyýazow, "Çaganyň gepleýşi diliniň düzetmek barada," *Mugallymlar gazeti*, 2 August 1962, 2.

72. Pennar, Bakalo, and Bereday, *Modernization and Diversity*, 176.

73. Berdi Kerbabaýew, "Diliň medeniýeti—uly iliň medeniýeti," *Edebiýat we Sungat*, 6 February 1963, 2.

74. He told readers he was so agitated by Kerbabaýew's article that he went to the newspaper's editor, submitted a rebuttal, and asked for there to be a public discussion on his assertions. When the editor of *Edebiýat we Sungat* did nothing, Annanurow turned to another newspaper: the official organ of the Turkmen Party, *Sowet Türkmenistan*.

75. A. Annanurow, "Ýoldaş Kerbabaýewiň dil hakyndaky makalasy," *Sowet Türkmenistan*, 16 March 1963, 3.

76. M. Hallyýew we A. Nurmuhammedow, "Rus we Turkmen dilleriniň deňeşdirme grammatikasy," *Mugallymlar gazeti*, 21 October 1964, 4.

77. Kreindler, "Soviet Language Planning," 52–53. For "cement," see Iu. Desheriev, "Russkii iazyk i razvitoe sotsialisticheskoe obshchestvo," *Russkii iazyk i literature v shkolakh SSSR* 5 (1977): 16; also Kreindler, "Non-Russian Languages," 356; Bilinsky, "Expanding the Use of Russian," 332.

78. Kreindler, "Missed Opportunity," 262.

79. L. I. Brezhnev, "Doklad L. I. Brezhneva o piaditesiatiletii Soiuza Sovetskikh Sotsialisticheskikh Respublik, *Kommunist* 18 (18 December 1972): 1, cited in Bohdan R. Bociurkiw, "Soviet Nationalities Policy and Dissent in the Ukraine," *World Today* 30, no. 5 (1974): 214.

80. L. I. Brezhnev, "On the Fiftieth Anniversary of the Union of Soviet Socialist Republics" (21 December 1972), translated in *Current Digest of the Soviet Press* 24, no. 51 (1973): 9.

81. Olcott, "Yuri Andropov," 105–6.

82. Lewis, "Bilingualism," 77.

83. S. Paşykow, "Rus dilinde uly söýgi," *Sovet Turkmenistan*, 10 April 1973, 4.

84. Kreindler, "Soviet Language Planning," 54.

85. Feldrugge, *Constitutions*, 98–99.

86. Kirkwood, "Language Planning," 2.

87. Desheriev, *Zakonomernosti*, 133.

88. Crisp, "Soviet Language Planning," 39.

89. This condition has implications for the conceptualization of the system as one of "bilingualism." Although this is the term used in Soviet literature and Western studies of the Soviet Union, we should instead think in terms of multilingualism, as there were many layers of languages throughout the USSR.

90. "Vsesoiuznaia nauchno-teoreticheskaia konferentsiia 'Russkii iazyk—iazyk druzhby i sotrudnichestva narodov SSSR' (Tashkent, Mai 1979 g.)," *Russkii iazyk v natsional'noi shkole* 4 (1979): 3.

91. Solchanyk, "Russian Language," 23.

92. Bilinsky, "Expanding the Use of Russian," 317; Solchanyk, "Russian Language," 31.

93. Bilinsky, "Expanding the Use of Russian," 317–18.

94. Sh. Rashidov, "Iazyk nashego edinstva i bratstva," *Russkii iazyk o natsional'noi shkole* 4 (1979): 6, 7–8; quoted in Bilinsky, "Expanding the Use of Russian," 318.

95. Bilinsky, "Expanding the Use of Russian," 321.

96. Solchanyk, "Russian Language," 32–33; A. Sh. Asadullin, "Vazhnoe zveno pervonachal'nogo obucheniia," *Russkii iazyk o natsional'noi shkole* 5 (1980): 61.

97. M. A. Prokofiev, "V protsesse sblizheniia natsii," *Russkii iazyk o natsional'noi shkole* 4 (1979): 12.

98. "Vsesoiuznaia perepis' naseleniia," *Vestnik statiskiki* 2 (1980): 24.

99. *Itogi vsesoiuznoi perepisi naseleniia 1970 goda*, 20; *Chislennost' i sostav naseleniia SSSR*, 71.

100. Solchanyk, "Russian Language," 24.

101. Kennedy, "Soviet Nationalities," 14.

102. Solchanyk, "Russian Language," 24.

103. Kreindler, "Soviet Language Planning," 57.

104. Lapidus, "Nationality Question," 101.

105. Kirkwood, "Glasnost'," 67.

106. Kreindler, "Soviet Language Planning," 56.

107. Kreindler, "Forging a Soviet People," 220. On the 1978 decree, see Roman Solchanyk, "Russification to Be Stepped Up," *Soviet Analyst*, 9 January 1980, 7–8.

108. S. Paşykow, "Rus dilinde uly söýgi," *Sovet Turkmenistan*, 10 April 1973, 4.

109. Lubomyr Hajda, "Ethnic Politics and Ethnic Conflict in the USSR and the Post-Soviet States," *Humboldt Journal of Social Relations* 19, no. 2 (1993): 227; Olcott, "Yuri Andropov," 114.

110. Kreindler, "Changing Status"; Isayev, *National Languages in the USSR*. For others, see Nazarow, *Türkmen dilinde*, 5; Anderson and Silver, "Equality, Efficiency," 1033.

Chapter 5: From Happy Socialism to Independence

Epigraph: O. Amantaganova and B. Bazarow, "Medeniýetlilikden nyşan," *Mugallymlar gazeti*, 22 May 1991, 3.

1. In 1989 and 1993 the United Nations Development Program (UNDP) and the Turkmen Academy of Science jointly estimated Turkmenistan's literacy rate at 99 percent. UNDP with assistance from the TSSR Academy of Sciences, *Turkmenistan Human Development Report 1996*.

2. Türkmenbaşy (Nyýazow's adopted title), *Bilimli nesil—kuwwatly Watan*, 33–34.

3. Of Turkmenistan's total population (3,522,717), 12 percent (421,015) regarded Russian as a native language. *Itogi vsesoiuznaia perepis' naselenia 1989 goda*, 68. In 1989 Turkmenistan's head of the Department of Ideological Work reported the population of Aşgabat to be made up of 41percent Turkmen, 41 percent Russians, and 18 percent other ethnicities. S. Bagdasarian, "'Agzybirlik' ne sostoialsia," *Komsomolets Turkmenistana*, 17 October 1989, 1.

4. Suny, *Revenge of the Past*, xv, 127–60.

5. Turkmen and Tatars, for example, remained peaceful and built upon their Soviet experiences, while Chechens and Tajiks fell into warfare, in part due to backlash against Soviet identity and borders. See Suny, *Revenge of the Past*; Brown, "Political Developments"; William Fierman, ed., special issue, "Implementing Language Laws: Perestroika and Its Legacy in Five Republics," *Nationalities Papers* 23, no. 3 (1995).

6. Annette Bohr, "Turkmenistan under Perestroika: An Overview," *Report on the USSR (Radio Liberty)* 2, no. 2 (1990): 20–30.

7. *Tebipçiligiň jübi kitapçasy—Lukman Hekimiň Emperi.* (This is a pocket version of traditional Turkic healing, with no date, no publisher; a Turkmen woman had obtained it in the early 1990s.)

8. Individuals from the Baltics surreptitiously trained Central Asians in how to organize mass public protests. See Beissinger, *Nationalist Mobilization*; Jones, "Georgian Language," 538; Jones, "Glasnost', Perestroika, and the Georgian SSR."

9. Wachtel, *Making a Nation*; Talattof, *Politics of Writing in Iran*; Greenberg, *Language and Identity*.

10. Kreindler, "Soviet Language Planning," 58.

11. Kirkwood, "Glasnost'," 71.

12. Kreindler, "Soviet Language Planning," 58.

13. William Fierman, "Problems of Language Law Implementation in Uzbekistan," *Nationalities Papers* 23, no. 3 (1995): 575. See also Landau and Kellner-Heinkele, "Language Politics," 62.

14. Kreindler, "Missed Opportunity," 269; V. M. Solontsev, "Natsional'no-iazykovye otnosheniia (Kruglyi stol)," *Voprosy istorii* 5 (1989): 46.

15. Starr, "Fate of Empire."

16. Pigolkin and Studenikina, "Republican Language Laws."

17. "Speech by Deputy S.A. Nyýazov, Bezmein, E.D., Turkmenian Republic," *Current Digest of the Soviet Press* 40, no. 51 (1989): 14.

18. "On the Basis of Leninist Principles, to a New Quality of Relations between Nationalities: Debate at the Plenary Session of the CPSU Central Committee," *Current Digest of the Soviet Press* 41, no. 39 (1989): 5–23. Nyýazov made this speech in Russian as he was among the leaders of the other Soviet states and that was the common language.

19. Peyrouse, *Turkmenistan*, 78.

20. S. Bagdasarian, "'Agzybirlik' ne sostoialsia," *Komsomolets Turkmenistana*, 17 October 1989, 1.

21. O. Amannyýazowa, "Iz plena ambitsii," *Turkmenskaia iskra*, 5 May 1988, 3.

22. S. Bagdasarian, "'Agzybirlik' ne sostoialsia," *Komsomolets Turkmenistana*, 17 October 1989, 1.

23. In 1988 Estonia and Lithuania established popular fronts, and Estonia declared itself a sovereign republic.

24. M. Volkov, "Presidents Elected," *Current Digest of the Soviet Press* 42, no. 3 (1990): 30.

25. *Human Rights and Democratization*, 178.

26. Fierman, "Introduction," 509.

27. Pigolkin and Studenikina, "Republican Language Laws"; Guboglo, *Perelomnye gody*, vol. 2. The law was repeated in the 1992 Constitution in Section I, Article 13. See also Oraz Ýagmyryň, "Ene dilim—eýe dilim," *Ýaş kommunist*, 15 February 1990, 1.

28. Tagangeldi Täçmyradow, "untitled" in the language section "Dil aladasy—il aladasy," *Edebiýat we sungat*, 13 April 1990, 1.

29. Author's field observations, 2001–2003, 2004.

30. Indeed, parents are distraught over the loss of what they feel is an important and valuable skill for getting on in the world, because their children, Turkmenistan's youth, do not speak Russian well.

31. Tagangeldi Täçmyradow, "Döwlet aladasy gerek," *Mugallymlar gazeti*, 1987, 2.

32. Tagangeldi Täçmyradow, "Untitled," in language section "Dil aladasy—il aladasy," *Edebiýat we sungat*, 13 April 1990, 1.

33. Söýegow, *Razvitie sintaktichskoi*.

34. Rejep Berdiýew, "Pikir etsen, oýlansaň . . . Dil hakyndaky kanuny durmuşa geçirmegiň käbir meseleleri," *Edebiýat we sungat*, 9 May 1991, 2–3.

35. Fuller, "Turkey's New Eastern Orientation"; Kirişçi, "Turkish Foreign Policy Behavior."

36. Atkin, "Islam as Faith."

37. Yavuz, "Turkish Identity Politics."

38. Proceedings from 18–20 November 1991 symposium held by the Türkiyat Araştırmaları Enstitüsü, Marmara University.

39. B. Karimov and S. Mutalov, *Urtaturk tili. "Ortaturk"—srednetiurkskii iazyk*. This is in Uzbek with Russian and English summary. There is a second version in English alone, titled *Urtaturk tili. "Ortaturk"—The Averaged Turkic Language*, with the thesis given also in German and French.

40. While I suspect that a large percentage of the populace was more comfortable with the idea of remaining safely within the Union, it is difficult to qualify this statistic as a reliable one.

41. CSCE Report, 2.

42. Beissinger, *Nationalist Mobilization*, 232; CSCE Report, 5.

43. Beissinger, *Nationalist Mobilization*, 232.

44. CSCE Report, 7.

45. The 1992 election voted Nyýazow to office for five years; the 1995 election extended his rule from five to ten years. The timing of Nyýazow's adoption of the title may have been connected to his role as head of the World Turkmen Association. *Dünýa Türkmenleri; Türkmen halkynyň gelip*.

46. Even when Turkmenistan joined the United Nations in 1995, declaring a status of "permanent neutrality" and signaling a strong desire to build some kind of relationship with the international community, what shape that might take was still not clear. Anceschi, *Turkmenistan's Foreign Policy*.

47. V. Kuleshov, "The Central Asian Republics and Kazakhstan Intend to Support the Commonwealth of Independent States," *Current Digest of the Soviet Press* 43 (1992): 8. Nyýazow also telephoned Mutalibov, president of Azerbaijan, but he declined the invitation. Turkmenistan later reduced its role in the Commonwealth of Independent States (CIS) to observer status.

48. CSCE Report, 5.

49. The Academy of Sciences was dismantled and considered closed down, but in reality it was reconstituted as separate institutes under the auspices of the president, and the library remained open. However, degrees in progress were canceled. There was no postgraduate education until President Berdimuhamedow reestablished the academy in 2007.

50. Nissman, "Searching for a National Identity."

51. N. Naryýew, "Latyn grafikasyna geçmek gerek," *Mugallymlar gazeti*, 16 December 1990, 3; R. Amangeldiew, "Diňe utuş bolar," *Mugallymlar gazeti*, 9 January 1991, 3; unsigned, "Oýlanyşykly çemeleşmek," *Edebiýat we Sungat*, 16 August 1991, 7.

52. Landau and Kellner-Heinkele, *Language Politics*.

53. Examples include Nurýady Nartyev, "Döwlet diline sarpa goýulmalydyr," *Edebiýat we Sungat*, 15 November 1991, 2; Juma Hydaýgulyew, "Tillerim," *Edebiýat we Sungat*, 27 December 1991, 2.

54. S. Fredrick Starr, "Civil Society in Central Asia," in *Civil Society in Central Asia*, ed. M. Holt Ruffin and Daniel Waugh (Seattle: University of Washington Press, 1999), 27.

55. For commentary on the "passive resistance of the illiterate masses" and "the ineffectiveness of mass literacy programmes," see Verne, "Literacy and Industrialization," 286.

56. Fieldwork observations 2001–2003, 2004, 2012. See also Clement, "Alphabet Changes in Turkmenistan."

57. As late as 2012 some people without prompting or solicitation were still complaining about the script reform, saying that it had been an expensive inconvenience that had cut Turkmen off from a great literary heritage. Conversations in Aşgabat and its environs, November 2012 (notes in author's possession).

58. This book was mandatory reading not only for schoolchildren but also for state workers. Thus, the majority of Turkmenistan's citizens would have seen these pages.

59. Liudmilla Rybkina, "Moldovada mekdep reformasy," *Mugallymlar gazeti*, 9 January 1991, 1.

60. G. Annamyradow, "Türkmen diliniň hepdeliginde," *Mugallymlar gazeti*, 9 January 1991, 3.

61. Author's interview with Seýhan Demiraliýew, principal of Türkmenabad School No. 35, May 21, 2004 (notes in author's possession).

62. Döwletmyrat Nurýew, "Göterildi bu ykbaly Türkmeniň," *Edebiýat we sungat*, 1 November 1991, 2.

63. P. Azymow we B. Çaryýarow, "Türkmen diliniň elipbiýini kämilleşdirmeli," *TSSR YA habarlary. Gumanitar ylymlaryň seriýasy* 3 (1990): 3–11.

64. A. Berdigylyjow, Hudaýberdi Begnazarow, and A. Hemzäew, "Biziň pikirimizçe," *Mugallymlar gazeti*, 6 January 1991, 3. In a section called "Voices," reserved for discussion, alphabet reform articles by teachers, a psychologist, and a student appeared: N. Hudayberenow, "Biziň arzuwymiz"; J. Gapbarow, Amangeldi Baýramow, and Ia. Saryew, "Pikirimizi aýtsak"; S. Allahanow, "Bähbitli taraplary köp"; O. Rejepow, "Diliň rowaçlanmagy ugrunda"; all in *Mugallymlar gazeti*, 25 January 1991, 3.

65. "Türkmen diliniň elibpiýini kämilleşdirmeli," *Mugallymlar gazeti*, 28 November 1990, 1.

66. Nurjan Amannepesow, "Elipbiýden söz açsak," *Edebiýat we sungat*, 15 February 1991, 2.

67. H. Maşadow, "Dilimiziň derwaýys meselesi," *Mugallymlar gazeti*, 12 June 1991, 1.

68. Taýtar Meregeldiýew, "Millilik çaklansyn: okuw kitaplarynyn ara alyp malahatlaşýarys," *Mugallymlar gazeti*, 19 June 1991, 4.

69. Semi-nomadic Turkmen had herded sheep and goats, keeping them for a food source and using their wool to make felt for yurts. But it was always the horse that held a near-sacred place in the heart of Turkmen. An old proverb advises, "When you wake in the morning first kiss your horse, then your father."

70. H. Maşadow, "Dilimiziň derwaýys meselesi," *Mugallymlar gazeti*, 12 June 1991, 1.

71. S. Berkeliýewa and Marks Berkeliýew, "Dil baýlygy—Il bayýlygy: Halk dilinden gözlemeli, *Edebiýat we sungat*, 12 April 1991, 7.

72. Pütz, Fishman, and Neff-van Aertselaer, *Along the Routes to Power*, 268.

73. S. Berkeliýewa and Marks Berkeliýew, "Dil baýlygy—Il bayýlygy: Halk dilinden gözlemeli," *Edebiýat we sungat*, 12 April 1991, 7.

74. Annameret Durdymämmedow, "Demokratlar we 'Demokratlar,'" *Edebýat we sungat*, 29 November 1991, 3; Kakabaý Ylýasow, "Bir ýagty ýoly gözäp . . . ," *Edebiýat we sungat*, 13 December 1991, 2.

75. O. Amantaganowa and B. Bazarow, "Medeniýetlilikden nyşan," *Mugallymlar gazeti*, 22 May 1991, 3.

76. A. Işanguliýew, "Ýaşlyk hem çagalyk," *Mugallymlar gazeti*, 19 June 1991, 4.

77. Nurjan Amannepesow, "Elipbiýden söz açsak," *Edebiýat we sungat*, 15 February 1991, 2. Russia also suffered from a paper shortage. Hosking, *Awakening of the Soviet Union*, 69.

78. Azymow and Söýegow, "Türkmen Elipbiýi," 73.

79. Conversations with Söýegow, 1997 (notes in author's possession).

80. Azymow and Söýegow, "Türkmen Elipbiýi," 74.

81. Azymow and Söýegow, "Türkmen Elipbiýi," 74.

82. International Turkic Language Congress, 26 September–1 October 1992, was sponsored by the *Türk Dil Kurumu*. See also *Sürekli Türk Dili Kurultayı*, Kültür Bak., 4–8 May 1992.

83. Azymow and Söýegow, "Türkmen Elipbiýi," 73, 75.

84. "Täze elipbiýe garaşylýar (gazetiň harbarçysy bilen söhbet)," *Watan*, 15 October 1992, 2; Myratgeldi Söýegow, "Allaguly Garahanow," *Türkmenistan Ylymlar aka-*

demiýasinyň habarlary 1 (1993): 94–96; Şeýdaýy, *Türkmen ahwaly* (Aşgabat: Ylymlar aka-demiýasy, 1993).

85. Azymow and Söýegow, "Türkmen Elipbiýi," 76–77.

86. "Elipbiýi barada: Türkmenistanyň dil hakyndaky kanuny nähili ýerine ýetirilýär," *Edebiýat we Sungat*, 11 October 1991, 2.

87. Azymow and Söýegow, "Türkmen Elipbiýi," 73.

88. Interview with Professor Söýegow, Aşgabat, November 26, 2012 (notes in author's possession); Azymow and Söýegow, "Türkmen Elipbiýi," 75.

89. This is especially notable in the modifications adopted in the 1996 alphabet, discussed below.

90. Gareth Winrow, "Regional Security and National Identity: The Role of Turkey in Former Soviet Central Asia," in *Turkey: Political, Social and Economic Challenges in the 1990s*, ed. Ciğdem Balım et al. (Leiden: E. J. Brill, 1995), 24.

91. *Türk Cumhuriyet . . . Protokolı,1992*. This protocol was mildly revised in 1996, but the intentions were the same. In 2012 the Turkish section in the Turkmenistan State Library was made part of the International Literature collection of the new Turkmen state library in Berzengi.

92. Azymow and Söýegow, "Türkmen Elibiýi," 74.

93. Azymow and Söýegow, "Türkmen Elibiýi," 74.

94. Türkmenbaşy, *Bilimli nesil—kuwwatly Watan*, 33–34.

95. Azymow and Söýegow, "Türkmen Elipbiýi," 73.

96. Türkmenbaşy, *Bilimli nesil—kuwwatly Watan*, 33–34.

97. S. Nyýazow, "Türkmenistanyň Prezidentiniň karary: Türkmen diliniň täze elipbiýi-ni kabul etmek hakynda," 12 April 1993, reprinted in *Türkmen Arhiwi* 1–2 (1994): 4–5.

98. "Türkmenistanyň Presidentiniň karary," *Türkmenistan gazeti*, 13 April 1993, 1.

99. Söýegow and Rejepow, *Täze Türkmen elipbiýi*.

100. Geoffrey Lewis, *The Turkish Language Reform: A Catastrophic Success* (Oxford: Oxford University Press, 1999), 34.

101. Azymow and Söýegow, "Türkmen Elipbiýi," 73.

102. Conversation, January 1997, with Myratgeldi Söýegow, who was a member of the Alphabet Commission.

103. In some parts of Central Asia, especially Tajikistan, there was discussion of whether to use the Arabic (or Perso-Arabic) script. The failure to pursue this in Turkmenistan was indicative of Aşgabat's desire to build a relationship with Ankara and take a westerly stance.

104. Reprinted in Söýegow et al., *Turkmen Dili*, 20–23.

105. Hezretguly Durdyýew, "Turkmen Milli elipbiýi: taryh we tejribe," *Türkmen Dili*, 4 March 2000, 2.

106. Söýegow and Rejepow, *Täze Türkmen elipbiýi*.

107. Nyýazow, "Türkmenistanyň Prezidentiniň karary," 5.

108. Timur Nizaýew, "Her bir mekdebe komputor klasy," *Mugallymlar gazeti*, 20 February 1991, 1.

109. Even as late as 2012, there was little access to the internet in Turkmenistan and where it was available (in luxury hotels in Aşgabat, for example) many of the most popular international sites were blocked. The state also restricted public internet sites set up by the United Nations, IREX and the British Embassy, and American Councils. Turkmen citizens slowly began gaining access to computers imported from Dubai and Abu Dhabi and internet connections via the state internet provider Turkmentelekom. Eventually, they began accessing the internet through phones.

110. Azymow and Söýegow, "Türkmen Elipbiýi," 74.

111. B. Öwezow and M. Söýegow, "Türkmen diliniň täze elipbiýi hakyndaky tekliplere garamak boýunça hökumet komissiásynyň agzalary," *Türkmentistan gazeti,* 11 January 1995, 1.

112. Author's fieldwork observations 1997, 2001–2003, 2004 (notes in author's possession).

113. Azymow and Söýegow, "Türkmen Elipbiýi," 73.

114. Anceschi, *Turkmenistan's Foreign Policy.*

115. *Türkmenistanyň Hemişelik Bitaraplygy,* 121. Nyýazow explained the concept of neutrality at a meeting of the Halk Maslahaty, on 27 December 1995. Text available in *Türkmenistanyň Hemişelik Bitaraplygy,* 133–38.

116. Adams, *Spectacular State,* 34.

Chapter 6: *Altyn Asyr Nesli*

Epigraphs: Azymow and Söýegow, "Türkmen Elipbiýi," 73; "Saparmurat Turkmenbashy, Turkmen Leader, Dies at 66," *New York Times,* 21 December 2006, retrieved from http://www.nytimes.com/2006/12/21/world/asia/21cnd-turkmen.html?pagewanted=2&_r=2/, accessed 28 September 2013.

1. My analysis contradicts the conclusions of Sebastien Peyrouse, who argues that "the regime did not seek to give birth to a new man and had no objective to undertake a social and national revolution." Peyrouse, *Turkmenistan,* 84.

2. Plamper, *Stalin Cult,* 205.

3. Article 45 of the Constitution of Türkmenistan, 1992.

4. Söýegow et al., *Turkmen Dili.* Use of Russian persisted behind closed doors, as many of Nyýazow's top advisors were ethnic Russians, and interaction with foreign entities such as embassies continued in Russian. Peyrouse, *Turkmenistan,* 74–75. No doubt interaction with such Turkish businessmen as Ahmet Çalık took place in Turkmen/Turkish, as these languages are not so different as to prevent understanding.

5. Hasan Kanbolat, "Garaşsız Türkmenistan," *Türk Dünyası: Dil ve edebiyat dergisi* 2 (1996): 452; Field observations, 2001–2003, 2004 (notes in author's possession). See also Nissman, "Just like the Old Times."

6. Pollard, *USSR Facts and Figures Annual,* 13:53.

7. Fieldwork observations, 2001–2006 (notes in author's possession).

8. Interviews with women who were teachers during the Soviet period and today work for the Ministry of Education, the National Library, or the Manuscript Institute (notes in author's possession).

9. This included ethnic Russians, Armenians, Ukrainians, Azerbaijanis, Poles, Jews—essentially anyone who was not ethnically Turkmen.

10. Fieldwork observations, 2001–2003, 2004 (notes in author's possession).

11. Bruce Pannier, "Nyýazow to Be Named President for Life," *Radio Free Europe/Radio Liberty (RFE/RL)*, 29 December 1999. In 2001 Nyýazow claimed that he was refusing the title and over the years gave timelines for presidential elections, but none ever took place. "Presidential Election to Be Held in 2009—Turkmen Leader," *BBC Monitoring Newsfile*, 8 April 2005. Shikhmuradow doubtless regretted this suggestion at the People's Council profoundly when he was jailed for an attempt against the president's life and treason in 2002.

12. Bruce Pannier, "Nyýazow to Be Named President for Life," *RFE/RL*, 29 December 1999.

13. Bonnell, *Iconography of Power*; Figes and Kolonitskii, *Russian Revolution*; Foucault, *Power/Knowledge*, 96–112, 119–22, 142, 197–98, 236.

14. Privatsky, *Muslim Turkistan*, discusses a similar notion among Kazakhs.

15. *Beýik Saparmyrat Türkmenbaşy Zamanasynyň Sözlügi* (Aşgabat: Türkmen döwlet neşirýat gullugy, 2002), 151.

16. The new word "*öwrümeç*" derives from the verb "*öwrümek*"—to grind up. Interview with Guwanç Garryýew, creator of the term, on 15 September 2001 (notes in author's possession).

17. Interviews with Dr. Hezretguly Durdyýev, September 2001 (notes in author's possession).

18. James Scott, *Domination and the Arts of Resistance: Hidden Transcripts* (New Haven: Yale University Press, 1990), 14–16.

19. Akhmet Salamov, "Sotsialnaia osnova vystrelov v Ashkhabade," from http://www.gundogar.org/, translated in "Cracks in the Marble: Turkmenistan's Failing Dictatorship," *Asia Report No. 44, International Crisis Group*, 17 January 2003, 26.

20. "Turkmenistan: 2004 Country Report on Human Rights Practices," US Department of State, 28 February 2005, retrieved from http://www.state.gov/j/drl/rls/hrrpt/2004/41714/htm/, accessed 10 August 2013.

21. Paul Goble, "Central Asia: Analysis from Washington—The Politics of Language," *RFE/RL*, 4 August 2000.

22. Fieldwork observations, 2001–2003, 2004 (notes in author's possession).

23. Field research 2001–2003, 2004 (notes in author's possession); see also "Turkmenistan: 2004 Country Report on Human Rights Practices," US Department of State, 28 February 2005, retrieved from http://www.state.gov/j/drl/rls/hrrpt/2004/41714/htm/, accessed 10 August 2013.

24. Conversations in September 2001 (notes in author's possession).

25. Unclassified memo E.O. 12958 US Embassy Ashgabat to Secretary of State in Washington, DC, dated 17 May 2004, 1.

26. Bourdieu and Passeron examine the role of the education system as an institutional mechanism for creating and sustaining inequality. See Bourdieu and Passeron, *Reproduction in Education*; Pierre Bourdieu and Jean-Claude Passeron, *The Inheritors: French Students and Their Relation to Culture*, trans. R. Nice (Chicago: University of Chicago Press, 1979).

27. Bob Simon, "60 Minutes," television program, *CBS*, 4 January 2004.

28. Conversations with ethnic Turkmen around the country 2001–2003, 2004 (notes in author's possession).

29. Bourdieu, *Language and Symbolic Power*, 55.

30. "Un-Turkmen Opera, Ballet Banned," *BBC News*, 4 April 2001.

31. Turkmen Initiative for Human Rights, *Education in Turkmenistan* (Vienna: Turkmen Initiative for Human Rights, 2006), retrieved from http://www.archive.chrono-tm.org/uploaded/2560683175898658.pdf/, accessed 10 August 2013; Steve Sabol, "Nations in Transit 2004: Turkmenistan," *Freedom House*, 2004, 7, retrieved from http://www.unpan1.un.org/intradoc/groups/public/documents/nispacee/unpan017052.pdf.

32. By 2005 more than two hundred thousand ethnic Russians had left Turkmenistan. Minority Rights Group International, "State of the World's Minorities 2006—Turkmenistan," retrieved from http://www.refworld.org/country/ANNUALREPORT,TKM,4562d8cf2,48abdd7548,0.html/, accessed 27 September 2013 (no longer available). See also "Focus on the Russian minority," *IRIN News*, retrieved from http://www.irinnews.org/report/20181/turkmenistan-focus-on-the-russian-minority/, accessed 27 September 2013.

33. This policy remained in place, but with uneven funding behind it, and schools achieved irregular results. Information retrieved from http://www.turkmenembassy.org.uk/about.html/, accessed 1 September 2013 (no longer available).

34. In 1997 interest in learning English was so high that complete strangers approached me at bazaars or in shared cabs offering free room and board in exchange for teaching their children English.

35. Türkmenbaşy, *Bilimli nesil-kuwwatly Watan*, 33–34.

36. He announced this on television. Fieldwork Aşgabat 2001 (notes in author's possession). See also Unclassified memo E.O. 12958 US Embassy Ashgabat to Secretary of State in Washington, DC, dated 17 May 2004, 1.

37. Fieldwork observations 2001–2003, 2004 (notes in author's possession). The arts and physical education were also eliminated from the curricula except in special schools that focused on music or art.

38. In an April 2002 televised meeting with university and institute rectors, he announced that English, for example, was removed from the curriculum of the Turkmenabad (Chärjew) Pedagogical Institute and French instruction was limited to the Azady World Languages Institute.

39. Unclassified memo, E.O. 12958, US Embassy Ashgabat to Secretary of State Washington, DC, 17 May 2004, 7. In addition to classes offered by the Turkish company Başkent and the supplementary activities of the Peace Corps, there were French and German language centers and also Persian language classes at the Iranian Cultural Center.

40. Corruption was extensive at all levels of Turkmen state administration and was no less so in education. Applicants paid five hundred dollars or more to take the admission exam to college. After passing such exams, they paid just to enter a particular education program. In 2012 "prices" for higher education ranged between seven thousand and ten thousand dollars. By 2016 "prices" ran in the tens of thousands. Similar problems existed on a smaller scale at the secondary school level. Communications with Turkmenistani citizens 2015–2016 (notes in author's possession).

41. Fieldwork 2001–2006 (notes in author's possession).

42. "Turkmenistan: 2004 Country Report on Human Rights Practices," US Department of State, 28 February 2005, retrieved from http://www.state.gov/j/drl/rls/hr rpt/2004/41714/htm/, accessed 10 August 2013.

43. Session of the Cabinet of Ministers of Turkmenistan, Watan TV News, 9 April 2002 (notes in author's possession).

44. My thanks to Mark Johnson for his assistance with this comparison.

45. "Turkmenistan: 2004 Country Report on Human Rights Practices," US Department of State, 28 February 2005, retrieved from http://www.state.gov/j/drl/rls/hr rpt/2004/41714/htm/, accessed 10 August 2013.

46. Fieldwork 2001–2003, 2004, 2006 (notes in author's possession).

47. Signs with phrases such as *Mukkades Ruhnama* (the holy *Ruhnama*) and *Halkyň Şamçyragy* (the people's lighthouse) and "The president's path is our path" were seen throughout the country.

48. Unclassified memo, E.O. 12958, US Embassy Aşgabat to Secretary of State Washington, DC, 17 May 2004, 6.

49. "Turkmenistan: 2004 Country Report on Human Rights Practices," US Department of State, 28 February 2005, retrieved from http://www.state.gov/j/drl/rls/hr rpt/2004/41714/htm/, accessed 10 August 2013.

50. In a country with petro-dollars it would have been possible for the state to stop its beautification of cities to allocate funds to teachers and nurses.

51. Interviews with Myratgeldi Soýegow, March 2002 (notes in author's possession).

52. Field observations, 2002–2003, 2004 (notes in author's possession).

53. Turkmen Initiative in Human Rights, "Education in Turkmenistan," 19, retrieved from http://www.archive.chrono-tm.org/uploaded/2560683175898658.pdf/, accessed 10 August 2013.

54. In 2003 educators were entitled to the one hundred dollar per month salary of state employees. However, teachers fell into a special category of being paid by the class. In 2002 President Nyýazow raised state salaries from fifty dollars per month to one hundred dollars, but among the teachers work also doubled. In the press and on television, President Nyýazow accused the local bureaucrats of corruption and promised to restore the salaries and punish the guilty. This epitomizes the manner in which Nyýazow used the rampant corruption to his own advantage.

55. Educators had been required to work thirty-five weeks a year, but this increase brought them to over forty. Interviews with Gaplan Esenamanow, former employee of the Ministry of Education's Department of Inspectors, May 2004 (notes in author's possession).

56. "Turkmenistan: 2004 Country Report on Human Rights Practices," US Department of State, 28 February 2005, retrieved from https://www.state.gov/j/drl/rls/hr rpt/2004/41714.htm/, accessed 31 January 2017.

57. Landau and Kellner-Heinkele, *Language Politics*, 154.

58. Interviews with Gaplan Esenamanow, former employee of Ministry of Education's Department of Inspectors, in May 2004 (notes in author's possession).

59. Interview with Seýhad Demiraliýew, principal of Türkmenabad School No. 35, on 21 May 2004 (notes in author's possession). The government of Kazakhstan donated hundreds of books, but schools were unable to use them because they were printed in the Kazakh language.

60. Unclassified memo, E.O. 12958, US Embassy Ashgabat to Secretary of State Washington, DC, 17 May 2004, 2.

61. ""Turkmenistan: 2004 Country Report on Human Rights Practices," US Department of State, 28 February 2005, retrieved from http://www.state.gov/j/drl/rls/hr rpt/2004/41714/htm/, accessed 31 January 2017.

62. Until 2005 it was typical for schoolchildren to work in the cotton fields each fall. But after the 1 February 2005 adoption of the law "On Guarantees of the Rights of Youth to Work," only some rural areas still saw children working in the fields. See *Neitral'nyi Turkmenistan*, no. 28, 2 February 2005.

63. Interviews with students 2003, 2004 (notes in author's possession).

64. Conversations, 2003 (notes in author's possession).

65. Interviews with students 2003, 2004 (notes in author's possession).

66. There were some exceptions, such as Architecture, which were five-year programs.

67. Interview with professor at the Police Academy, 16 March 2004 (notes in author's possession).

68. Fieldwork observations 2003, 2004 (notes in author's possession).

69. Interview with Maya Meredowa, 17 May 2004 (notes in author's possession).

70. Interviews with Gaplan Esenamanow, former employee of the Ministry of Education's Department of Inspectors, May 2004 (notes in author's possession).

71. Unclassified memo, E.O. 12958, US Embassy Ashgabat to Secretary of State Washington, DC, 17 May 2004, 3.

72. "Cracks in the Marble: Turkmenistan's Failing Dictatorship," *Asia Report No. 44*, International Crisis Group, 17 January 2003, 26.

73. By the 2014/2015 academic year there were approximately 25,600 students enrolled in higher education institutes.

74. "Repression and Regression in Turkmenistan: A New International Strategy," *International Crisis Group*, 4 November 2004, https://www.crisisgroup.org/europe-central-asia/

central-asia/turkmenistan/repression-and-regression-turkmenistan-new-international-strategy/, accessed 21 October 2017.

75. In 2004 there were 116 vocational schools in Turkmenistan, of which 11 were in Aşgabat, 19 in Ahal wilaýet, 12 in Balkan wilaýet, 20 in Daşoguz wilaýet, 24 in Mary wilaýet, and 30 in Lebap wilaýet. In 2003, there were 51,437 students enrolled in them. This was an increase from 21,746 in 1998. These schools offered six- to eight-month-long courses and operated solely on tuition with no government subsidies. There were also fifteen professional colleges in Turkmenistan; thirteen were government funded and two privately funded from tuition and fees and sponsors. Government-funded schools consisted of three pedagogical schools (in Aşgabat, Daşoguz, and Mary), five medical schools (Aşgabat, Türkmenbaşy, Daşoguz, Türkmenabat, and Mary), and five music/art schools (Aşgabat, Daşoguz, Mary, Lebap). Interview with Professor Niýazberdi Rejepow, textbook author and senior editor for the Ministry of Education, 6 July 2004 (notes in author's possession). The tuition-based schools focused on management and banking. In 2003 there were nearly four thousand students enrolled in the latter. Unclassified memo, E.O. 12958, US Embassy Ashgabat to Secretary of State Washington, DC, 17 May 2004, 7–8.

76. Based on the classes that were eliminated, art, physical education, and foreign languages seemed to be what he was referring to.

77. Turkmenistan Project Open Society Institute, *Weekly News Brief on Turkmenistan*, 12–18 December 2003, 9, citing excerpts from Turkmen TV first channel, Aşgabat, in Turkmen 1600 GMT, 11 December 2003.

78. "Türkmenistanyň Bilim Işgärleriniň Hünär synagy Hakynda Düzgünnama," *Mugallamlar Gazetesi*, 13 February, 2001, 1–3.

79. Interview with Professor Niýazberdi Rejepow, textbook author and senior editor for the Ministry of Education, 6 July 2004 (notes in author's possession).

80. In 2003, a total of 4,774 people applied to thirteen professional schools: 362 (6.8 percent) had two years' work experience; 2,380 (49.8 percent) were 2003 high school graduates; 27.1 percent were male; 72.9 percent were female; 94.5 percent were native Turkmen. There were 1,140 students admitted (which shows there were 4.2 applicants per slot), 115 with more than two years' work experience; 553 were new high school graduates; 313 male and 827 female; 1,086 Turkmen and 54 non-Turkmen. Unclassified memo, E.O. 12958, American Embassy to Secretary of State Washington, DC, 17 May 2004, 6.

81. "'Labour Army' in the Alarming Time of the News," *Turkmenistan.ru*, retrieved from http://www.turkmenistan.ru/en/node/3604/, accessed 31 January 2017.

82. Decree No. 5913, September 10, 2002; see Saparmyrat Nyýazow, "Beýik Saparmyrat Türkmenbaşynyň Altyn Bilim Syýasaty" (Aşgabat: Bilim Ministirligi, 2003), 70.

83. "Turkmenistan: 2004 Country Report on Human Rights Practices," US Department of State, 28 February 2005, retrieved from http://www.state.gov/j/drl/rls/hr rpt/2004/41714/htm/, accessed 31 January 2017.

84. Conversations, 2001–2004 (notes in author's possession).

85. The year 2004 marked the tenth anniversary of the Peace Corps in Turkmenistan. "Peace Corps Week in Turkmenistan," *Neitral'nyi Turkmenistan*, 2 March 2004, 2, though in 2012 the Peace Corps left Turkmenistan because of a lack of interest from the Turkmen government, which over the years requested fewer and fewer volunteers until it became financially unfeasible to maintain an office in Aşgabat.

86. Yavuz, "Turkish Identity Politics."

87. *Türk Cumhuriyet Bakanlıklığı ve Türkmenistan arasında Eğitim İş Protokolı, 1992*; this was mildly revised by a 1996 protocol, but the intentions were the same. The Turkish government hoped that Central Asian students who studied in Turkey would "return to their native countries to constitute a Turkish-speaking elite that will replace the Russian-speaking elite." Demir, Balcı, and Akkok, "Role of Turkish Schools," 142.

88. Between 1993 and 2003, 1,847 certificates had been awarded by the Turkish Language Center (TÖMER). In 2003 there were 249 students and 5 teachers. In 2003 a three-month-long course cost three hundred thousand manats (thirteen dollars). In 2003 a total of 1,760 graduates had received certificates from the Vocational Training Center (YAMEN). In 2004, there were 259 students. All of these institutes were in Aşgabat. A four-month program cost two hundred thousand manats (under ten dollars). Interview with officials from Turkey's embassy in Turkmenistan, 1 June 2004 (notes in author's possession).

89. Demir, Balcı, and Akkok, "Role of Turkish Schools," 141–55. These schools were nationalized in 2011.

90. Apay, "Turkish Higher Education."

91. I taught at the university in 1997 and visited most of the high schools in spring 2004.

92. See Yavuz and Esposito, *Turkish Islam.*

93. Gülen became infamous during his years in exile in the United States, especially in summer 2016 when Turkey's president Erdoğan accused Gülen of fomenting the 15 July coup attempt in Turkey.

94. Agai, "Ethic of Education," 50.

95. Agai, "Ethic of Education," 49. See also Silova, "Reclaiming the Empire," 8; Turam, "National Loyalties."

96. Özdalga, "Fethullah Gülen," 85.

97. Clement, "Faith-Based Schools."

98. Personal observations 2001–2002 (notes in author's possession).

99. Personal observations 1997, 2002 (notes in author's possession).

100. For greater detail on this, see Clement, "Central Asia's Hizmet Schools."

101. "V Turkmenistane zakryvaiut turetskie shkoly," *Chronicles of Turkmenistan*, 14 August 2011, retrieved from http://www.chrono-tm.org/2011/08/v-turkmenistane-zakry ivayut-turetskie-sh/, accessed 2 September 2013.

102. "Saparmurat Turkmenbashy, Turkmen Leader, Dies at 66," *New York Times*, 21 December 2006, retrieved from http://www.nytimes.com/2006/12/21/world/asia/21 cnd-turkmen.html?pagewanted=2&_r=2/, accessed 28 September 2013.

103. "President for Life—Turkmenistan," *Journeyman Pictures*, August 2005, retrieved from https://www.youtube.com/watch?v=KNJS2-Zv-Tc/, accessed 21 October 2017; Ilan Greenberg, "When a Kleptocratic, Megalomaniacal Dictator Goes Bad," *New York Times*, 5 January 2003, retrieved from http://www.nytimes.com/2003/01/05/magazine/when-a-kleptocratic-megalomanuacal-dictator-goes-bad.html/, accessed 21 October 2017. This had come to be greatly ironic as Nyýazow arrested and tortured Shikhmuradow for being the leader of a 2002 assassination attempt against him. Shikhmuradow was Turkmenistan's minister of foreign affairs in 1995–2000; he remains imprisoned.

104. Ansari, *Modern Iran*, 21.

105. "Turkmenistan: 2004 Country Report on Human Rights Practices," US Department of State, 28 February 2005, retrieved from https://www.state.gov/j/drl/rls/hrrpt/2004/41714.htm/, accessed 31 January 2017.

106. The critical source for understanding this chapter is Nyýazow's *Ruhnama*. It has been translated into English but lends more to the analysis if one can read it in the language in which the Turkmen people read it, especially as that book was the source of so many neologisms. See also Bouma, "Turkmenistan: Epics in Place of Historiography," 559–85.

Chapter 7: The Era of Might and Happiness, 2007–2014

1. Slavomir Horák, "Turkmenistan posle Turkmenbashi: K voprosu o transformatsii rezhimov lichnoi vlasti," *Politeks* 1 (2008): 63–79.

2. Berdimuhamedow had been minister of health since 1997, deputy prime minister since 2001, and head of the state commission for admission to the institutions of higher education. A dentist by training, he also acted as Nyýazow's personal dentist.

3. "New Turkmenistan President Promises Social Reform," *Jane's Intelligence Watch Report—Daily Update*, 14 February 2007; "The Turkmen Choice," *Turkmenistan.ru*, 15 February 2007, retrieved from http://www.turkmenistan.ru/en/node/5296/, accessed 17 April 2012.

4. Peyrouse, *Turkmenistan*, 109.

5. "President Turkmenistana prizval chinovnikov ot obrazovaniia myslit' po-novomy," *Turkmenistan.ru*, 9 February 2008, retrieved from http://www.turkmenistan.ru/?page_id=3&lang_id=ru&elem_id=13510&type=event&sort=date_desc/, accessed 25 January 2017.

6. Jennifer Gandhi, *Political Institutions under Dictatorships* (Cambridge: Cambridge University Press, 2008), xv.

7. "Gurbanguly Berdymukhammedov Introduces Major Education Reform in Turkmenistan," *Turkmenistan.ru*, 15 February 2007, retrieved from http://www.turkmenistan.ru/en/node/5301/, accessed 21 June 2015.

8. "Statement of the Chairman of the Khalk Maslakhaty of Turkmenistan President of Turkmenistan Gurbanguly Berdimuhamedow at the XXI Khalk Maslakhaty Special Session," 26 September 2008, in *Demokratiýa we Hukuk* (Aşgabat: Ylym, 2008), 99.

9. Turkmen Initiative for Human Rights, *Turkmenistan: The Reform of the Education*

System (Vienna: TIHR, 2009), retrieved from http://www.archive.chrono-tm.org/upload ed/1671390621977742.pdf/, accessed 9 March 2016.

10. For the first year that the academy was back in operation, it went without state funding. In June 2008, the president announced that the Academy of Sciences would receive funding from the state. He signed a decree formalizing this on 12 June 2009. Eleven institutes, one central scientific library, and the Ylym publishing house all operate under the auspices of the Academy of Sciences of Turkmenistan; see http://www.science.gov.tm/.

11. "Prezident Turkmenii vossozdal Akademii nauk," 13 June 2007, retrieved from http://www.lenta.ru/news/2007/06/13/academy/, accessed 12 March 2016 (quotation); *World Data on Education, VII Ed. 2010/2011* (Aşgabat: UNESCO-International Bureau of Education, 2011), 3.

12. No author, "Admission to Postgraduate and Doctoral Studies Announced in Turkmenistan," *Turkmenistan.ru*, 25 January 2012, retrieved from http://www.turkmenistan .ru/en/articles/15829.html/, accessed 21 June 2015. In 2008, under presidential decree, seventy-eight people were admitted to postgraduate studies, thirty-three to postgraduate clinical training (medical workers must be under thirty-five years old), and twenty-seven to doctoral studies. "Turkmenistan's Higher Education Establishments Begin Entrance Examinations," *Turkmenistan.ru*, 2 August 2013, retrieved from http://www.turkmenistan.ru/ en/articles/17322.html/, accessed 21 June 2015.

13. "Turkmenistan Announces Postgraduate Studies Admissions," *Turkmenistan.ru*, 1 April 2008, retrieved from http://www.turkmenistan.ru/en/node/6850/, accessed 9 March 2016.

14. "Turkmenistan Reinstates Physical Culture Classes," *Turkmenistan.ru*, 4 March 2007, retrieved from http://www.turkmenistan.ru/en/node/5394/, accessed 9 March 2016.

15. President Berdimuhamedow opened a handful of movie theaters in Turkmenistan and began to allow public space to host cultures other than Turkmen. In October 2007, the US embassy and the Ministry of Culture, Television, and Radio joined together to organize a week-long film festival, "Discover America." The state also began allowing publishers from more than twenty countries to gather for international exhibitions. See "Turkmenistan: New Social Policy Yields First Results," *Oxford Analytica Daily Brief Service*, 20 November 2007.

16. "Visits of Turkmen, Iranian Leaders Put Columbia University in the Spotlight," *Eurasianet*, retrieved from http://www.eurasianet.org/departments/insight/articles/eav09250 7.shtml/, accessed 6 March 2016.

17. "The *Rukhnama* Is Gone Forever," *Chronicles of Turkmenistan*, 1 August 2013, retrieved from http://www.chrono-tm.org/en/2013/08/the-rukhnama-is-gone-forever/, accessed 21 June 2016.

18. Berdimuhamedow, *To New Heights of Progress* 6:8, 64.

19. Annette Bohr, *Turkmenistan: Power, Politics and Petro-authoritarianism* (London: Royal Institute of International Affairs, 2016), 4, 11.

20. Catherine A. Fitzpatrick, "Turkmenistan Weekly Roundup," *Eurasianet*, 30 August 2011, retrieved from http://www.EurasiaNet.org/, accessed 15 January 2013; "Turk-

menistan: President Gurbanguly Berdmukhammedov Is Awarded the Status of Arkadag—Protector," 1 February 2011, retrieved from http://www.enews.fergananews.com/news .php?id=2003&print=1/, accessed 26 January 2017.

21. Naz Nazar, "Window Dressing," *Transitions Online*, 7 January 2010, retrieved from http://www.tol.org/client/article/21056-window-dressing.html/, accessed 2 September 2010.

22. Aisha Khan, "Turkmenistan's Clannish Leader," *IWPR*, 23 November 2010, retrieved from https://www.iwpr.net/global-voices/turkmenistans-clannish-leader/, accessed 31 January 2017; "Growing Tribalism," *Chronicles of Turkmenistan,* retrieved from http:// www.en.chrono-tm.org/2016/03/growing-tribalism/, accessed 31 January 2017; "Turkmenistan," *Nations in Transit* 2012, retrieved from https://www.freedomhouse.org/report/ nations-transit/2012/turkmenistan/, accessed 31 January 2017.

23. Telephone interview with citizen of Turkmenistan, 25 July 2016.

24. Prior to 2014, the only university that charged tuition was the International Turkmen-Turkish University (ITTU) in Aşgabat, which closed in 2011. Some Turkmen believe that this move toward charging tuition could stem the tide of "gift giving" and bribery in higher educational institutions. If students are already paying tuition, and the number of spaces available for students continues to increase as it has, it is unlikely that families will be inclined to pay further. Still, other observers doubt that other universities will begin charging tuition as there are too many people with a vested interest in corruption.

25. Number retrieved from http://www.transparency.org/country/TKM/, accessed 26 January 2017.

26. "Turkmenistan: President Fumes at Graft in Energy Sector," *Eurasianet*, 7 March 2016, retrieved from http://www.eurasianet.org/node/77686/, accessed 7 March 2016.

27. "Uzbekistan, Turkmenistan: Corruption, Shmorruption," *Eurasianet*, 2 February 2016, retrieved from http://www.eurasianet.org/node/77121/, accessed 7 March 2016.

28. "Turkmenistan: Top Official Fired, and Possibly Jailed," *Eurasianet*, 8 February 2016, retrieved from http://www.eurasianet.org/node/77216/, accessed 7 March 2016.

29. Percentages retrieved from http://www.indexmundi.com/turkmenistan/age_struc ture.html/, accessed 26 January 2017.

30. Turkmenistan possesses the world's fourth-largest reserves of natural gas and has a population of only about five million. The statistical yearbook of Turkmenistan gives the number 6,746,500 of the total population (3,193,000 urban and 3,553,500 rural). See Türkmenistanyň Milli döwlet hasabaty we maglumatlar instituty, *Türkmenistanyň ýyllylk hasabat neşiri, 2000–2005*. But academic consensus is that these numbers are inflated; statistics coming out of Turkmenistan are notoriously unreliable.

31. Telephone interview with citizen of Turkmenistan, 25 July 2016.

32. "Teaching in Russian Banned," *Chronicles of Turkmenistan,* 12 September 2013, retrieved from http://www.chrono-tm.org/en/2013/09/teaching-in-russian-banned/, accessed 20 June 2015.

33. Obtained in Aşgabat, November 2015.

34. Embassy, Ashgabat (Turkmenistan) "Turkmenistan: Why English Matters," *Wikileaks,* Wikileaks cable: 09ASHGABAT303, 6 March 2009, 1 September 2011, retrieved from http://www.wikileaks.org/cable/2009/03/09ASHGABAT303.html/, accessed 11 August 2015.

35. State News Agency of Turkmenistan, "National Education: Achievements and Development Prospects Are under Discussion," 8 January 2015, retrieved from http://www.turkmenistan.gov.tm/_eng?id=4378/, accessed 20 June 2016.

36. "B Turkmenistane razrabotaiut gosudarstvennye standarty obrazovanie," retrieved from http://www.asgabat.net/novosti/v-turkmenistane-razrabotayut-gosudarstvenye-standarty-obrazovanija.html/, accessed 21 March 2016.

37. "Turkmenistan: Is This Education Reform We Can Believe In?," *Eurasianet*, 27 January 2012, retrieved from http://www.eurasianet.org/node/64918/, accessed 6 March 2016.

38. *Turkmenistan the Golden Age*, 8 January 2015, retrieved from http://www.turkmenistan.gov.tm/_eng?id=4378/, accessed 30 June 2016.

39. As of 2012/2013, under intergovernmental agreements, over one thousand students from Turkmenistan were being educated in 120 high schools in Turkey. High school students also study in Germany, China, Russia, Ukraine, India, and Malaysia. M. Meredova, "Turkmenistan: Reforming the Education System," in *Education in West Central Asia*, ed. M. Ahmed (London: Bloomsbury, 2013), 277. In that same year, seven thousand students studied in Ukraine, and the same number went to Belarus for higher education. Berdimuhamedow, *To New Heights of Progress*, 63.

40. Bradley Jardine, "In Turkmenistan, Border Woes Trump Education," retrieved from http://www.thediplomat.com/2015/07/in-turkmenistan-border-woes-trump-education/, accessed 25 January 2017.

41. Naz Nazar, "Window Dressing," retrieved from http://www.tol.org/client/article/21056-window-dressing.html/, accessed 31 January 2017.

42. "Will Turkmenistan's Education Reform Work?," *Eurasianet*, 5 March 2013, retrieved from http://www.eurasianet.org/66637/, accessed 21 June 2015.

43. "Vystupleniie prezidenta Turkmenistana Gurbanguly Berdimukhamedova na zasedanii Soveta stareishin Turkmenistana," *Neitral'nyi Turkmenistan*, 24 October 2012, 2.

44. "President of Turkmenistan Poses a Number of Tasks on Reformation of National Science," *Turkmenistan.ru*, 13 June 2007, retrieved from http://www.turkmenistan.ru/en/node/5768/, accessed 21 June 2015.

45. Estimates on the number of internet users in Turkmenistan include 2,000 users in the year 2000 and 64,800 users in the year 2007. Internet World Stats, retrieved from http://www.internet worldstats.com/asia/tm.htm/, accessed 20 June 2015. In 2012, there were approximately 252,742 users, but Facebook, Twitter, and Youtube were all blocked. Viktoriya Zhavoronkova, "Beyond 'www': Life without Internet Exists," *Chronicles of Turkmenistan,* retrieved from http://www.chrono-tm.org/en/2014/02/beyond-www-life-without-internet-exists/, accessed 20 June 2015.

46. "Protection of Fundamental Rights in Central Asia," *Chronicles of Turkmenistan,* retrieved from http://www.chrono-tm.org/en/2014/7/protection-of-fundamental-rights -in-central-asia-update-on-developments-in-April-June-2014/, accessed 20 June 2015.

47. Berdimuhamedow, *To New Heights of Progress*, 65.

48. Adams, *Spectacular State.*

49. "Turkmenistan: Festivities and Life," *Chronicles of Turkmenistan*, 19 October 2011, retrieved from http://www.chrono-tm.org/en/2011/10/turkmenistan-festivities-and-life/, accessed 20 June 2015.

50. "Will Turkmenistan's Education Reform Work?" Eurasianet, 5 MArch 2013, retrieved from http://www.eurasianet.org/print/66637/, accessed 21 June 2015.

51. "Generation 'Ch,'" *Chronicles of Turkmenistan*, 11 October 2013, retrieved from http://www.chrono-tm.org/en/2013/10/generation-ch/, accessed 20 June 2015.

Conclusion

1. Kotkin, *Magnetic Mountain*, 18.

2. Martin, "Modernization or Neo-traditionalism?" 162.

3. "Russian" included not only ethnic Russians but also Armenians, Ukrainians, Azerbaijanis, Poles, Jews—essentially anyone who was not ethnically Turkmen.

4. Minority Rights Group International, *State of the World's Minorities 2006—Turkmenistan*, 22 December 2005. See also "Focus on the Russian minority," *IRIN News*, retrieved from http://www.irinnews.org/report/20181/turkmenistan-focus-on-the-russian-mi nority/, accessed 27 September 2013.

5. Swartz, *Culture and Power*, 43.

6. Clement, "Changes in Turkmen Alphabets."

7. T. Täçmyradow, "Söz manysy sözlükden gözlenýär," *Mugallymlar gazeti*, 25 September 1987, 2–3.

8. David L. Hoffmann, "European Modernity and Soviet Socialism," in Hoffmann and Kotsonis, *Russian Modernity*, 245–60.

9. Collins and Blot, *Literacy and Literacies*, 36.

10. Fortna comes to a similar conclusion about reading. He writes, "Reading is both constructive and illustrative of modernity." Fortna, *Learning to Read*, 209.

Bibliography

Primary Sources

Archival Sources

Moscow, Russia

Fond—collection; *opis'*—inventory; *delo*—file; *list*—page

Gosudarstvennyi arkhiv Rossiisskoi Federatsii (GARF). State Archive of the Russian Federation

    Fond 1235. Otdel natsional'nostei VTsIK. Central Executive Committee Bureau of Nationalities

    Fond 1318. Narkomnats. People's Commissariat for the Nationalities (RSFSR 1917–1924)

    Fond 3316. Tsentral'nyi Ispolnitel'nyi Komitet TsIK SSSR. Central Executive Committee

    Fond 5402. M. P. Pavlovich

    Fond 7543. Vsesoiuznoi tsentral'nyi komitet novogo alfavita. All-Union Central Committee for the New Alphabet

Rossiiskii Gosudarstvennyi Arkhiv Sotsial'no-politicheskoi Istorii (RGASPI; formerly RTsKhIDNI). Russian State Archive of Social-Political History

    Fond 17. Tsentral'nyi Komitet KPSS. Central Committee of the Soviet Communist Party

    Fond 62. Sredneaziatskoe Buro TsK VKP [b]. Central Asian Bureau

    Fond 122. Turkkomissiia TsK RKP [b]. Turkestan Commission

Arkhiv Rossiiskoi Akademii Nauk (ARAN). Archive of the Russian Academy of Sciences

    Fond 350. Communist Academy

    Fond 676. *Vsesoiuznyi* Tsentral'nyi Komitet Novogo Alfavita. All-Union Central Committee for the New Alphabet

    Fond 688. V. A. Gordlevskii

Turkmenistan

Türkmen Döwlet Milli Arhiwi (TDMA). Turkmen State National Archive
   Fond 1. Merkezi Komitet, 1924–1991. Central Committee
   Fond 150. Turkmenistanyň Magaryf Ministerligi, 1924–1991. Turkmenistan's Education Ministry
Magtumguly adyndaky Dil we Edebiýat Institutynyň golýazmalar fondy. Ashgabat, Turkmenistan. (Manuscript holdings of the Language and Literature Institute named after Magtumguly, no. 160, folder no. 10. Ashgabat, Turkmenistan

Stenographic Records

Amansaryýew, J. *Türkmen diliniň lingvistik terminlerini düzgüne salmak hakynda.* Aşgabat: TSSR Academy of Sciences, 1951.
Iazyk i pis'mennost' narodov SSSR. Stenograficheskii otchet 1-go vsesoiuznogo plenuma Nauchnogo Soveta VTsK NA 15–19 fevralia 1933. Moscow, 1933.
Pervyi vsesoiuznyi tiurkologicheskii s'ezd 26 fevralia–5 marta 1926 g. Stenograficheskii otchet. Baku, 1926.
Pervyi vseturkmenskii s'ezd sovetov rabochikh, dekhanskikh i krasno armeiskikh deputatov. 14–24 February 1925. Aşgabat, 1926.
Polozhenie sovetov rabochikh, dekhkanskikh, i krasnoarmeiskikh deputatov TSSR. Aşgabat: TsIK TSSR, 1926.
Postanovleniia 3-go vseturkmenskogo s'ezd sovetov. Aşgabat: TsIK TSSR, 1929.
Rezoliutsia II Lingvisticheskogo s'ezda TSSR po punktuatsii Turkmenskogo literaturnogo iazyka (6–9 oktiabria, 1954). Ashkhabad: Izd. Akademii nauk TSSR, 1955.
Rezoliutsia II Lingvisticheskogo s'ezda TSSR po terminologii Turkmenskogo literaturnogo iazyka (6–9 oktiabria, 1954). Ashkhabad: Izd. Akademii nauk TSSR, 1955.
Rezoliutsia II Lingvisticheskogo s'ezda TSSR po orfografii Turkmenskogo literaturnogo iazyka (6–9 oktiabria, 1954). Ashkhabad: Izd. Akademii nauk TSSR, 1955.
Stenograficheskii otchet chetvertogo plenuma vsesoiuznogo komiteta novogo tiurkskogo alfavita. Moscow, 1931.
Stenograficheskii otchet pervogo plenuma vsesoiuznogo komiteta novogo tiurkskogo alfavita, zasedavshego v Baku ot 3-ego do 7-go iunia 1927 goda. Moscow, 1927.
Stenograficheskii otchet piatogo plenuma vsesoiuznogo komiteta novogo tiurkskogo alfavita. Moscow, 1932.
Stenograficheskii otchet vtorogo plenuma vsesoiuznogo komiteta novogo tiurkskogo alfavita, zasedavshego v g. Tashkente ot 7-go po 12-e ianvaria 1928 goda. Baku, 1929.
Türk Cumhuriyet Bakanlıklığı ve Türkmenistan arasında Eğitim İş Protokolı, 1992.
Türkmen edebi diliniň orfografiýasy TSSR-iň II liňgvistik gurultaýynyň rezolýutsiýasy (6–9 October, 1954). Aşgabat: Academy of Sciences, 1955.

Türkmen edebi diliniň punktuatsiýasy TSSR-iň II liňgvistik gurultaýynyň rezolýutsiýasy (6–9 October, 1954). Aşgabat: Academy of Sciences, 1955.

Türkmen edebi diliniň terminologiýasy TSSR-iň II liňgvistik gurultaýynyň rezolýutsiýasy. Aşgabat: Academy of Sciences, 1955.

Türkmen halkynyň gelip çykyşynyň dünýä ýaraýşynyň we onyň döwletiniň tarihiniň problemalary: Halkara ylmy konferentsiýanyň dokladlarynynň we habarlarynyň. Aşgabat: Ruh, 1993.

Türkmenistan 1-inji ylmy konferentsiýasiniň edebi dil, adalga, hem imla dogrusynda çykaran karary. Aşgabat: TSSR-TTEMK, 1930.

Türkmenistan SSR-niň ähli medentiýet işgärlerine medeni aň-bilim edaralary işgärleriniň Birinji gurultaýynyň ýüzlenmesi. Aşgabat: Turkmenistan SSR Cultural Ministry, 1958.

Türkmenistanyň Milli döwlet hasabaty we maglumatlar instituty. *Türkmenistanyň ýyllylk hasabat neşiri, 2000–2005.* Aşgabat: Türkmenmillihasabat, 2006.

Ýgyndyda: Türkmen diliniň orfografiýa, punktuatsiýa we terminologiýa meseleleri. Aşgabat: Academy of Sciences, 1955.

Newspapers and Journals

Turkmen language:

Edebiýat we Sungat

Gyzyl ýol

Medeni ynkylap

Mugallymlar gazeti

Ruznama-i Mawera-i Bahr-i Hazar

Sowatlyk ugrunda göreş

Şuralar Türkmenistanyn

Tokmak

Türkmen Dili

Türkmen ili

Türkmenistan gazeti

Türkmen medeniýeti

Watan

Ýaş kommunist

Russian language:

Kommunist

Kul'tura i pis'mennost' vostoka

Neitral'nyi Turkmenistan

Novyi Vostok

Revolutsiia i natsionalnosti
Russkii iazyk o natsional'noi shkole
Turkmenovedenie
Turkmenskaia iskra
Zhizn' natsional'nostei
Zhurnal ministerstva narodnogo prosveshcheniia (ZhMNP)

Turkish language:

bilig
Bülten Press—Uluslararası Türkmen Türk Üniversitesi yayın organı.
Defter

Azymow, Pigam, and Mıratgeldi Söyegow. "Türkmen Elipbiýi: Düýni, şu güni, ertiri." In
  Uluslararası Türk Dili Kongresi 1992 (26 Eylül 1992–1 Ekim 1992), 69–77. Ankara:
  Türk Dil Kurumu Yayınları, 1996.
Azymow, P. "Türkmen diliniň käbir meseleleri hakynda." In *Ýgyndyda: Türkmen diliniň
  orfografiýa, punktuatsiýa we terminologiýa meseleleri*, 9–10. Aşgabat: Academy of Sci-
  ences, 1955.
Böriýew, Kumuşaly. "Türkmen dili." *Türkmen medeniýeti* 3–4 (1931): 40–44.
Böriýew, Kumuşaly. "Türkmenistan ylmy konferentsiasynyň degişli." *Türkmenistan*, 20
  April 1930, 2–3.
Böriýew, Kumuşaly. "Türkmenistanyň birinji ylmy konferentsiýasy." *Türkmenistan*, 6 April
  1930, 2–3.
Celilov, Feridun. "Ortak Türk Dili." Paper presented at symposium held at the Türkiyat
  Araştırmaları Enstitüsü (Turkic Institute), Marmara University, on 18–20 November
  1991.
Chislennost' i sostav naseleniia SSSR. Moscow, 1984.
Choreklieva, Aina. "Tempus Programme in Turkmenistan." Twelfth OSCE Economic Fo-
  rum, Prague, 31 May–4 June 2004.
*Direktivy VKP(b) i postanovleniia Sovetskogo pravitel'stva o narodnom obrazovanii, vypusk
  2-i. Is-tvo Ak. Peknauk RSFSR*. Moscow, 1947.
Dünýa Türkmenleri (Doly takyklanmadyk ylmy maglumatlar. Aşgabat: Ruh, 1994.
Geldiýew, Muhammet, and Gibad Alparow. *Türkmen diliň grammatykasy*. Aşgabat:
  Türkmenistan Döwlet Neşiraty, 1929.
*Itogi vsesoiuznaia perepis' naselenia 1989 goda, tom I, chislennost' i razmeshchenie naseleniia
  SSSR*. Minneapolis: East View Publications, 1992.
Itogi vsesoiuznoi perepisi naseleniia 1970 goda. Vol. 4. Moscow, 1973.
Itogo vsesoiuznoi perepisi naseleniia 1959 goda Turkmenskaia SSR. Moscow: Gosstatizdat,
  1963.

Krushchev, N. S. *On Strengthening the Ties of the School with Life, and Further Developing the System of Public Education.* Soviet Booklet, no. 42. Moscow, 1958.

Lenin, V. I. *Polnoe sobranie sochinenii.* Vol. 24. Moscow, 1961.

Nazarov, O., and Ia. Charyiarov. *Turkmensko-russkoe dvuiazychie na sovremennom etape.* Aşgabat: Ylym, 1990.

Nyýazow, S. "Türkmenistanyň Prezidentiniň karary: Türkmen diliniň täze elipbiýini kabul etmek hakynda." 12 April 1993. Reprinted in *Türkmen Arhiwi* 1–2 (1994): 4–5.

O nachal'noi i srednei shkole postanovlenie TsK KP(b)T "O vypolnenii direktiv po nachal'noi i srednei shkole" ot 5 sentiabria 1933. Aşgabat: Türkmenpartneşir, 1999.

Ostroumov, Nikolai Petrovich. *Konstantin Petrovich fon-Kaufman, ustroitel' Turkestanskogo krai.* Tashkent, 1899.

Pedagogicheskii slovar. Moscow, 1960.

Potseluevksii, Aleksandr Petrovich. *Rukhovodstvo dlia izucheniia turkmenskogo iazyka.* Aşgabat: Turkmengosizdat, 1929.

Potseluevksii, Aleksandr Petrovich. *Fonetika turkmenskogo iazyka.* Aşgabat, 1936.

Programma po russkomu iazyku dlia turkmenskikh nachal'nykh i nepolnykh srednikh shkol. Ashkhabad: Turkmengosizdat, 1937.

Sürekli Türk Dili Kurultayı (Permanent Turkish Language Council). Kültür Bak., 4–8 May 1992, and at the International Turkic Language Congress, 26 September–1 October 1992. Ankara: Turk Dil Kurumu, 1992.

Tsentral'noe statisticheskoe upravlenie pri Sovete ministrov SSSR. *Itogi vsesoiuznoi perepisi naseleniia 1959 goda: SSSR.* Moscow, 1962.

Tsentral'noe statisticheskoe upravlenie SSSR. *Narodnoe prosveshchenie v SSSR, 1926/27 uchebnyi god.* Moscow, 1929.

Tsentral'noe statisticheskoe upravlenie Turkmenskoi SSR. *Kul'turnoe stroitel'stvo Turkmenskoi SSR: Statistichskoe sbornik.* Ashkhabad, 1960.

Türkmenbaşy, Saparmurat. *Bilimli nesil—kuwwatly Watan.* Aşgabat: Magaryf, 1994.

Türkmenbaşy, Saparmurat. *Ruhnama.* Aşgabat: Turkmen dowlet nesiryat gullugy, 2001.

Türkmen diliň gramatykasy. Aşgabat: Türkmenistan Döwlet Neşiraty, 1929.

Türkmen diliniň lingvistik terminlerini düzgüne salmak hakynda (TSSR-iň II lingvistik gurultaýyna materiýallar). Aşgabat: Türkmenistan SSR Ylymlar Akademiýasy, 1951.

Türkmenistan Birinji ylmy konferensiýasyniň edebi dil, adalga hem imla dogrusnda çykaran karary. Aşgabat, 1930.

Türkmenistanyň Hemişelik Bitaraplygy. Aşgabat, 2005.

Secondary Sources

Abaeva, A. M. "Nekatorye voprosy razvitiia sotsialisticheskikh natsii v period razvernutogo stroitelstva kommunizma." *Izvestiia Akademii Nauk Turkmenskoi SSR* 6 (1963): 40–53.

Abendroth, Mark, and Peter McLaren. *Rebel Literacy: Cuba's National Literacy Campaign and Critical Global Citizenship.* Duluth, MN: Litwin Books, 2009.

Adams, Laura L. "Modernity, Postcolonialism, and Theatrical Form in Uzbekistan." *Slavic Review* 64, no. 2 (2005): 333–54.

Adams, Laura L. *The Spectacular State: Culture and National Identity in Uzbekistan.* Durham: Duke University Press, 2010.

Agai, Bekim. "The Gülen Movement's Islamic Ethic of Education." In Yavuz and Esposito, *Turkish Islam*, 48–68.

Agazade, A., and K. Karakashli. *Ocherk po istorii razvitiia dvizhenie novogo alfavita i ego dostizheniia.* Kazan, 1928.

Aliyeva, Hatyra A. "Birinci Türkoloji Kurultayı ve Ortak Türk Yazı Dili Üzerine." In *Üçünci Uluslar arası Türk Dil Kurultayı 1996*, 105–7. Ankara: TDK, 1999.

Allworth, Edward A., ed. *Central Asia, 130 Years of Russian Dominance: A Historical Overview.* Durham: Duke University Press, 1994.

Allworth, Edward A. *The Modern Uzbeks from the Fourteenth Century to the Present: A Cultural History.* Stanford: Hoover Institution Press, 1990.

Altstadt, Audrey, L. *The Azerbaijani Turks: Power and Identity under Russian Rule.* Stanford: Hoover Institute Press, 1992.

Altstadt, Audrey, L. *The Politics of Culture in Soviet Azerbaijan, 1920–1940.* London: Routledge, 2016.

Amansaryýew, B. *Türkmenistan Täze Galkanyş Eýýamynda: Ylym we Bilim.* Aşgabat: Türkmen döwlet neşirýat gullugy, 2009.

Anceschi, Luca. *Turkmenistan's Foreign Policy: Positive Neutrality and the Consolidation of the Turkmen Regime.* London: Routledge, 2009.

Anderson, Barbara, and Brian D. Silver. "Equality, Efficiency, and Politics in Soviet Bilingual Education Policy, 1934–1980." *American Political Science Review* 78, no. 4 (1984): 1019–39.

Annagurdow, M. D. *Ocherki po istorii likvidatsii negramotnosti v sovetskom turkmenistane.* Ashkhabad, 1961.

Annagurdow, M. D. *Sowet Türkmenistanynda Sowatsyzlygyň ýok ediliş Taryhyndan oçerkler.* Aşgabat, 1960.

Ansari, Ali M. *Modern Iran since 1921: The Pahlavis and After.* London: Pearson Education, 2003.

Apay, A. "Turkish Higher Education Initiatives toward Central Asia." In *The Challenge of Education in Central Asia*, edited by S. P. Heyneman and A. J. DeYoung, 81–96. Greenwich, CT: InfoAgePub.

Arnove, Robert F. "The Nicaraguan National Literacy Crusade of 1980." *Comparative Education Review* 25 (1981): 244–59.

Arnove, Robert F., and Harvey J. Graff, eds. *National Literacy Campaigns: Historical and Comparative Perspectives.* New York: Plenum Press, 1987.

Ascoli, Albert Russell, and Krystyna von Henneberg, eds. *Making and Remaking Italy: The Cultivation of National Identity around the Risorgimento.* Oxford: Berg, 2001.

Atabaki, Touraj, ed. *Modernity and Its Agencies: Young Movements in the History of the South*. New Delhi: Manohar, 2010.

Atkin, Muriel. "Islam as Faith, Politics and Bogeyman in Tajikistan." In *The Politics of Religion in Russia and the New States of Eurasia*, edited by M. Bordeaux, 260–65. Armonk, NY: M. E. Sharpe, 1995.

"Azeri Türkçesi." *Inönü Ansiklopedisi*, 4: 437.

Azimov, P. A., and Iu. D. Desheriev. *Sovetskii opyt razvitiia natsinal'nykh kul'tur na baze rodnykh iazykov*. Moscow, 1972.

Azimov, Pigam. *Orfografiia turkmeskogo iazyka: kratkii spravochnik*. Aşgabat, 1959.

B. N., ed. *Pygamberler, Dört Çaryýarlar, Perişdeler*. Aşgabat, 1991.

Baldauf, Ingeborg. "Jadidism in Central Asia within Reformism and Modernism in the Muslim World." *Die Welt des Islams* 41, no. 1 (2000): 72–88.

Basilov, V. N. "Blessing in a Dream. A Story Told by an Uzbek Musician." *Turcica* 27 (1995): 237–46.

Bauman, Zygmunt. *Modernity and the Holocaust*. Cambridge: Polity Press, 1989.

Beissinger, Mark. *Nationalist Mobilization and the Collapse of the Soviet State*. Cambridge: Cambridge University Press, 2002.

Beissinger, Mark. "The Relentless Pursuit of the National State: Reflections on Soviet and Post-Soviet Experiences." In *Global Convulsions: Race, Ethnicity, and Nationalism at the End of the Twentieth Century*, edited by Winston A. Van Horne, 227–46. Albany: State University of New York Press, 1997.

Bendrikov, K. E. *Ocherki po istorii narodnogo obrazovaniia v Turkestane, 1865–1925 gody*. Moscow: Izd. Akademii pedagochieskikh nauk, 1960.

Bennigsen, Alexandre, and Chantal Lemercier-Quelquejay. *La Presse et le Mouvement National chez les Musulmans de Russie avant 1920*. Paris: Mouton de Gruyter, 1964.

Bennigsen, Alexandre, and S. Enders Wimbush. *Mystics and Commissars: Sufism in the Soviet Union*. Berkeley: University of California Press, 1985.

Berdichevsky, Norman. *Nations, Language and Citizenship*. Jefferson, NC: McFarland, 2004.

Berdiýew, T. B. *Ocherki po istorii shkoly Turkmenskoi SSR*. Askhabad: Akademii Nauk TSSR, 1960.

Berdimuhamedow, Gurbanguly. *To New Heights of Progress*. Vol. 6 of *Selected Works*. Ashgabat: Turkmen State Publishing Service, 2013.

Berman, Marshall. *All That Is Solid Melts into Air: Experiences with Modernity*. London: Verso, 1983.

Bermel, Neil. *Linguistic Authority, Language Ideology, and Metaphor: The Czech Orthography Wars*. Berlin: Mouton de Gruyter, 2007.

Bilinsky, Yaroslav. "Education of the Non-Russian Peoples in the USSR, 1917–1967: An Essay." *Slavic Review* 27, no. 3 (1968): 411–37.

Bilinsky, Yaroslav. "Expanding the Use of Russian or Russification." *Russian Review* 40, no. 3 (1981): 317–32.

Bilinsky, Yaroslav. "The Soviet Education Laws of 1958–1959 and Soviet Nationality Policy." *Soviet Studies* 14, no. 2 (1962): 138–57.

"Birleşik Devletlet Topluluğu'nda Türkçe." *Dil Dergisi* 4 (January 1992): 38–43.

Blackwell, Carole. *Tradition and Society in Turkmenistan: Gender, Oral Culture, and Song.* Richmond, Surrey, UK: Curzon Press, 2001.

Blank, Stephen. *Sorcerer as Apprentice: Stalin as Commissar of Nationalities, 1917–1924.* Westport, CT: Greenwood Press, 1994.

Blank, Stephen. *Turkmenistan and Central Asia after Niyazov.* Carlisle: Strategic Studies Institute, 2007.

Bonnell, Victoria. *Iconography of Power: Soviet Political Posters under Lenin and Stalin.* Berkeley: University of California Press, 1997.

Boone, Elizabeth Hill, and Walter D. Mignolo, eds. *Writing without Words: Alternative Literacies in Mesoamerica and the Andes.* Durham: Duke University Press, 1994.

Bouma, Amieke. "Turkmenistan: Epics in Place of Historiography." *Jahrbücher Osteuropäischer Geschichte* 59, no. 4 (2011): 559–85.

Bourdieu, Pierre. "Cultural Reproduction and Social Reproduction." In *Knowledge, Education and Cultural Change*, edited by Richard Brown. London: Tavistock, 1973.

Bourdieu, Pierre. *The Field of Cultural Production: Essays on Art and Literature.* Edited and introduced by Randal Johnson. New York: Columbia University Press, 1993.

Bourdieu, Pierre. *Language and Symbolic Power.* Cambridge, MA: Harvard University Press, 2003.

Bourdieu, Pierre. "Systems of Education and Systems of Thought." *International Social Science Journal* 19 (1967): 338–58.

Bourdieu, Pierre, and Jean-Claude Passeron. *Reproduction in Education, Society and Culture.* Translated by Richard Nice. London: Sage, 2000.

Bowen, James. *Soviet Education: Anton Makarenko and the Years of Experiment.* Madison: University of Wisconsin University Press, 1962.

Brandt, Deborah. "Literacy and Knowledge." In *The Right to Literacy*, edited by Andrea Lunsford, Helene Moglen, and James F. Slevin, 189–96. New York: Modern Language Association of America, 1990.

Brandt, Deborah. "Sponsors of Literacy." In *Literacy and Historical Development: A Reader*, edited by Harvey Graff, 357–78. Carbondale: University of Illinois Press, 2007.

Brass, Paul. *Language, Religion and Politics in North India.* London, 1974.

Braude, Benjamin. "Foundation Myths of the *Millet* System." In *Christians and Jews in the Ottoman Empire: The Functioning of a Plural Society*, edited by Benjamin Braude and Bernard Lewis, 69–88. New York: Holmes and Meier, 1982.

Bregel, Yuri. *Khorezmskie Turkmeny v XIX veke.* Moskva: Izdatel'stvo vostochnoi lit., 1961.

Brenner, Louis. *Controlling Knowledge: Religion, Power and Schooling in a West African Muslim Society.* Bloomington: Indiana University Press, 2001.

Brooks, Jeffrey. *When Russia Learned to Read: Literacy and Popular Literature, 1861–1917.* Princeton, NJ: Princeton University Press, 1985.

Brower, Daniel. *Turkestan and the Fate of the Russian Empire*. London, 2003.

Brower, Daniel R., and Edward J. Lazzerini, eds. *Russia's Orient: Imperial Borderlands and Peoples, 1700–1917*. Bloomington: Indiana University Press, 1997.

Brown, Bess. "Political Developments in Soviet Central Asia: Some Aspects of the Restructuring Process in Turkmenistan, Kirgizia and Kazakhstan in the Late 1980s." In *Political and Economic Trends in Central Asia*, edited by Shirin Akiner, 62–74. London: I. B. Tauris, 1994.

Brubaker, Rogers. *Nationalism Reframed: Nationhood and the National Question in the New Europe*. Cambridge: Cambridge University Press, 1996.

Calhoun, Craig. *Nationalism*. Minneapolis: Open University Press, 1997.

Carlisle, Donald S. "Modernization, Generations and the Uzbek Soviet Intelligentsiia." In *The Dynamics of Soviet Politics*, edited by Paul Cocks, Robert V. Daniels, and Nancy Whittier Heer, 220–46. Cambridge, MA: Harvard University Press, 1976.

Carrère d'Encausse, Hélène. *Decline of an Empire: The Soviet Socialist Republics in Revolt*. 2nd ed. Translated by Martin Sokolinsky and Henry A. La Farge. New York: Harper and Row, 1982.

Carron, G., and Anil Bordia, eds. *Issues in Language Planning and Implementing National Literacy Programmes*. Paris: UNESCO and IIEP, 1985.

Chatham House. *REP Seminar Summary: Turkmenistan's Domestic and Foreign Policy*, 12 October 2011. London: Chatham House, 2011.

Chatterjee, Partha. *The Nation and Its Fragments: Colonial and Postcolonial Histories*. Princeton, NJ: Princeton University Press, 1993.

Chatterjee, Partha. "Talking about Our Modernity in Two Languages." In *A Possible India: Essays in Political Criticism*, 263–85. New Delhi: Oxford University Press, 1997.

Chen, Ping. *Modern Chinese: History and Sociolinguistics*. Cambridge: Cambridge University Press, 1999.

Çinar, Alev. *Modernity, Islam, and Secularism in Turkey: Bodies, Places, and Time*. Minneapolis: University of Minnesota, 2005.

Ciscel, Matthew H. *The Language of the Moldovans: Romania, Russia, and Identity in an Ex-Soviet Republic*. Lanham: Lexington Books, 2007.

Clark, Larry. *Turkmen Reference Grammar*. Wiesbaden: Harrassowitz Verlag, 1998.

Clement, Victoria. "Alphabet Changes in Turkmenistan: State, Society, and the Everyday, 1904–2004." In *Everyday Life in Central Asia: Past and Present*, edited by Jeff Sahadeo and Russel Zanca, 266–80. Bloomington: Indiana University Press, 2007.

Clement, Victoria. "Articulating National Identity in Turkmenistan: Inventing Tradition through Myth, Cult and Language." *Nations & Nationalism* 20, no. 3 (2014): 546–62.

Clement, Victoria. "Central Asia's Hizmet Schools." In *The Muslim World and Politics in Transition: Creative Contributions of the Gülen Movement*, edited by Greg Barton, Paul Weller, and Ihsan Yılmaz, 154–67. London: Bloomsbury Publishing, 2013.

Clement, Victoria. "Emblems of Independence: Script Choice in Post-Soviet Turkmenistan." *International Journal of the Sociology of Language* 192 (July 2008): 171–85.

Clement, Victoria. "Faith-Based Schools in Post-Soviet Türkmenistan." *European Education* 43, no. 1 (2011): 76–92.

Clement, Victoria. "Grassroots Educational Initiatives in Türkmenistan." In *Globalization on the Margins: Education and Post-socialist Transformations in Central Asia*, edited by Iveta Silova, 345–62. Charlotte: Information Age Publishing, 2010.

Clement, Victoria. "Secular and Religious Trends in Turkmen Education." Unpublished study for Eurasia Policy Studies Program, National Bureau of Asian Research, August 2004. In author's possession.

Clement, Victoria. "Türkmenistan's New Challenges: Can Stability Co-exist with Reform? A Study of Gülen Schools in Central Asia." In *Muslim World in Transition: Contributions of the Gülen Movement*, edited by Greg Barton, Paul Weller, and Ihsan Yılmaz, 572–83. London: Leeds Metropolitan University Press, 2007.

Cole, David, and Linda J. Graham, eds. *The Power in/of Language*. Malden: Wiley Blackwell, 2012.

Collins, James, and Richard K. Blot. *Literacy and Literacies: Texts, Power, and Identity*. Cambridge: Cambridge University Press, 2009.

Comte, Auguste. *System of Positive Polity*. 4 vols. London: Longmans Green, 1875–1877.

Cooper, Robert. *Language Planning and Social Change*. Cambridge: Cambridge University Press, 1989.

Coulmas, Florian, ed. *Language Adaptation*. Cambridge: Cambridge University Press, 1989.

Coulson, N. J. *A History of Islamic Law*. Edinburgh: Edinburgh University Press, 1997.

"Cracks in the Marble: Turkmenistan's Failing Dictatorship." *Asia Report No. 44*. International Crisis Group, 2003.

Crews, Robert. *For Prophet and Tsar: Islam and Empire in Russia and Central Asia*. Cambridge, MA: Harvard University Press, 2009.

Crisp, Simon. "Soviet Language Planning, 1917–1953." In Kirkwood, *Language Planning*, 23–45.

CSCE Report on Turkmenistan's Referendum on Independence, October 26, 1991. Ashkhabad, Turkmenistan, 27 November 1991.

Cummings, Sally, ed. *Power and Change in Central Asia*. London: Routledge, 2002.

Dadabaev, Timur. *Identity and Memory in Post-Soviet Central Asia: Uzbekistan's Soviet Past*. London: Routledge, 2016.

Danev, A. M., ed. *Narodnoe obrazovanie: osnovnye postanovleniia, prikazy i instruktsii*. Moscow: MNP, 1948.

David-Fox, Michael. *Revolution of the Mind: Higher Learning among the Bolsheviks, 1918–1929*. Ithaca: Cornell University Press, 1997.

David-Fox, Michael. "What Is Cultural Revolution?" *Russian Review* 58, no. 2 (1999): 181–201.

Demidov, M. S. *Postsovetskii Turkmenistan*. Moscow: Natalis, 2002.

Demir, Cennet Engin, Ayse Balci, and Fusun Akkok. "The Role of Turkish Schools in the Educational System and Social Transformation of Central Asian Countries: The Case of Turkmenistan and Kyrgyzstan." *Central Asian Survey* 19, no. 1 (2000): 141–55.

Denison, Michael. "The Art of the Impossible: Political Symbolism, and the Creation of National Identity and Collective Memory in Post-Soviet Turkmenistan." *Europe-Asia Studies* 61, no. 7 (September 2009): 1167–87.

Desheriev, Iu. D. "Russkii iazyk i razvitoe sotsialisticheskoe obshchestvo." *Russkii iazyk i literature v shkolakh SSSR* 5 (1977): 14–29.

Desheriev, Iu. D. *Zakonomernosti razvitiia literaturnykh iazykov narodov SSSR v sovetskuiu epokhu: Razvitie obshchestvennykh funktsii literaturnykh iazykov.* Moscow: Izdatel'stvo Nauka, 1976.

Deutsch, Karl W. *Nationalism and Social Communication.* New York: John Wiley and Sons, 1953.

Dirlik, Arif. "Revisioning Modernity: Modernity in Eurasian Perspectives." *Inter-Asia Cultural Studies* 12, no. 2 (2011): 284–305.

Disch, Robert, ed. *The Future of Literacy.* Englewood Cliffs, NJ: Prentice-Hall, 1973.

Division of International Education. *Education in the USSR.* Bulletin 1957, No. 14. Washington, DC: Government Printing Office, 1957.

Droeber, Julia. "Ramadan in Kyrgyzstan: An Ethnographer's Gaze on Fasting." *ISIM Newsletter* 12 (2002): 56.

Duara, Prasajit. *Rescuing History from the Nation: Questioning Narratives of Modern China.* Chicago: University of Chicago Press, 1996.

Dunlop, John. *The New Russian Nationalism.* New York: Praeger, 1985.

Durdyýew, M., and Sh. Kadyrow. *Dünýädäki Türkmenler: Taryhy-Demografik Syn.* Aşgabat: Harp, 1991.

Durdyýew, Tagan. *Formirovanie i razvitie turkmenskoe sovetskoi intelligentsia, 1917–1958.* Aşgabat: Ylym, 1972.

Durdyýew, Hezretguly. *Ýigriminji Ýyllarda Türkmen Dil Biliminiň Ösüşi.* Aşgabat, 1995.

Edgar, Adrienne Lynn. "Emancipation of the Unveiled: Turkmen Women under Soviet Rule, 1924–1929." *Russian Review* 62, no. 1 (2003): 132–49.

Edgar, Adrienne Lynn. "The Fragmented Nation: Genealogy, Identity, and Social Hierarchy in Turkmenistan." In *Race and Nation: Ethnic Systems in the Modern World*, edited by Paul Spickard, 257–72. New York: Routledge, 2005.

Edgar, Adrienne Lynn. "Genealogy, Class, and 'Tribal Policy' in Soviet Turkmenistan, 1924–1934." *Slavic Review* 60, no. 2 (2001): 266–88.

Edgar, Adrienne Lynn. "Nationality Policy and National Identity: The Turkmen Soviet Socialist Republic, 1924–1929." *Journal of Central Asian Studies* 1 (Spring–Summer 1997): 2–20.

Edgar, Adrienne Lynn. *Tribal Nation: The Making of Soviet Turkmenistan.* Princeton, NJ: Princeton University Press, 2004.

Egengeldiýew, E., and O. Abdyrahmanow. *Bilnäýmeli, Bilinmeýän zatlar.* Aşgabat: Abaman, 1995.

Eisenstadt, Shmuel Noah. "Multiple Modernities." *Daedalus* 129, no. 1 (2000): 1–29.

Eisenstadt, Shmuel Noah. *Multiple Modernities.* Piscataway, NJ: Transaction, 2002.

Eisenstadt, Shmuel Noah. *Russian Peasant Schools: Officialdom, Village Culture, and Popular Pedagogy, 1861–1914.* Berkeley: University of California Press, 1986.

Eklof, Ben. "Russian Literacy Campaigns, 1861–1939." In Arnove and Graff, *National Literacy Campaigns*, 123–46.

Eklof, Ben, ed. *School and Society in Tsarist and Soviet Russia.* London: Macmillan, 1993.

Elias, Norbert. *On Civilization, Power and Knowledge.* Chicago: Chicago University Press, 1998.

Ercilasun, Ahmet B. "Latin Alfabesi Konusunda Gelişmeler." *Türk Dili* (July 1995): 523.

Ermolaev, Herman. *Censorship in Soviet Literature, 1917–1991.* Lanham: Rowman and Littlefield, 1997.

Ertük, Nergis. *Grammatology and Literary Modernity in Turkey.* Oxford: Oxford University Press, 2011.

Estraikh, Gennady. *Soviet Yiddish: Language Planning and Linguistic Development.* Oxford: Oxford University Press, 1999.

Evered, Emine Ö. *Empire and Education under the Ottomans: Politics, Reform and Resistance from the Tanzimat to the Young Turks.* New York: I. B. Tauris, 2012.

Ewing, E. Thomas. *Separate Schools: Gender, Policy, and Practice in Postwar Soviet Education.* DeKalb: Northern University Press, 2010.

Feldrugge, F. J. M., ed. *The Constitutions of the USSR and the Union Republics.* Alphen aan den Rijn: Sithoff and Nordhoff, 1979.

Ferguson, Charles A. "Diglossia." *Word* 15 (1959): 325–40.

Fierman, William. "Independence and the Declining Priority of Language Law Implementation in Uzbekistan." In *Muslim Eurasia: Conflicting Legacies*, edited by Yaacov Ro'i, 205–30. Portland: Frank Cass, 1995.

Fierman, William. "Introduction: Division of Linguistic Space." In "Implementing Language Laws: Perestroika and Its Legacy in Five Republics." Special issue, *Nationalities Papers* 23, no. 3 (1995): 507–13.

Fierman, William. "Language Development in Soviet Uzbekistan." In *Sociolinguistic Perspectives on Soviet National Languages: Their Past, Present, and Future*, edited by Isabelle Kreindler, 205–33. Berlin: Mouton de Gruyter, 1985.

Fierman, William. *Language Planning and National Development: The Uzbek Experience.* Berlin: Mouton de Gruyter, 1991.

Figes, Orlando, and Boris Kolonitskii. *Interpreting the Russian Revolution: The Language and Symbols of 1917.* New Haven: Yale University Press, 1999.

Findley, Carter Vaughn. *The Turks in World History.* Oxford: Oxford University Press, 2005.

Fishman, Joshua A., ed. *Advances in Language Planning.* The Hague: Mouton de Gruyter, 1974.

Fishman, Joshua A., ed. *Advances in the Creation and Revision of Writing Systems*. The Hague: Mouton de Gruyter, 1977.

Fishman, Joshua A. "Sociolinguistics: More Power(s) to You! On the Explicit Study of Power in Sociolinguistic Research." In *"Along the Routes to Power": Explorations of Empowerment through Language*, edited by Martin Pütz, Joshua A. Fishman, and JoAnne Neff-van Aertselaer, 1–11. Berlin: Mouton de Gruyter, 2006.

Fishman, J. A., C. A. Ferguson, and J. Das Gupta, eds. *Language Problems of Developing Nations*. New York: Wiley, 1968.

Fitzpatrick, Sheila. *The Commissariat of Enlightenment: Soviet Organization of Education and the Arts under Lunacharsky, October 1917–1921*. Cambridge: Cambridge University Press, 1970.

Fitzpatrick, Sheila, ed. *The Cultural Front: Power and Culture in Revolutionary Russia*. Ithaca: Cornell University Press, 1992.

Fitzpatrick, Sheila. *Cultural Revolution in Russia, 1928–1931*. Bloomington: Indiana University Press, 1978.

Fitzpatrick, Sheila. *Education and Social Mobility in the Soviet Union, 1921–1934*. Cambridge: Cambridge University Press, 1979.

Fitzpatrick, Sheila. *The Russian Revolution, 1917–1932*. Oxford: Oxford University Press, 2008.

Fortna, Benjamin F. *Learning to Read in the Late Ottoman Empire and the Early Turkish Republic*. New York: Palgrave Macmillan, 2011.

Foucault, Michel. *The Archaeology of Knowledge and the Discourse on Language*. Translated by A. M. Sheridan Smith. New York: Pantheon Books, 1972.

Foucault, Michel. *Power/Knowledge: Selected Interviews and Other Writings, 1972–1977*. Edited and translated by Colin Gordon. Brighton, Sussex: Harvester Press, 1980.

Fuller, Graham E. "Turkey's New Eastern Orientation." In *Turkey's New Geopolitics: From the Balkans to Western China*, edited by Graham E. Fuller and Ian O. Lesser, 37–98. Boulder: Westview, 1993.

Galantı, Avram. "Arap ve Japon Yazıları." In *Tanzimat'tan Cumhuriyet'e Alfabe Tartışmaları*, edited by Hüseyin Yorulmaz, 150–56. Istanbul: Kitabevi, 1995.

Garcia, Ofelia, Rakhmiel Peltz, Harod Schiffman, and Joshua Fishman. *Language Loyalty, Continuity and Change: Joshua Fishman's Contributions to International Sociolinguistics*. Clevedon, UK: Multilingual Matters, 2006.

Geertz, Clifford. "Linguistic Etiquette." In *The Religion of Java*, edited by Clifford Geertz, 286–90. Glencoe: Free Press, 1960.

Geiss, Paul Georg. *Pre-tsarist and Tsarist Central Asia: Communal Commitment and Political Order in Change*. London: Routledge, 2003.

Geiss, Paul Georg. "Turkmen Tribalism." *Central Asian Survey* 18, no. 3 (1999): 347–57.

Geldimyradow, A. *Çeper edebiýatyň dili we edebi norma*. Aşgabat: Ylym, 1989.

Geldimyradow, A. *Türkmen edebi dilinde variantlaşma*. Aşgabat: Ylym, 1983.

Gellner, Ernest. *Nations and Nationalism*. Ithaca: Cornell University Press, 1983.

242 Bibliography

Geraci, Robert. "Russian Orientialism at an Impasse: Tsarist Education Policy and the 1910 Conference on Islam." In *Russia's Orient: Imperial Borderlands and Peoples, 1700–1917*, edited by Daniel R. Brower and Edward Lazzerini, 138–61. Bloomington: Indiana University Press, 1997.

Geraci, Robert. *Window on the East: National and Imperial Identities in Late Tsarist Russia.* Ithaca: Cornell University Press, 2001.

Getty, J. Arch. *Practicing Stalinism: Bolsheviks, Boyars, and the Persistence of Tradition.* New Haven: Yale University Press, 2013.

Ghandi, Jennifer. *Political Institutions under Dictatorships.* Cambridge: Cambridge University Press, 2008.

Gibb, H. A. R. *The Arab Conquests in Central Asia.* 1929. Reprint, New York: AMS Press, 1970.

Giddens, Anthony. *The Consequences of Modernity.* Stanford: Stanford University Press, 1990.

Golden, Peter. *An Introduction to the History of the Turkic Peoples: Ethnogenesis and State-Formation in Medieval and Early Modern Eurasia and the Middle East.* Weisbaden: Otto Harrassowitz, 1992.

Golden, Peter. "The Migrations of the Oguz." *Archivum Ottomanicum* 4 (1972): 47–81.

Goldhagen, Erich, ed. *Ethnic Minorities in the Soviet Union.* New York: Praeger, 1968.

Goldman, Wendy, ed. *Women, the State and Revolution: Soviet Family Policy and Social Life, 1917–1936.* Cambridge: Cambridge University Press, 1993.

Gorham, Michael S. *Speaking in Soviet Tongues: Language Culture and the Politics of Voice in Revolutionary Russia.* DeKalb: Northern Illinois University Press, 2003.

Graff, Harvey J. "Assessing the History of Literacy: Themes and Questions." In *Understanding Literacy in Its Historical Contexts: Socio-cultural History and the Legacy of Egil Johansson*, edited by Harvey J. Graff, Alison Mackinnon, Bengt Sandin, and Ian Winchester, 243–64. Lund, Sweden: Nordic Academic Press, 2009.

Graff, Harvey J. *The Labyrinths of Literacy: Reflections on Literacy Past and Present.* Pittsburgh: University of Pittsburgh Press, 1995.

Graff, Harvey J. *The Legacies of Literacy: Continuities and Contradictions in Western Society and Culture.* Bloomington: Indiana University Press, 1986.

Graff, Harvey J. "Literacy." In *Social Science Encyclopedia*, edited by Adam Kuper and Jessica Kuper, 587–89. 3rd ed. Vol. 2. London: Routledge, 2004.

Graff, Harvey J. *Literacy and Social Development in the West: A Reader.* Cambridge: Cambridge University Press, 1981.

Graff, Harvey J. *The Literacy Myth: Cultural Integration and Social Structure in the Nineteenth Century.* New Brunswick, NJ: Transaction Publishers, 1991.

Grant, Nigel. *Soviet Education.* 4th ed. Harmondsworth, England: Penguin, 1979.

Greenberg, Robert. *Language and Identity in the Balkans.* Oxford: Oxford University Press, 2004.

Grenoble, Lenore A. *Language Policy in the Soviet Union.* Dordrecht: Kluwer Academic, 2003.

Guboglo, Mikhail, ed. *Perelomnye gody, vol. II, Iazykovaia reforma-1989: dokumenty i materialy*. Moscow: Rossiisaia akademiia nauk, Institut etnologii i antropologii, 1994.

Haciyev, Toqif. "Ortaq Türkcə Deyilən Ədəbi Dil Mövzusunda." *Dil Kurutayı* 3 (1999): 503–9.

Haeri, Niloofar. *Sacred Language, Ordinary People: Dilemmas of Culture and Politics in Egypt*. New York: Palgrave Macmillan, 2003.

Hall, Chatwood. "Education among Three Soviet National Minorities." *Phylon* 2, no. 3 (1941): 218–22.

Haugen, Arne. *The Establishment of National Republics in Soviet Central Asia*. London: Palgrave, 2003.

Hayford, Charles W. "Literacy Movements in Modern China." In Arnove and Graff, *National Literacy Campaigns*, 147–71.

Henze, Paul B. "Politics and Alphabets of Inner Asia." In Fishman, *Language Planning*, 382–402.

Heyd, Uriel. *Language Reform in Modern Turkey*. Jerusalem: Israel Oriental Society, 1954.

Hirsch, Francine. *Empire of Nations: Ethnographic Knowledge and the Making of the Soviet Union*. Ithaca: Cornell University Press, 2005.

Hirshon, Sheryl L., with Judith Butler. *And Also Teach Them to Read*. Westport, CT: Lawrence Hill, 1983.

Hoffmann, David L. *Stalinist Values: The Cultural Norms of Soviet Modernity, 1917–1941*. Ithaca: Cornell University Press, 2003.

Hoffmann, David L., and Yanni Kotsonis, eds. *Russian Modernity: Politics, Knowledge, Practices*. New York: St. Martin's Press, 2000.

Horák, Slavomír. "Educational Reforms in Turkmenistan: Good Framework, Bad Content?" *Central Asia Policy Brief* no. 11. George Washington University, Washington, 2013.

Horák, Slavomír. "The Elite in Post-Soviet and Post-Niyazow Turkmenistan: Does Political Culture Form a Leader?" *Demokratizatsiya: The Journal of Post-Soviet Democratization* 20, no. 4 (2012): 371–86.

Horák, Slavomír. "Turkmenistan posle Turkmenbashi: K voprosu o transformatsii rezhimov lichnoi vlasti." *Politeks* 1 (2008): 63–79.

Holmes, Larry E. *The Kremlin and the Schoolhouse: Reforming Education in Soviet Russia, 1917–1931*. Bloomington: Indiana University Press, 1991.

Hosking, Geoffrey. *The Awakening of the Soviet Union*. London: Heinemann, 1990.

Houston, Rab. "The Literacy Campaign in Scotland, 1560–1803." In Arnove and Graff, *National Literacy Campaigns*, 49–98.

Houston, Rab. *Literacy in Early Modern Europe*. London: Longman, 2002.

Human Rights and Democratization in the Newly Independent States of the Former Soviet Union. Washington, DC: Commission on Security and Cooperation in Europe, 1993.

Huskey, Eugene. "The Politics of Language in Kyrgyzstan." *Nationalities Papers* 23 (1995): 549–72.

İğmen, Ali. *Speaking Soviet with an Accent: Culture and Power in Kyrgyzstan*. Pittsburgh: University of Pittsburgh Press, 2012.

Irons, William. *The Yomut Speaking Turkmen: A Study of Social Organization among a Central Asian Turkic-Speaking Population*. Ann Arbor: University of Michigan Press, 1975.

Isayev, M. I. *National Languages in the USSR: Problems and Solutions*. Moscow: Progress, 1977.

Istoriia Sovetskogo Turkmenistana: chast' pervaia (1917–1937). Ashkhbad: Ylym, 1970.

Ivanova, A. M. *Chto dala Sovetskaia vlast' po likvidatsii negramostnosti sredi vzroslykh*. Moscow, 1949.

Jernudd, Björn H., and Michael J. Shapiro, eds. *The Politics of Language Purism*. Berlin: Mouton de Gruyter, 1989.

Johansson, Egil. "Literacy Campaigns in Sweden." In Arnove and Graff, *National Literacy Campaigns*, 49–98.

Johnson, William H. E. *Russia's Educational Heritage: A Study of the Major Educational Policies and Programs Characterizing the Last Three Centuries of the Tsarist Regime*. Pittsburgh: Carnegie Institute of Technology, 1950.

Jones, Stephen F. "The Georgian Language State Program and Its Implications." *Nationalities Papers* 23, no. 3 (1995): 535–48.

Jones, Stephen F. "Glasnost', Perestroika, and the Georgian SSR." *Armenian Review* 43, nos. 2–3 (1990): 127–52.

Jusdanis, Gregory. *Belated Modernity and Aesthetic Culture: Inventing National Literature*. Minneapolis: University of Minnesota Press, 1991.

Kadyrov, Shokhrat. *"Natsiia" Plemen: Etnicheskie istoki, transformatsiia, perspektivy gosudarstvennosti v Turkmenistane*. Moscow: Norway Country Council Department of Regional Development, 2003.

Kamali, Masoud. *Multiple Modernities, Civil Society and Islam: The Case of Iran and Turkey*. Liverpool: Liverpool University Press, 2006.

Kamp, Marianne. "Between Women and the State: *Mahalla* Committees and Social Welfare in Uzbekistan." In *The Transformation of Central Asia: States and Societies from Soviet Rule to Independence*, edited by Pauline Jones Luong, 29–58. Ithaca: Cornell University Press, 2004.

Kamp, Marianne. *The New Uzbek Woman in Uzbekistan: Islam Modernity and Unveiling under Communism*. Seattle: University of Washington Press, 2006.

Kanbolat, Hasan. "Garaşsız Türkmenistan." *Türk Dünyası: Dil ve edebiyat dergisi* 2 (1996): 452.

Karimov, B., and S. Mutalov. *Urtaturk tili. "Ortaturk"—srednetiurkskii iazyk*. Tashkent: Mekhnat, 1992.

Kaya, Ibrahim. "Modernity, Openness, Interpretation: A Perspective on Multiple Modernities." *Social Science Information* 43, no. 1 (2004): 35–57.

Keller, Shoshana. "The Central Asian Bureau: An Essential Tool in Governing Soviet Turkestan." *Central Asian Survey* 22, no. 2–3 (2003): 281–97.

Keller, Shoshana. *To Moscow, Not Mecca: The Soviet Campaign against Islam in Central Asia, 1917–1941*. Westport, CT: Praeger, 2001.

Keller, Shoshana. "Trapped between State and Society: Women's Liberation and Islam in Soviet Uzbekistan, 1926–1941." *Journal of Women's History* 10, no. 1 (1998): 20–44.

Kelly, Catriona. *Children's World: Growing Up in Russia, 1989–1991*. New Haven: Yale University Press, 2007.

Kenez, Peter. *The Birth of the Propaganda State: Soviet Methods of Mass Mobilization, 1917–1929*. London: Cambridge University Press, 1985.

Kenez, Peter. "Liquidating Illiteracy in Revolutionary Russia." *Russian History* 9, pts. 2–3 (1982): 173–86.

Kennedy, Craig. "Soviet Nationalities: The Economic Dilemma." *Harvard International Review* 4, no. 2 (1981): 13–15.

Khalid, Adeeb. "Backwardness and the Quest for Civilization: Early Soviet Central Asia in Comparative Perspective." *Slavic Review* 65, no. 2 (2006): 231–51.

Khalid, Adeeb. "Being Muslim in Soviet Central Asia, or an Alternative History of Muslim Modernity." *Journal of the Canadian Historical Association* 18, no. 2 (2007): 123–43.

Khalid, Adeeb. *Islam after Communism: Religion and Politics in Central Asia*. Berkeley: University of California Press, 2007.

Khalid, Adeeb. *Making Uzbekistan: Nation, Empire, and Revolution in the Early USSR*. Ithaca: Cornell University Press, 2015.

Khalid, Adeeb. "Muslim Printers in Tsarist Central Asia: A Research Note." *Central Asian Survey* 11, no. 3 (1992): 111–18.

Khalid, Adeeb. "Nationalizing the Revolution: The Transformation of Jadidism, 1917–1920." In *A State of Nations: Empire and Nation-Making in the Age of Lenin and Stalin*, edited by Ron Grigor Suny and Terry Martin, 145–62. New York: Oxford University Press, 2001.

Khalid, Adeeb. *The Politics of Muslim Cultural Reform: Jadidism in Central Asia*. Berkeley: University of California Press, 1998.

Khalid, Adeeb. "A Secular Islam: Nation, State, and Religion in Uzbekistan." *International Journal of Middle East Studies* 35, no. 4 (2003): 573–98.

Khalid, Adeeb. "Tashkent, 1917: Muslim Politics in Revolutionary Turkestan." *Slavic Review* 55, no. 3 (1996): 270–96.

Khasanov, Mansur. *Galimjan Ibragimov*. Kazan, 1969.

Khlevniuk, Oleg. "Les mécanismes de la 'grande terreur' des années 1937–1938 au Turkménistan." *Cahiers du Monde Russe* 39, nos. 1–2 (January–June 1998): 197–208.

King, Christopher R. *One Language, Two Scripts: The Hindi Movement in Nineteenth-Century North India*. New Delhi: Oxford University Press, 1994.

Kırımlı, Hakan. *National Movements and National Identity among the Crimean Tatars (1905–1916)*. Leiden: E. J. Brill, 1996.

Kirişçi, Kemal. "New Patterns of Turkish Foreign Policy Behavior." In *Turkey: Political, Social and Economic Challenges in the 1990s*, edited by Ciğdem Balım, E. Kalaycioglu, B. Karataş, G. Winrow, and F. Yasamee, 1–21. Leiden: E. J. Brill, 1995.

Kirkwood, Michael. "Glasnost', 'the National Question,' and Soviet Language Policy." *Soviet Studies* 43, no. 1 (1991): 61–81.

Kirkwood, Michael. "Language Planning: Some Methodological Preliminaries." In Kirkwood, *Language Planning*, 1–22. Kirkwood, Michael, ed. *Language Planning in the Soviet Union*. New York: Palgrave Macmillan, 1990.

Korkmaz, Zeynep. "Türk Dünyası ve Ortak Yazı Dili Konusu." In *Uluslararası Türk Dili Kongresi 1992 (26 Eylül 1992–1 Ekim 1992)*, 189–97. Ankara: Türk Dil Kurumu Yayınları, 1996.

Kotkin, Stephen. *Magnetic Mountain: Stalinism as a Civilization*. Berkeley: University of California Press, 1995.

Kotkin, Stephen. "Modern Times: The Soviet Union and the Interwar Conjuncture." *Kritika* 2, no. 1 (2001): 111–64.

Kozol, Jonathan. *Children Are the Revolution*. New York: Delacorte Press, 1978.

Krasovitskaia, Tamara Iusupovna. *Vlast' i Kultura: Istoricheskii opyt organizatsii gosudarstvennogo rukovodstva natsional'no-kul'turnym stroitel'stvom*. Moscow: Nauk, 1992.

Kreindler, Isabelle T. "The Changing Status of Russian in the Soviet Union." *International Journal of the Sociology of Language* 33 (1982): 7–40.

Kreindler, Isabelle T. "Educational Policies toward the Eastern Nationalities in Tsarist Russia: A Study of Il'minskii's System." PhD dissertation, Columbia University, 1969.

Kreindler, Isabelle T. "Forging a Soviet People: Ethnolinguistics in Central Asia." In *Soviet Central Asia: The Failed Transformation*, edited by William Fierman, 219–31. Boulder: Westview, 1991.

Kreindler, Isabelle T. "The Non-Russian Languages and the Challenge of Russian: The Eastern versus the Western Tradition." In *Sociolinguistic Perspectives on Soviet National Languages: Their Past, Present, and Future*, edited by Isabelle Kreindler, 345–67. Berlin: Mouton de Gruyter, 1985.

Kreindler, Isabelle T. "A Second Missed Opportunity: Russian in Retreat as a Global Language." *International Political Science Review* 14, no. 3 (1993): 257–74.

Kreindler, Isabelle T. "Soviet Language Planning since 1953." In Kirkwood, *Language Planning*, 46–63. New York: St. Martin's Press, 1990.

Kreindler, Isabelle T. "Soviet Muslims Gains and Losses as a Result of Soviet Language Planning." *Muslim Eurasia: Conflicting Legacies*, ed. Yaacov Ro'i, 187–204. Portland: Frank Cass, 1995.

Krylova, Anna. "Soviet Modernity: Stephen Kotkin and the Bolshevik Predicament." *Contemporary European History* 23, no. 2 (2014): 167–92.

Kulturnoe stroitelstvo SSSR. Moscow: Nauka, 1940.

Kurbanov, A. A. "Obuchenie v konfessional'nykh i russko-tuzemnykh shkolakh b. Zakaspiiskii oblasti." *Uchenye Zapiski Turkmenskogo Gosudarstvennogo Universiteta im. A. M. Gor'kogo* 8 (1956): 37–92.

Kurbanov, A. A., and O. D. Kuz'min. *Ocherki po istorii razvitiia pedagogicheskoi mysli v turkmenistane*. Ashkhabad, 1973.

Kurbanov, A. M. *Türkoloji Dilcilik*. Baku: ADPU'nun Neşirat, 1993.

Kurtulan, Ildeniz. "Azerbaycan'ın Abece Sorunu." *Defter* 15 (1990): 29–33.

Kuru, Ahmet T. "Between the State and Cultural Zones: Nation Building in Turkmenistan." *Central Asian Survey* 21, no. 1 (2002): 71–90.

Kurzman, Charles, ed. *Modernist Islam, 1840–1940: A Sourcebook*. Oxford: Oxford University Press, 2002.

Kuttner, Thomas. "Russian Jadidism and the Islamic World: Ismail Gasprinskii in Cairo, 1908." *Cahiers du Monde Russe et Soviétique* 16, nos. 3–4 (1979): 383–424.

Labov, William. "Phonological Correlates of Social Stratification." *American Anthropologist* 66 (1964): 164–76.

Laitin, David. *Identity in Formation: The Russian-Speaking Populations in the Near Abroad*. Ithaca: Cornell University Press, 1998.

Landau, Jacob, and Barbara Kellner-Heinkele. *Language Politics in Contemporary Central Asia: National and Ethnic Identity and the Soviet Legacy*. New York: I. B. Tauris, 2012.

Landau, Jacob, and Barbara Kellner-Heinkele. *Politics of Language in the Ex-Soviet Muslim States*. Ann Arbor: University of Michigan Press, 2001.

Lapidus, Gail Warshofsky. "Educational Strategies and Cultural Revolution: The Politics of Soviet Development." In Fitzpatrick, *Cultural Revolution*, 78–104.

Lapidus, Gail W. "The Nationality Question and the Soviet System." *Proceedings of the Academy of Political Science* 35, no. 3 (1984): 98–112.

Lazzerini, Edward. "The Debate over Instruction of Muslims in Post-1905 Russia: A Local Perspective." In *Religious and Secular Forces in Late Tsarist Russia: Essays in Honor of Donald W. Treadgold*, edited by Charles E. Timberlake, 230–40. Seattle: University of Washington Press, 1992.

Lazzerini, Edward. "Ğadidism at the Turn of the Twentieth Century: A View from Within." *Cahiers du Monde Russe et Soviétique* 16, no. 2 (1975): 245–77.

Lazzerini, Edward. "Ismail Bey Gasprinskii and Muslim Modernism in Russia, 1873–1914." PhD dissertation, University of Washington, 1973.

Lazzerini, Edward. "Ismail Bey Gasprinskii's *Perevodchik/Tercuman*: A Clarion of Modernism." In *Central Asian Monuments*, edited by H. B. Paksoy, 143–66. Istanbul: Isis Press, 1992.

Lee, Raymond. "Reinventing Modernity: Reflexive Modernization vs Liquid Modernity vs Multiple Modernities." *European Journal of Social Theory* 9, no. 3 (2006): 355–68.

Leiser, Gary, ed. *A History of the Seljuks*. Carbondale: Southern Illinois University Press, 1988.

Lewis, David. *The Temptations of Tyranny in Central Asia*. New York: Columbia, 2008.

Lewis, Geoffrey, trans. *The Book of Dede Korkut*. Harmondsworth, UK: Penguin, 1974.

Lewis, E. Glyn. "Bilingualism as Language Planning in the Soviet Union." In *Western Perspectives on Soviet Education in the 1980s*, edited by J. J. Tomiak, 75–96. New York: St. Martin's Press, 1986.

Lewis, E. Glyn, ed. *Multilingualism in the Soviet Union: Aspects of Language Policy and Implementation*. The Hague: Mouton de Gruyter, 1972.

Lomakin, A. *Obychno pravo Turkmen (Adat)*. 2nd ed. Aşgabad: Ylym, 1994.

Long, Delbert H., and Roberta A. Long. *Education of Teachers in Russia*. Westport: Greenwood Press, 1999.

Low, Alfred D. "Soviet Nationality Policy and the New Program of the Communist Party of the Soviet Union." *Russian Review* 22, no. 1 (1963): 3–29.

Martin, Terry. *The Affirmative Action Empire: Nations and Nationalism in the Soviet Union, 1923–1939*. Ithaca: Cornell University Press, 2001.

Martin, Terry. "Modernization or Neo-traditionalism? Ascribed Nationality and Soviet Primordialism." In Hoffmann and Kotsonis, *Russian Modernity*, 161–82.

Medlin, William, William Cave, and Finley Carpenter, eds. *Education and Development in Central Asia: A Case Study on Social Change in Uzbekistan*. Leiden: E. J. Brill, 1971.

Mel'kumov, V. G. *Ocherki istorii partorganizatsii Turkmenskoi oblasti Turkesktanskoi ASSR*. Aşgabat: Turkmengosizdat, 1959.

Michaels, Paula. *Curative Powers: Medicine and Empire in Stalin's Soviet Central Asia*. Pittsburgh: University of Pittsburgh Press, 2003.

Mickiewicz, Ellen Propper. *Soviet Political Schools: The Communist Party Adult Instruction System*. New Haven: Yale University Press, 1967.

Miller, Valerie. *Between Struggle and Hope: The Nicaraguan Literacy Crusade*. Boulder: Westview, 1985.

Mingolo, Walter D. *Local Histories/Global Designs: Coloniality, Subaltern Knowledges, and Border Thinking*. Princeton, NJ: Princeton University Press, 2000.

Moos, Elizabeth. *Soviet Schools Visited*. New York: National Council of American-Soviet Friendship, 1961.

Murat, Aman Berdi. "Turkmenistan and the Turkmen." In *Handbook of Major Soviet Nationalities*, edited by Zev Katz, Rosmarie Rogers, and Frederic T. Harned, 262–82. New York: Free Press, 1975.

Murra, John V., Rubert M. Hankin, and Fred Holling, trans. *The Soviet Linguistic Controversy*. New York: King's Crown Press, 1951.

Musaev, K. M. *Alfavity iazykov narodov SSSR*. Moscow: Izdatel'stvo Nauka, 1965.

Myer, Will. *Islam and Colonialism: Western Perspectives on Central Asia*. London: Routledge Curzon, 2002.

Nazarow, O. *Türkmen dilinde Rus alynma Sözleri*. Aşgabat: Ylym, 1981.

Nissman, David B. "Turkmenistan: Just like the Old Times." In *New States, New Politics: Building the Post-Soviet Nations*, edited by Ian Bremmer and Ray Taras, 635–53. Cambridge: Cambridge University Press, 1997.

Nissman, David B. "Turkmenistan: Searching for a National Identity." In *Nations and Politics in the Soviet Successor States*, edited by Ian Bremmer and Ray Taras, 384–97. Cambridge: Cambridge University Press, 1993.

Northrop, Douglas. *Veiled Empire: Gender and Power in Stalinist Central Asia*. Ithaca: Cornell University Press, 2004.

Olcott, Martha Brill. "Yuri Andropov and the 'National Question.'" *Soviet Studies* 37, no. 1 (1985): 103–17.

Öner, Mustafa. "Notes on the Joint Turkish Alphabet." *Eurasian Studies* 13 (Spring 1998): 70.

Ornstein, Jacob. "Soviet Language Policy: Continuity and Change." *Ethnic Minorities in the Soviet Union*, edited by Erich Goldhagen, 121–46. New York: Praeger, 1968.

Özdalga, Elisabeth. "Following in the Footsteps of Fethullah Gülen: Three Women Tell Their Stories." In Yavuz and Esposito, *Turkish Islam*, 85–114.

Pal'vanova, Bibijan. *Tragichskie 30-e.* Aşgabat: Turkmenistan, 1991.

Pennar, Jaan. "Five Years after Khrushchev's School Reform." *Comparative Education Review* 8, no. 1 (1964): 73–77.

Pennar, Jaan, Ivan I. Bakalo, and George Z. F. Bereday. *Modernization and Diversity in Soviet Education with Special Reference to Nationality Groups.* New York: Praeger, 1971.

Perry, John R., and Rachel Lehr, trans. *The Sands of the Oxus: Boyhood Reminiscences of Sadriddin Aini.* Costa Mesa: Mazda, 1998.

Peterson, Glen. *The Power of Words: Literacy and Revolution in South China, 1949–95.* Vancouver: University of British Columbia Press, 1997.

Petrone, Karen. *Life Has Become More Joyous, Comrades: Celebrations in the Time of Stalin.* Bloomington: Indiana University Press, 2000.

Petros, Tiffany. "Islam in Central Asia: The Emergence and Growth of Radicalism in the Post-Communist Era." In *The Tracks of Tamerlane: Central Asia's Path to the Twenty-First Century*, edited by Daniel Burghart and Theresa Sabonis-Helf, 143–45. Washington, DC: National Defense University, Center for Technology and National Security Policy, 2004.

Peyrouse, Sebastien. "Berdy Mukhammedov's Turkmenistan: A Modest Shift in Domestic and Social Politics." *Journal of Central Asian Studies* 19, no. 1 (2010): 77–96.

Peyrouse, Sebastien. *Turkmenistan, Strategies of Power, Dilemmas of Development.* Armonk, NY: M. E. Sharpe, 2012.

Pigolkin, Albert, and Marina S. Studenikina. "Republican Language Laws in the USSR: A Comparative Analysis." *Journal of Soviet Nationalities* 2, no. 1 (1991): 38–76.

Pipes, Richard. *The Formation of the Soviet Union: Communism and Nationalism, 1917–1923.* 6th ed. Cambridge, MA: Harvard University Press, 1997.

Plamper, Jan. *The Stalin Cult: A Study in the Alchemy of Power.* New Haven: Yale University Press, 2012.

Potseluevskii, Aleksandr Petrovich. *Dialekty turkmenskogo iazyka.* Aşgabat: Turkmengosizdat, 1936.

Potseluevskii, Aleksandr Petrovich. "Dil we edebiýat ugrunda Türkmenkultyň eden işleri." *Türkmen Medeniýeti* 3 (1930): 10–11.

Potseluevskii, Aleksandr Petrovich. "Iazykovoe stroitel'stvo Turkmenii i ego osnovnye problemy." *Revoliutsiia i Natsional'nosti* 9 (1935): 42–50.

Potseluevskii, Aleksandr Petrovich. *Izbrannye Trudy*. Aşgabat: Ylym, 1975.

Potseluevskii, Aleksandr Petrovich. "Lingvisticheskaia ekspeditsiia GUSa." *Turkmenovedenie* 6, no. 2 (1928): 25–28.

Potseluevskii, Aleksandr Petrovich. "Razvitie Turkmenskogo iazyka." *Turkmenovedenie* 10–11 (1929): 71–72.

Potseluevksii, Aleksandr Petrovich. *Rukovodstvo dlia izucheniia turkmenskogo iazyka*. Aşgabat: Turkmengosizdat, 1929.

Prinsloo, M., and M. Breier, eds. *The Social Uses of Literacy: Theory and Practice in Contemporary South Africa*. Philadelphia: John Benjamins, 1996.

Privatsky, Bruce. *Muslim Turkistan: Kazak Religion and Collective Memory*. Richmond, Surrey: Curzon Press, 2001.

Pütz, Martin, Joshua Fishman, and JoAnne Neff-van Aertselaer, eds. *"Along the Routes to Power": Explorations of Empowerment through Language*. Berlin: Mouton de Gruyter, 2006.

Rabinowitch, Alexander. *The Bolsheviks in Power: The First Year of Soviet Rule in Petrograd*. Bloomington: Indiana University Press, 2007.

Rakowska-Harmstone, Teresa. *Russia and Nationalism in Central Asia: The Case of Tajikistan*. Baltimore: Johns Hopkins University Press, 1970.

Rappaport, Joanne, and Tom Cummins. *Beyond the Lettered City: Indigenous Literacies in the Andes*. Durham: Duke University Press, 2011.

Raun, Toivo U. "The Estonian SSR Language Law (1989): Background and Implementation." *Nationalities Papers* 23, no. 3 (1995): 515–34.

Rejepow, N. *Okatjagyň özara işjeňlik (interaktiw) usuly: Türkmenistanyň Bilim ministrligi tarapyndan hödürlenildi*. Aşgabat: Türkmen dölet neşiriýet gullugy, 2007.

Riordan, Jim, ed. *Soviet Youth Culture*. Bloomington: Indiana University Press, 1989.

Rodoslovnaia Turkmen: Sochinenie Abu-l-Gazi Khana Khivinskogo. Moscow: Izdatel'stvo Akademii Nauk SSSR, 1958.

Ro'i, Yaacov. *Islam in the Soviet Union: From the Second World War to Gorbachev*. New York: Columbia University Press, 2000.

Rorlich, Azade-Ayşe. *The Volga Tatars: A Profile in National Resilience*. Stanford: Hoover Institution Press, 1986.

Rosen, Seymour. *Education and Modernization in the USSR*. Reading, MA: Addison-Wesley, 1971.

Rosen, Seymour. *Education in the USSR: Recent Legislation and Statistics*. Washington, DC: US Government Printing House, 1975.

Roy, Olivier. *The New Central Asia: The Creation of Nations*. London: I. B. Tauris, 2000.

Rywkin, Michael. "Religion, Modern Nationalism and Political Power in Soviet Central Asia." *Canadian Slavonic Papers* 17, nos. 2–3 (1975): 271–85.

Rzaev, A. K. *Akhundov: Iz istorii politicheskoi i provovoi mysli*. Moscow: Iuridicheskaia literatura, 1980.

Sabol, Steve. "The Creation of Soviet Central Asia: The 1924 National Delimitation." *Central Asian Survey* 14, no. 2 (1995): 225–41.

Sabol, Steve. *Russian Colonization and the Genesis of Kazak National Consciousness*. New York: Palgrave Macmillan, 2003.

Sabol, Steve. "Turkmenbashi: Going It Alone." *Problems of Post-Communism* 50, no. 5 (2003): 48–57.

Saray, Mehmet. *The Turkmens in the Age of Imperialism: A Study of the Turkmen People and Their Incorporation into the Russian Empire*. Ankara: Turkish Historical Society Printing House, 1989.

Schamiloglu, Uli. "Formation of Tatar Historical Consciousness: Şihabäddin Märcani and the Image of the Golden Horde." *Central Asian Survey* 9, no. 2 (1990): 39–49.

Segars, Andrew. "Nation Building in Turkey and Uzbekistan: The Use of Language and History in the Creation of National Identity." In *Central Asia: Aspects of Transition*, edited by Tom Everett-Heath, 80–105. London: Routledge, 2003.

Serdyuchenko, G. P. "The Eradication of Illiteracy and the Creation of New Written Languages in the USSR." *International Journal of Adult and Youth Education* 14, no. 1 (1962): 23–29.

Shore, Maurice J. *Soviet Education: Its Psychology and Philosophy*. New York: Philosophical Library, 1947.

Siegelbaum, Lewis, and Andrei Sokolov. *Stalinism as a Way of Life: A Narrative in Documents*. New Haven: Yale University Press, 2000.

Silova, Iveta. "Reclaiming the Empire: Turkish Education Initiatives in Central Asia and Azerbaijan." In *South–South Transfer: Cooperation and Unequal Development in Education*, edited by L. Chisolm and G. Steiner-Khamsi, 173–91. New York: Teachers College Press, 2008.

Simon, Gerhard. *Nationalism and Policy toward the Nationalities in the Soviet Union: From Totalitarian Dictatorship to Post-Stalinist Society*. Translated by Karen Forster and Oswald Forster. Boulder: Westview, 1991.

Şimşir, Bilal. *Türk Yazı Devrimi*. Ankara: Türk Tarih Kurumu Basimevi, 1992.

Šir, Jan, with Slavomír Horák. *Dismantling Totalitarianism? Turkmenistan under Berdimuhamedow*. Washington, DC: Central Asia-Caucasus Institute, 2009.

Slezkine, Yuri. *Arctic Mirrors: Russia and the Small Peoples of the North*. Ithaca: Cornell University Press, 1994.

Slezkine, Yuri. "N. Ia. Marr and the National Origins of Soviet Ethnogenetics." *Slavic Review* 55, no. 4 (1996): 826–62.

Slezkine, Yuri. "The USSR as a Communal Apartment, or How a Socialist State Promoted Ethnic Particularism." *Slavic Review* 53, no. 2 (1994): 414–52.

Smith, Graham, Vivien Law, Andrew Wilson, Annette Bohr, and Edward Allworth. *Nation-Building in the Post-Soviet Borderlands: The Politics of National Identities*. Cambridge: Cambridge University Press, 1998.

Smith, Jeremy. *The Bolsheviks and the National Question, 1917–1923*. Houndmills, UK: Palgrave, 1999.

Smith, Michael G. *Language and Power in the Creation of the USSR, 1917–1953*. Berlin: Mouton de Gruyter, 1998.

Smith, Scott B. *Captives of Revolution: The Socialist Revolutionaries and the Bolshevik Dictatorship, 1918–1923*. Pittsburgh: University of Pittsburgh Press, 2011.

Solchanyk, Roman. "Russian Language and Soviet Politics." *Soviet Studies* 34, no. 1 (1982): 23–42.

Sovet Türkmenistanynyň medeniýetiniň taryhy (1917–1970). Aşgabat: Ylym neşirýaty, 1975.

Söýegow, Myratgeldi. "Bilim Kurucusu ve Dilbilimci: Kümüsali Börüoglu." *Bülten Press* 1 (1999): 6.

Söýegow, Myratgeldi. "Collected Works." Unpublished.

Söýegow, Myratgeldi. "Ilk Türkmen Kıtabı Yazarı: Alışbek Aliev." *Bülten Press* 1 (1999): 9.

Söýegow, Myratgeldi. "Istanbul Üniversitesi 1918 yılı mezunu Türkmen yazarı: Orazmammet Vepayev." *Bülten Press* 2 (2001): 32.

Söýegow, Myratgeldi. *On çynar: ilkinji Türkmen dilchileri we edebiýatçylary hakynda ocherkler*. Aşgabat: Kuýaş, 1993.

Söýegow, Myratgeldi. *Razvitie sintaksichskoi sistemy turkmenskogo literaturnogo iazyka v sovetskuiu epokhu*. Aşgabat: Ylym, 1991.

Soegov, Muratgeldi. "Stranitsy iz istorii turkmenskoi i kyrgyzskoi filologii v sud'bakh ee predstavitelei." *Türkoloji Üzerine Araştırımalar* 1 (2012): 133.

Söýegow, Myratgeldi. "Tek Dramıyıa Edebiyat Tarihine Girmiş Olan Yazar: Ayıcan Haldurdiyev." *Bülten Press* 3 (2001): 34.

Söýegow, Myratgeldi, et al. *Turkmen Dili* 6. Istanbul: MEB Basımevi, 1996.

Söýegow, Myratgeldi. "Türkmen edebiýatında ceditçilik dönemi hakkynda bazi tesbitler ve yeni mlumatlar." *bilig* 7 (1998): 112–18.

Söýegow, Myratgeldi, and Nyýazberdi Rejepow. *Täze Türkmen elipbiýi*. Aşgabat: Ruh, 1993.

Spolsky, Bernard. *Language Policy: Key Topics in Sociolinguistics*. Cambridge: Cambridge University Press, 2004.

Starr, Fredrick. "The Fate of Empire in Post-tsarist Russia and in the Post-Soviet Era." In *The End of Empire? The Transformation of the USSR in Comparative Perspective*, edited by Karen Dawisha and Bruce Parrot, 243–60. Armonk, NY: M. E. Sharpe, 1997.

Stites, Richard. *Revolutionary Dreams: Utopian Vision and Experimental Life in the Russian Revolution*. Oxford: Oxford University Press, 1991.

Suny, Ronald Grigor. *The Revenge of the Past: Nationalism, Revolution, and the Collapse of the Soviet Union*. Stanford: Stanford University Press, 1993.

Suny, Ronald Grigor. *The Soviet Experiment: Russia, the USSR, and the Successor States*. Oxford: Oxford University Press, 2011.

Suny, Ronald Grigor, and Terry Martin, eds. *A State of Nations: Empire and Nation-Making in the Age of Lenin and Stalin*. New York: Oxford University Press, 2001.

Swartz, David. *Culture and Power: The Sociology of Pierre Bourdieu*. Chicago: University of Chicago, 1997.

Täçmyradow, Tagangeldi. *Muhammet Geldiýewiň ömri we döredijiligi*. Aşgabat: Ylym, 1989.

Täçmyradow, Tagangeldi. *Türkmen edebi diliniň leksikasynyň sowet döwründe normalanysy*. Aşgabat: Ylym, 1971.

Täçmyradow, Tagangeldi. *Türkmen Edebi Diliniň Orfoepiýasy*. Aşgabat: Ylym, 1976.

Täçmyradow, Tagangeldi. *Türkmen edebi diliniň Sowet döwründe ösüşi we normalanyşy*. Aşgabat: Ylym, 1984.

Talattof, Kamran. *The Politics of Writing in Iran: A History of Modern Persian Literature*. Syracuse: Syracuse University Press, 2000.

Taylor, Charles. *Modern Social Imaginaries*. 3rd ed. Durham: Duke University Press, 2005.

Tekin, Talat. *A Grammar of Orkhon Turkic*. Bloomington: Uralic Altaic Series, 1968.

Thomas, Lawrence L. *The Linguistic Theories of N. Ja. Marr*. Berkeley: University of California Press, 1957.

Tillett, Lowell. *The Great Friendship: Soviet Historians on the Non-Russian Nationalities*. Chapel Hill: University of North Carolina Press, 1969.

Tod, J. K. "The Malleson Mission to Transcaspia in 1918." *Journal of the Royal Asiatic Society* 27, part 1 (1940): 53–72.

Turam, Berna. "National Loyalties and International Undertakings: The Case of the Gülen Community in Kazakhstan." In Yavuz and Esposito, *Turkish Islam*, 184–207.

Turkmen Initiative for Human Rights (TIHR). *Education in Turkmenistan*. Vienna: TIHR, 2006.

Turkmen Initiative for Human Rights (TIHR). *Turkmenistan: The Reform of the Education System*. Vienna: TIHR, 2009.

"Turkmenistan: 2004 Country Report on Human Rights Practices." US Department of State, 28 February 2005. https://www.state.gov/j/drl/rls/hrrpt/2004/41714.htm/.

Uddin, Sufia M. *Constructing Bangladesh: Religion, Ethnicity, and Language in an Islamic Nation*. Chapel Hill: University of North Carolina Press, 2006.

Unbegaun, B. O. "Some Recent Studies on the History of the Russian Language." *Oxford Slavonic Papers*, 5:117–32. Oxford: Clarendon Press, 1954.

United Nations Development Program with assistance from the Academy of Sciences of Turkmenistan. *Turkmenistan Human Development Report 1996*. Ankara: Ajans-Türk Matbaacılılk Sanayii A.Ş., 1996.

Vaidyanath, R. *The Formation of the Soviet Central Asian Republics*. New Delhi, 1967.

Van Leeuwen, Richard. *Waqfs and Urban Structure: The Case of Damascus*. Leiden: E. J. Brill, 1999.

Vansina, Jan. *Paths in the Rainforest: Toward a History of Political Tradition in Equatorial Africa*. Madison: University of Wisconsin Press, 1990.

Vardys, Stanley. "Soviet Nationality Policy since the XXII Party Congress." *Russian Review* 24, no. 4 (1965): 323–40.

Verne, E. "Literacy and Industrialization: The Dispossession of Speech." In Graff, *Literacy and Social Development in the West*, 286–303.

Veselkov, G. "Pis'mo tov. Stalina i borba za proletarskuiu khudozhestvennuii literature v Turkmenii." *Turkmenovedenie* 10–12 (1931): 44–47.

Vinokur, G. O. *The Russian Language: A Brief History*. Cambridge: Cambridge University Press, 1971.

Volkov, Vadim. "The Concept of Kul'turnost; Notes on the Stalinist Civilizing Process." In *Stalinism New Directions: Rewriting Histories*, edited by Sheila Fitzpatrick, 210–30. London: Routledge, 2000.

Vorshev, V. "Osnovnye etapy razvitiia partorganizatsii Turkmenistana." *Revoliutsiia i natsional'nosti* 12 (1934): 79.

Wachtel, Andrew. *Making a Nation, Breaking a Nation: Literature and Cultural Politics in Yugoslavia*. Stanford: Stanford University Press, 1998.

Wagner, Daniel A. *Literacy, Culture, and Development: Becoming Literate in Morocco*. Cambridge: Cambridge University Press, 1993.

Winner, Thomas. *The Oral Art and Literature of the Kazaks of Russian Central Asia*. Durham: Duke University Press, 1958.

World Data on Education, VII Ed. 2010/2011. Turkmenistan. UNESCO-International Bureau of Education, 2011.

Yavuz, M. Hakan. "Turkish Identity Politics and Central Asia." In *Islam in Central Asia: An Enduring Legacy or an Evolving Threat?* edited by Roald Sagdeev and Susan Eisenhower, 193–211. Washington, DC: Center for Political and Strategic Studies, 2000.

Yavuz, M. Hakan, and John L. Esposito, eds. *Turkish Islam and the Secular State: The Gülen Movement*. Syracuse: Syracuse University Press, 2003.

Ziny, Muhammed Ibn Djamil'. *Stolpy Islama i very*. Moscow: Vsemirnoi Assamblei Islamskoi Molodezhi, 1992.

Zürcher, Erik Jan. "Institution Building in the Kemalist Republic Compared with Pahlevi Iran." In *Men of Order: Authoritarian Modernization under Atatürk and Reza Shah*, edited by Touraj Atabaki and Erik Jan Zürcher, 98–112. London: I. B. Tauris, 2004.

Index